CONCLUD

OUT THERE

VOLUME THREE: REUNION

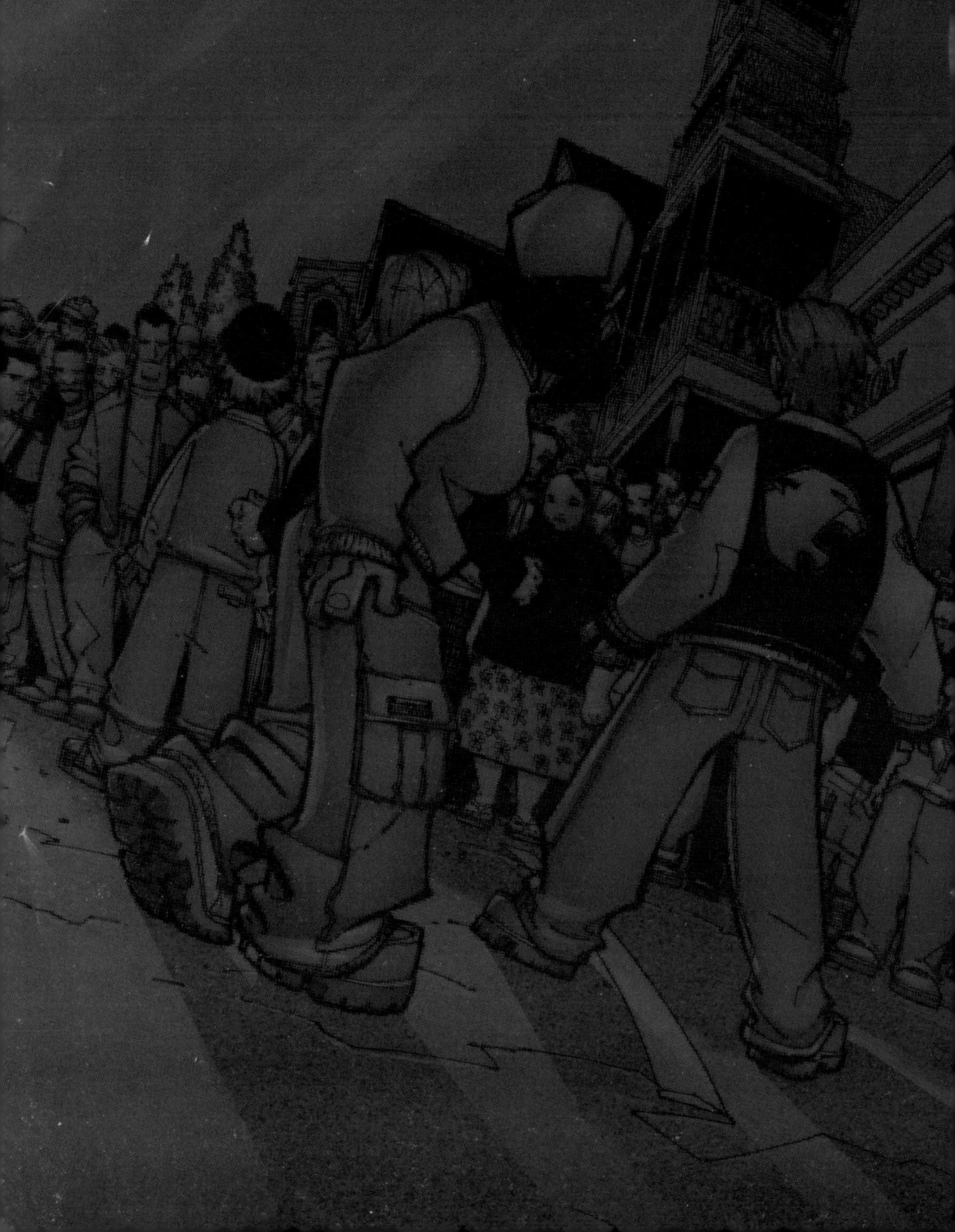

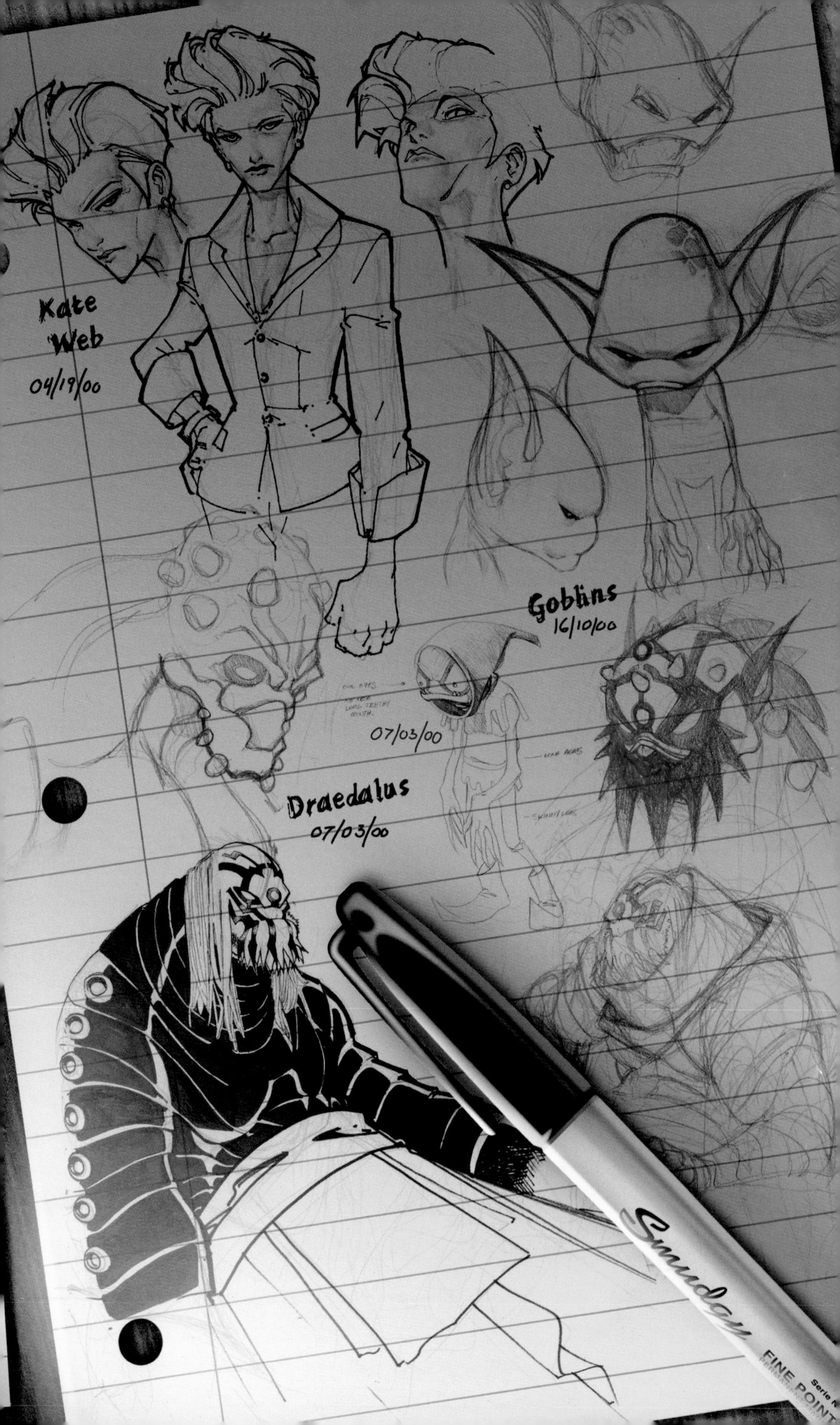
Kate
Web
04/19/00
Goblins
16/10/00
07/03/00
Draedalus
07/03/00
Sharpie
FINE POINT

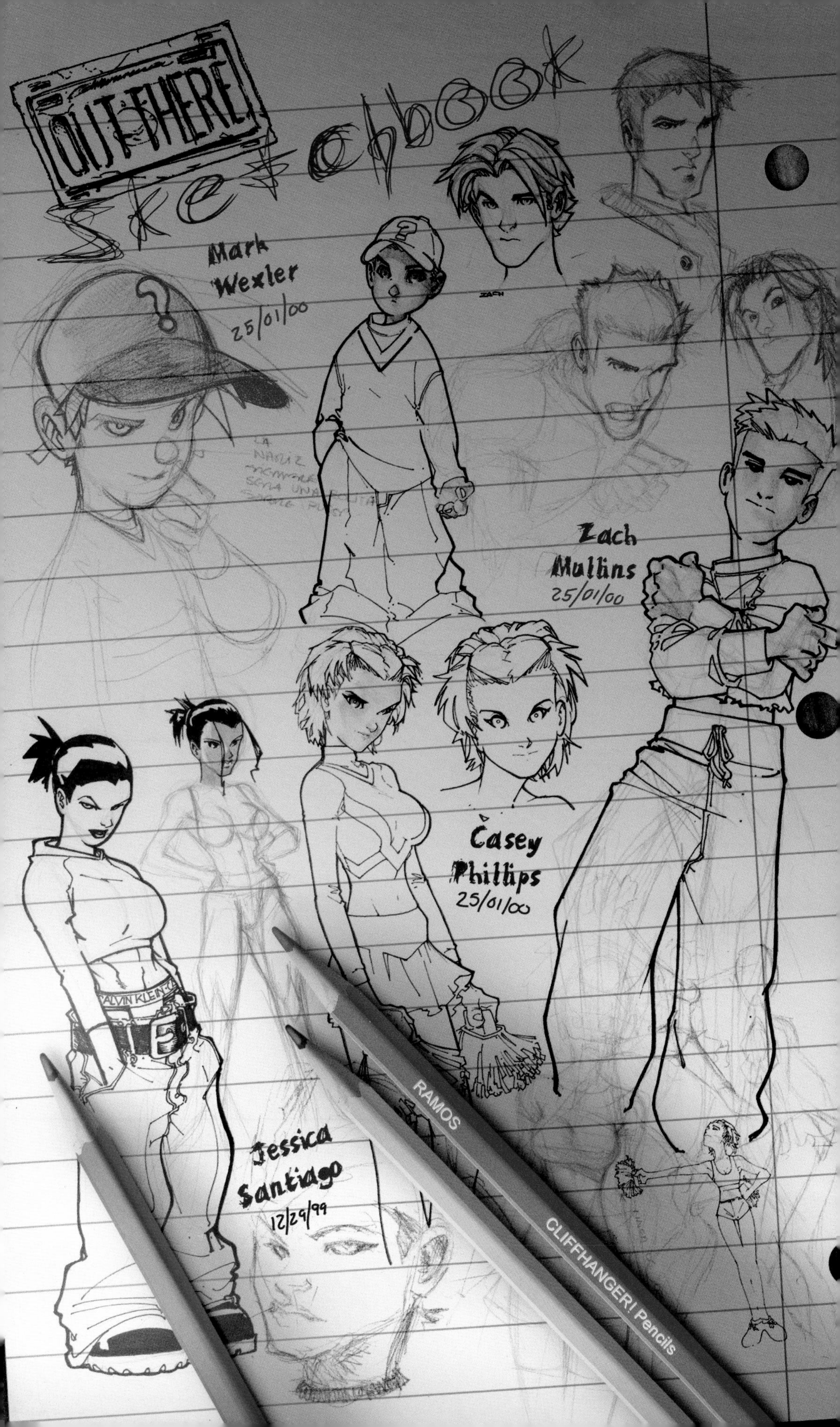
OUT THERE
Sketchbook
Mark Wexler
25/01/00
ZACH
Zach Mullins
25/01/00
Casey Phillips
25/01/00
Jessica Santiago
12/29/99
RAMOS
CLIFFHANGER! Pencils

SKETCH GALLERY

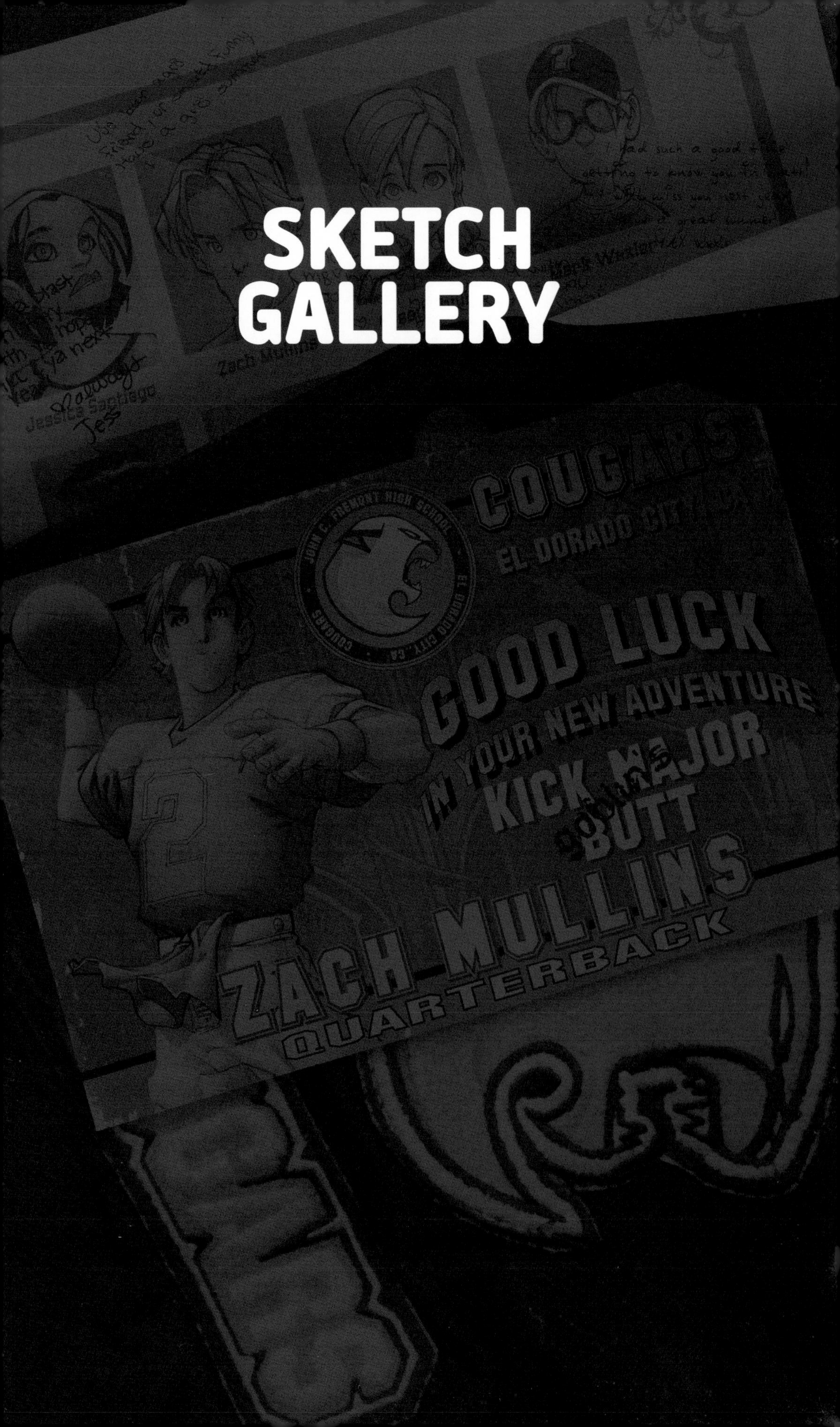
COUGARS
EL DORADO CITY
JOHN C. FREMONT HIGH SCHOOL
GOOD LUCK
IN YOUR NEW ADVENTURE
KICK MAJOR BUTT
ZACH MULLINS
QUARTERBACK

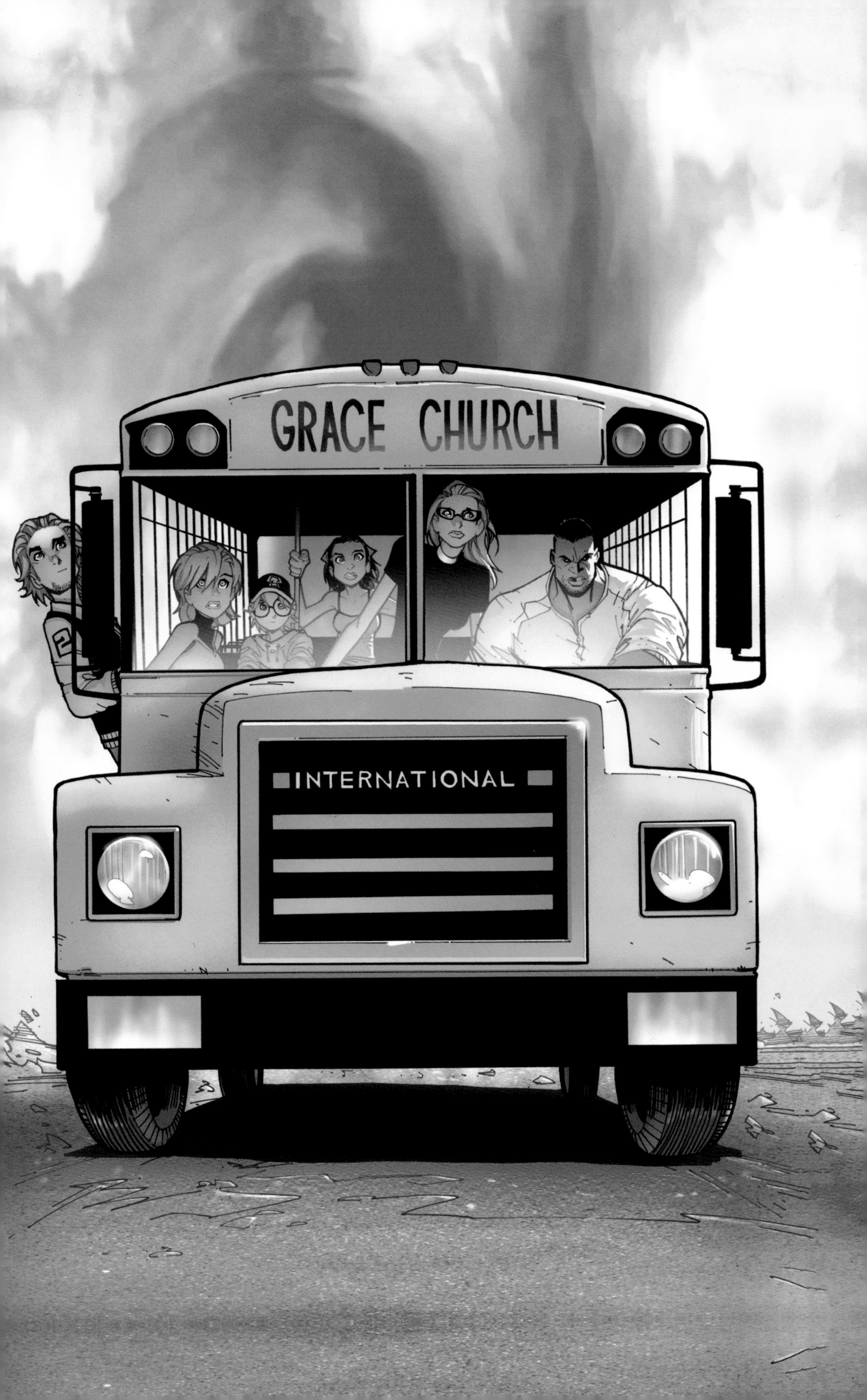
GRACE CHURCH
INTERNATIONAL

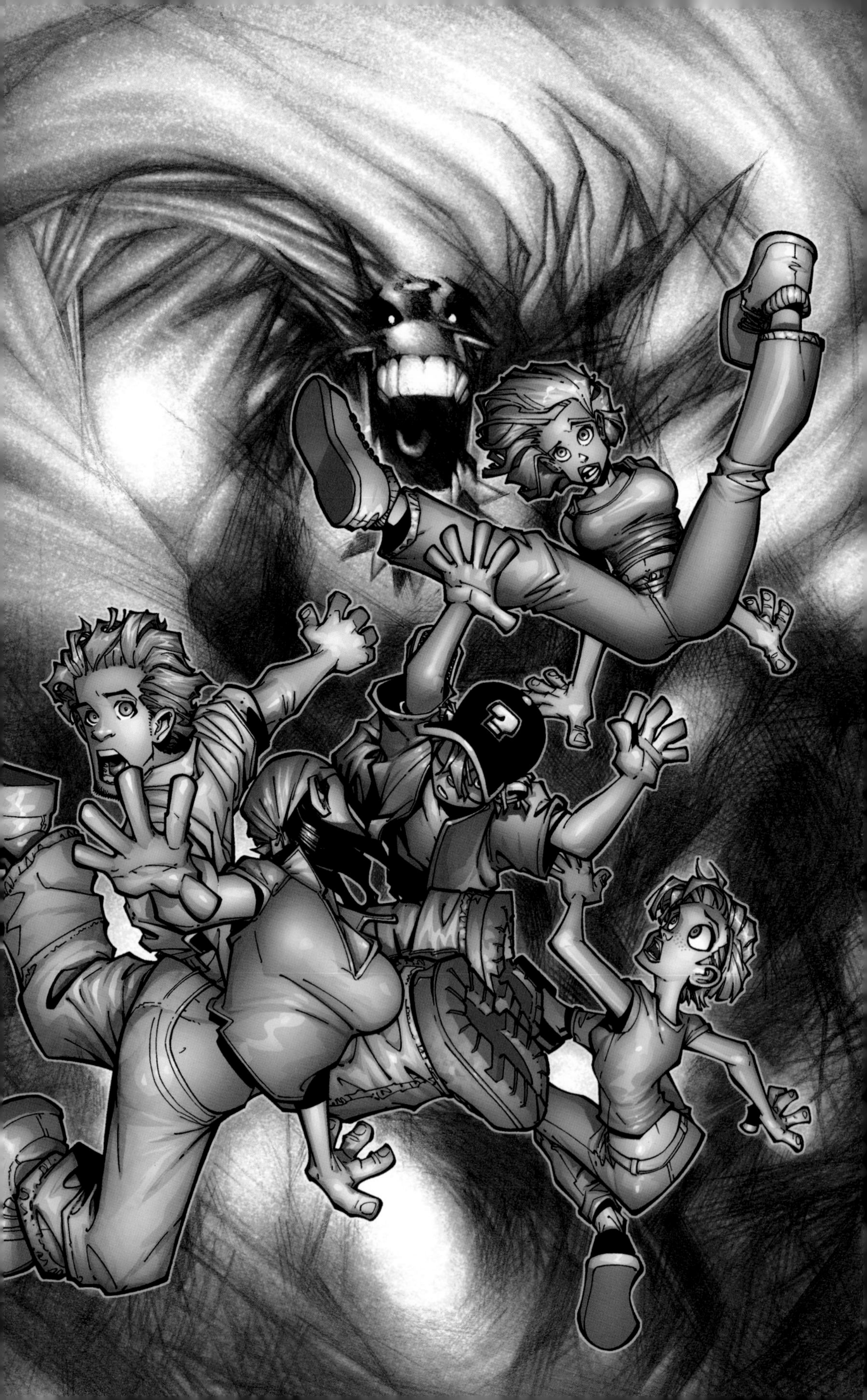

ISSUE ELEVEN COVER PENCILS BY **HUMBERTO RAMOS** INKS BY **SANDRA HOPE** COLORS BY **EDGAR DELGADO**

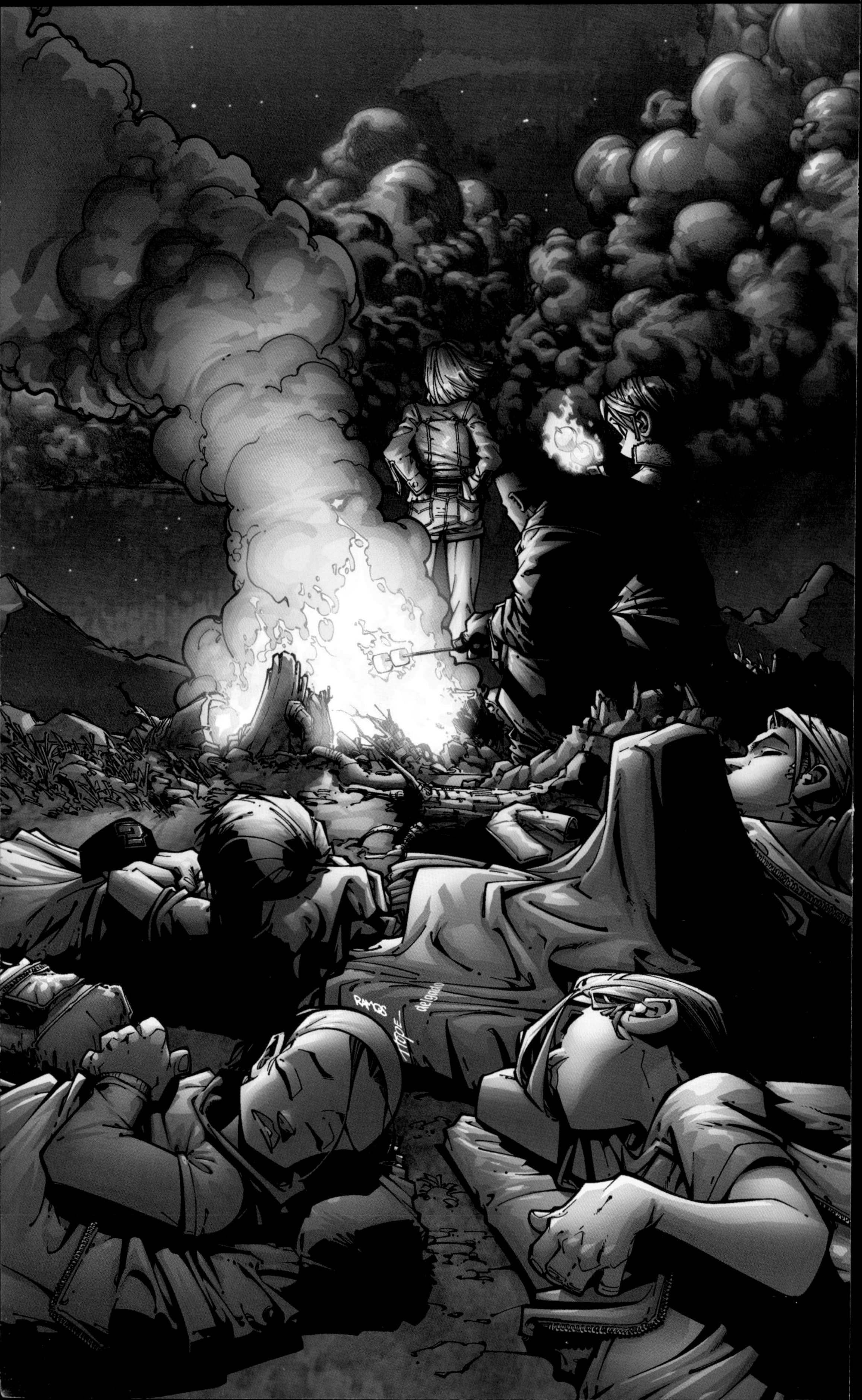

ISSUE TEN COVER PENCILS BY HUMBERTO RAMOS INKS BY [illegible] COLORS BY EDGAR DELGADO

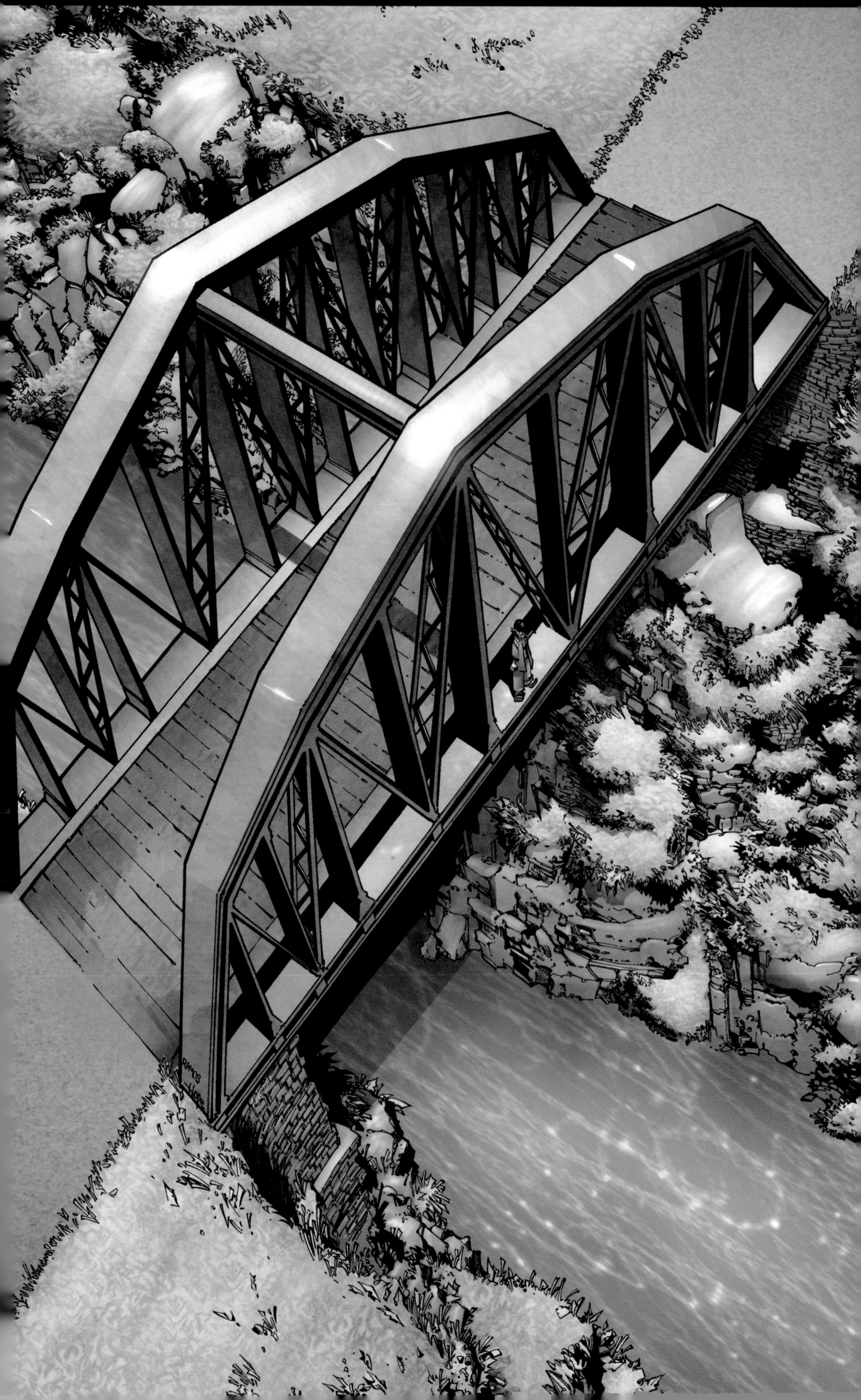

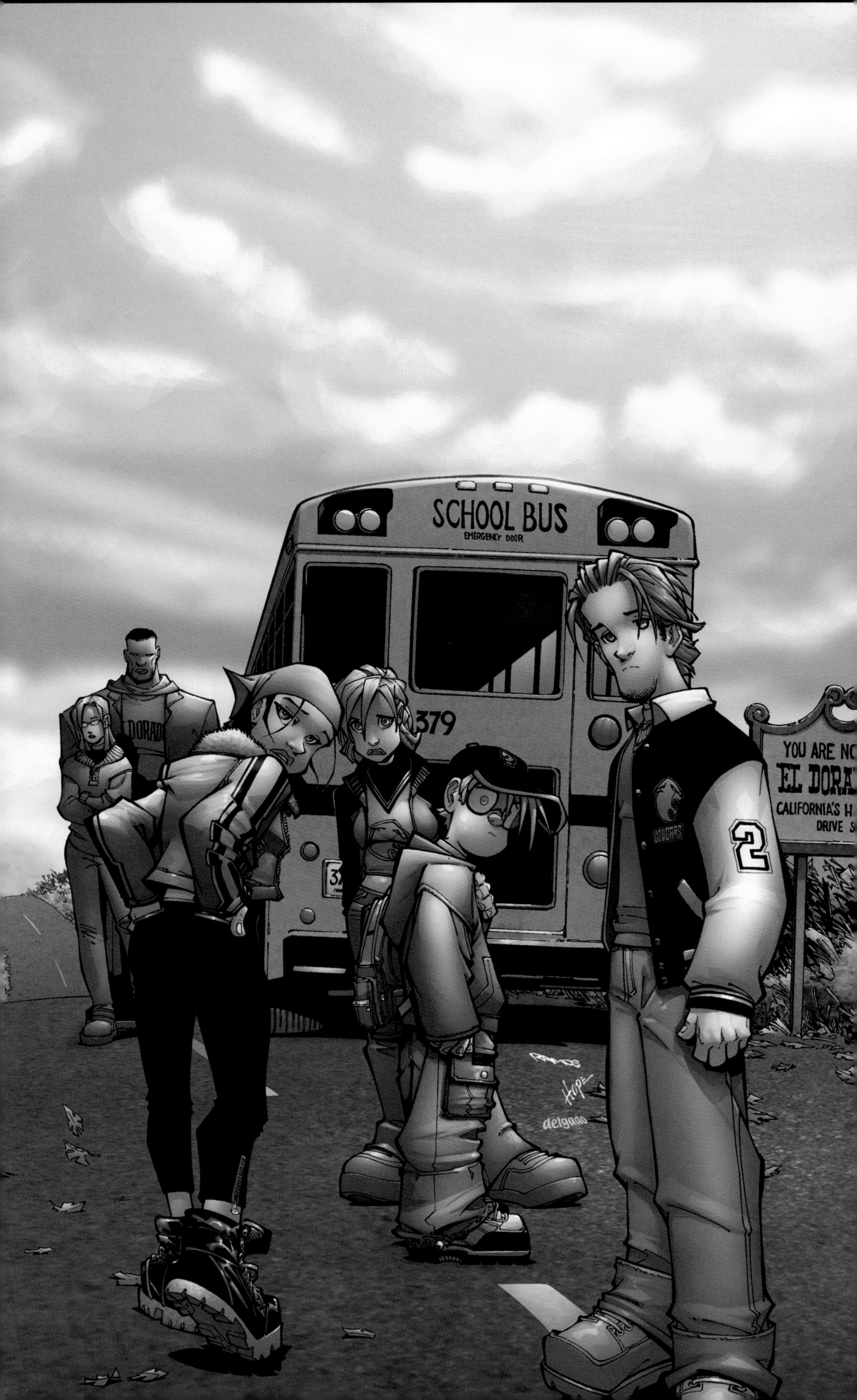
SCHOOL BUS
EMERGENCY DOOR
379
COUGARS
2
Ramos
Hope
delgado

COVER GALLERY

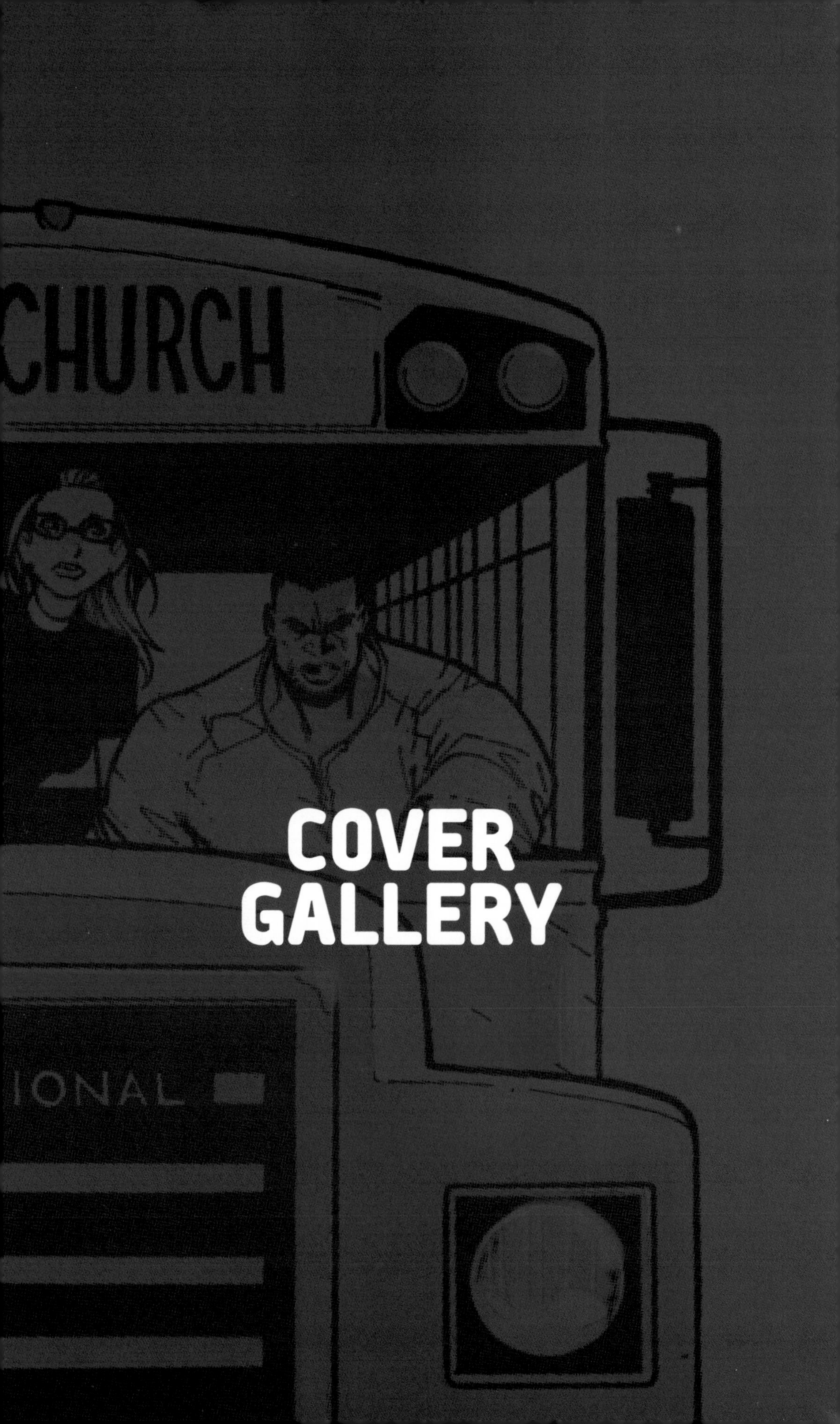
CHURCH
IONAL

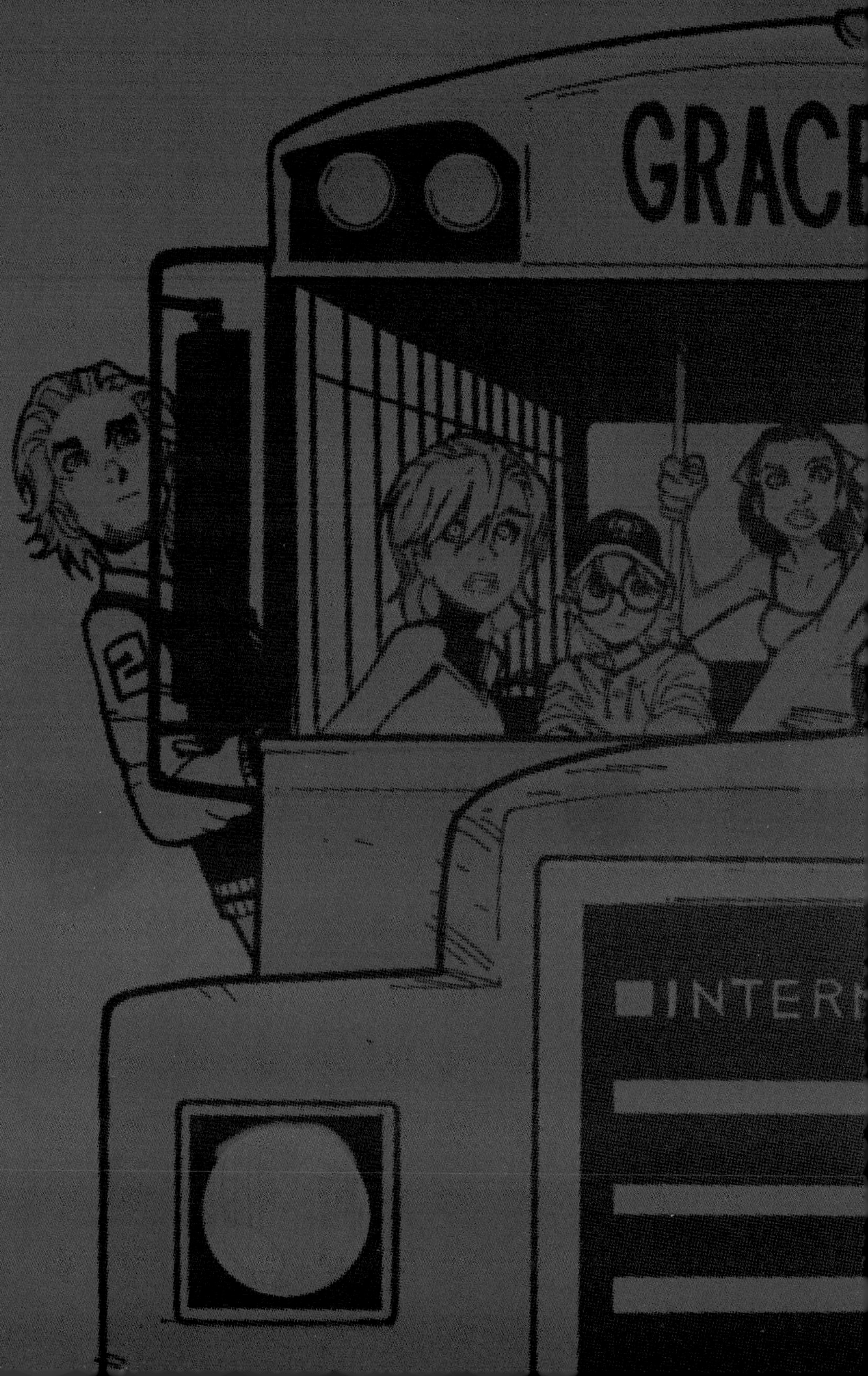
GRACE
INTERN

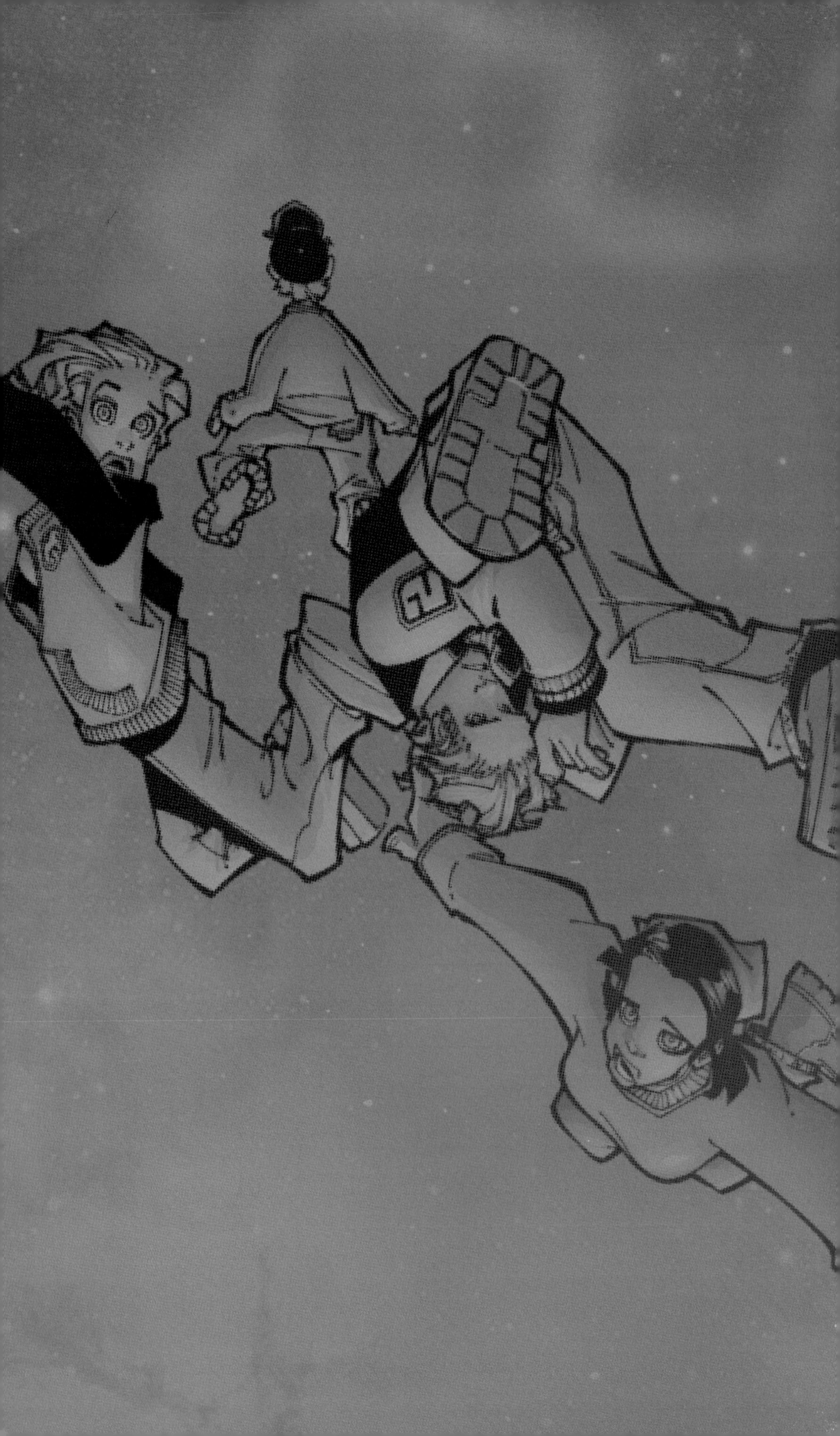

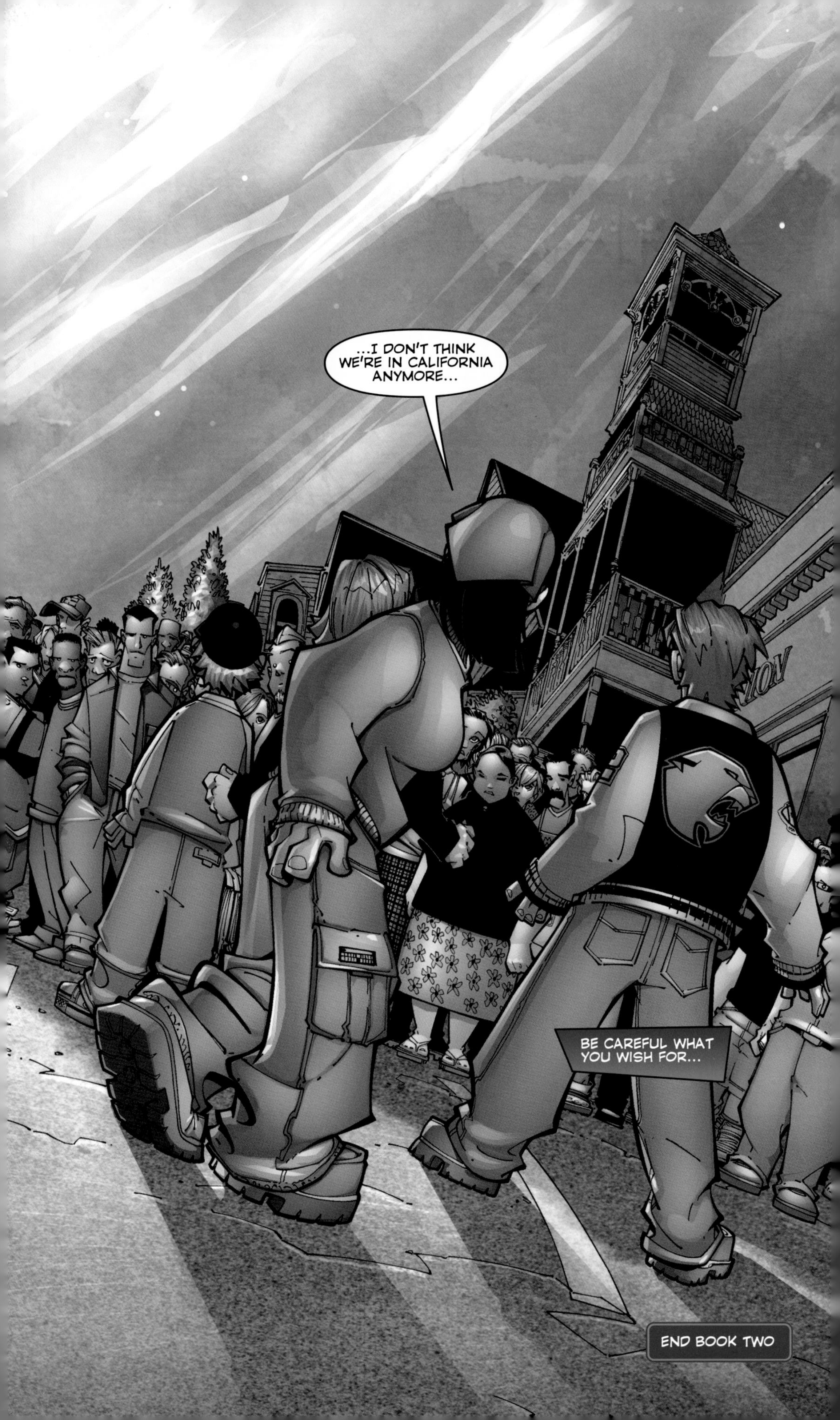
...I DON'T THINK WE'RE IN CALIFORNIA ANYMORE...
BE CAREFUL WHAT YOU WISH FOR...
END BOOK TWO

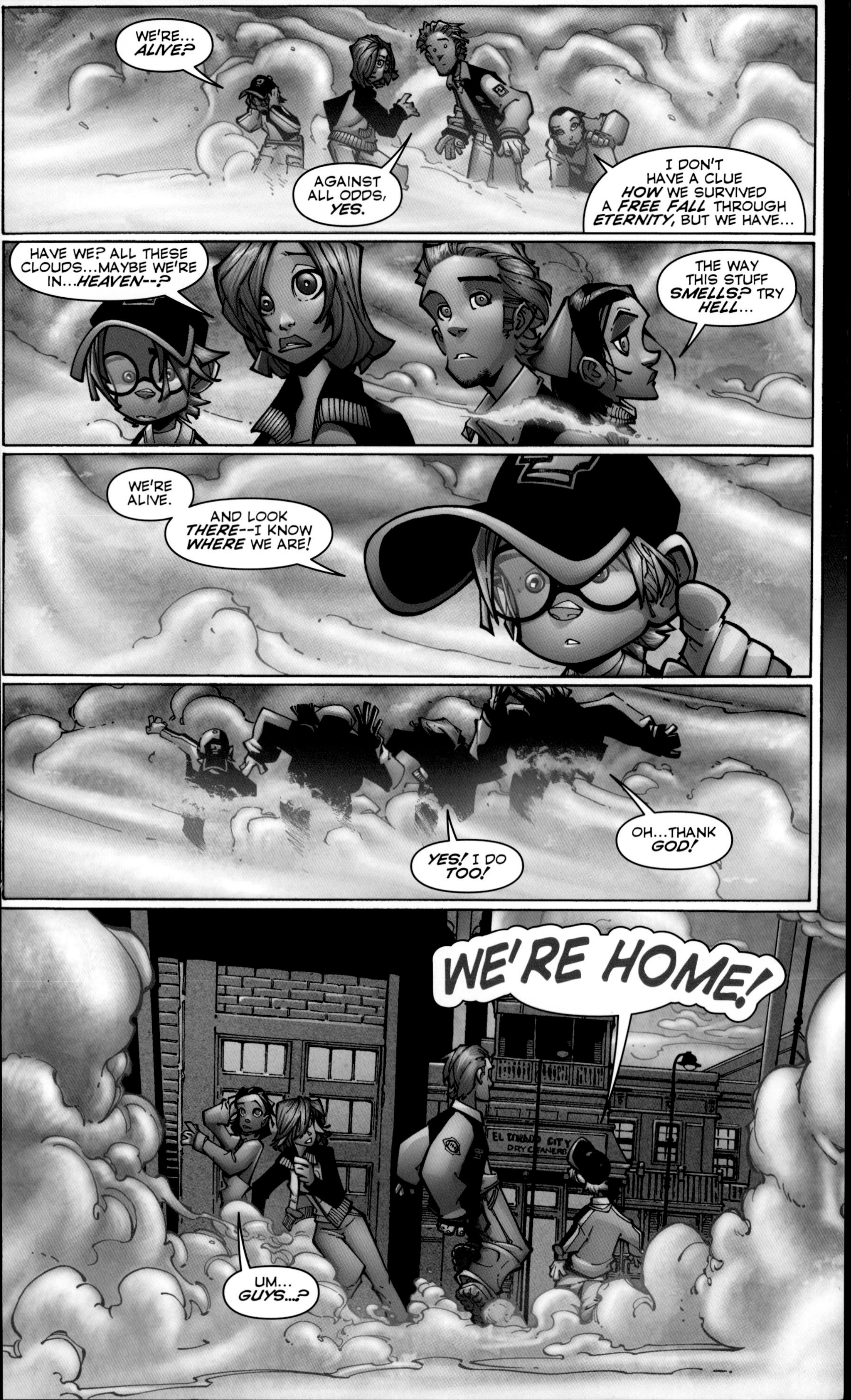
WE'RE... ALIVE?
AGAINST ALL ODDS, YES.
I DON'T HAVE A CLUE HOW WE SURVIVED A FREE FALL THROUGH ETERNITY, BUT WE HAVE...
HAVE WE? ALL THESE CLOUDS...MAYBE WE'RE IN...HEAVEN--?
THE WAY THIS STUFF SMELLS? TRY HELL...
WE'RE ALIVE.
AND LOOK THERE--I KNOW WHERE WE ARE!
YES! I DO TOO!
OH...THANK GOD!
WE'RE HOME!
EL DORADO CITY DRY CLEANERS
UM... GUYS...?

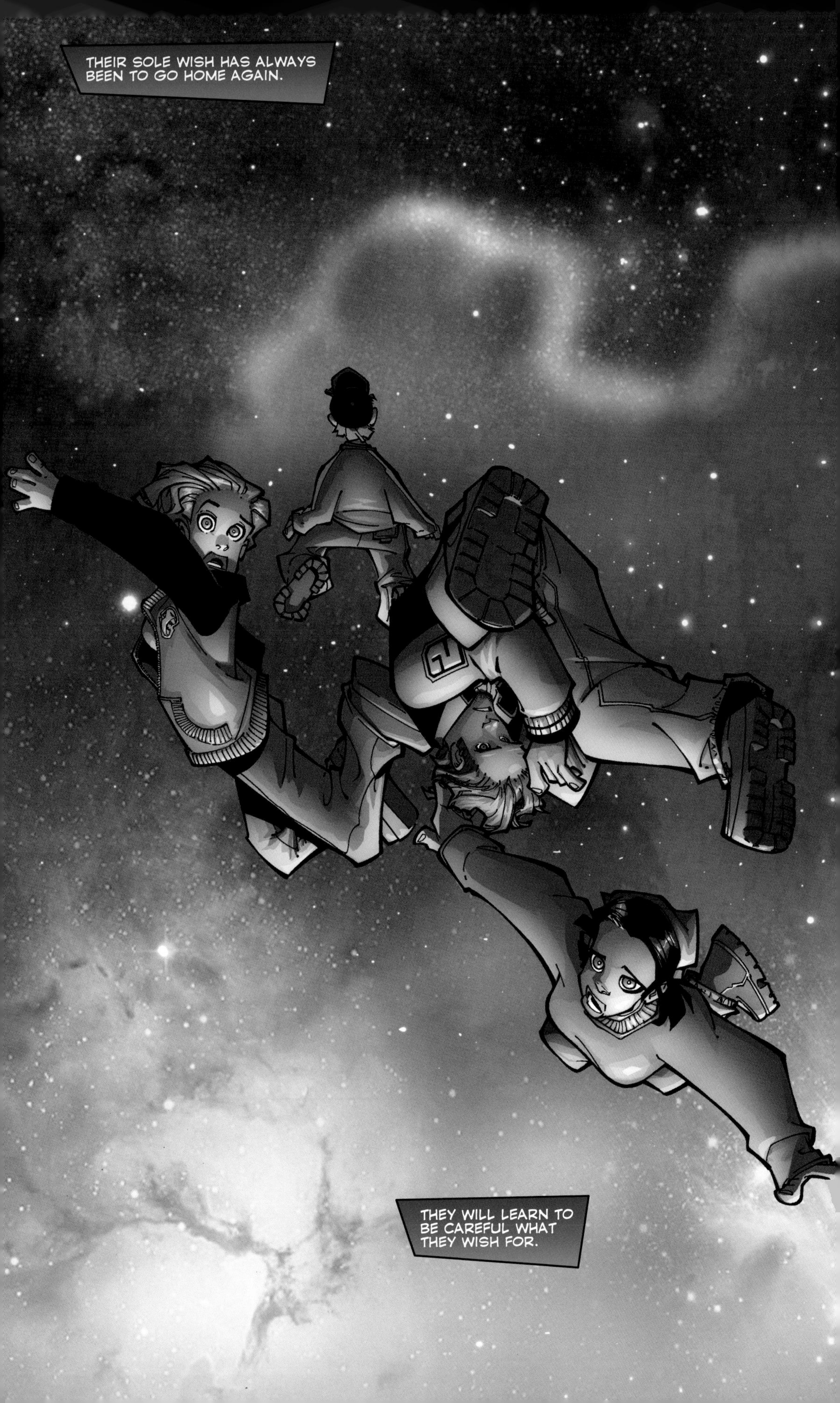
THEIR SOLE WISH HAS ALWAYS BEEN TO GO HOME AGAIN.
THEY WILL LEARN TO BE CAREFUL WHAT THEY WISH FOR.

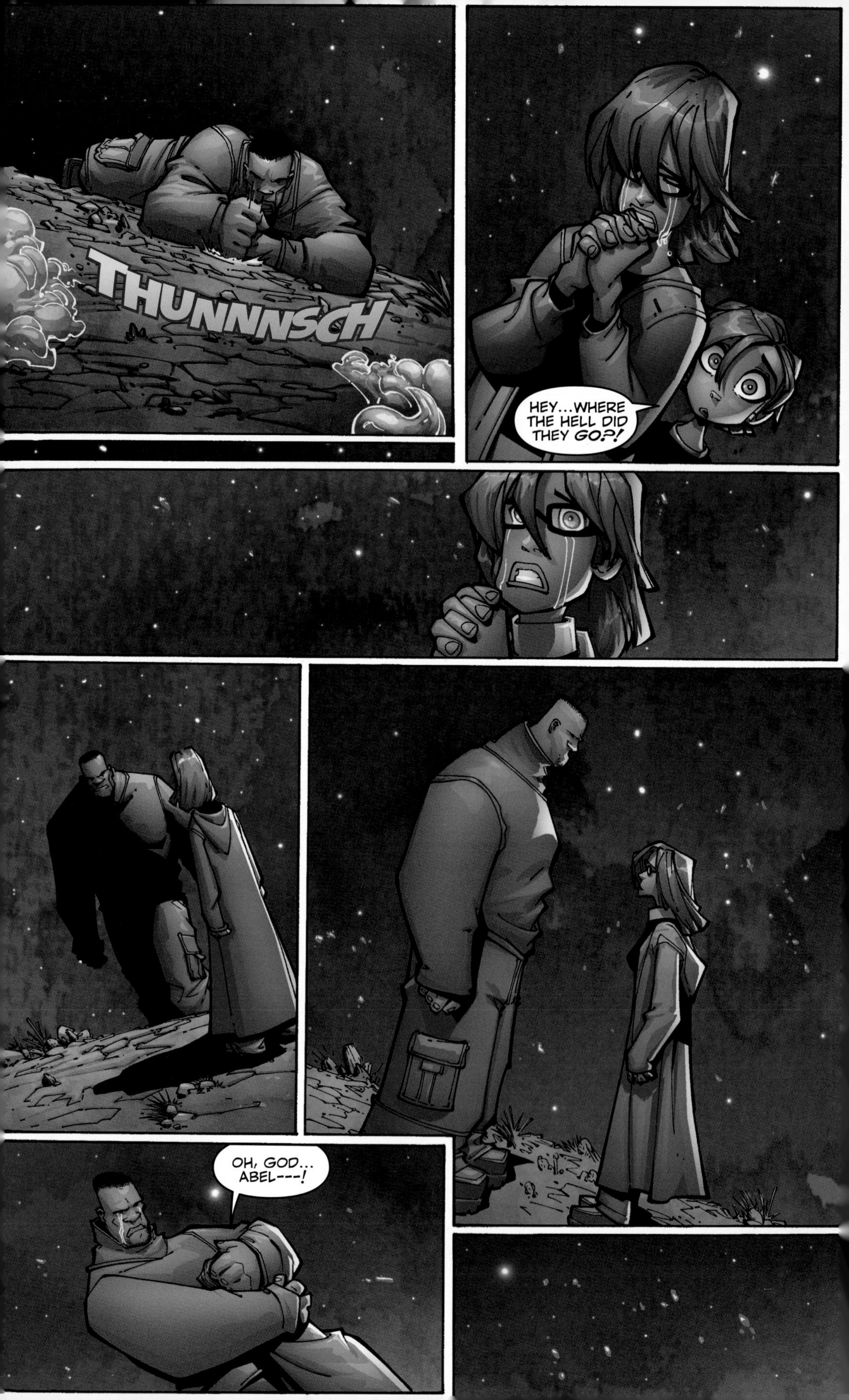
THUNNNSCH
HEY...WHERE THE HELL DID THEY GO?!
OH, GOD... ABEL---!

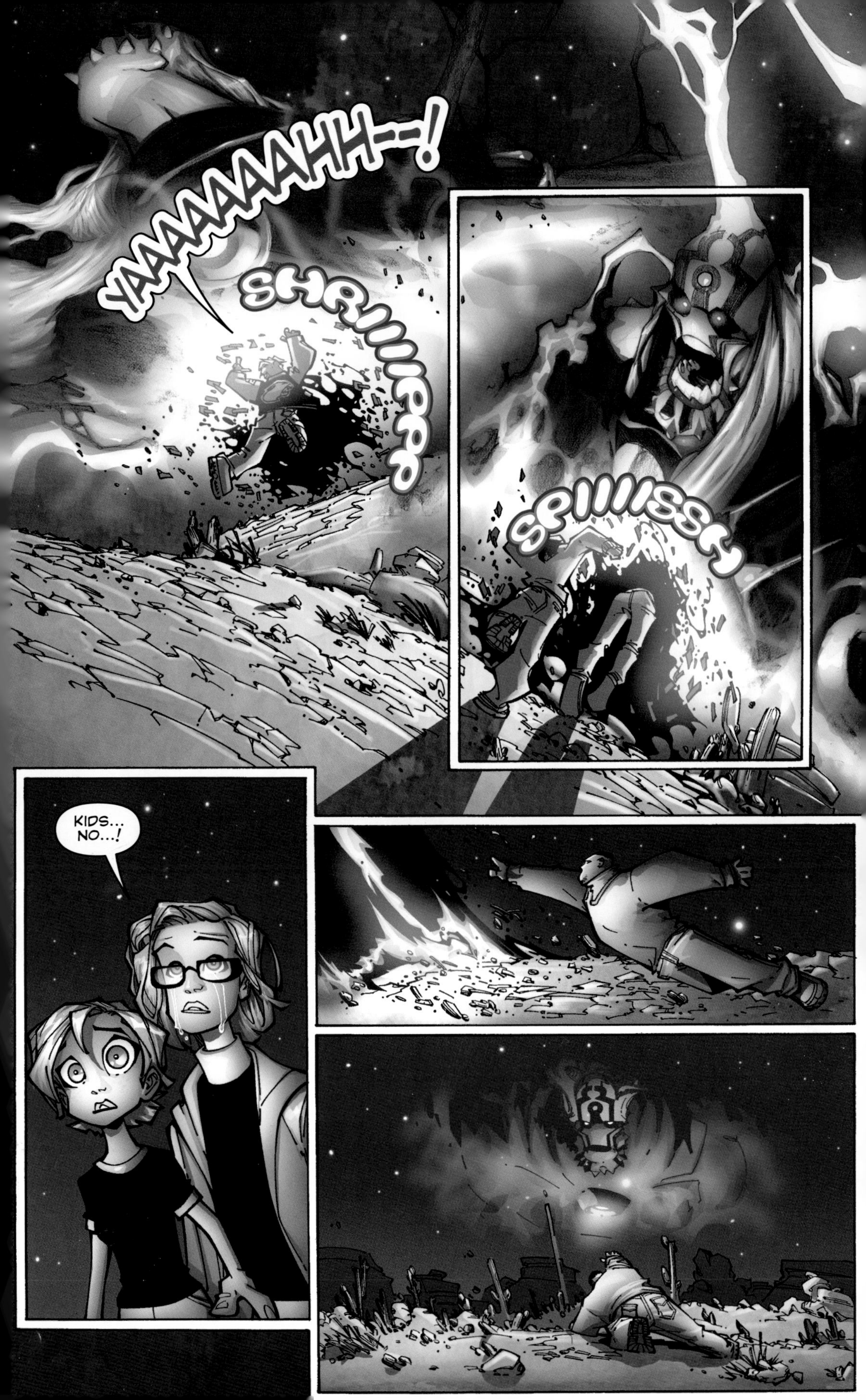
YAAAAAAAHH--!
SHRIIIIIPPP
SPIIIISSSH
KIDS... NO...!

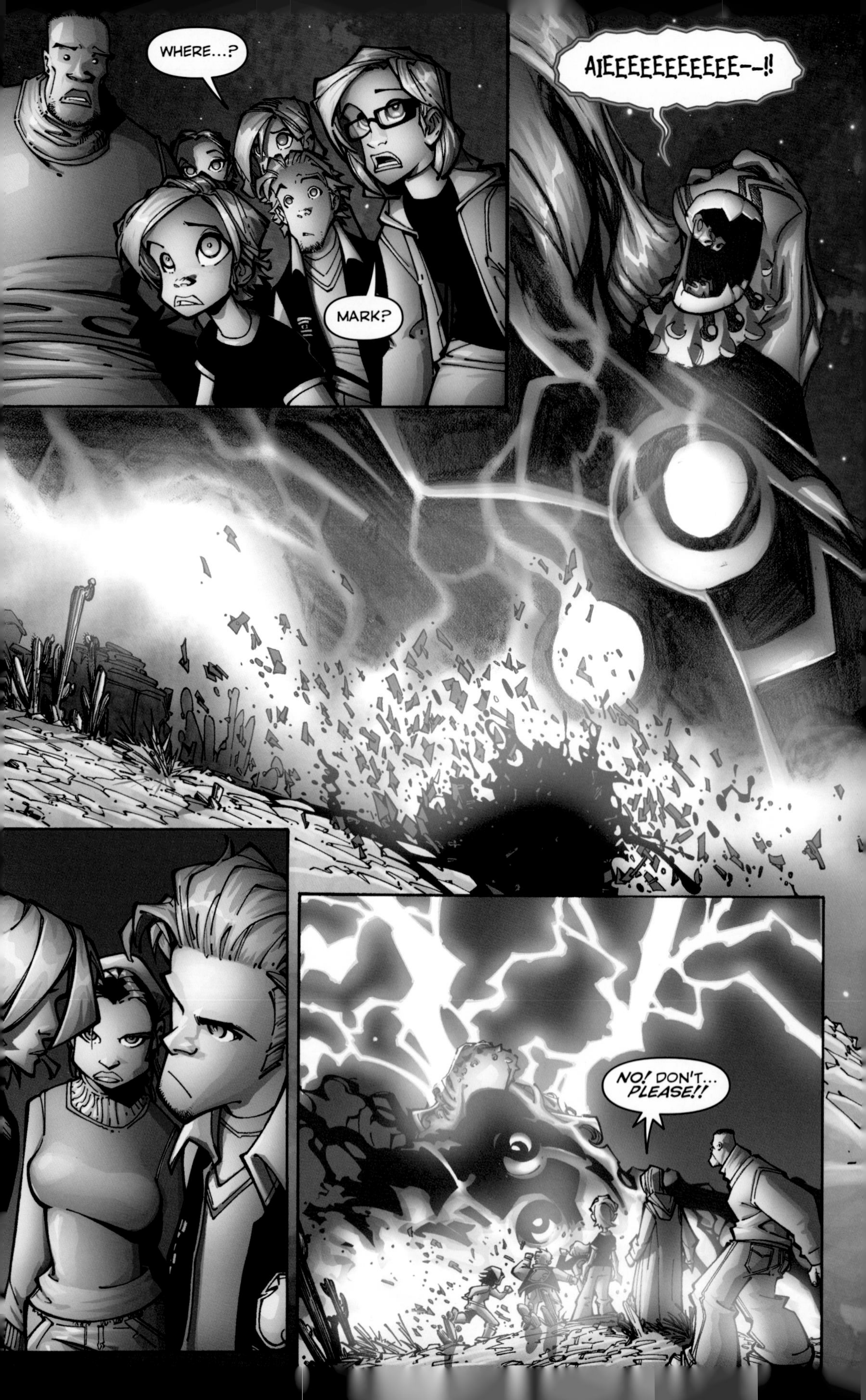
WHERE...?
MARK?
AIEEEEEEEEEEE--!!
NO! DON'T... PLEASE!!

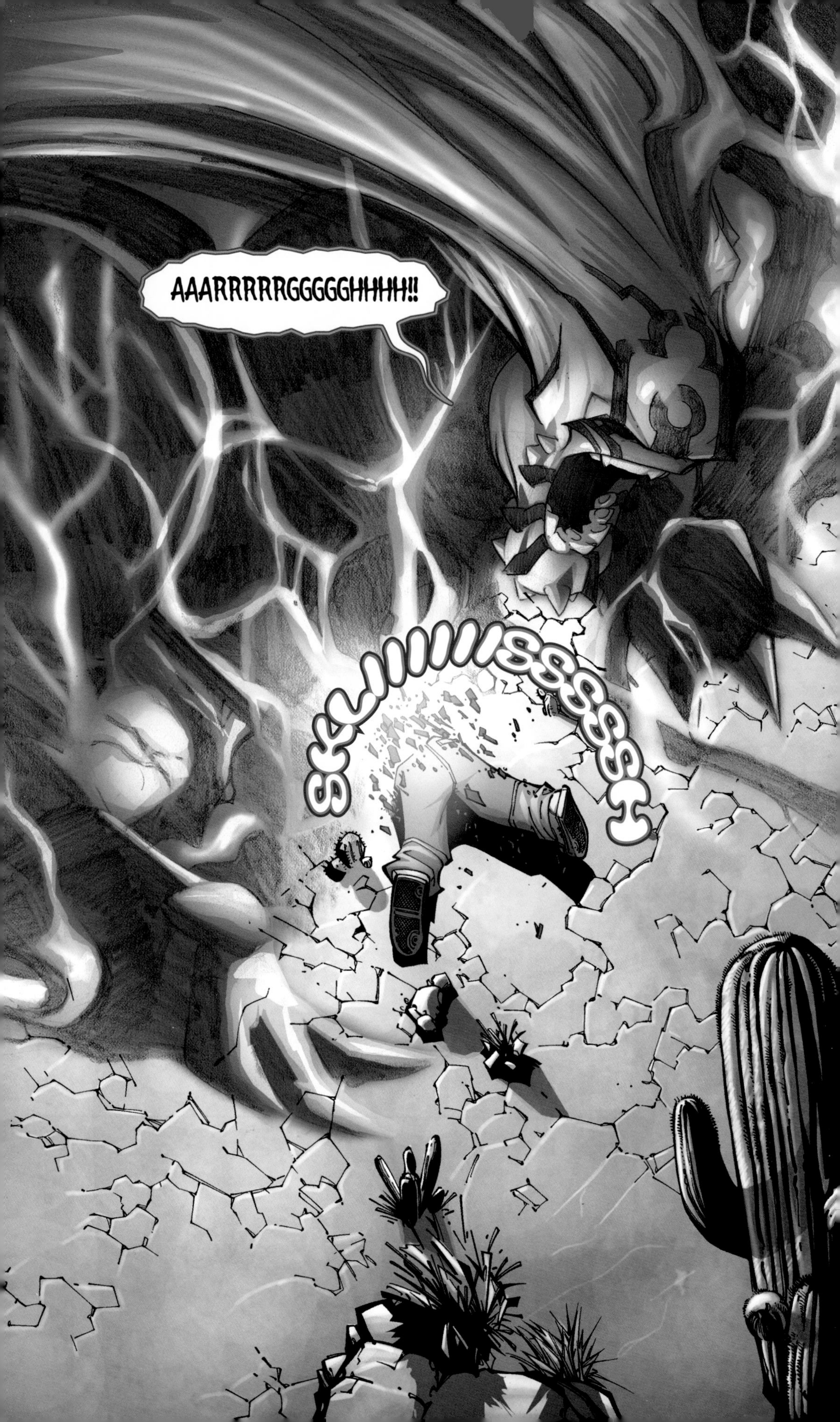
AAARRRRRGGGGGHHHH!!
SKLIIIIIISSSSSH

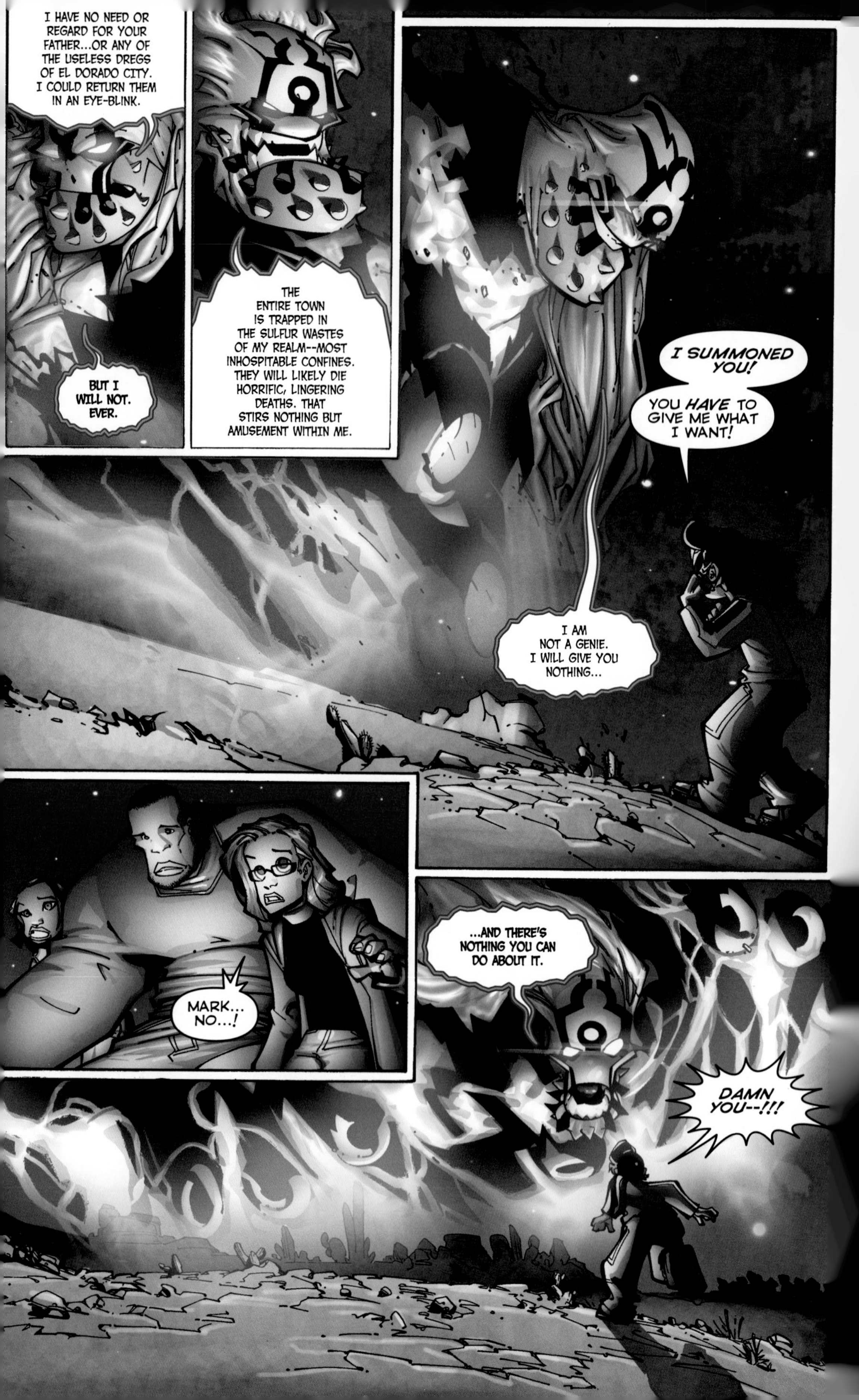
I HAVE NO NEED OR REGARD FOR YOUR FATHER...OR ANY OF THE USELESS DREGS OF EL DORADO CITY. I COULD RETURN THEM IN AN EYE-BLINK.
BUT I WILL NOT. EVER.
THE ENTIRE TOWN IS TRAPPED IN THE SULFUR WASTES OF MY REALM--MOST INHOSPITABLE CONFINES. THEY WILL LIKELY DIE HORRIFIC, LINGERING DEATHS. THAT STIRS NOTHING BUT AMUSEMENT WITHIN ME.
I SUMMONED YOU!
YOU HAVE TO GIVE ME WHAT I WANT!
I AM NOT A GENIE. I WILL GIVE YOU NOTHING...
MARK... NO...!
...AND THERE'S NOTHING YOU CAN DO ABOUT IT.
DAMN YOU--!!!

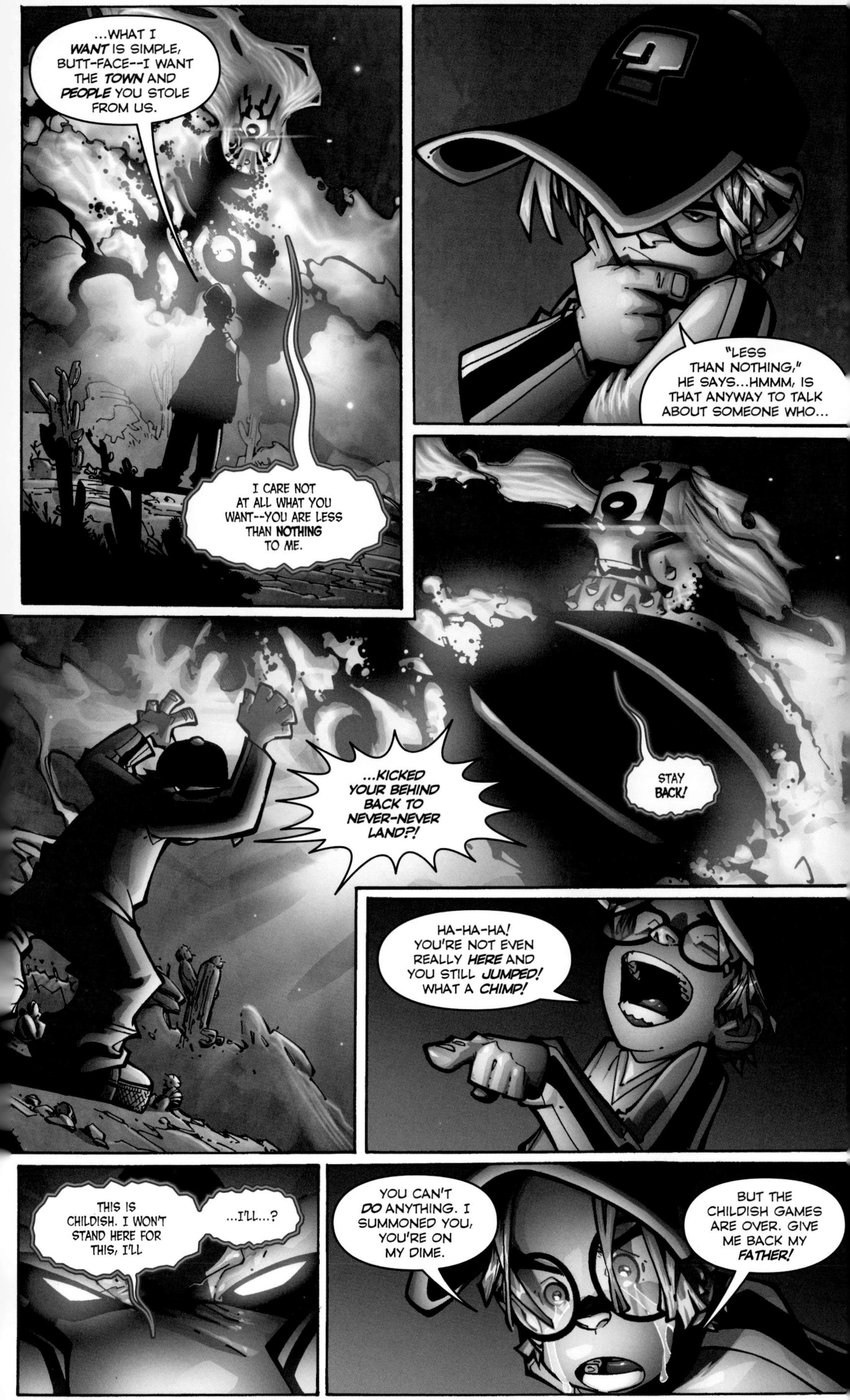
...WHAT I WANT IS SIMPLE, BUTT-FACE--I WANT THE TOWN AND PEOPLE YOU STOLE FROM US.
I CARE NOT AT ALL WHAT YOU WANT--YOU ARE LESS THAN NOTHING TO ME.
"LESS THAN NOTHING," HE SAYS...HMMM, IS THAT ANYWAY TO TALK ABOUT SOMEONE WHO...
...KICKED YOUR BEHIND BACK TO NEVER-NEVER LAND?!
STAY BACK!
HA-HA-HA! YOU'RE NOT EVEN REALLY HERE AND YOU STILL JUMPED! WHAT A CHIMP!
THIS IS CHILDISH. I WON'T STAND HERE FOR THIS, I'LL
...I'LL...?
YOU CAN'T DO ANYTHING. I SUMMONED YOU, YOU'RE ON MY DIME.
BUT THE CHILDISH GAMES ARE OVER. GIVE ME BACK MY FATHER!

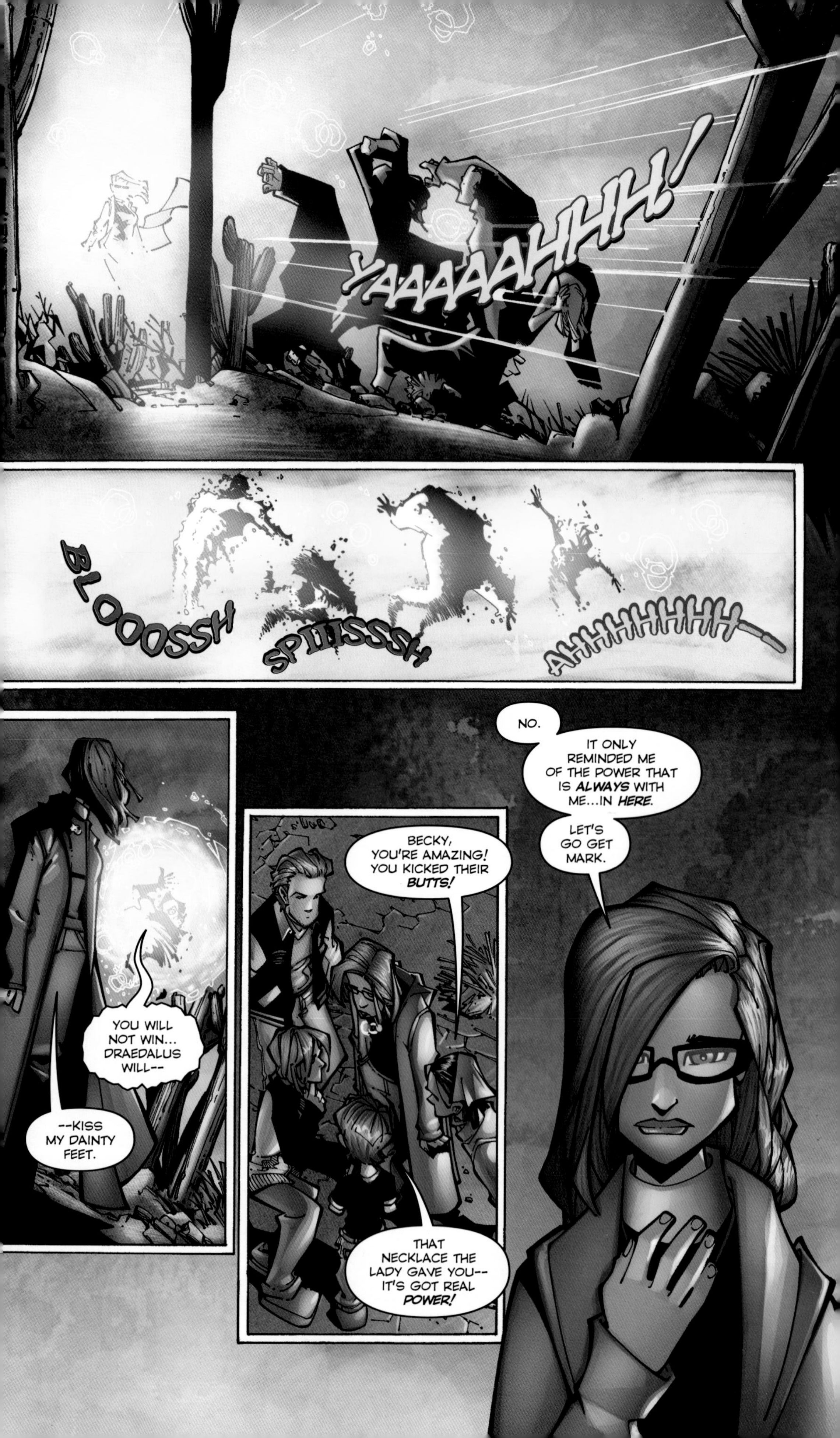
YAAAAAHHHH!
BLOOOSSH
SPIIISSSH
AHHHHHHHH--
YOU WILL NOT WIN... DRAEDALUS WILL--
--KISS MY DAINTY FEET.
BECKY, YOU'RE AMAZING! YOU KICKED THEIR BUTTS!
THAT NECKLACE THE LADY GAVE YOU-- IT'S GOT REAL POWER!
NO.
IT ONLY REMINDED ME OF THE POWER THAT IS ALWAYS WITH ME...IN HERE.
LET'S GO GET MARK.

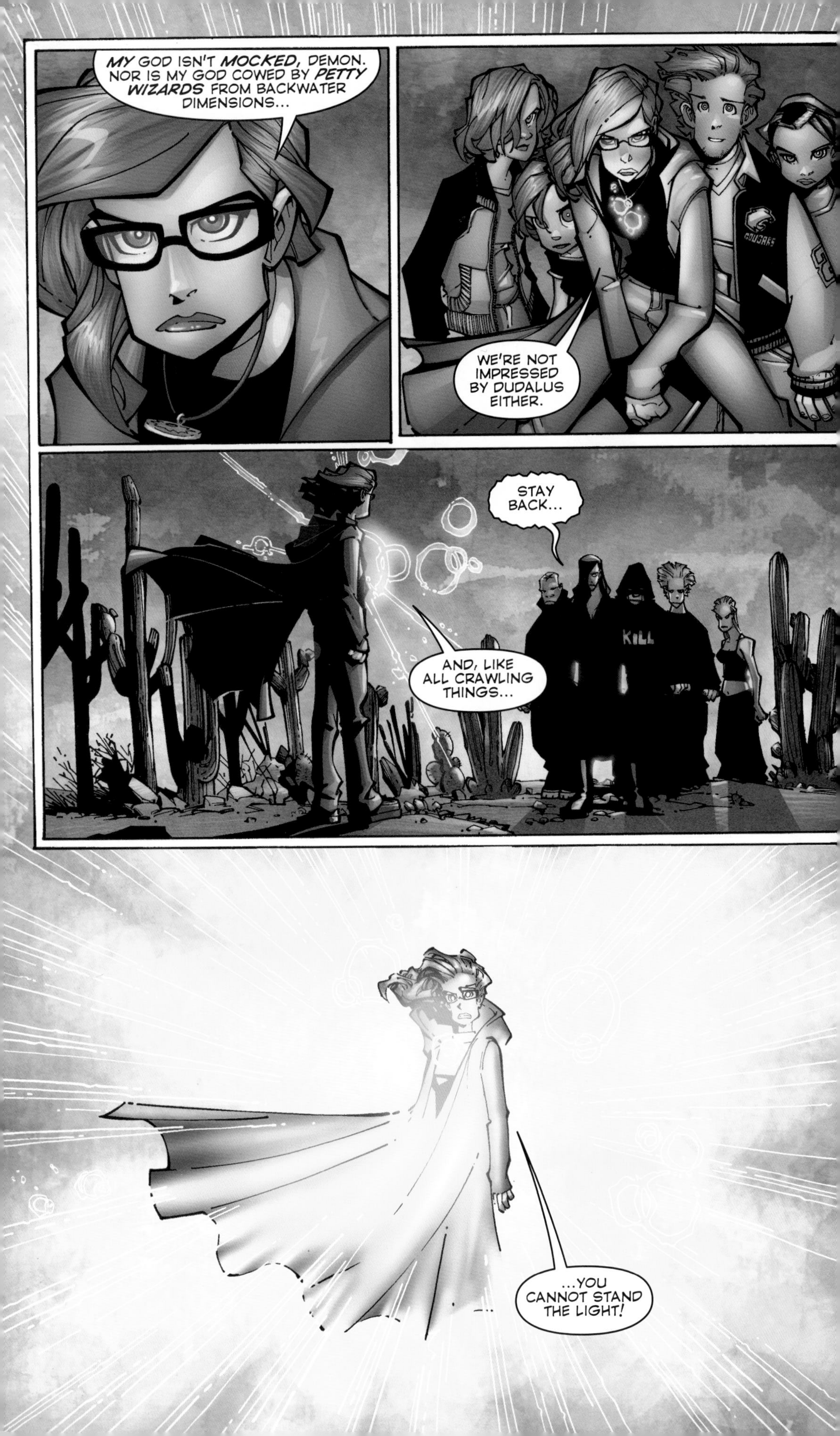
MY GOD ISN'T MOCKED, DEMON. NOR IS MY GOD COWED BY PETTY WIZARDS FROM BACKWATER DIMENSIONS...
WE'RE NOT IMPRESSED BY DUDALUS EITHER.
STAY BACK...
AND, LIKE ALL CRAWLING THINGS...
...YOU CANNOT STAND THE LIGHT!

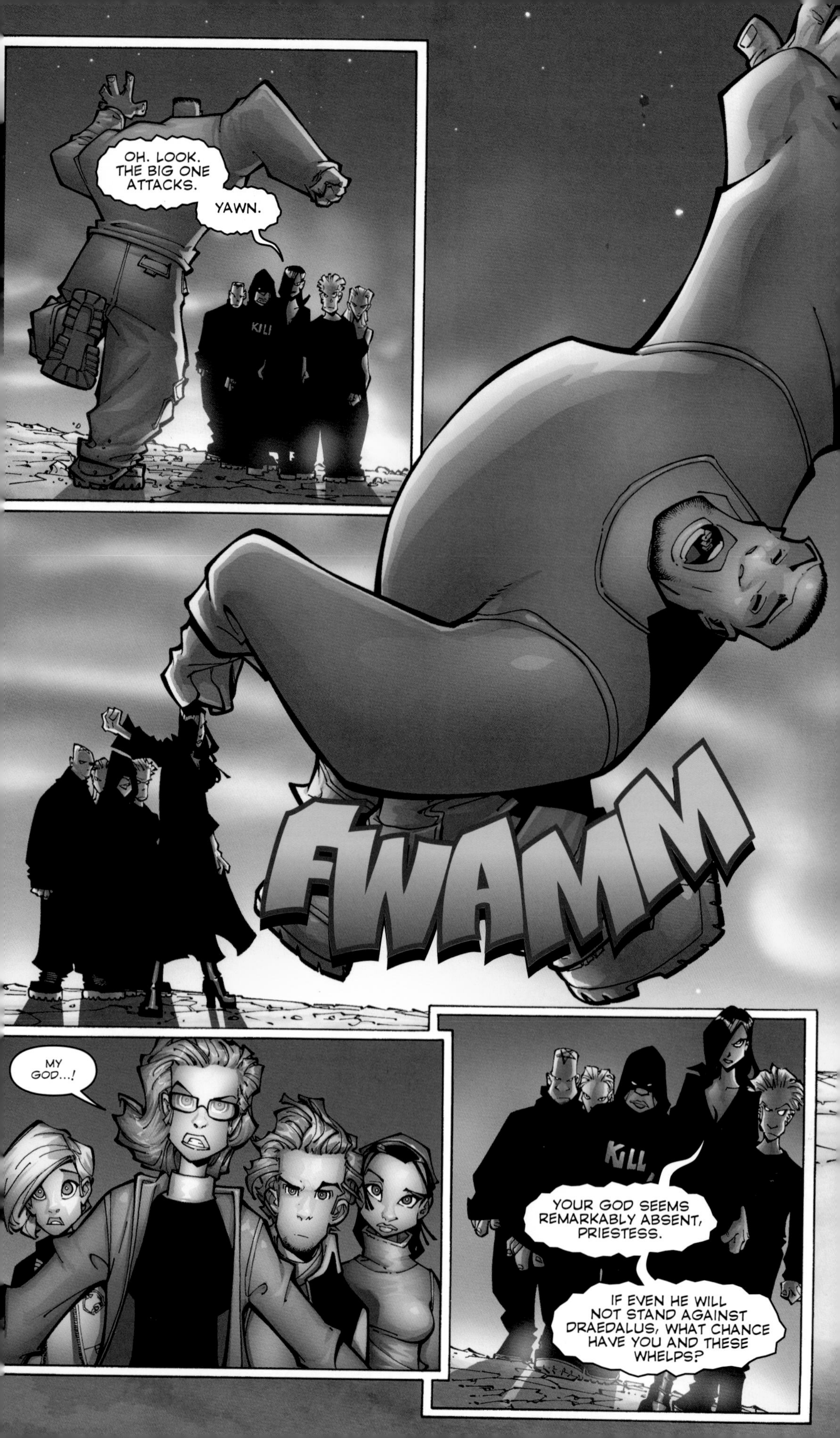

OH. LOOK. THE BIG ONE ATTACKS.
YAWN.
KILL
FWAMM
MY GOD...!
KILL
YOUR GOD SEEMS REMARKABLY ABSENT, PRIESTESS.
IF EVEN HE WILL NOT STAND AGAINST DRAEDALUS, WHAT CHANCE HAVE YOU AND THESE WHELPS?

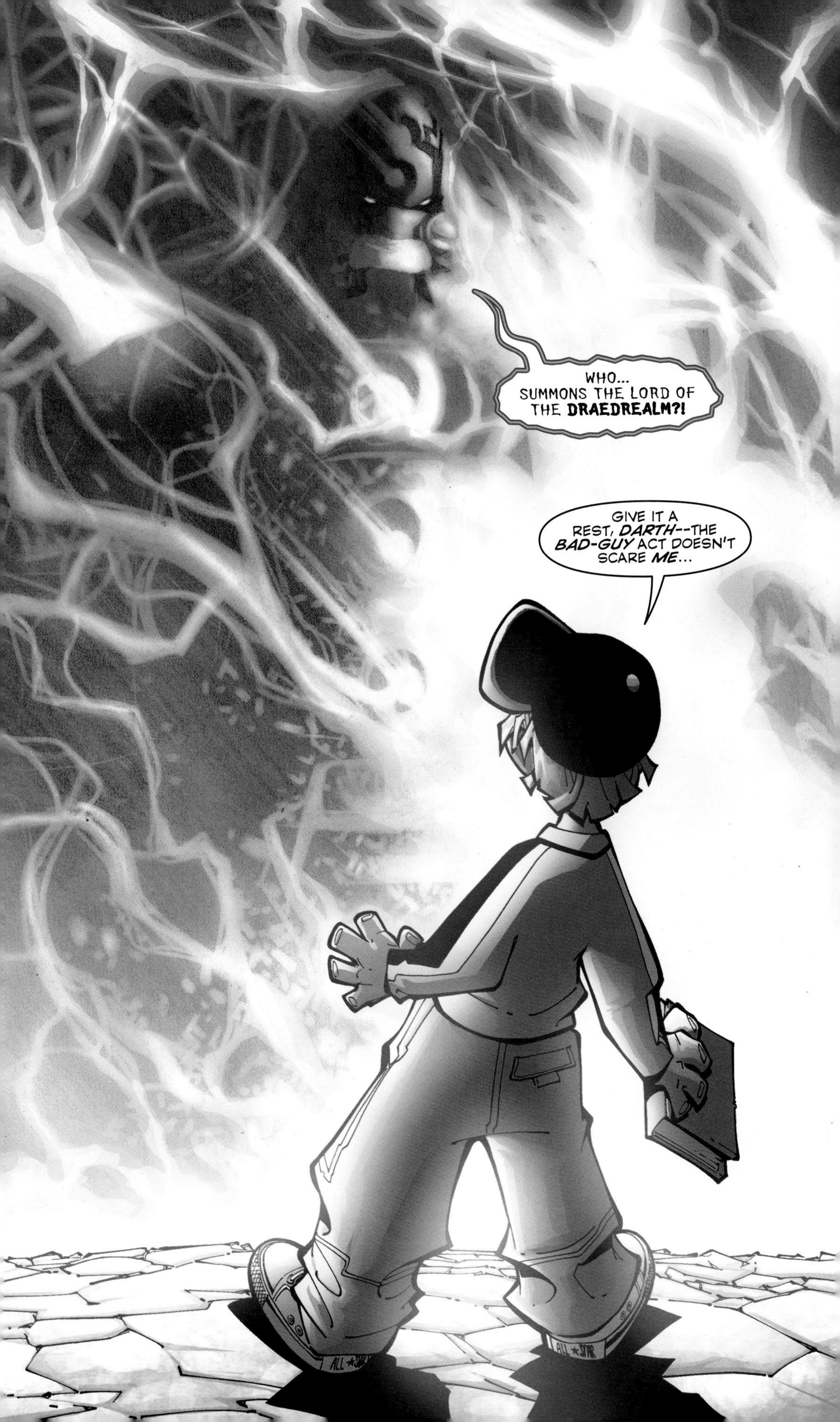
WHO... SUMMONS THE LORD OF THE **DRAEDREALM?!**
GIVE IT A REST, ***DARTH***--THE ***BAD-GUY*** ACT DOESN'T SCARE ***ME***...

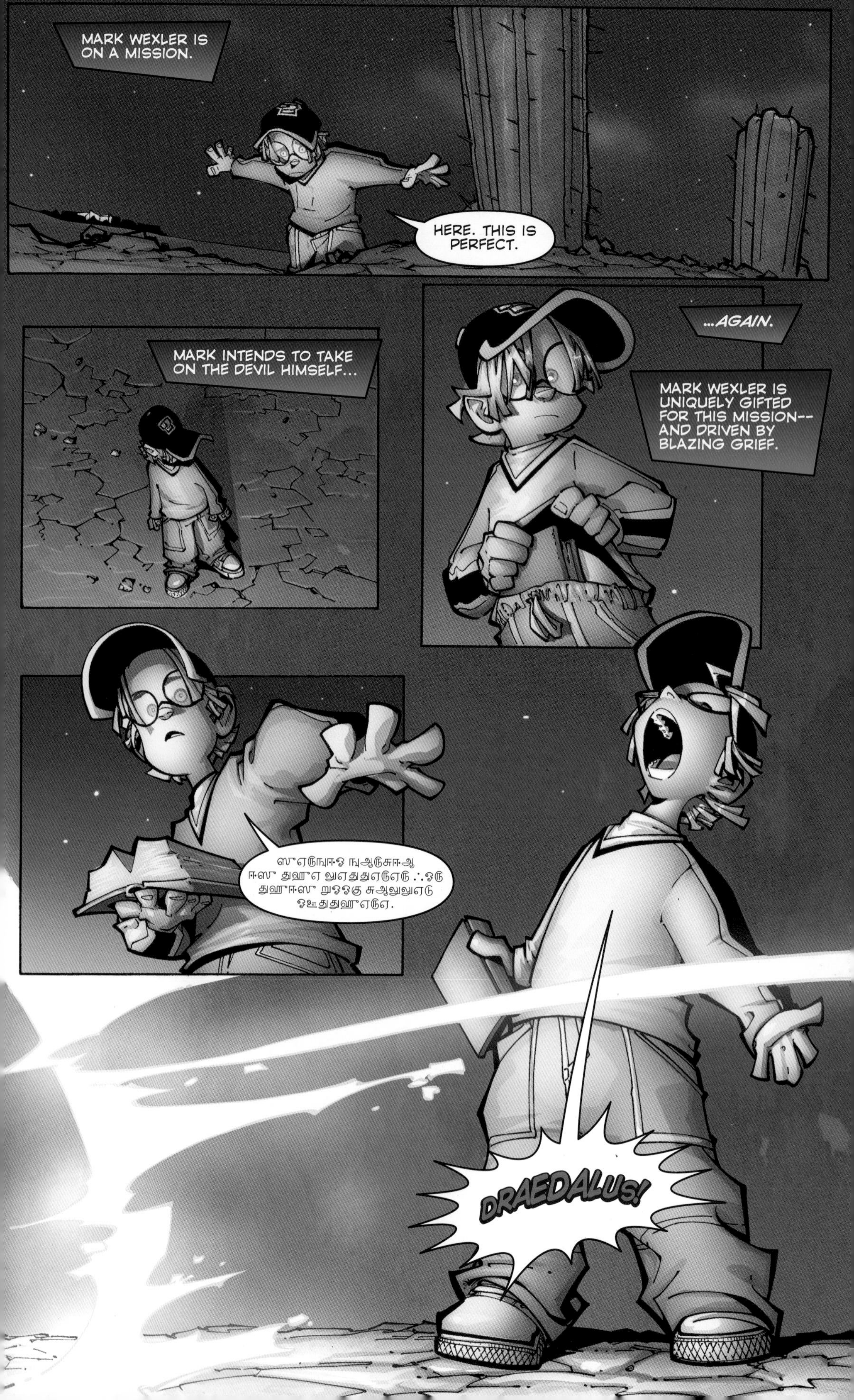
MARK WEXLER IS ON A MISSION.
HERE. THIS IS PERFECT.
MARK INTENDS TO TAKE ON THE DEVIL HIMSELF...
...AGAIN.
MARK WEXLER IS UNIQUELY GIFTED FOR THIS MISSION-- AND DRIVEN BY BLAZING GRIEF.
DRAEDALUS!

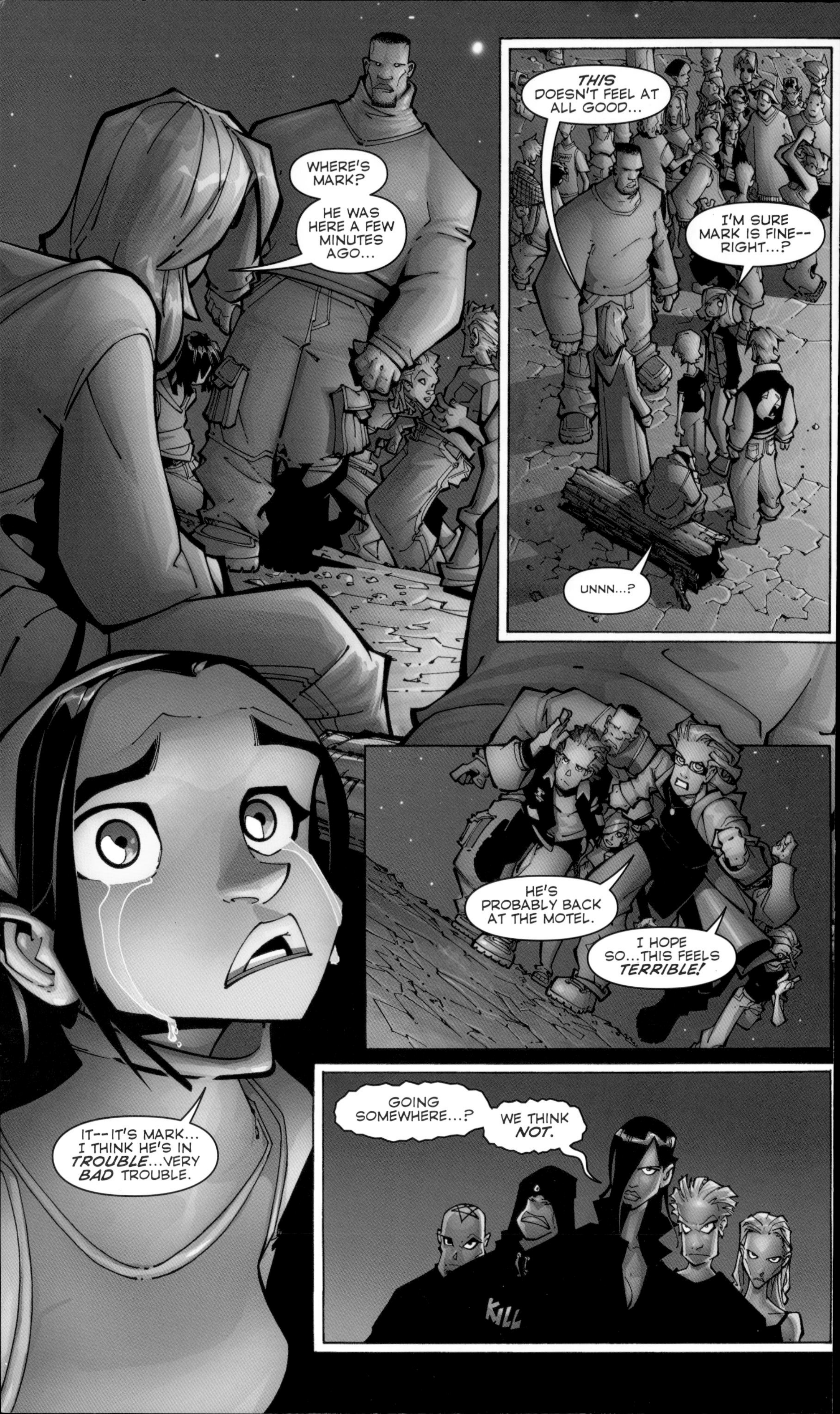
WHERE'S MARK?
HE WAS HERE A FEW MINUTES AGO...
THIS DOESN'T FEEL AT ALL GOOD...
I'M SURE MARK IS FINE-- RIGHT...?
UNNN...?
HE'S PROBABLY BACK AT THE MOTEL.
I HOPE SO...THIS FEELS *TERRIBLE!*
IT--IT'S MARK... I THINK HE'S IN *TROUBLE*...VERY *BAD* TROUBLE.
GOING SOMEWHERE...?
WE THINK *NOT*.
KILL

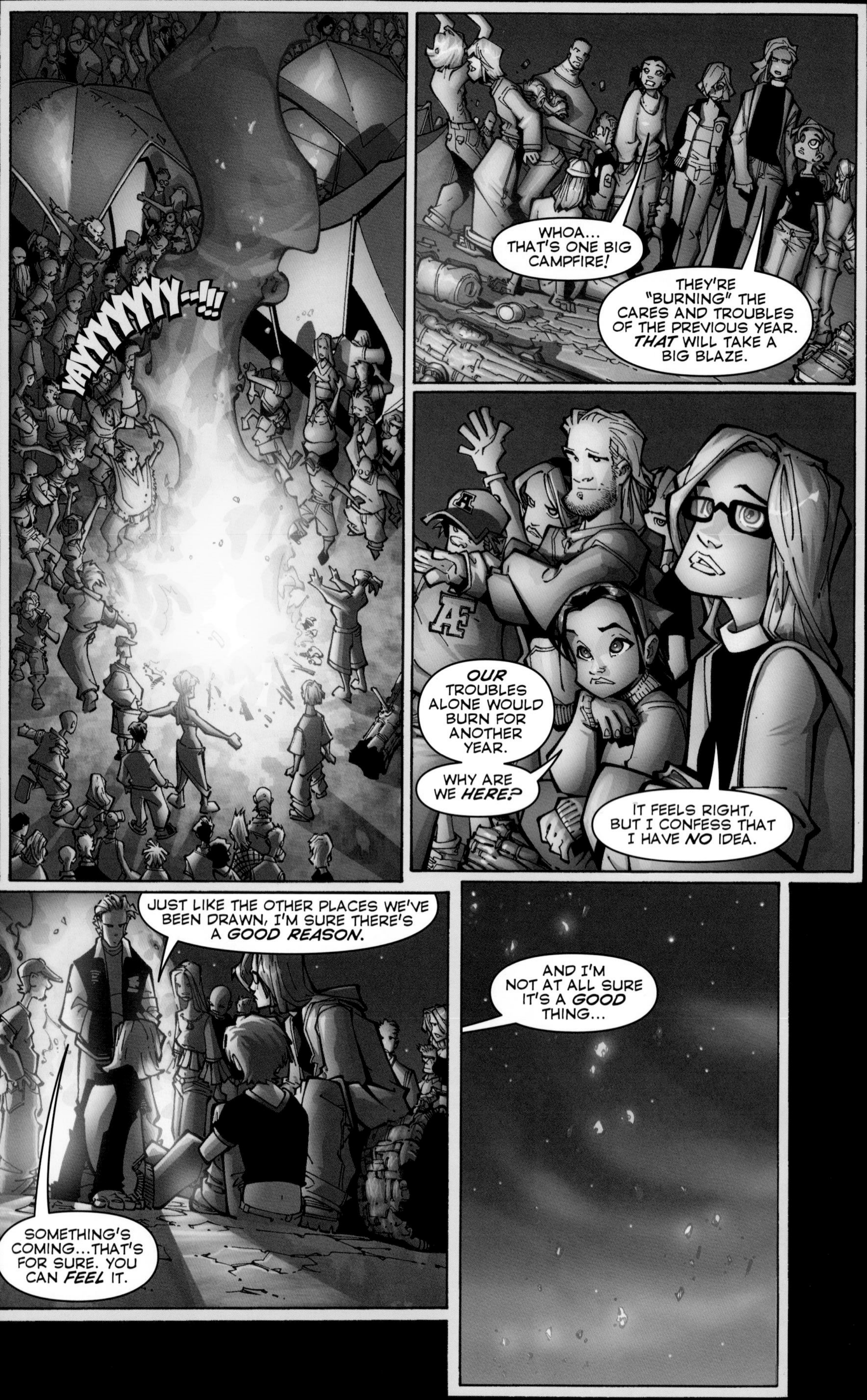
YAYYYYYYY--!!!
WHOA... THAT'S ONE BIG CAMPFIRE!
THEY'RE "BURNING" THE CARES AND TROUBLES OF THE PREVIOUS YEAR. THAT WILL TAKE A BIG BLAZE.
OUR TROUBLES ALONE WOULD BURN FOR ANOTHER YEAR.
WHY ARE WE HERE?
IT FEELS RIGHT, BUT I CONFESS THAT I HAVE NO IDEA.
JUST LIKE THE OTHER PLACES WE'VE BEEN DRAWN, I'M SURE THERE'S A GOOD REASON.
SOMETHING'S COMING...THAT'S FOR SURE. YOU CAN FEEL IT.
AND I'M NOT AT ALL SURE IT'S A GOOD THING...

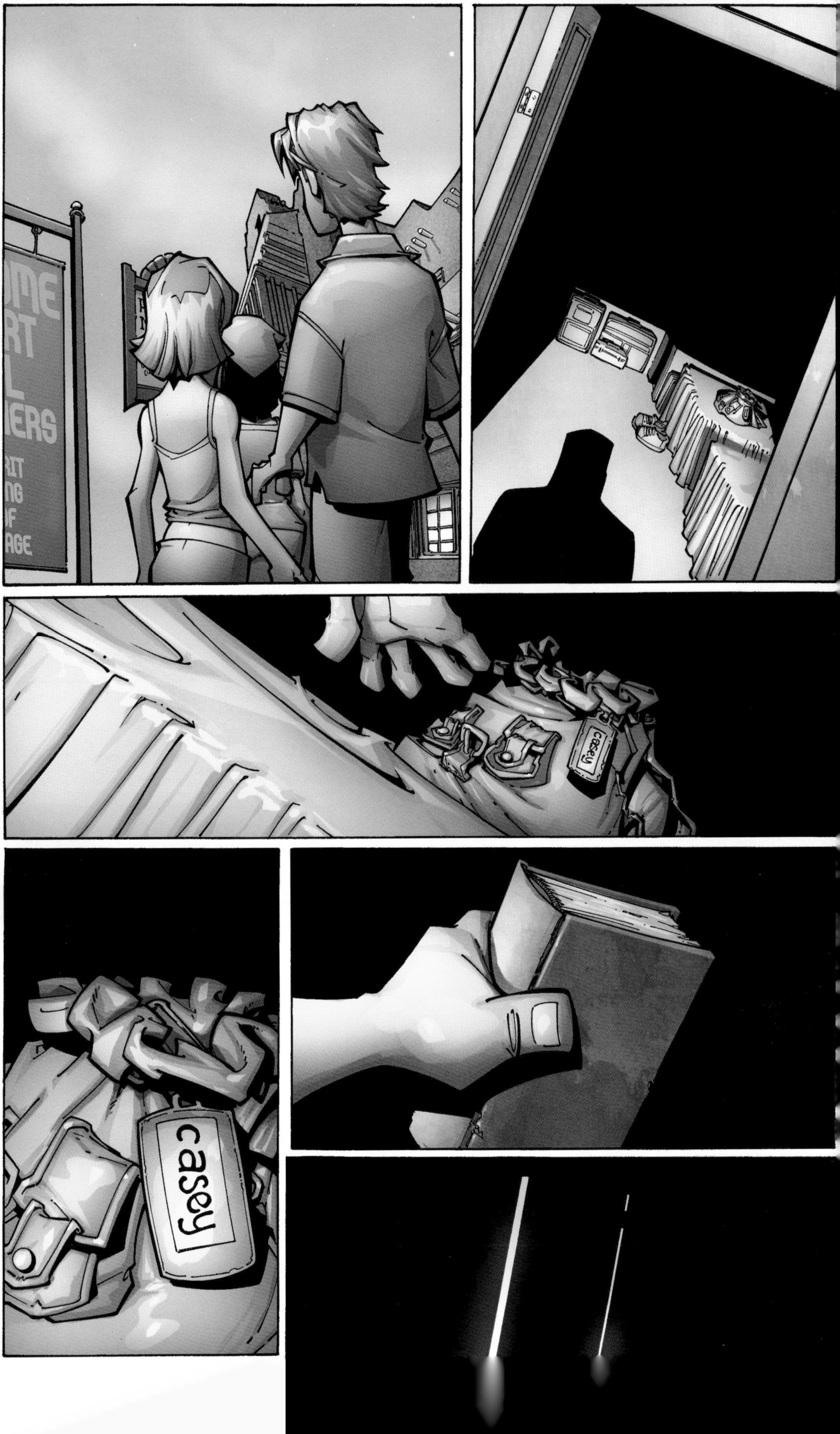
casey
casey

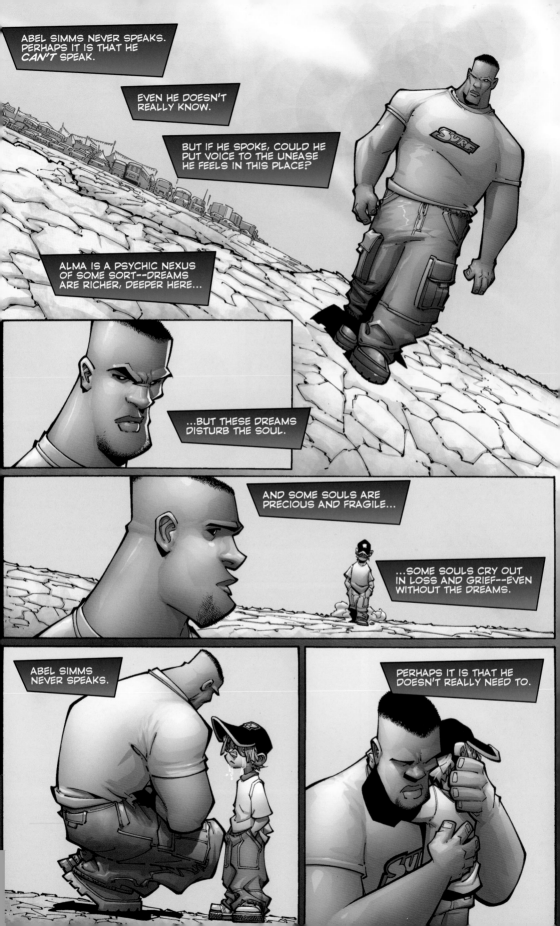

ABEL SIMMS NEVER SPEAKS. PERHAPS IT IS THAT HE *CAN'T* SPEAK.

EVEN HE DOESN'T REALLY KNOW.

BUT IF HE SPOKE, COULD HE PUT VOICE TO THE UNEASE HE FEELS IN THIS PLACE?

ALMA IS A PSYCHIC NEXUS OF SOME SORT--DREAMS ARE RICHER, DEEPER HERE...

...BUT THESE DREAMS DISTURB THE SOUL.

AND SOME SOULS ARE PRECIOUS AND FRAGILE...

...SOME SOULS CRY OUT IN LOSS AND GRIEF--EVEN WITHOUT THE DREAMS.

ABEL SIMMS NEVER SPEAKS.

PERHAPS IT IS THAT HE DOESN'T REALLY NEED TO.

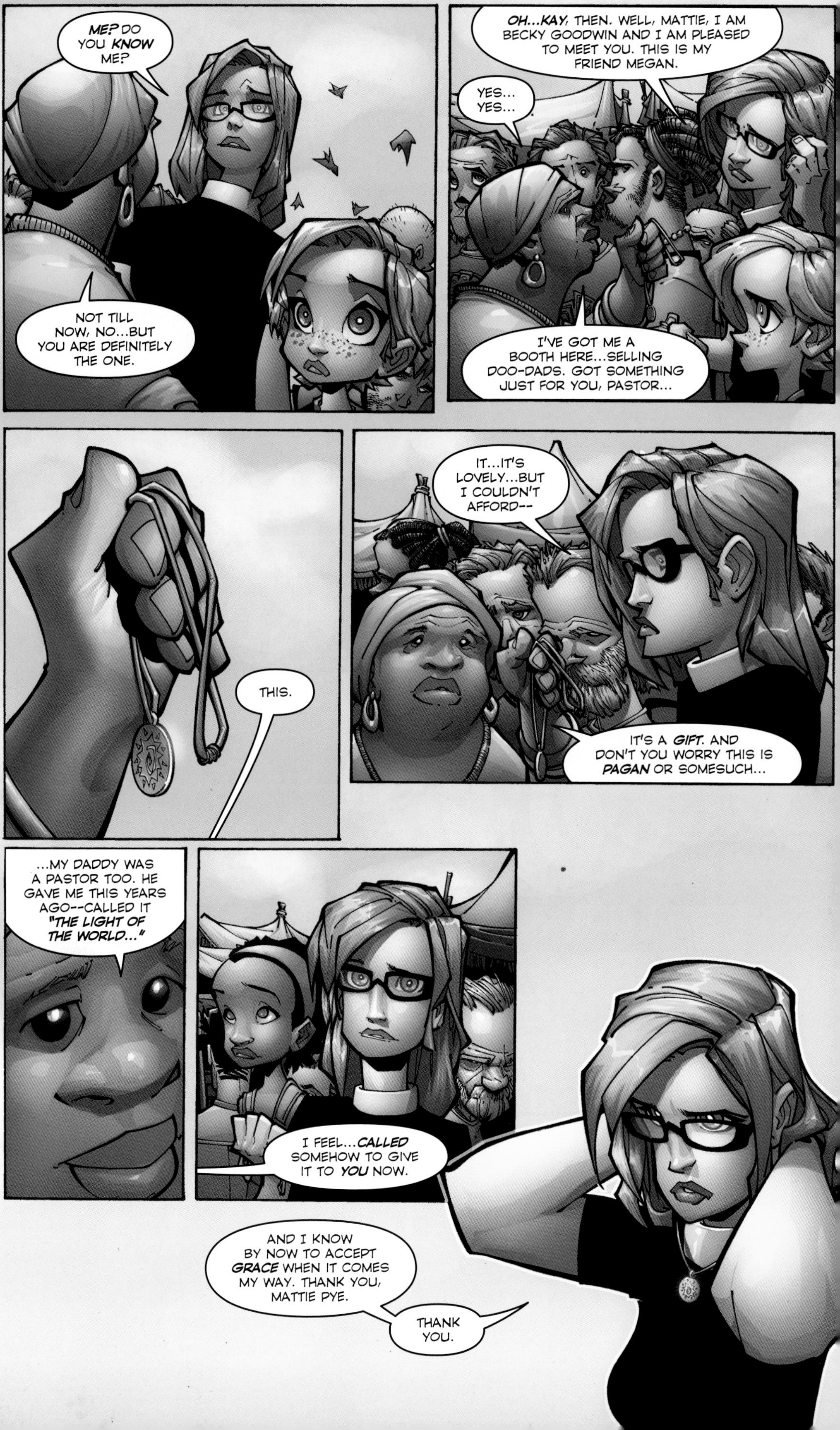

ME? DO YOU KNOW ME?
NOT TILL NOW, NO...BUT YOU ARE DEFINITELY THE ONE.
OH...KAY, THEN. WELL, MATTIE, I AM BECKY GOODWIN AND I AM PLEASED TO MEET YOU. THIS IS MY FRIEND MEGAN.
YES... YES...
I'VE GOT ME A BOOTH HERE...SELLING DOO-DADS. GOT SOMETHING JUST FOR YOU, PASTOR...
THIS.
IT...IT'S LOVELY...BUT I COULDN'T AFFORD--
IT'S A GIFT. AND DON'T YOU WORRY THIS IS PAGAN OR SOMESUCH...
...MY DADDY WAS A PASTOR TOO. HE GAVE ME THIS YEARS AGO--CALLED IT "THE LIGHT OF THE WORLD..."
I FEEL...CALLED SOMEHOW TO GIVE IT TO YOU NOW.
AND I KNOW BY NOW TO ACCEPT GRACE WHEN IT COMES MY WAY. THANK YOU, MATTIE PYE.
THANK YOU.

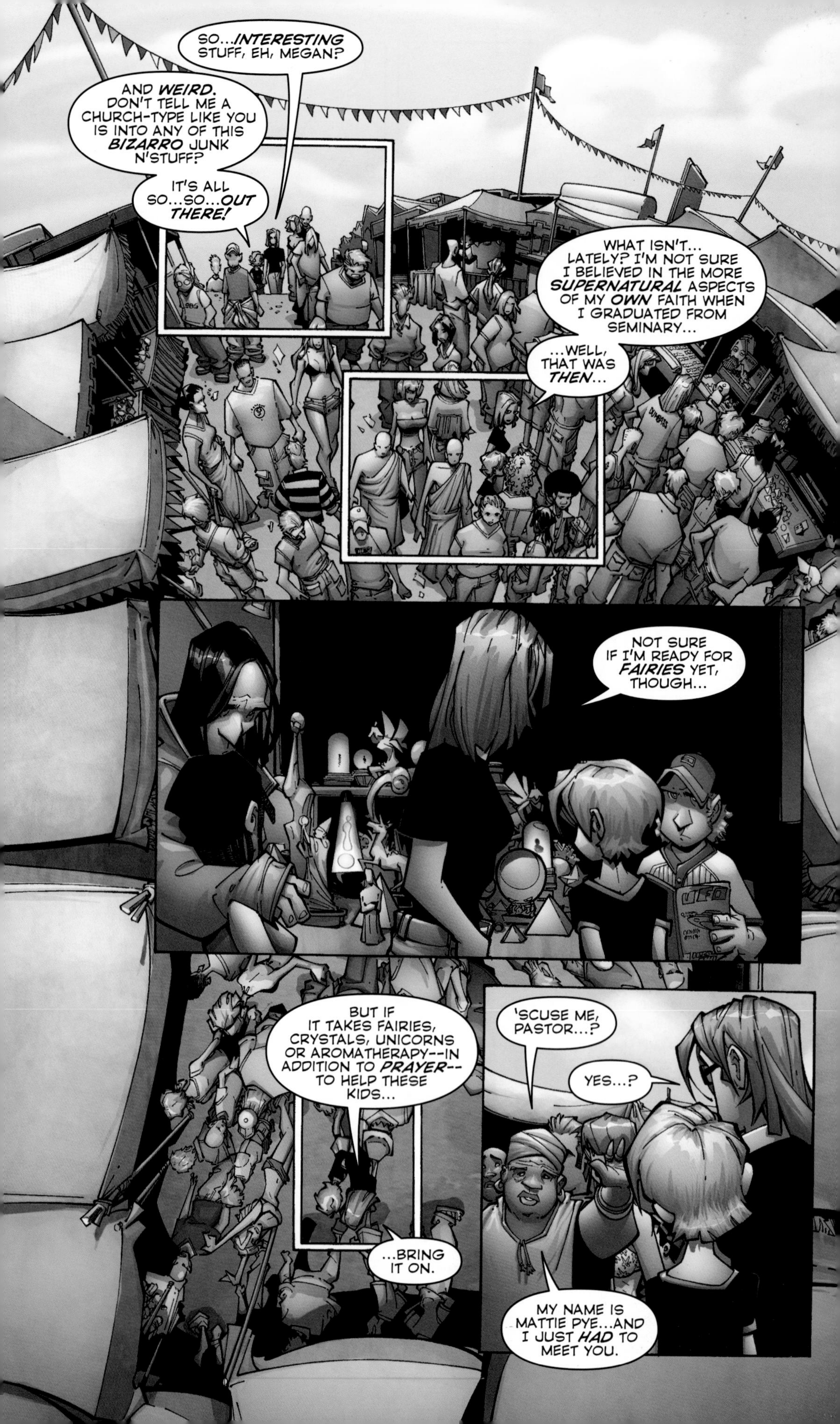

SO...*INTERESTING* STUFF, EH, MEGAN?
AND *WEIRD.* DON'T TELL ME A CHURCH-TYPE LIKE YOU IS INTO ANY OF THIS *BIZARRO* JUNK N'STUFF?
IT'S ALL SO...SO...*OUT THERE!*
WHAT ISN'T... LATELY? I'M NOT SURE I BELIEVED IN THE MORE *SUPERNATURAL* ASPECTS OF MY *OWN* FAITH WHEN I GRADUATED FROM SEMINARY...
...WELL, THAT WAS *THEN*...
NOT SURE IF I'M READY FOR *FAIRIES* YET, THOUGH...
UFO
BUT IF IT TAKES FAIRIES, CRYSTALS, UNICORNS OR AROMATHERAPY--IN ADDITION TO *PRAYER*-- TO HELP THESE KIDS...
...BRING IT ON.
'SCUSE ME, PASTOR...?
YES...?
MY NAME IS MATTIE PYE...AND I JUST *HAD* TO MEET YOU.

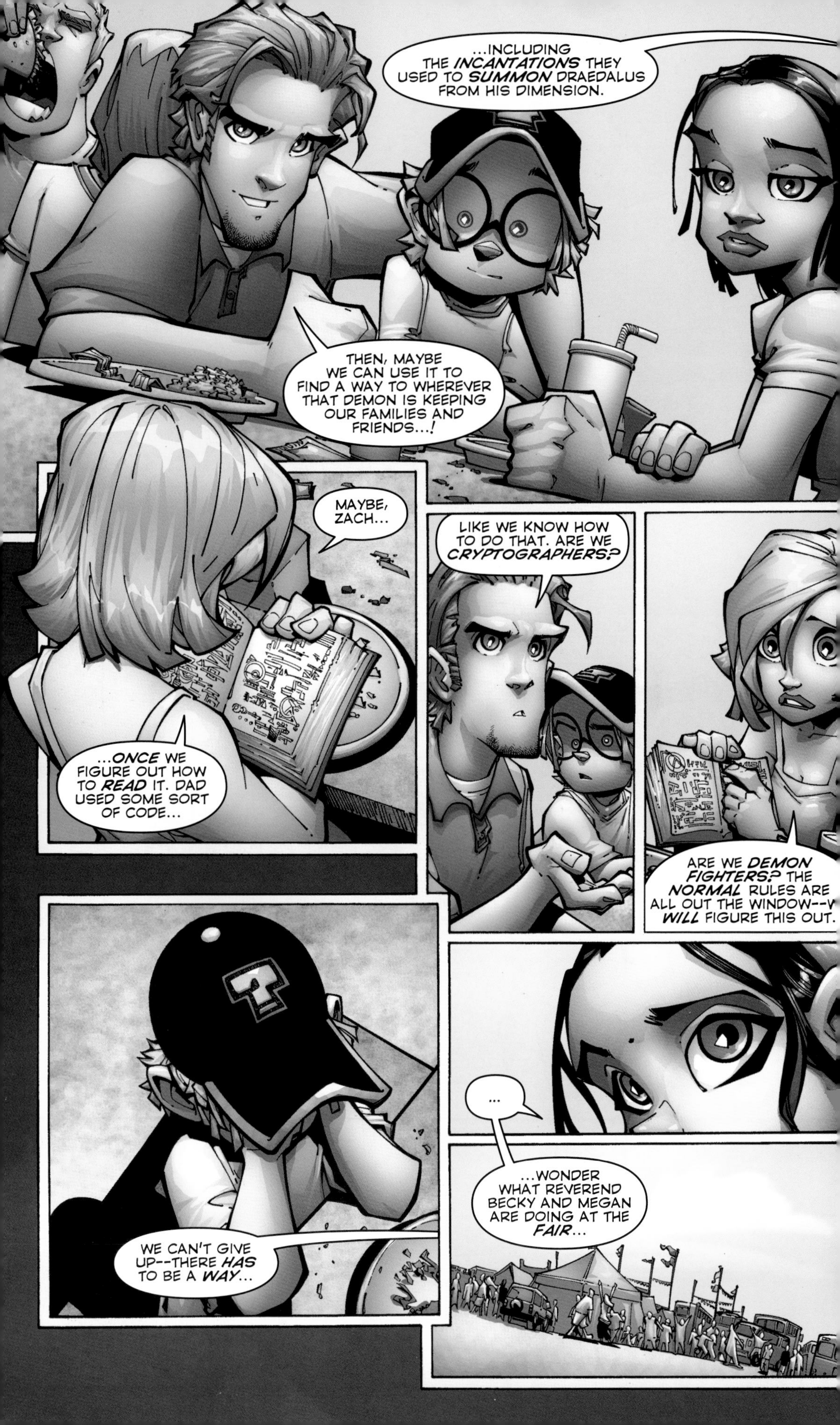
...INCLUDING THE *INCANTATIONS* THEY USED TO *SUMMON* DRAEDALUS FROM HIS DIMENSION.
THEN, MAYBE WE CAN USE IT TO FIND A WAY TO WHEREVER THAT DEMON IS KEEPING OUR FAMILIES AND FRIENDS...!
MAYBE, ZACH...
...*ONCE* WE FIGURE OUT HOW TO *READ* IT. DAD USED SOME SORT OF CODE...
LIKE WE KNOW HOW TO DO THAT. ARE WE *CRYPTOGRAPHERS?*
ARE WE *DEMON FIGHTERS?* THE *NORMAL* RULES ARE ALL OUT THE WINDOW--W *WILL* FIGURE THIS OUT.
WE CAN'T GIVE UP--THERE *HAS* TO BE A *WAY*...
...
...WONDER WHAT REVEREND BECKY AND MEGAN ARE DOING AT THE *FAIR*...

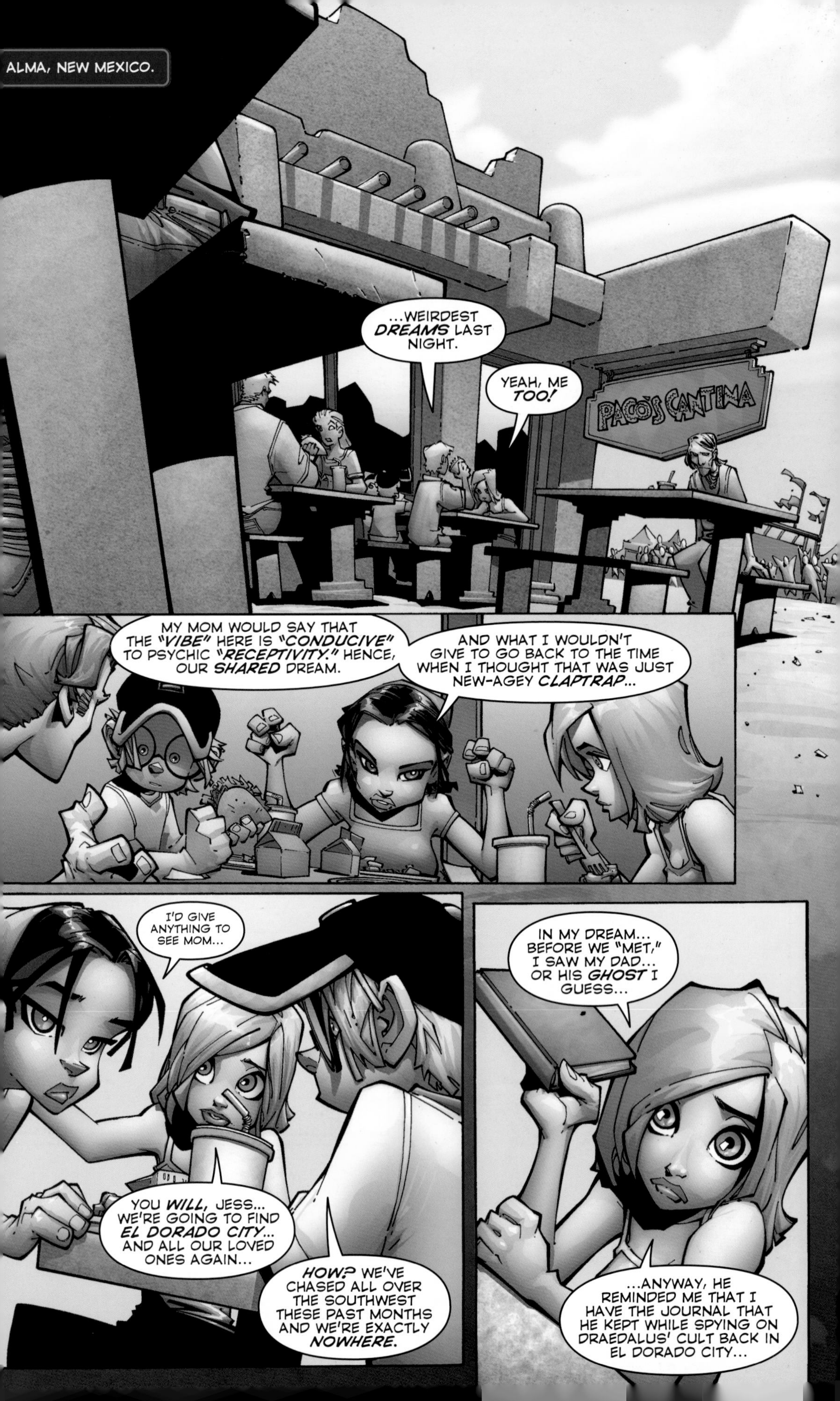

ALMA, NEW MEXICO.
...WEIRDEST DREAMS LAST NIGHT.
YEAH, ME TOO!
PACO'S CANTINA
MY MOM WOULD SAY THAT THE "VIBE" HERE IS "CONDUCIVE" TO PSYCHIC "RECEPTIVITY." HENCE, OUR SHARED DREAM.
AND WHAT I WOULDN'T GIVE TO GO BACK TO THE TIME WHEN I THOUGHT THAT WAS JUST NEW-AGEY CLAPTRAP...
I'D GIVE ANYTHING TO SEE MOM...
YOU WILL, JESS... WE'RE GOING TO FIND EL DORADO CITY... AND ALL OUR LOVED ONES AGAIN...
HOW? WE'VE CHASED ALL OVER THE SOUTHWEST THESE PAST MONTHS AND WE'RE EXACTLY NOWHERE.
IN MY DREAM... BEFORE WE "MET," I SAW MY DAD... OR HIS GHOST I GUESS...
...ANYWAY, HE REMINDED ME THAT I HAVE THE JOURNAL THAT HE KEPT WHILE SPYING ON DRAEDALUS' CULT BACK IN EL DORADO CITY...

CHAPTER TWELVE
WHERE THE HEART IS

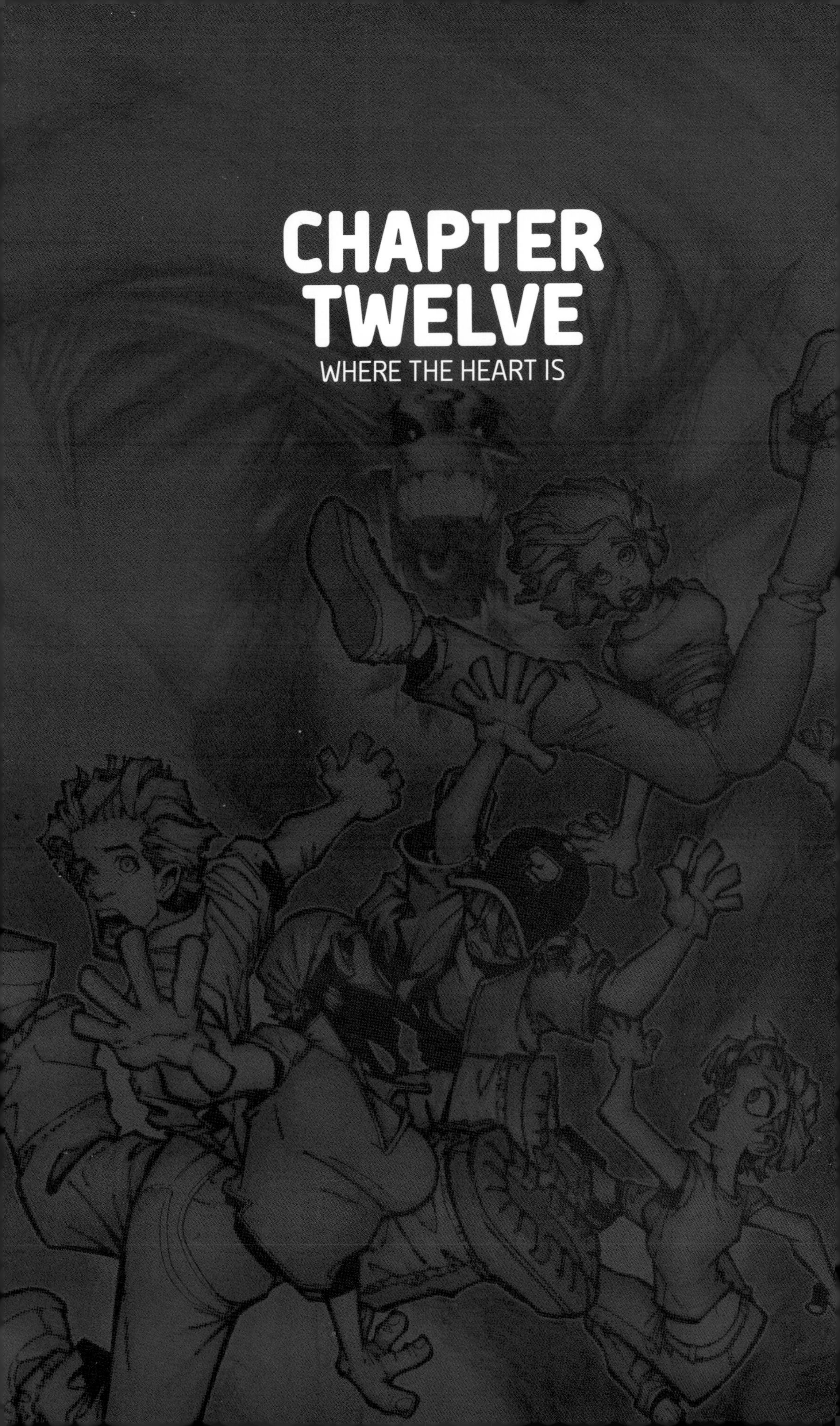

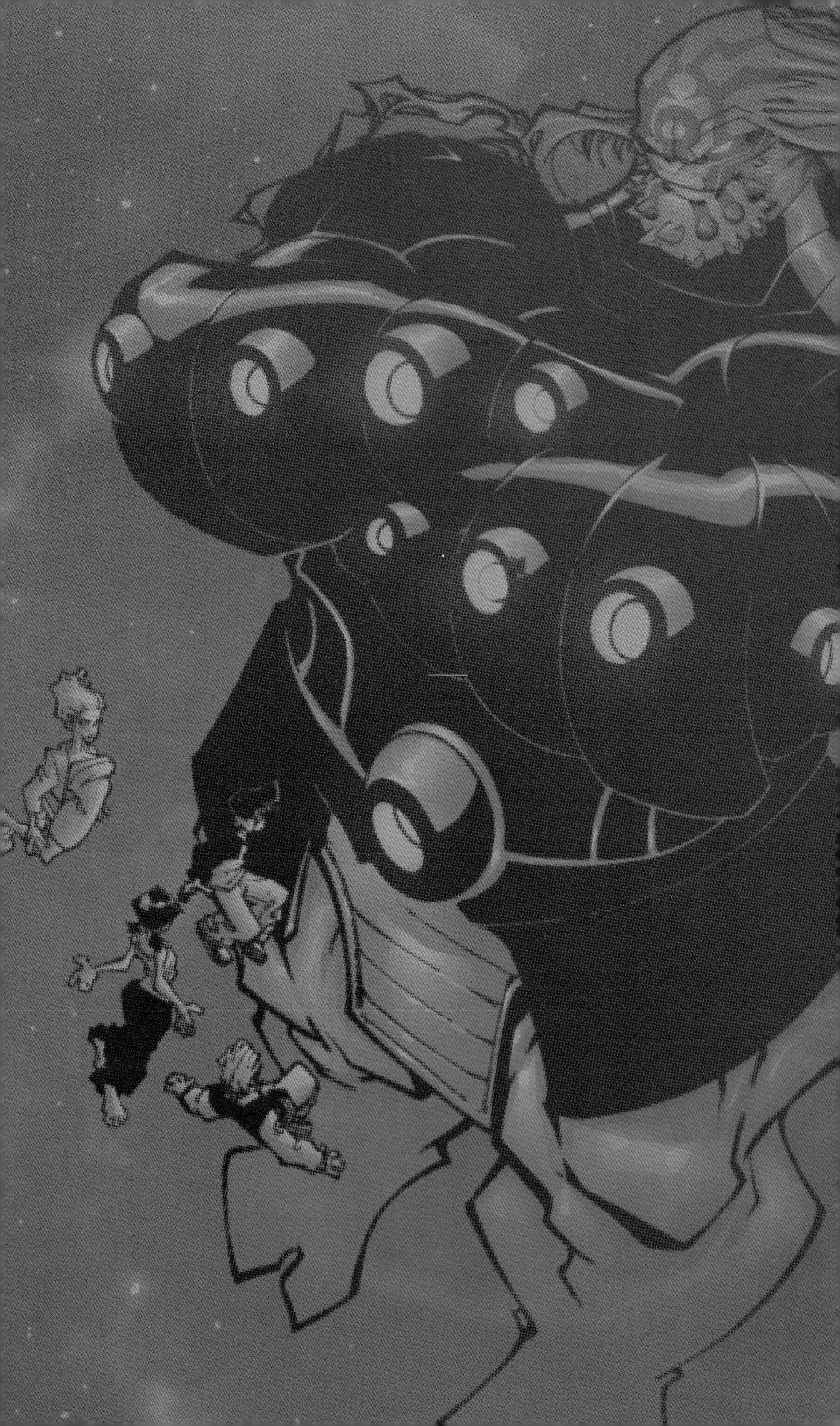

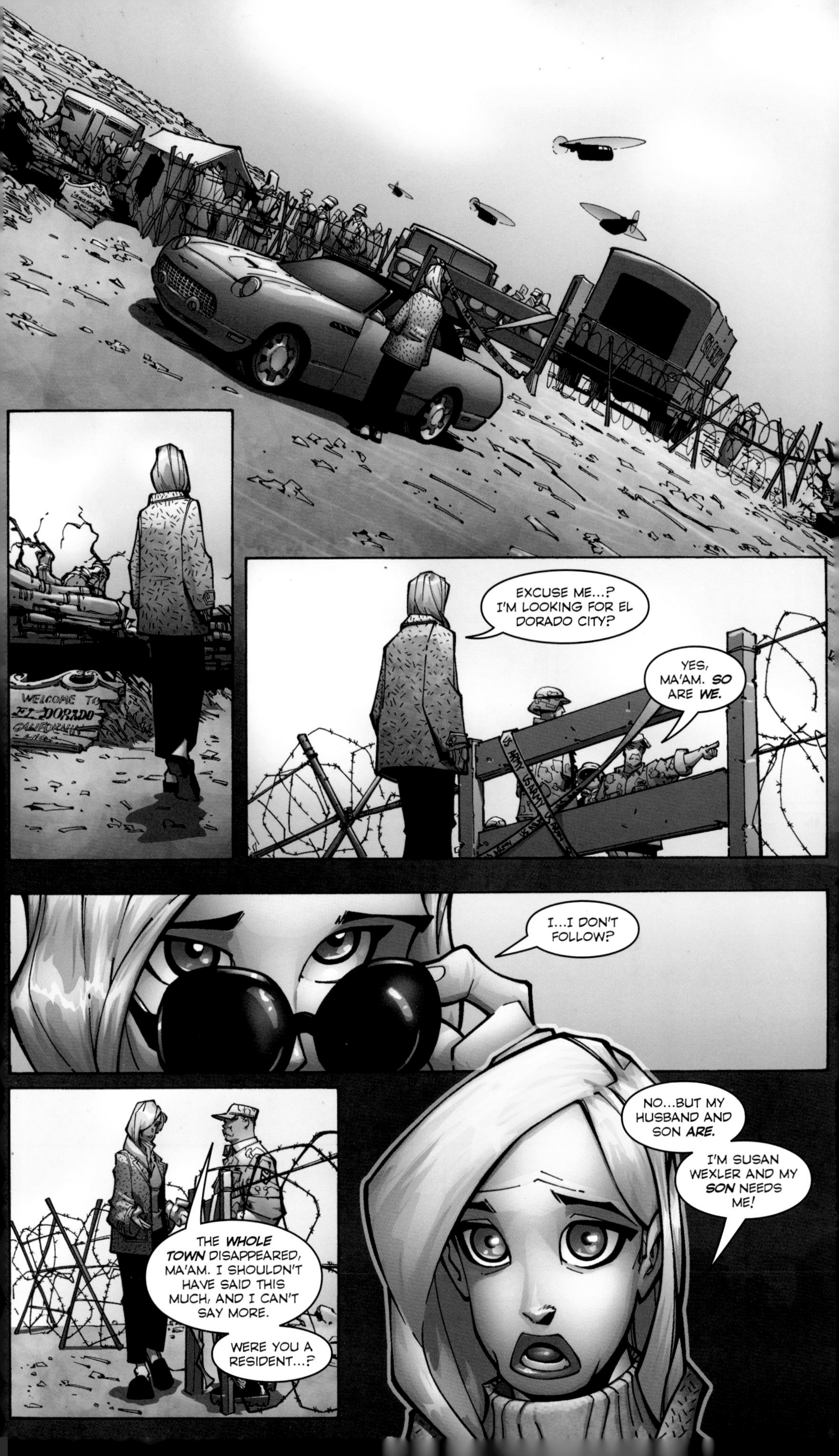
WELCOME TO
EL DORADO
CALIFORNIA
EXCUSE ME...? I'M LOOKING FOR EL DORADO CITY?
YES, MA'AM. **SO** ARE **WE.**
US ARMY
I...I DON'T FOLLOW?
THE **WHOLE TOWN** DISAPPEARED, MA'AM. I SHOULDN'T HAVE SAID THIS MUCH, AND I CAN'T SAY MORE.
WERE YOU A RESIDENT...?
NO...BUT MY HUSBAND AND SON **ARE.**
I'M SUSAN WEXLER AND MY **SON** NEEDS ME!

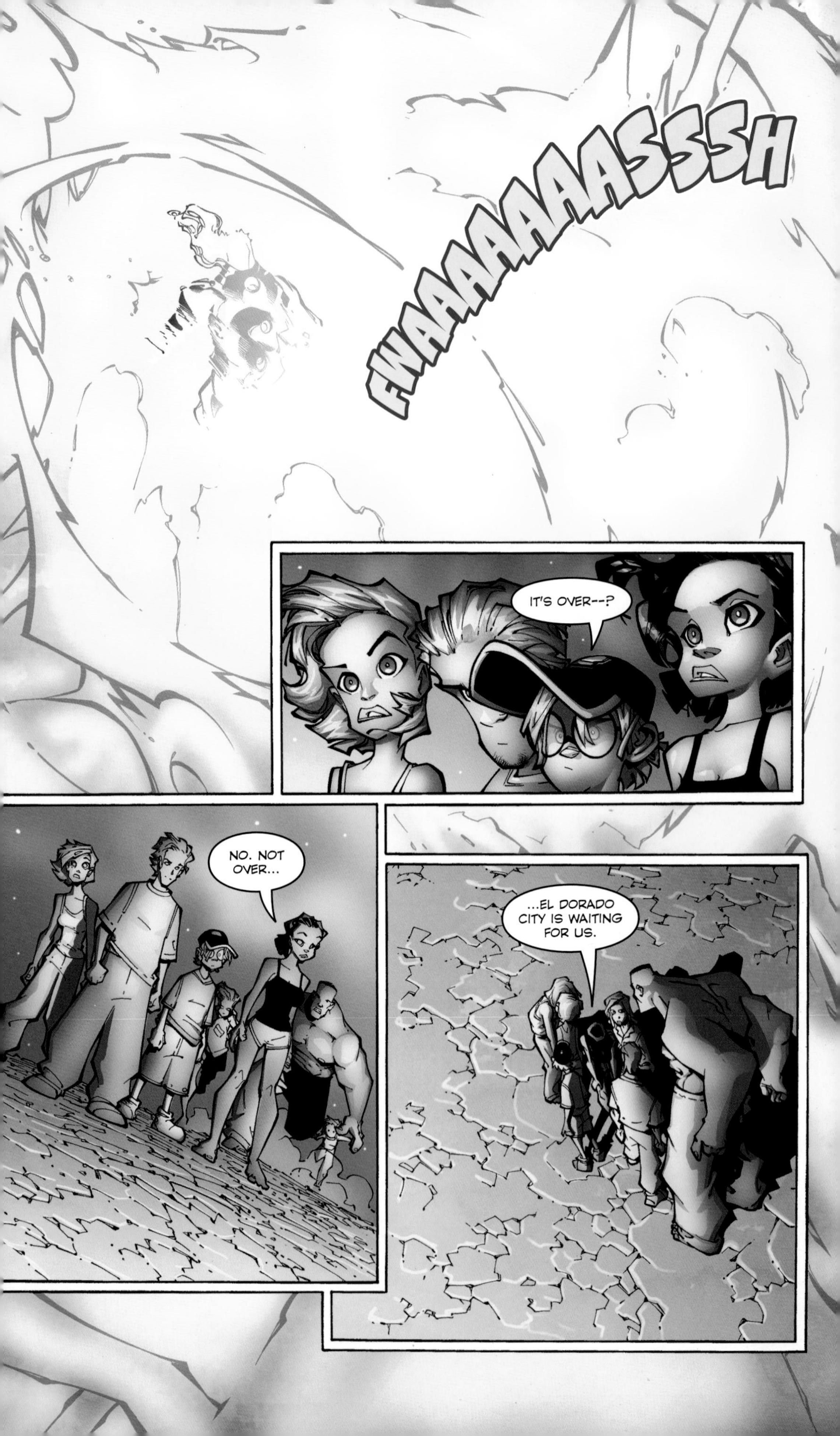
FWAAAAAAASSSH
IT'S OVER--?
NO. NOT OVER...
...EL DORADO CITY IS WAITING FOR US.

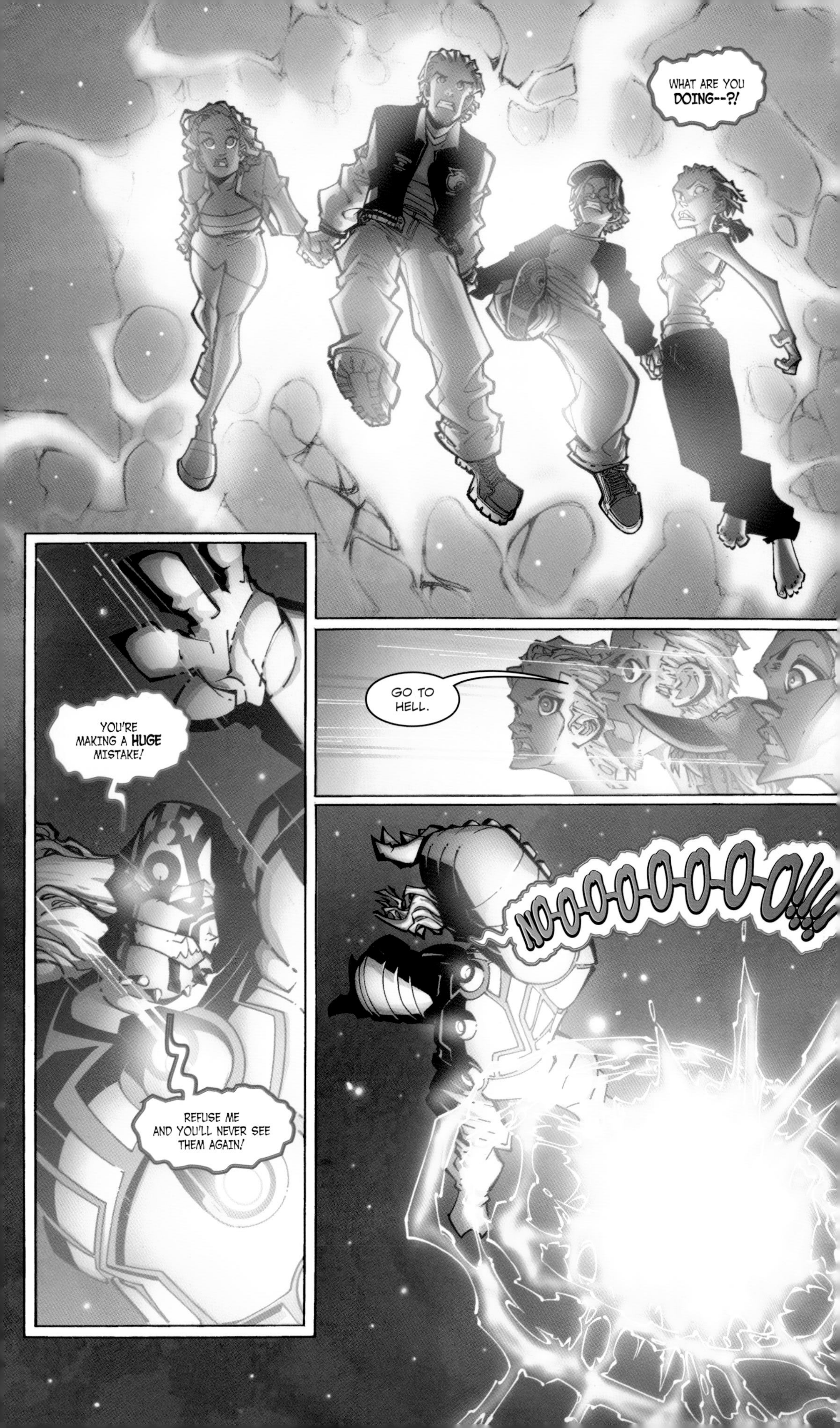
WHAT ARE YOU DOING--?!
YOU'RE MAKING A HUGE MISTAKE!
GO TO HELL.
REFUSE ME AND YOU'LL NEVER SEE THEM AGAIN!
NO-O-O-O-O-O-O-O-O-O!!!

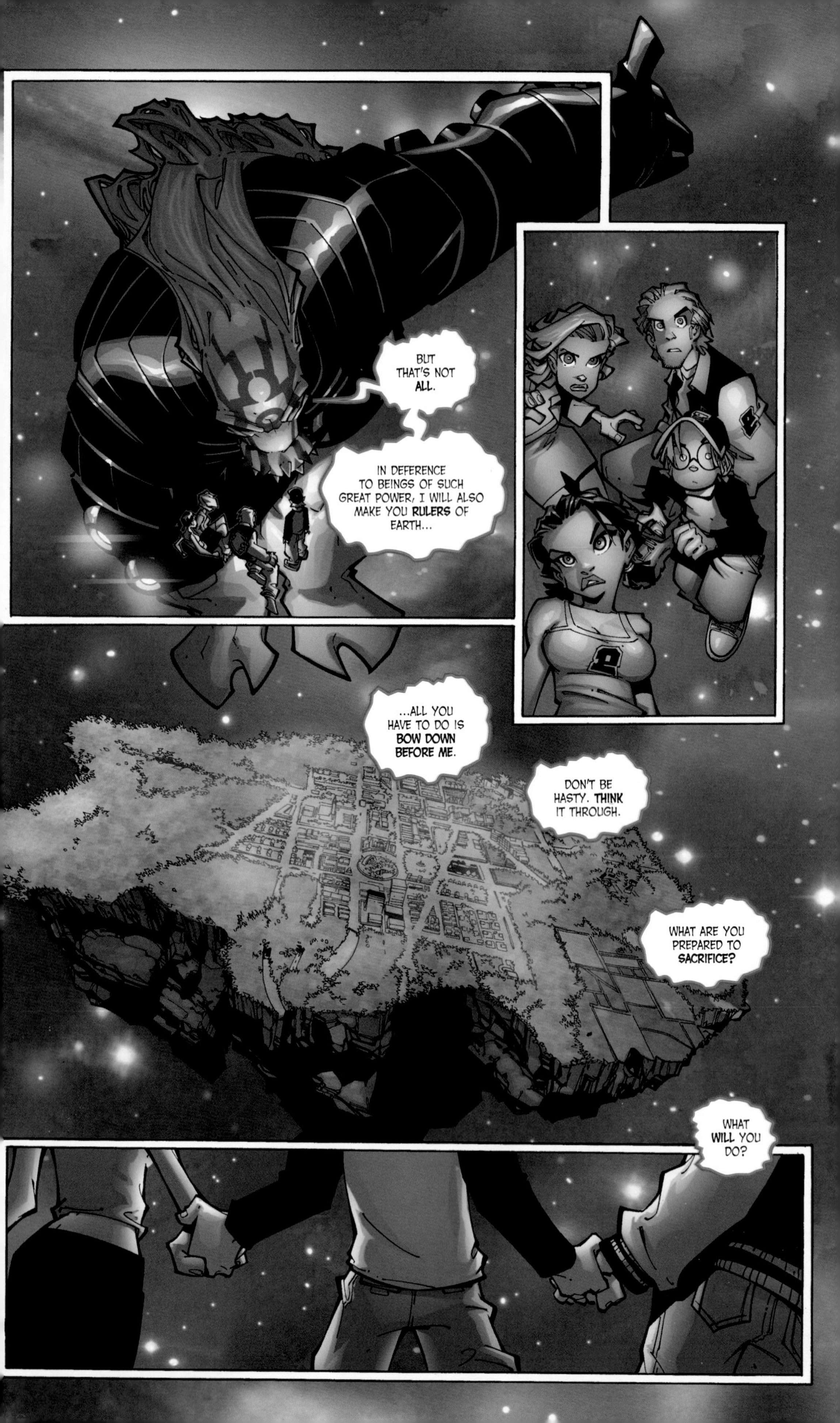
BUT THAT'S NOT **ALL**.
IN DEFERENCE TO BEINGS OF SUCH GREAT POWER, I WILL ALSO MAKE YOU **RULERS** OF EARTH...
...ALL YOU HAVE TO DO IS **BOW DOWN BEFORE ME**.
DON'T BE HASTY. **THINK** IT THROUGH.
WHAT ARE YOU PREPARED TO **SACRIFICE?**
WHAT **WILL** YOU DO?

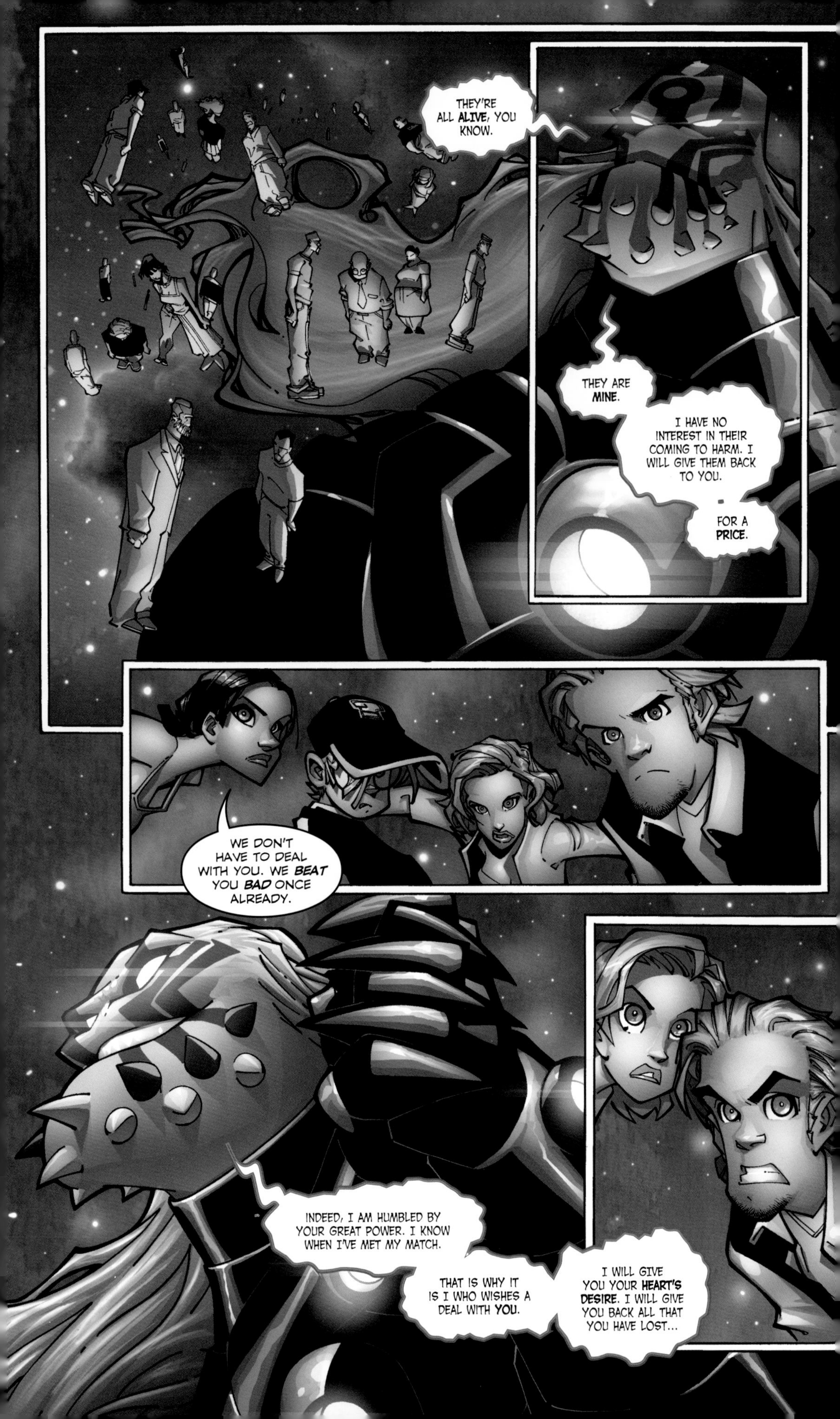

THEY'RE ALL **ALIVE**, YOU KNOW.
THEY ARE **MINE**.
I HAVE NO INTEREST IN THEIR COMING TO HARM. I WILL GIVE THEM BACK TO YOU.
FOR A **PRICE**.
WE DON'T HAVE TO DEAL WITH YOU. WE ***BEAT*** YOU ***BAD*** ONCE ALREADY.
INDEED, I AM HUMBLED BY YOUR GREAT POWER. I KNOW WHEN I'VE MET MY MATCH.
THAT IS WHY IT IS I WHO WISHES A DEAL WITH **YOU**.
I WILL GIVE YOU YOUR **HEART'S DESIRE**. I WILL GIVE YOU BACK ALL THAT YOU HAVE LOST...

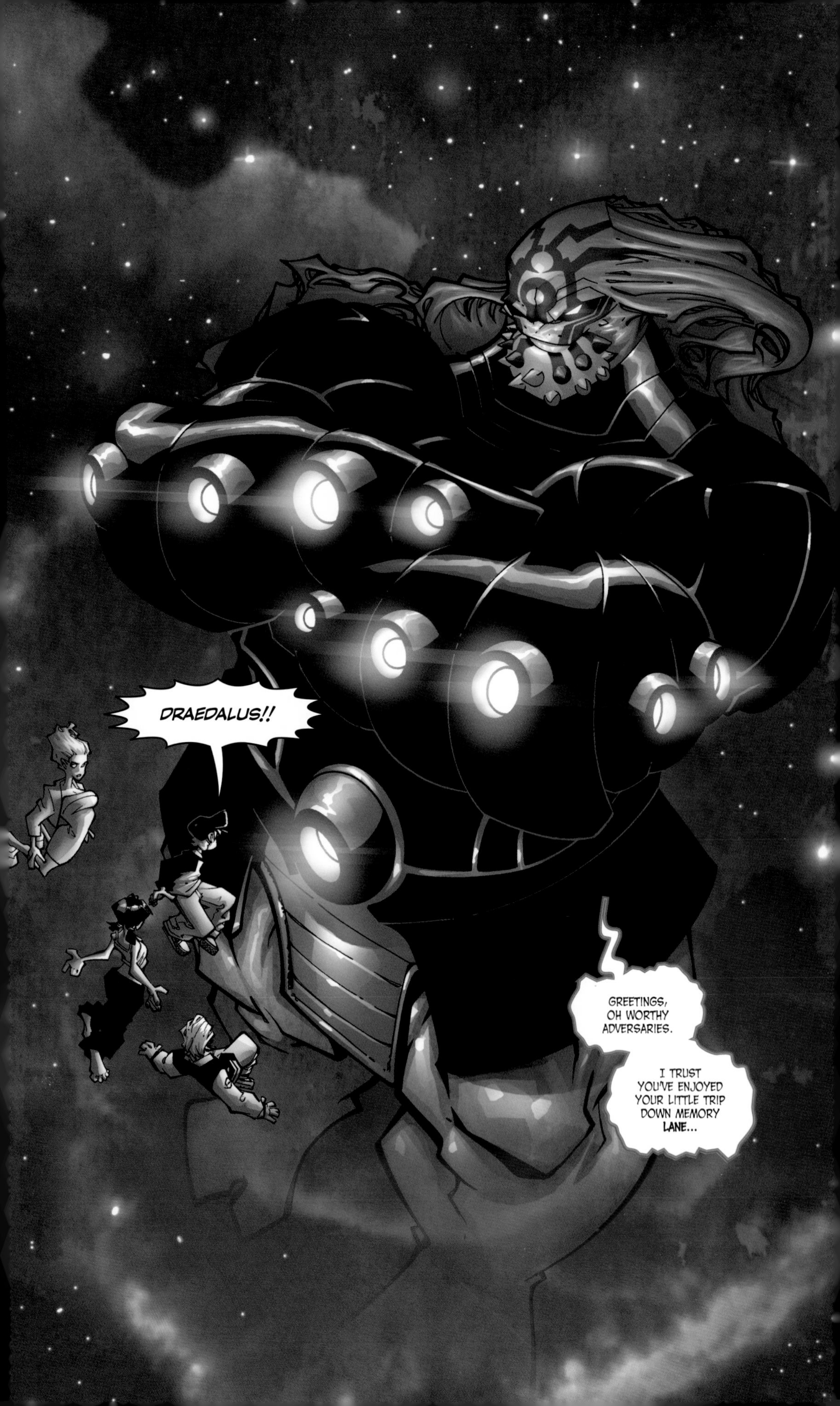
DRAEDALUS!!
GREETINGS, OH WORTHY ADVERSARIES.
I TRUST YOU'VE ENJOYED YOUR LITTLE TRIP DOWN MEMORY LANE...

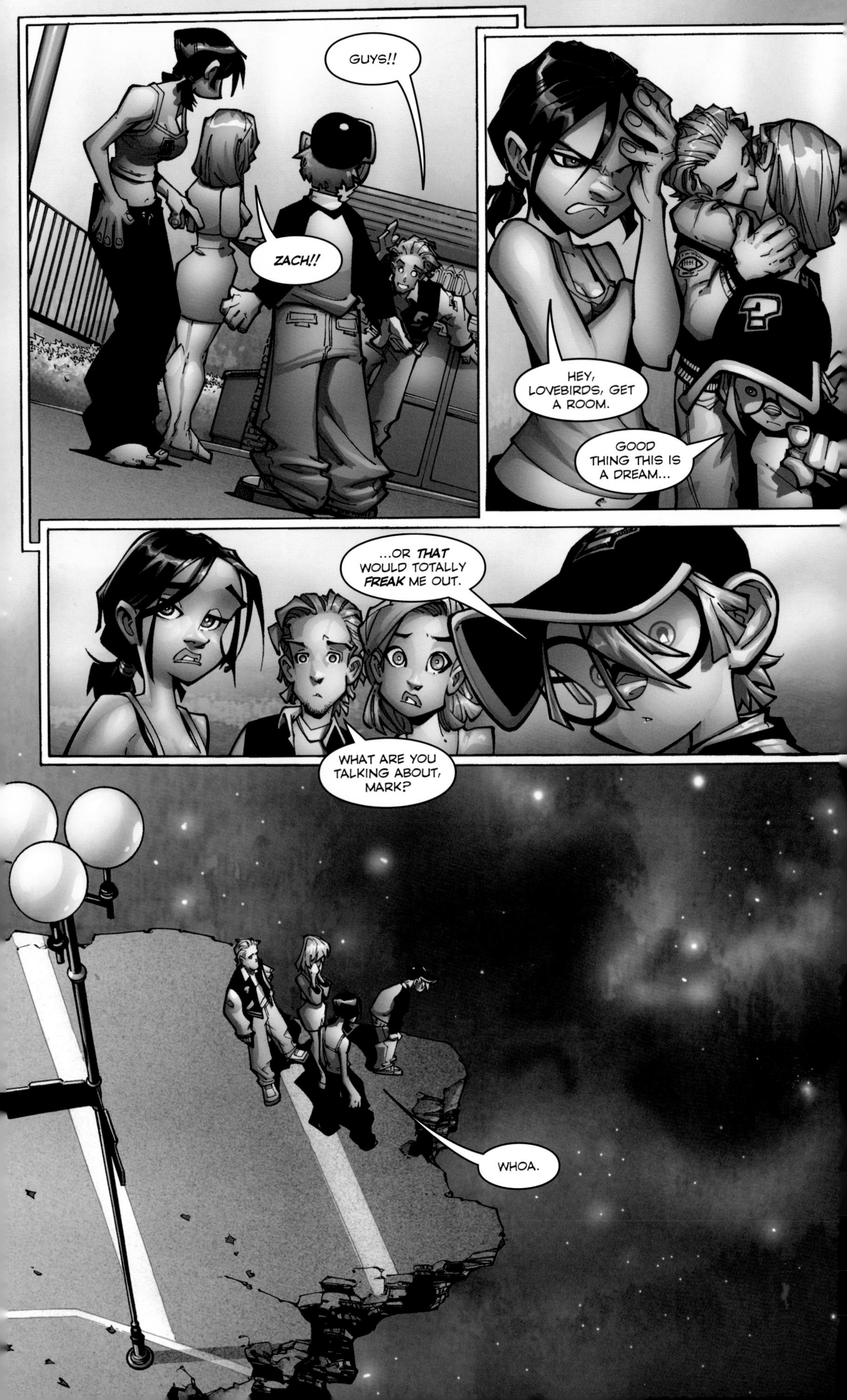
GUYS!!
ZACH!!
HEY, LOVEBIRDS, GET A ROOM.
GOOD THING THIS IS A DREAM...
...OR THAT WOULD TOTALLY FREAK ME OUT.
WHAT ARE YOU TALKING ABOUT, MARK?
WHOA.

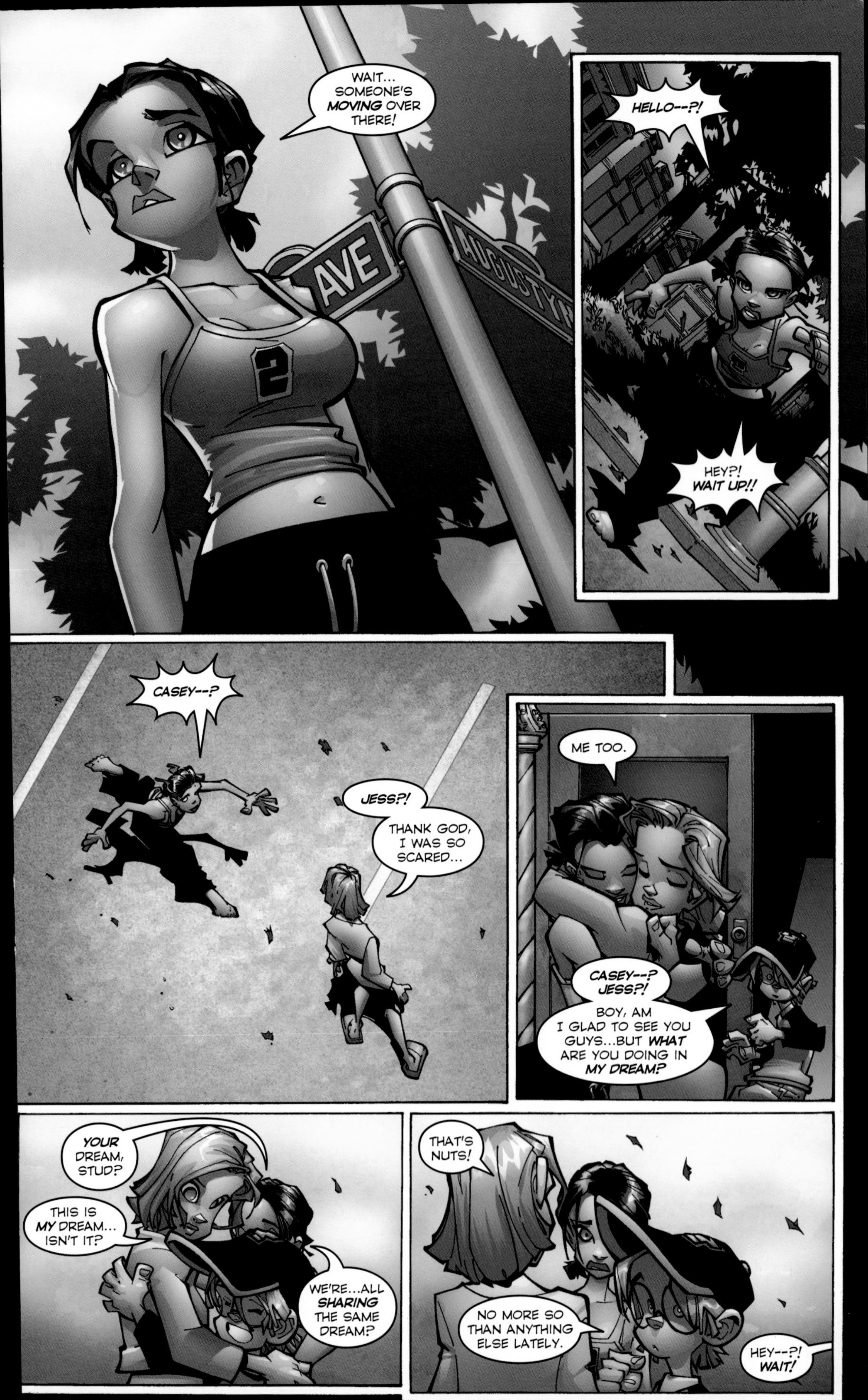
WAIT... SOMEONE'S MOVING OVER THERE!
AVE
AUGUSTYN
HELLO--?!
HEY?! WAIT UP!!
CASEY--?
JESS?!
THANK GOD, I WAS SO SCARED...
ME TOO.
CASEY--? JESS?!
BOY, AM I GLAD TO SEE YOU GUYS...BUT WHAT ARE YOU DOING IN MY DREAM?
YOUR DREAM, STUD?
THIS IS MY DREAM... ISN'T IT?
WE'RE...ALL SHARING THE SAME DREAM?
THAT'S NUTS!
NO MORE SO THAN ANYTHING ELSE LATELY.
HEY--?! WAIT!

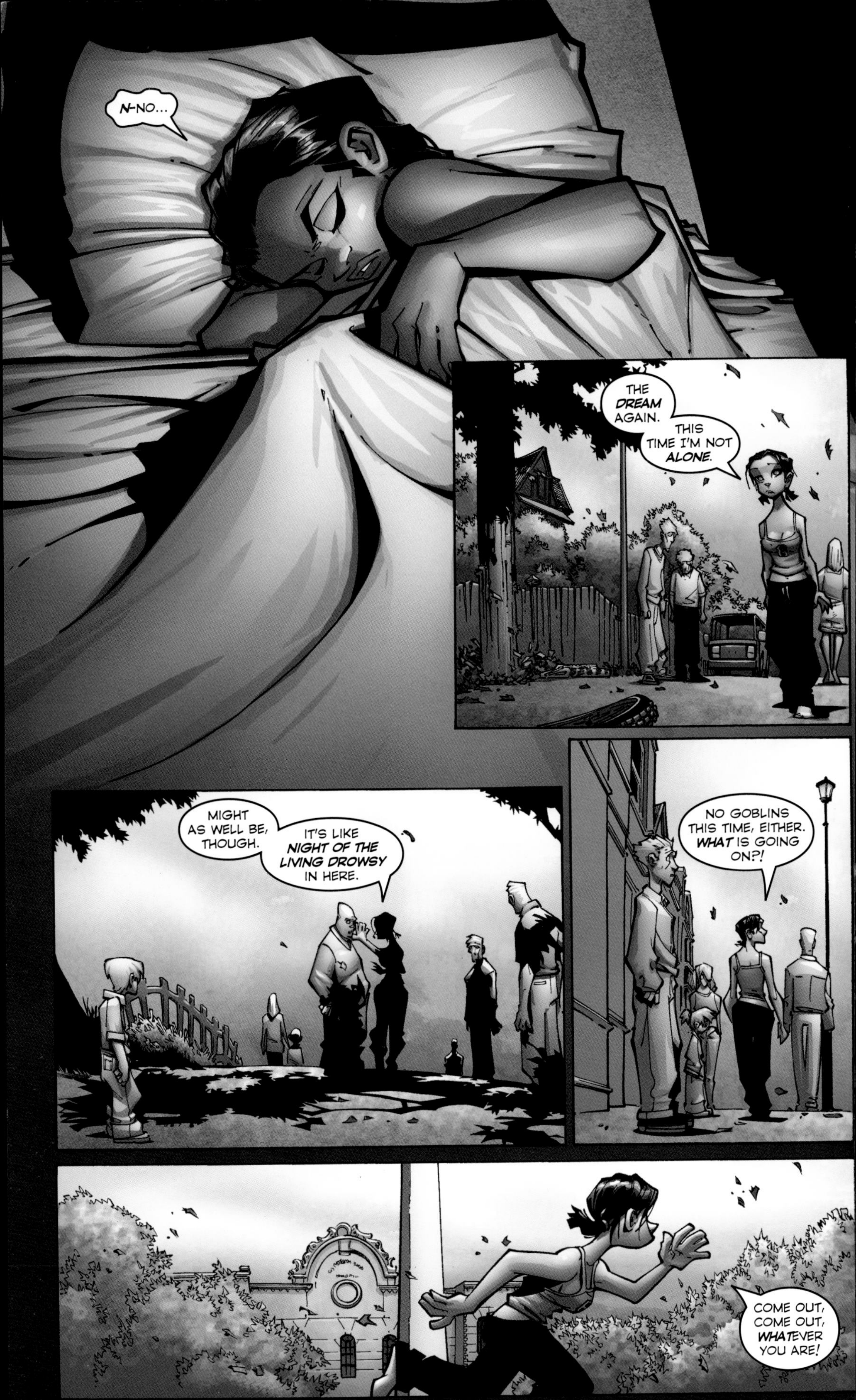
N-NO...
THE DREAM AGAIN.
THIS TIME I'M NOT ALONE.
MIGHT AS WELL BE, THOUGH.
IT'S LIKE NIGHT OF THE LIVING DROWSY IN HERE.
NO GOBLINS THIS TIME, EITHER. WHAT IS GOING ON?!
COME OUT, COME OUT, WHATEVER YOU ARE!

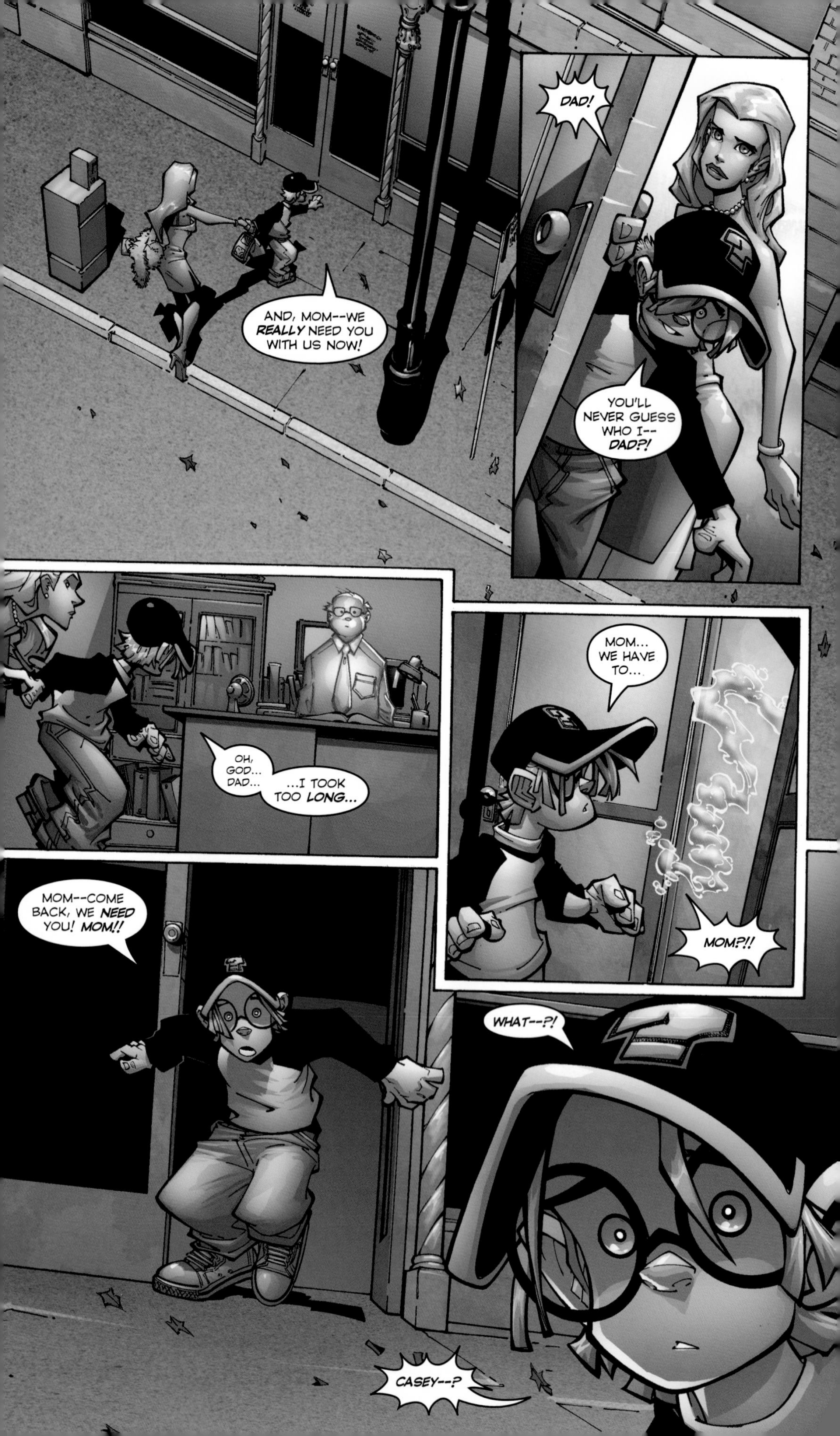
DAD!
AND, MOM--WE REALLY NEED YOU WITH US NOW!
YOU'LL NEVER GUESS WHO I-- DAD?!
OH, GOD... DAD...
...I TOOK TOO LONG...
MOM... WE HAVE TO...
MOM?!!
MOM--COME BACK, WE NEED YOU! MOM!!
WHAT--?!
CASEY--?

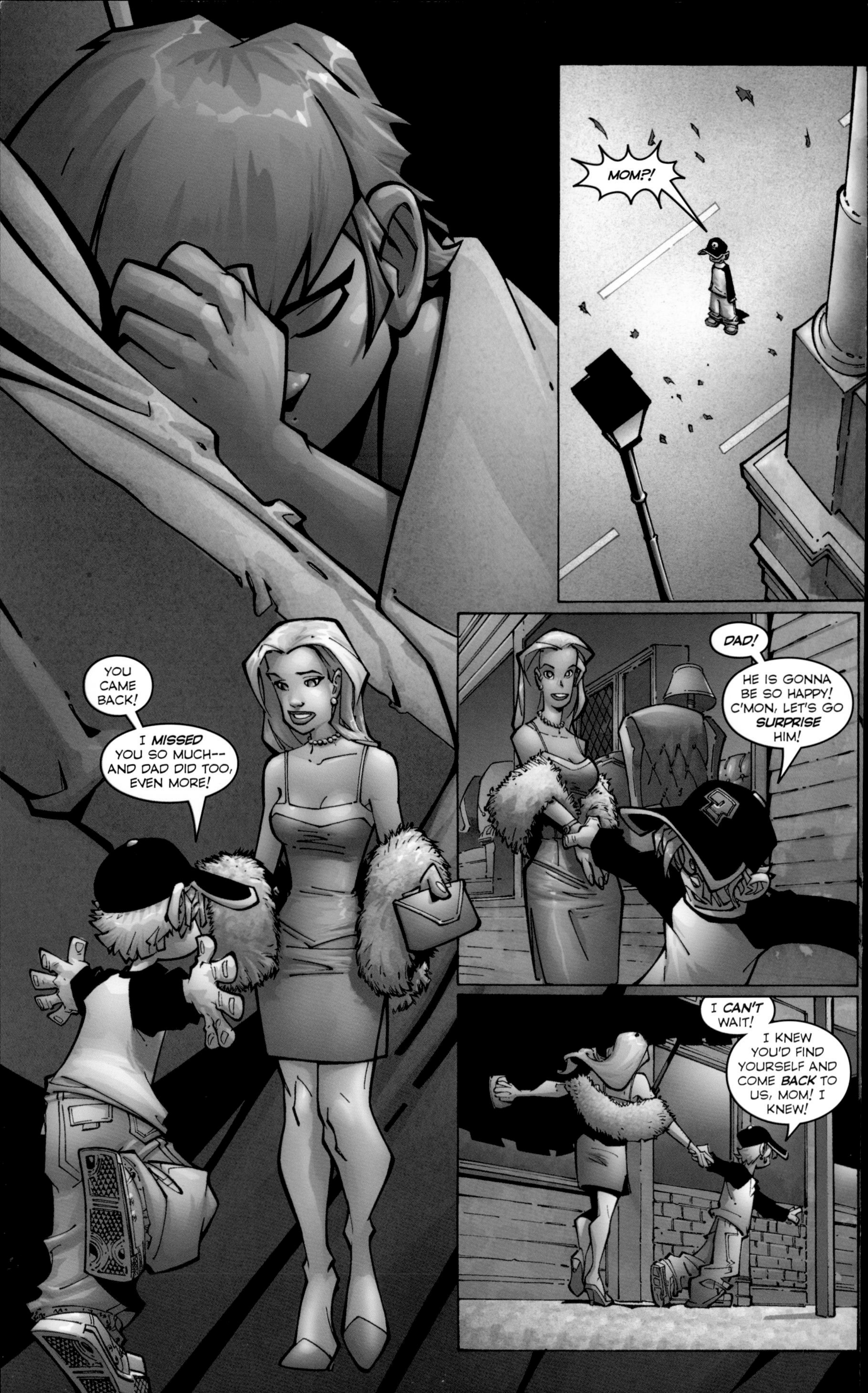
MOM?!
YOU CAME BACK!
I MISSED YOU SO MUCH-- AND DAD DID TOO, EVEN MORE!
DAD!
HE IS GONNA BE SO HAPPY! C'MON, LET'S GO SURPRISE HIM!
I CAN'T WAIT!
I KNEW YOU'D FIND YOURSELF AND COME BACK TO US, MOM! I KNEW!

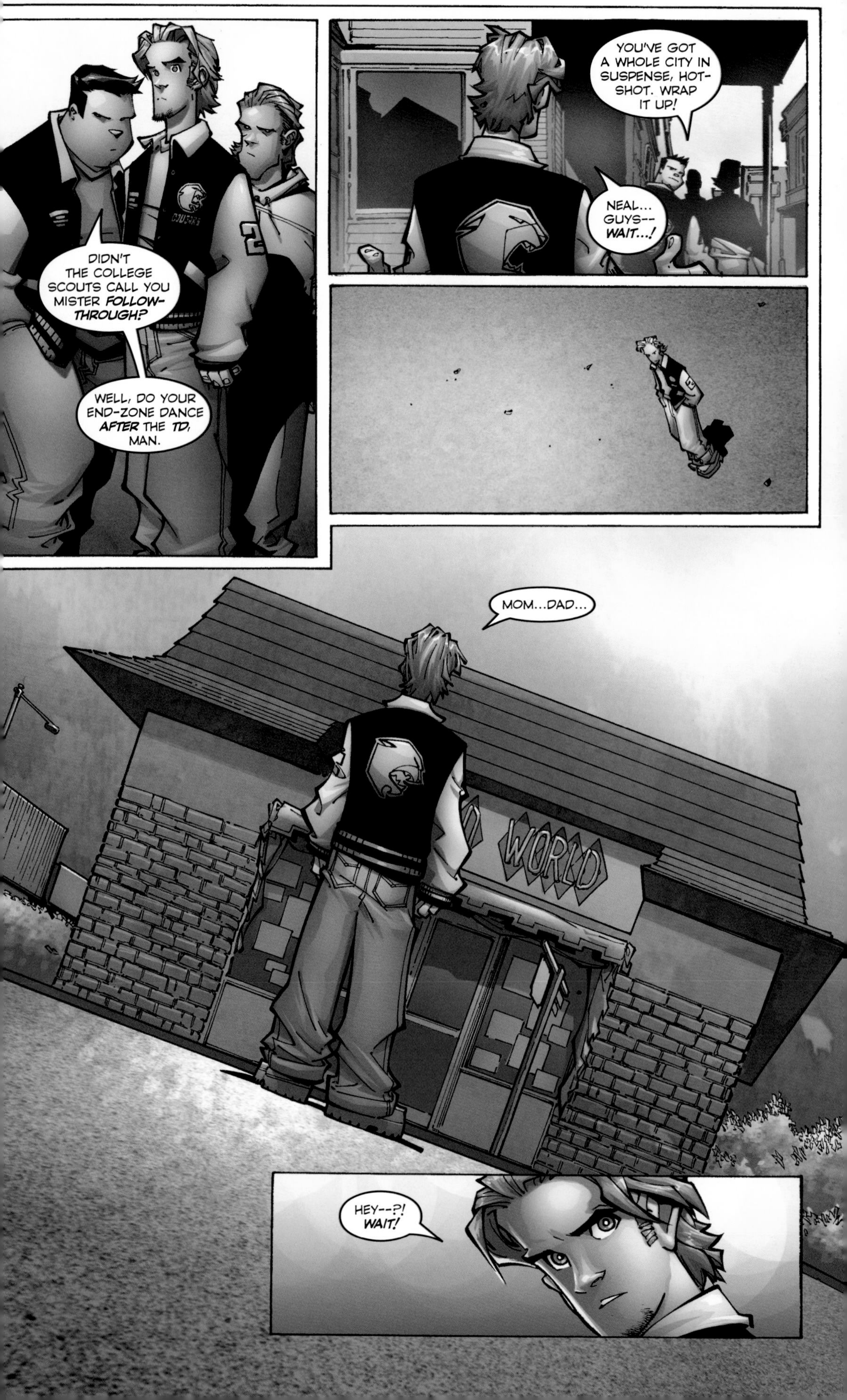
DIDN'T THE COLLEGE SCOUTS CALL YOU MISTER FOLLOW-THROUGH?
WELL, DO YOUR END-ZONE DANCE AFTER THE TD, MAN.
YOU'VE GOT A WHOLE CITY IN SUSPENSE, HOT-SHOT. WRAP IT UP!
NEAL... GUYS-- WAIT...!
MOM...DAD...
WORLD
HEY--?! WAIT!

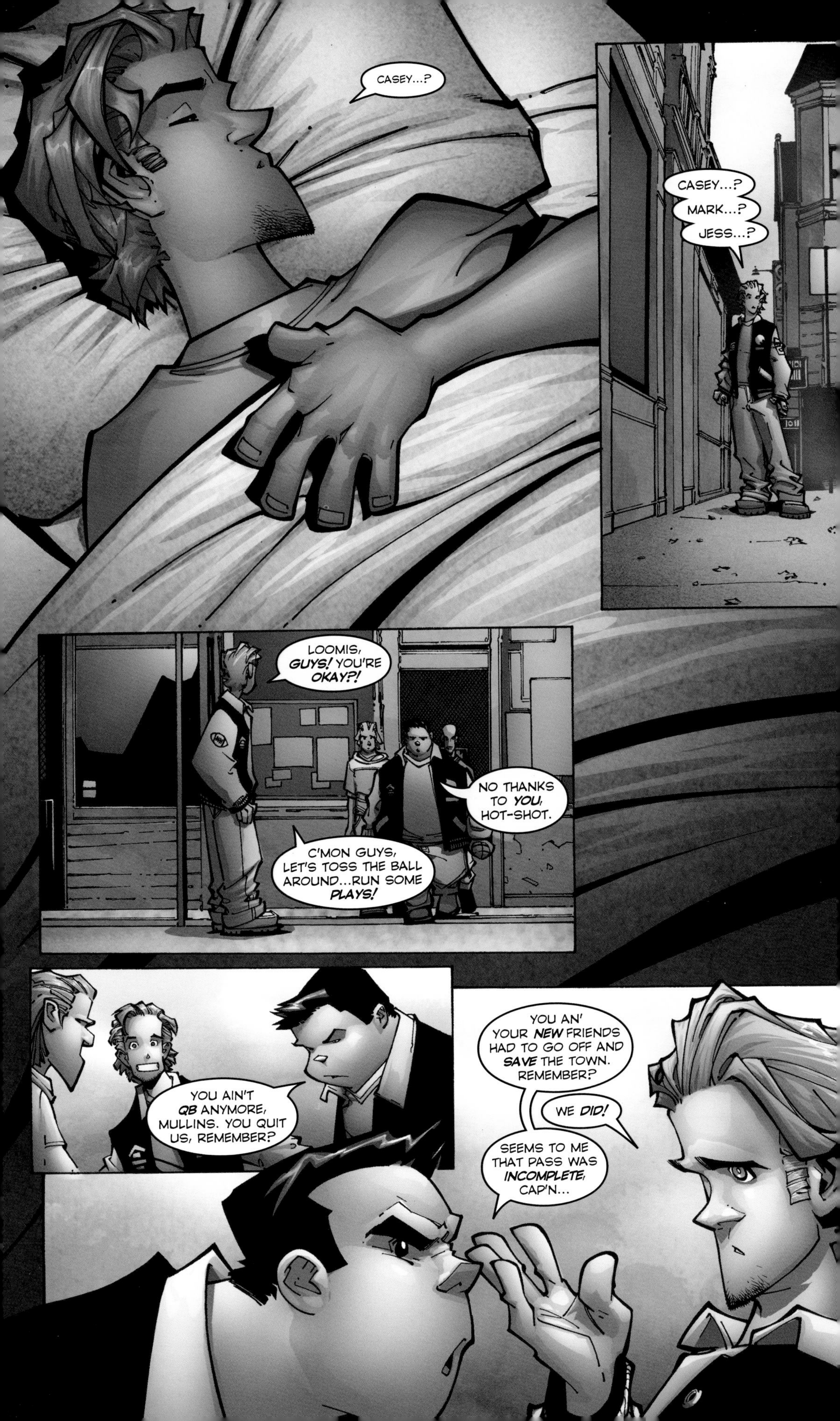

CASEY...?
CASEY...?
MARK...?
JESS...?
LOOMIS, GUYS! YOU'RE OKAY?!
NO THANKS TO YOU, HOT-SHOT.
C'MON GUYS, LET'S TOSS THE BALL AROUND...RUN SOME PLAYS!
YOU AIN'T QB ANYMORE, MULLINS. YOU QUIT US, REMEMBER?
YOU AN' YOUR NEW FRIENDS HAD TO GO OFF AND SAVE THE TOWN. REMEMBER?
WE DID!
SEEMS TO ME THAT PASS WAS INCOMPLETE, CAP'N...

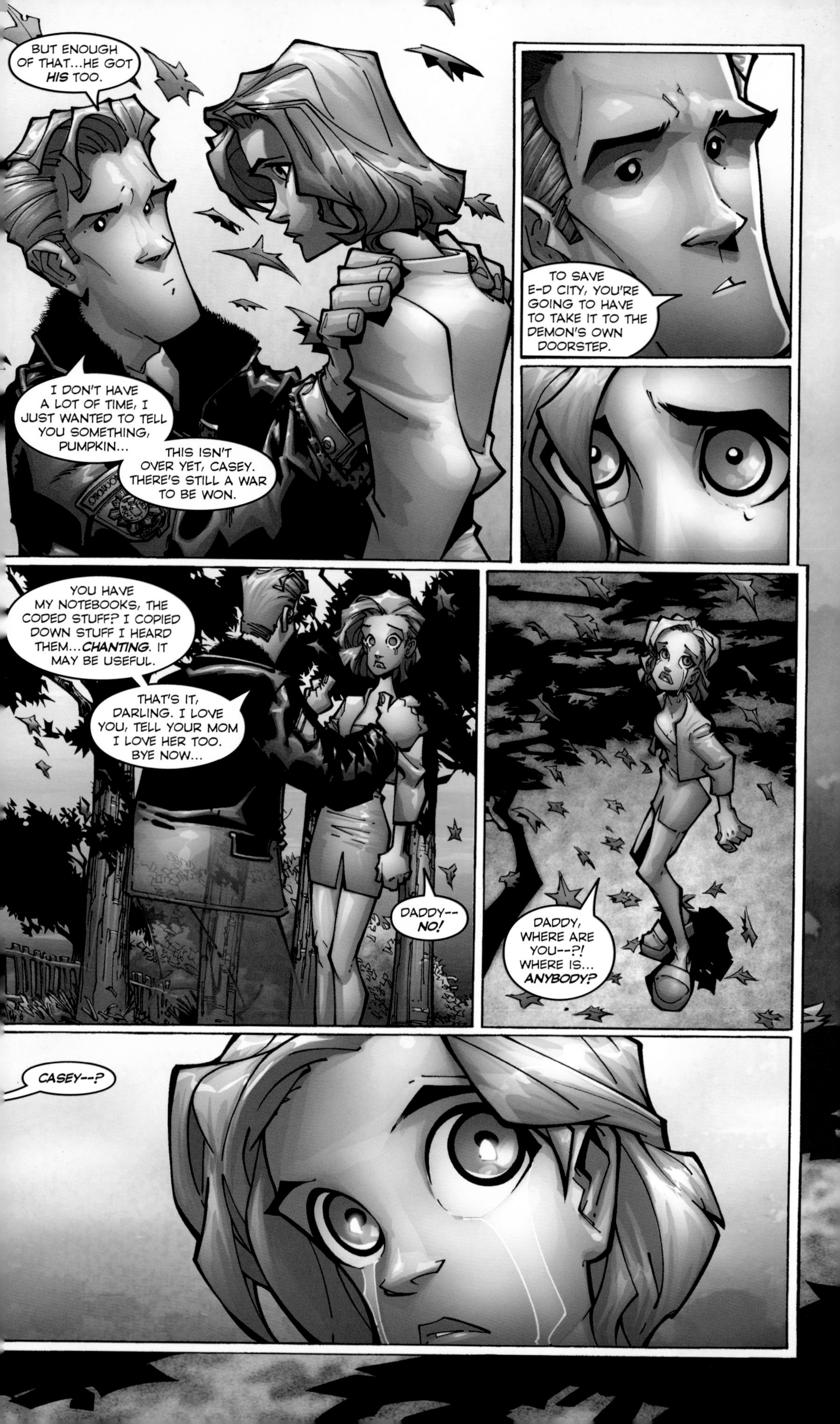
BUT ENOUGH OF THAT...HE GOT *HIS* TOO.
I DON'T HAVE A LOT OF TIME, I JUST WANTED TO TELL YOU SOMETHING, PUMPKIN...
THIS ISN'T OVER YET, CASEY. THERE'S STILL A WAR TO BE WON.
TO SAVE E-D CITY, YOU'RE GOING TO HAVE TO TAKE IT TO THE DEMON'S OWN DOORSTEP.
YOU HAVE MY NOTEBOOKS, THE CODED STUFF? I COPIED DOWN STUFF I HEARD THEM...*CHANTING*. IT MAY BE USEFUL.
THAT'S IT, DARLING. I LOVE YOU, TELL YOUR MOM I LOVE HER TOO. BYE NOW...
DADDY-- *NO!*
DADDY, WHERE ARE YOU--?! WHERE IS... *ANYBODY?*
CASEY--?

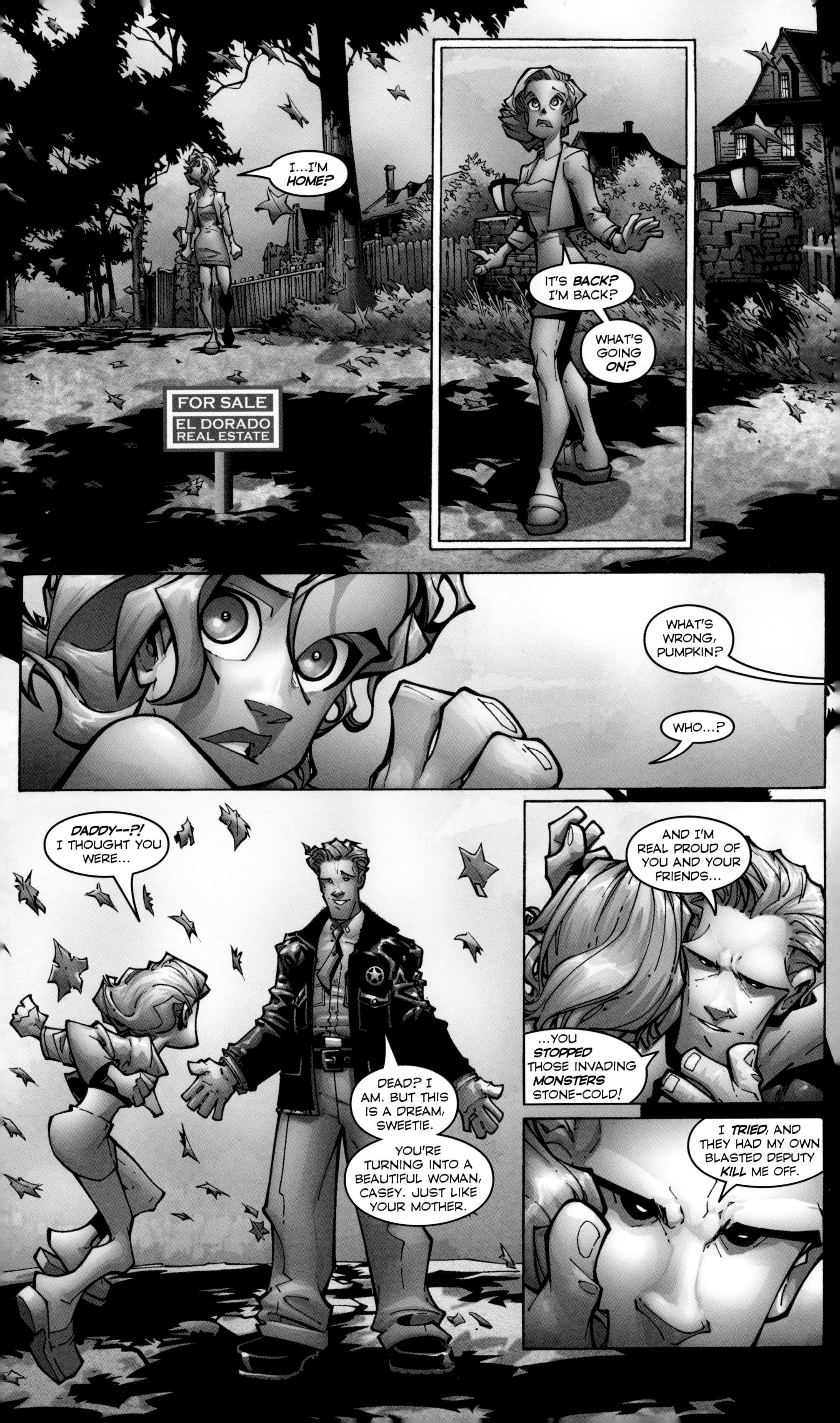
I...I'M HOME?
FOR SALE
EL DORADO REAL ESTATE
IT'S BACK? I'M BACK?
WHAT'S GOING ON?
WHAT'S WRONG, PUMPKIN?
WHO...?
DADDY--?! I THOUGHT YOU WERE...
DEAD? I AM. BUT THIS IS A DREAM, SWEETIE.
YOU'RE TURNING INTO A BEAUTIFUL WOMAN, CASEY. JUST LIKE YOUR MOTHER.
AND I'M REAL PROUD OF YOU AND YOUR FRIENDS...
...YOU STOPPED THOSE INVADING MONSTERS STONE-COLD!
I TRIED, AND THEY HAD MY OWN BLASTED DEPUTY KILL ME OFF.

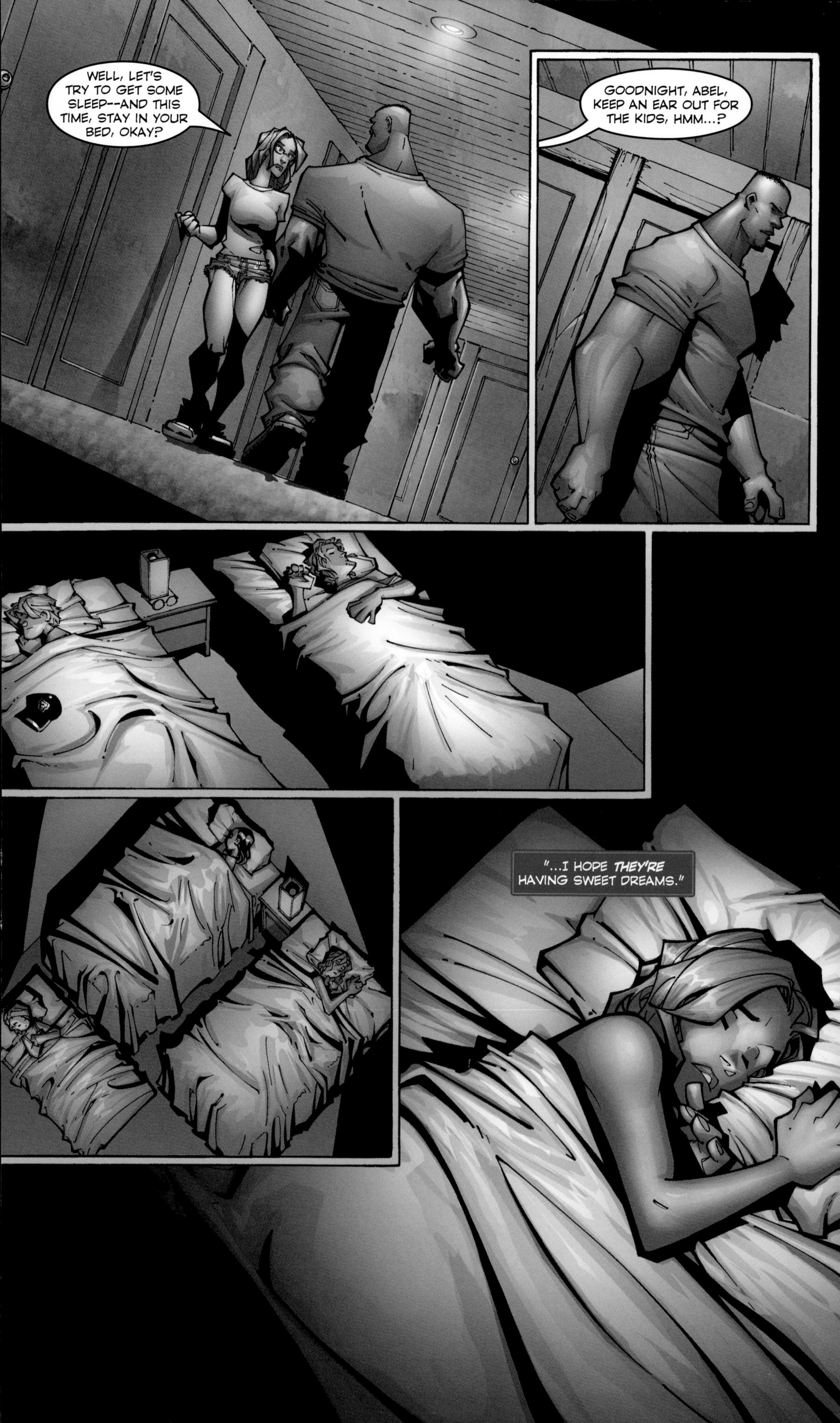
WELL, LET'S TRY TO GET SOME SLEEP--AND THIS TIME, STAY IN YOUR BED, OKAY?
GOODNIGHT, ABEL, KEEP AN EAR OUT FOR THE KIDS, HMM...?
"...I HOPE THEY'RE HAVING SWEET DREAMS."

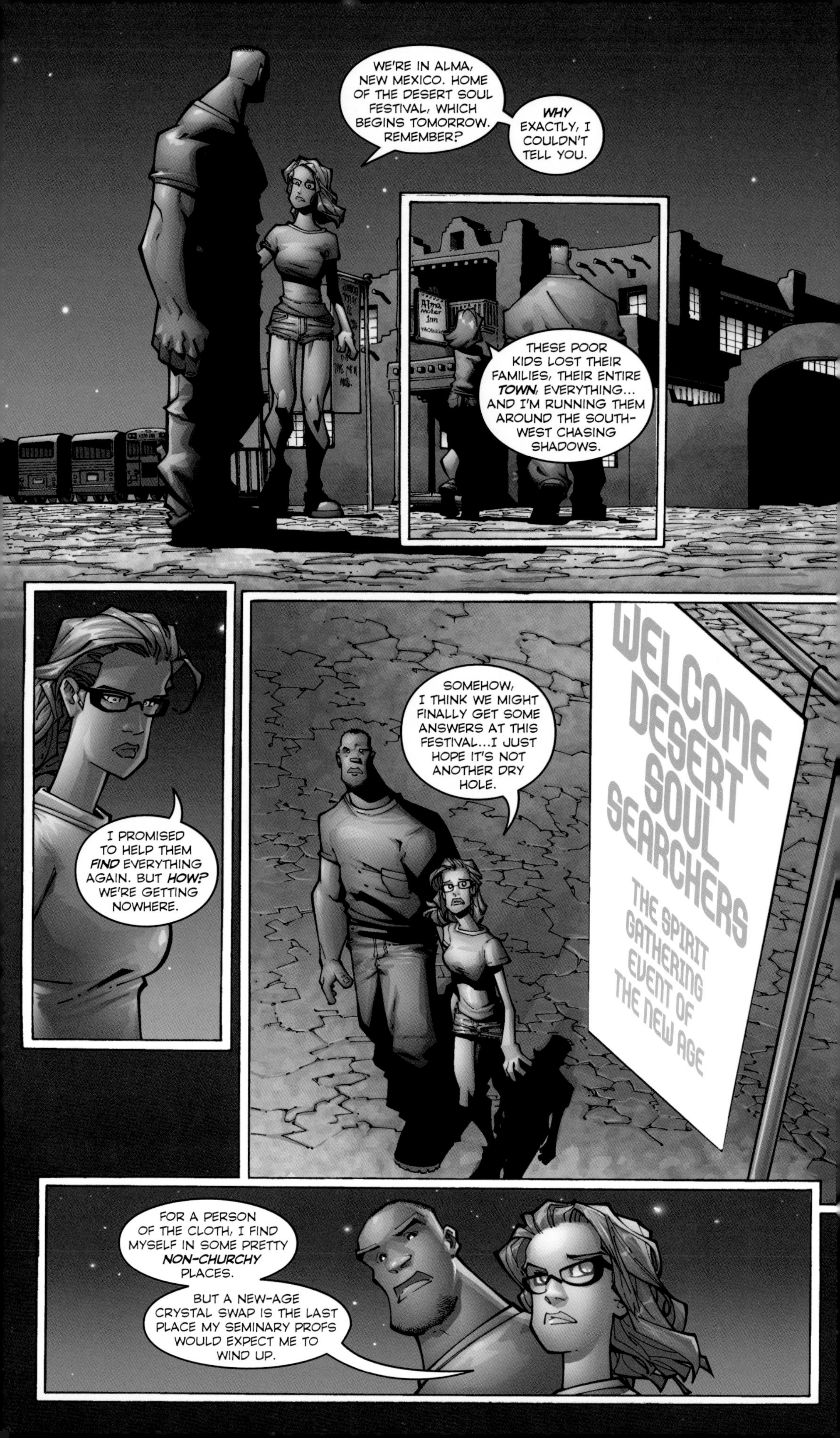
WE'RE IN ALMA, NEW MEXICO. HOME OF THE DESERT SOUL FESTIVAL, WHICH BEGINS TOMORROW. REMEMBER?
WHY EXACTLY, I COULDN'T TELL YOU.
THESE POOR KIDS LOST THEIR FAMILIES, THEIR ENTIRE TOWN, EVERYTHING... AND I'M RUNNING THEM AROUND THE SOUTH-WEST CHASING SHADOWS.
I PROMISED TO HELP THEM FIND EVERYTHING AGAIN. BUT HOW? WE'RE GETTING NOWHERE.
SOMEHOW, I THINK WE MIGHT FINALLY GET SOME ANSWERS AT THIS FESTIVAL...I JUST HOPE IT'S NOT ANOTHER DRY HOLE.
WELCOME DESERT SOUL SEARCHERS
THE SPIRIT GATHERING EVENT OF THE NEW AGE
FOR A PERSON OF THE CLOTH, I FIND MYSELF IN SOME PRETTY NON-CHURCHY PLACES.
BUT A NEW-AGE CRYSTAL SWAP IS THE LAST PLACE MY SEMINARY PROFS WOULD EXPECT ME TO WIND UP.

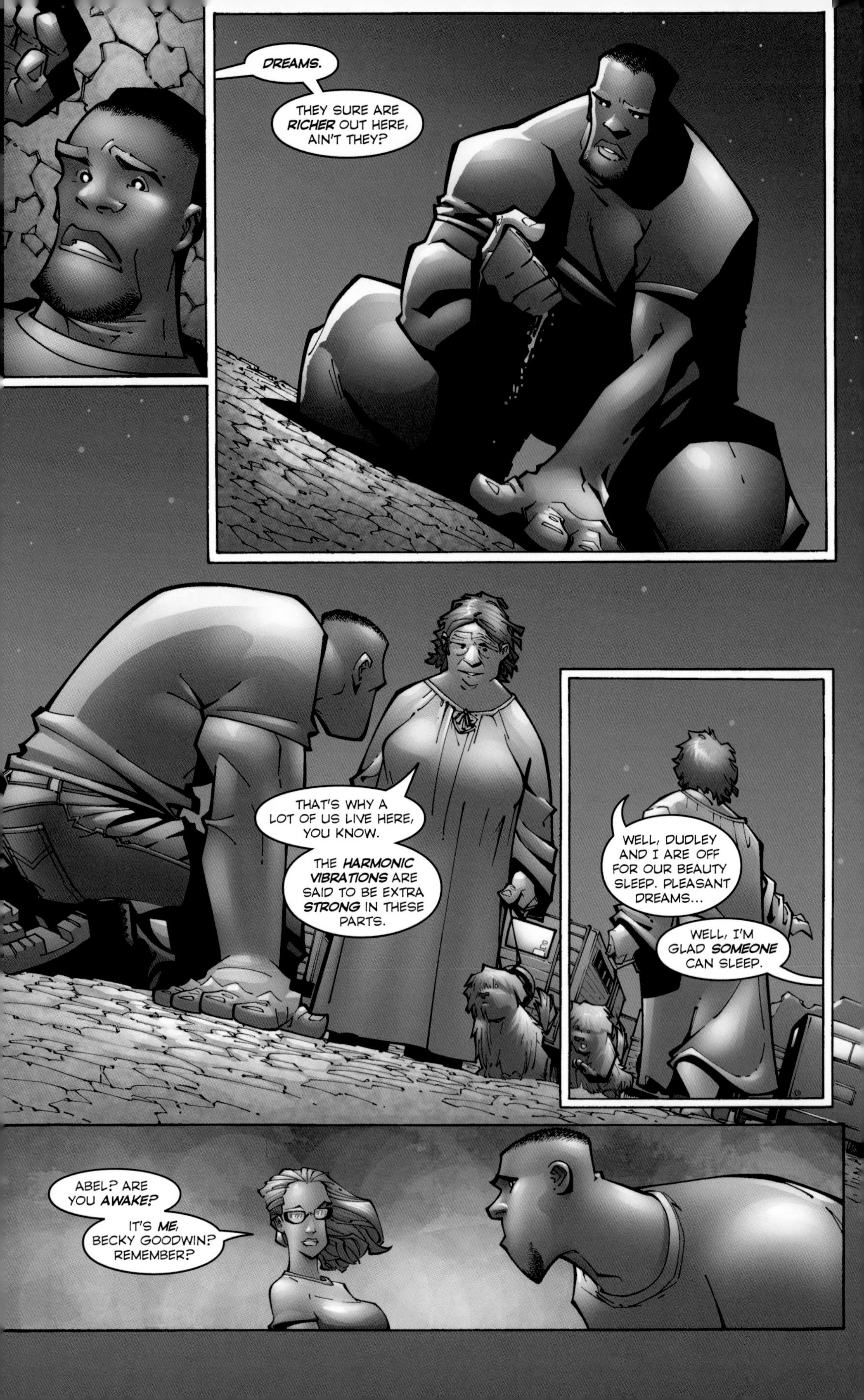
DREAMS.
THEY SURE ARE RICHER OUT HERE, AIN'T THEY?
THAT'S WHY A LOT OF US LIVE HERE, YOU KNOW.
THE HARMONIC VIBRATIONS ARE SAID TO BE EXTRA STRONG IN THESE PARTS.
WELL, DUDLEY AND I ARE OFF FOR OUR BEAUTY SLEEP. PLEASANT DREAMS...
WELL, I'M GLAD SOMEONE CAN SLEEP.
ABEL? ARE YOU AWAKE?
IT'S ME, BECKY GOODWIN? REMEMBER?

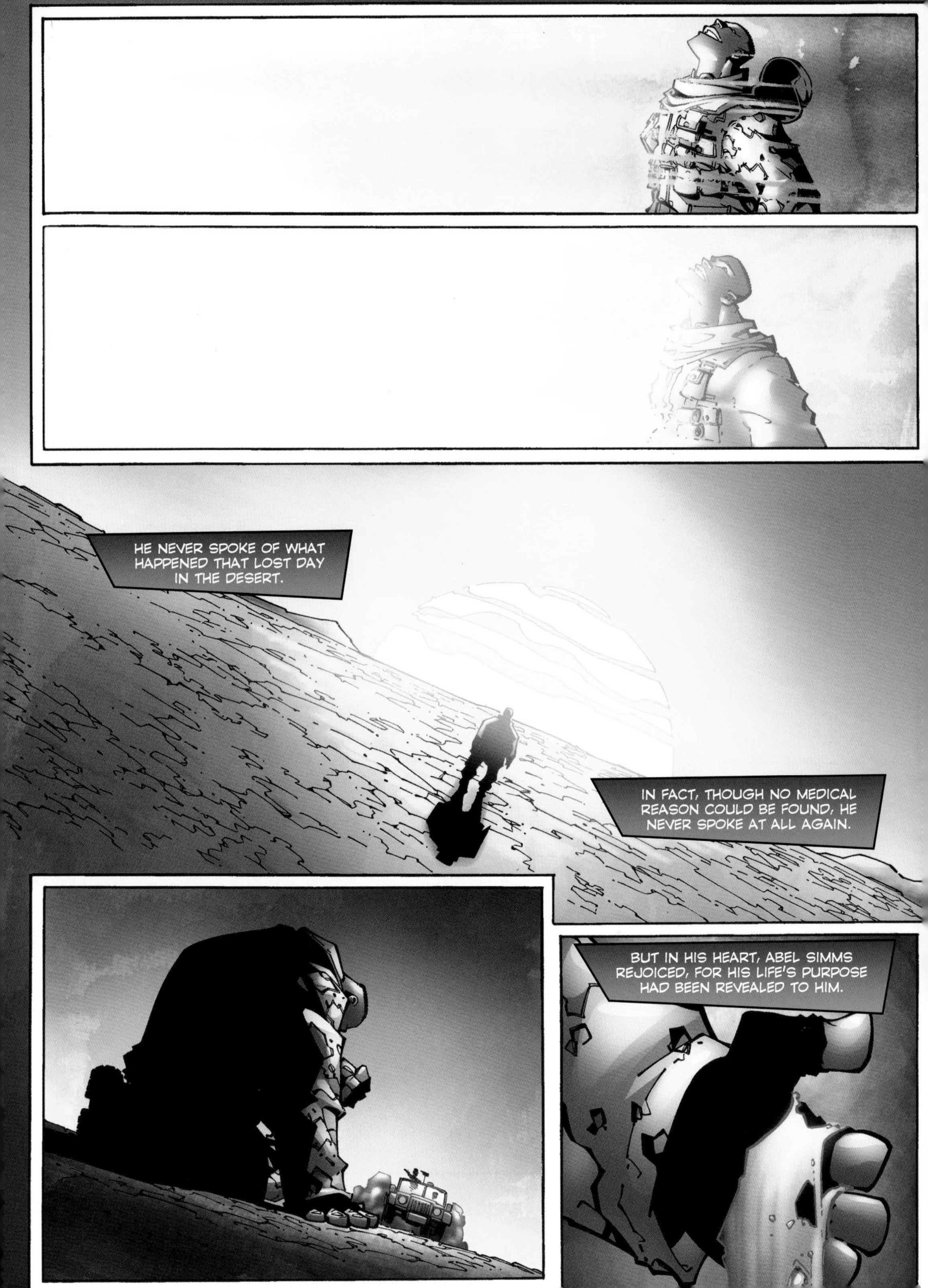
HE NEVER SPOKE OF WHAT HAPPENED THAT LOST DAY IN THE DESERT.
IN FACT, THOUGH NO MEDICAL REASON COULD BE FOUND, HE NEVER SPOKE AT ALL AGAIN.
BUT IN HIS HEART, ABEL SIMMS REJOICED, FOR HIS LIFE'S PURPOSE HAD BEEN REVEALED TO HIM.

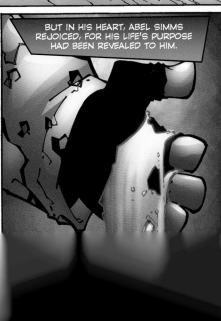

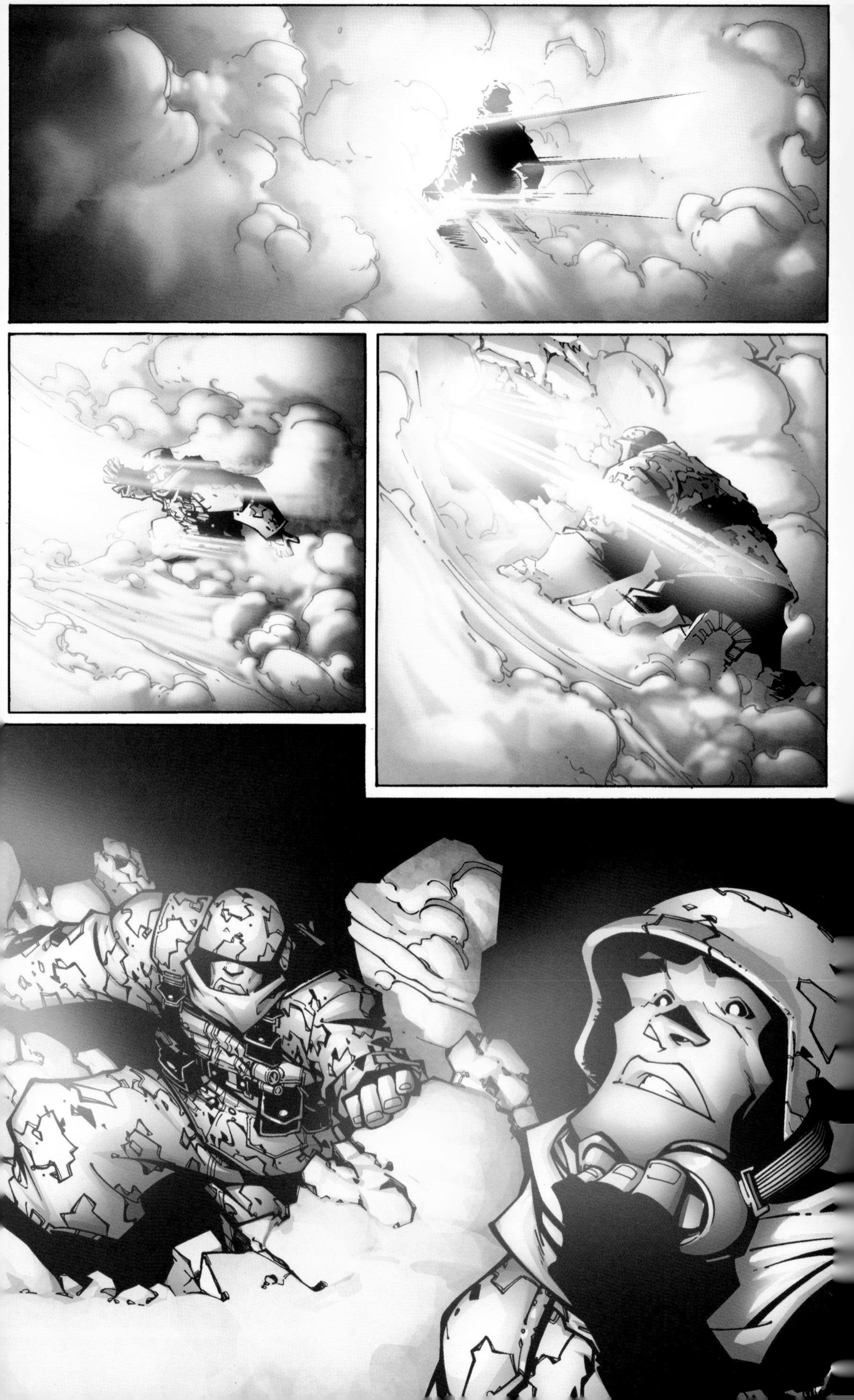

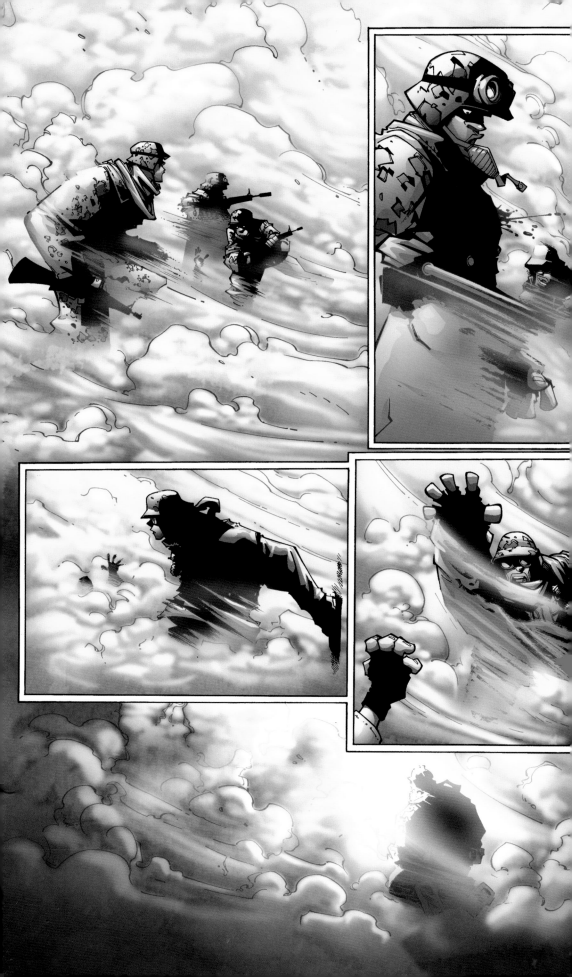

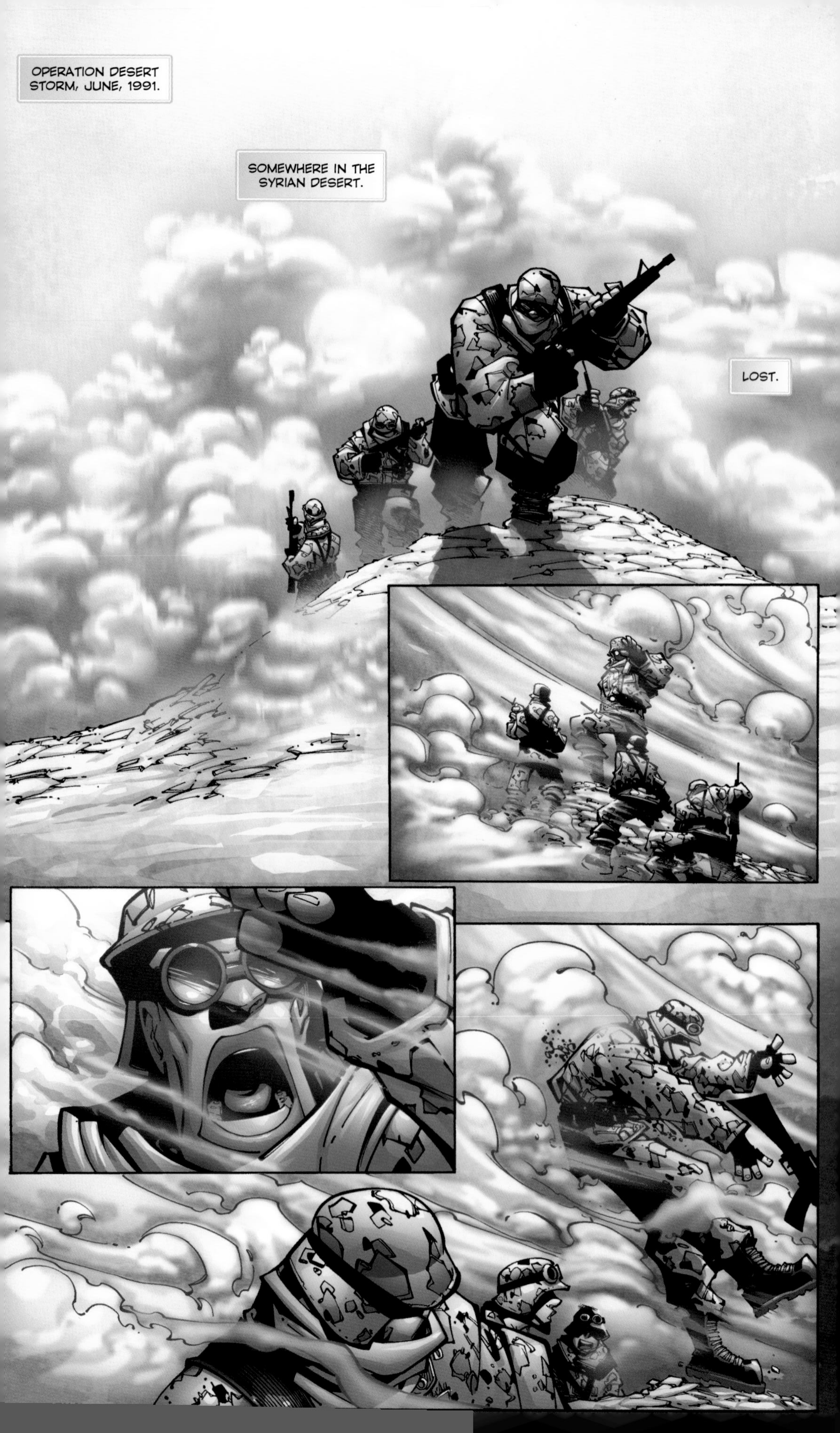
OPERATION DESERT STORM, JUNE, 1991.
SOMEWHERE IN THE SYRIAN DESERT.
LOST.

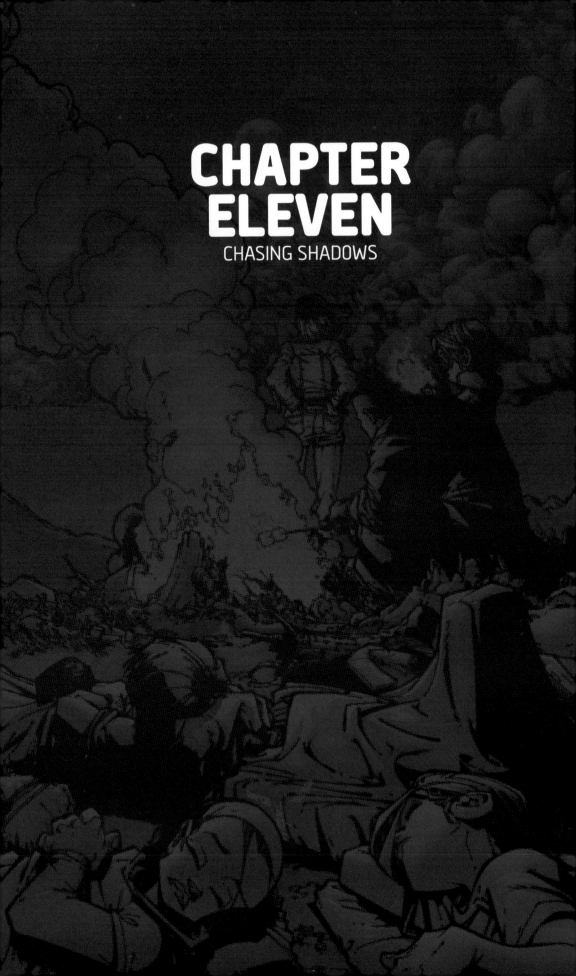

CHAPTER ELEVEN
CHASING SHADOWS

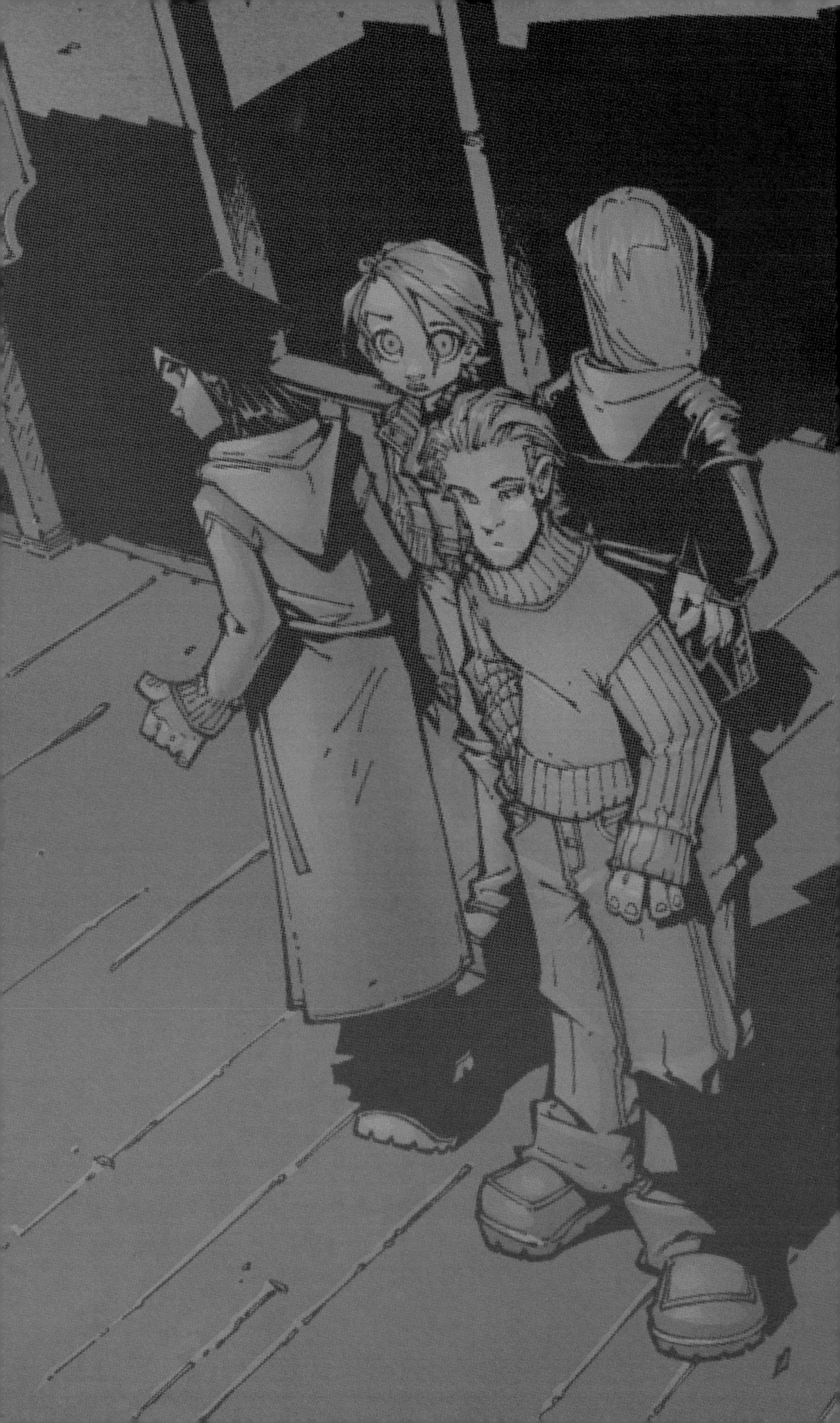

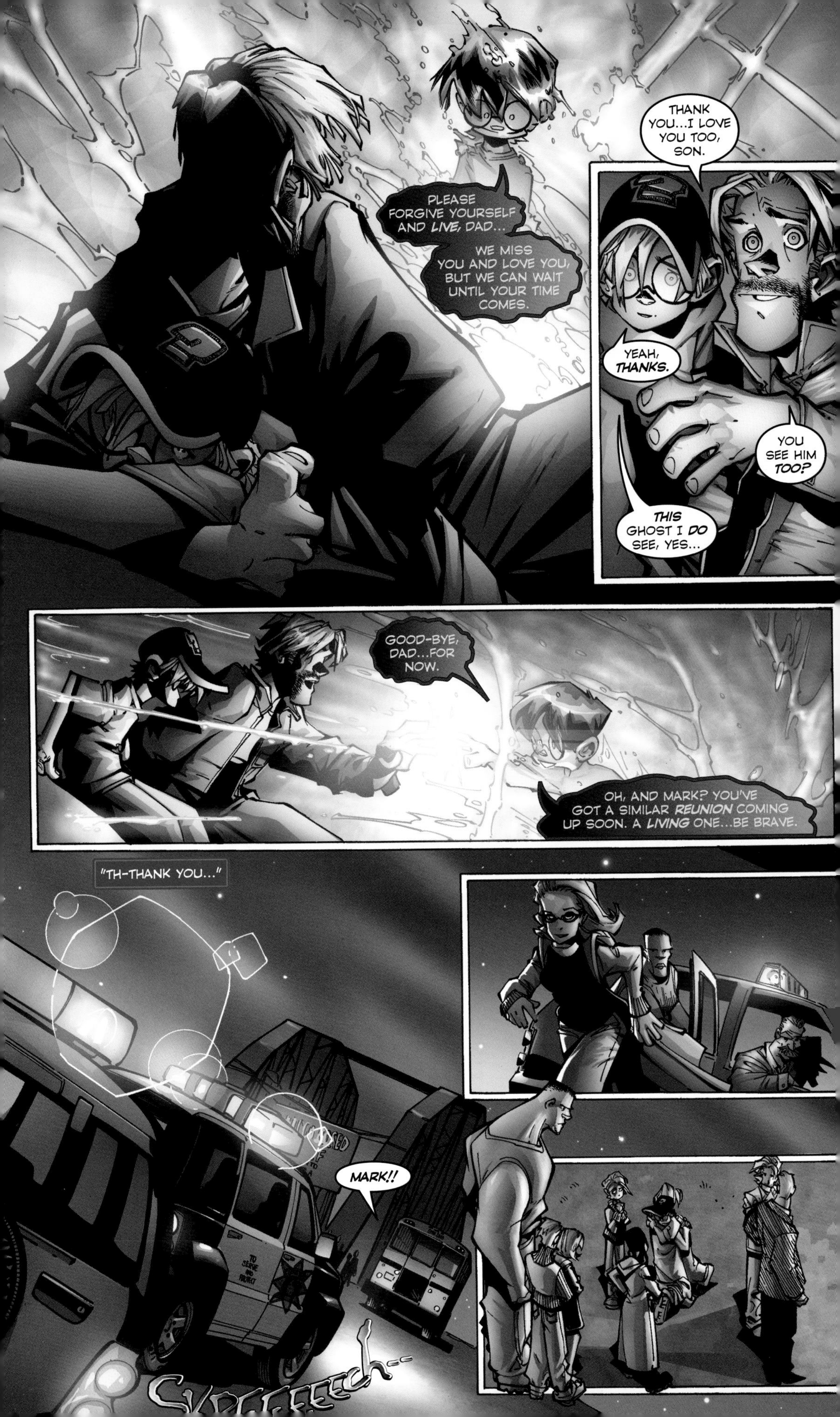
PLEASE FORGIVE YOURSELF AND LIVE, DAD...
WE MISS YOU AND LOVE YOU, BUT WE CAN WAIT UNTIL YOUR TIME COMES.
THANK YOU...I LOVE YOU TOO, SON.
YEAH, THANKS.
YOU SEE HIM TOO?
THIS GHOST I DO SEE, YES...
GOOD-BYE, DAD...FOR NOW.
OH, AND MARK? YOU'VE GOT A SIMILAR REUNION COMING UP SOON. A LIVING ONE...BE BRAVE.
"TH-THANK YOU..."
MARK!!
TO SERVE AND PROTECT
CVREEEEECH--

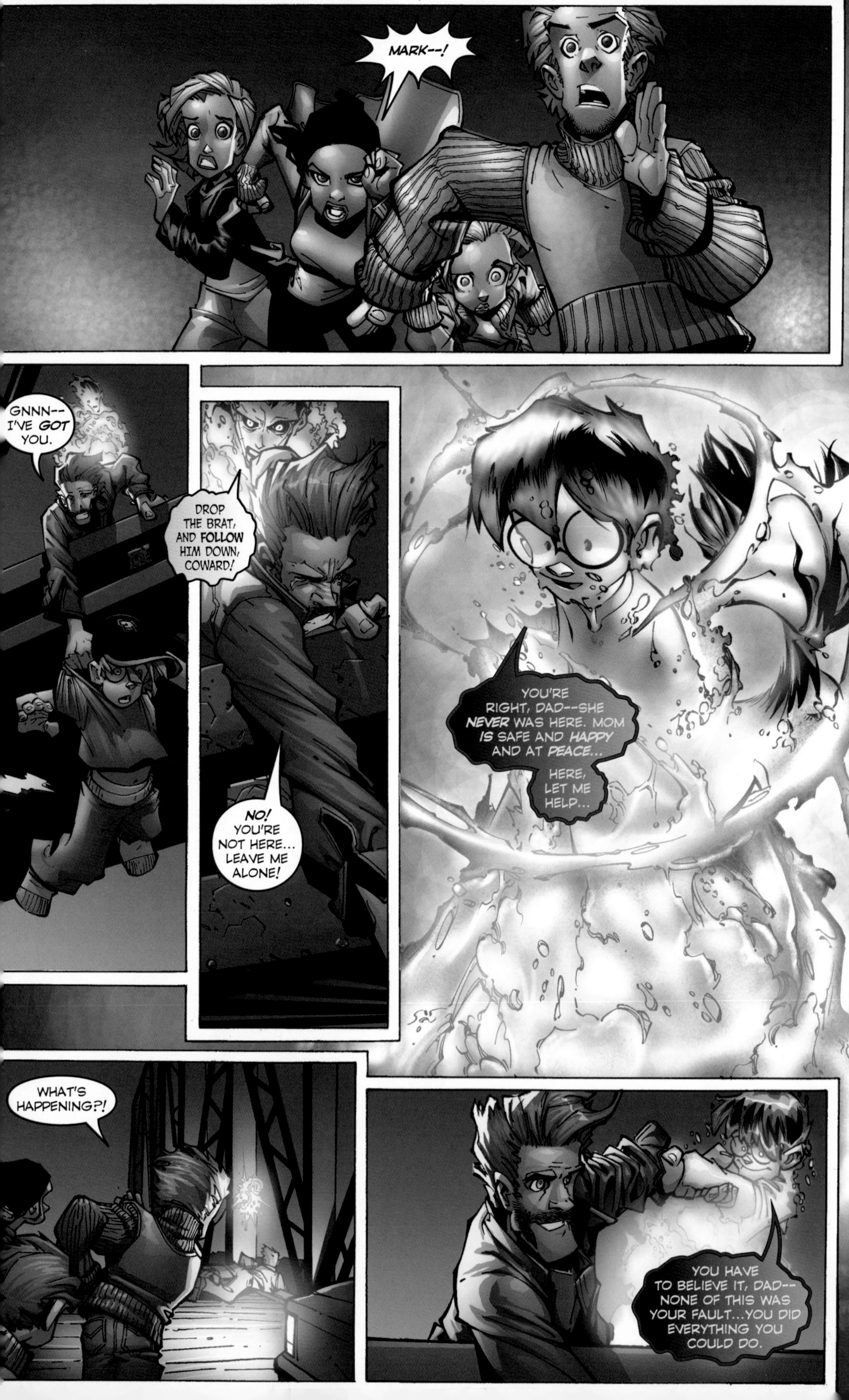

MARK--!
GNNN-- I'VE GOT YOU.
DROP THE BRAT, AND FOLLOW HIM DOWN, COWARD!
NO! YOU'RE NOT HERE... LEAVE ME ALONE!
YOU'RE RIGHT, DAD--SHE NEVER WAS HERE. MOM IS SAFE AND HAPPY AND AT PEACE...
HERE, LET ME HELP...
WHAT'S HAPPENING?!
YOU HAVE TO BELIEVE IT, DAD-- NONE OF THIS WAS YOUR FAULT...YOU DID EVERYTHING YOU COULD DO.

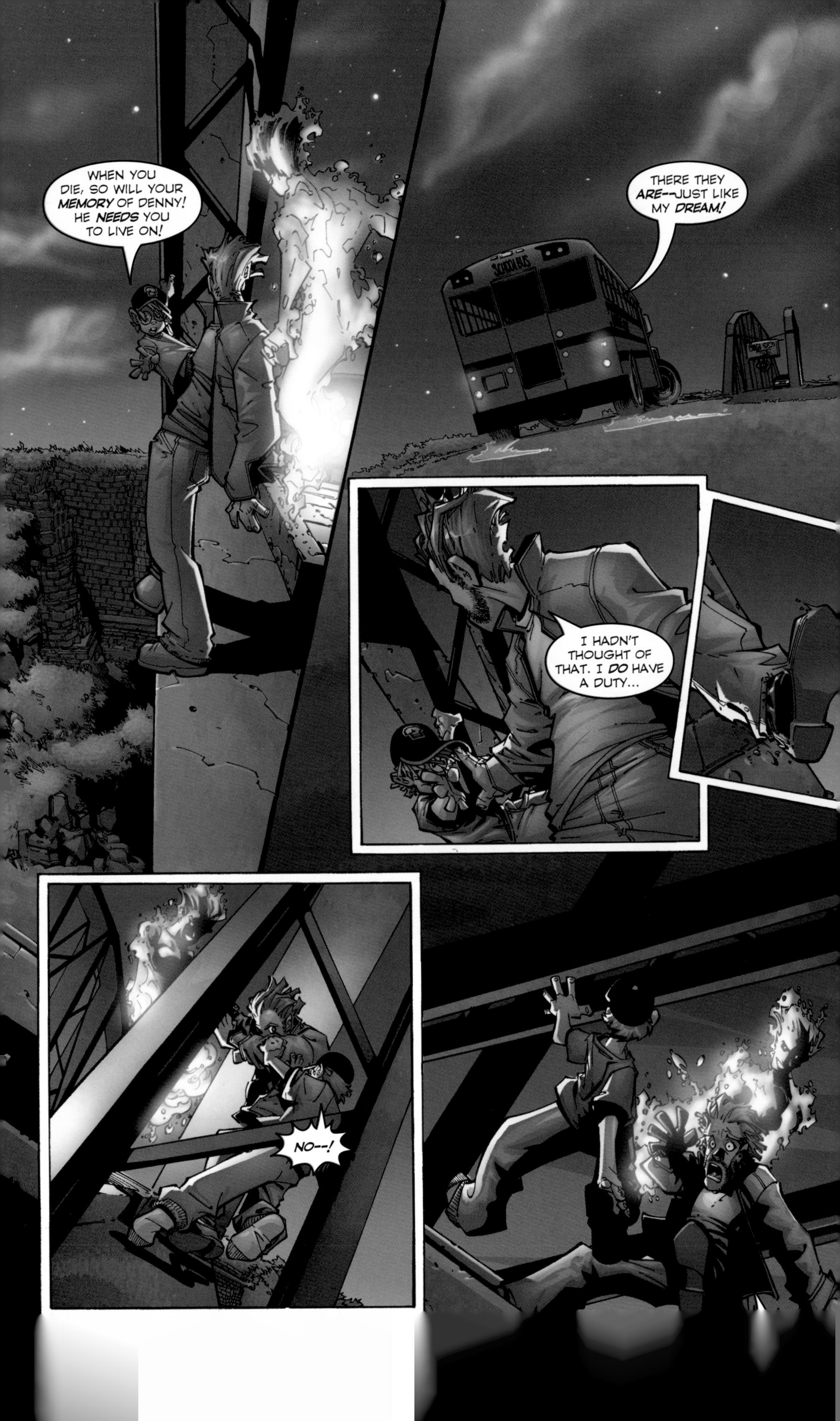
WHEN YOU DIE, SO WILL YOUR MEMORY OF DENNY! HE NEEDS YOU TO LIVE ON!
THERE THEY ARE--JUST LIKE MY DREAM!
I HADN'T THOUGHT OF THAT. I DO HAVE A DUTY...
NO--!

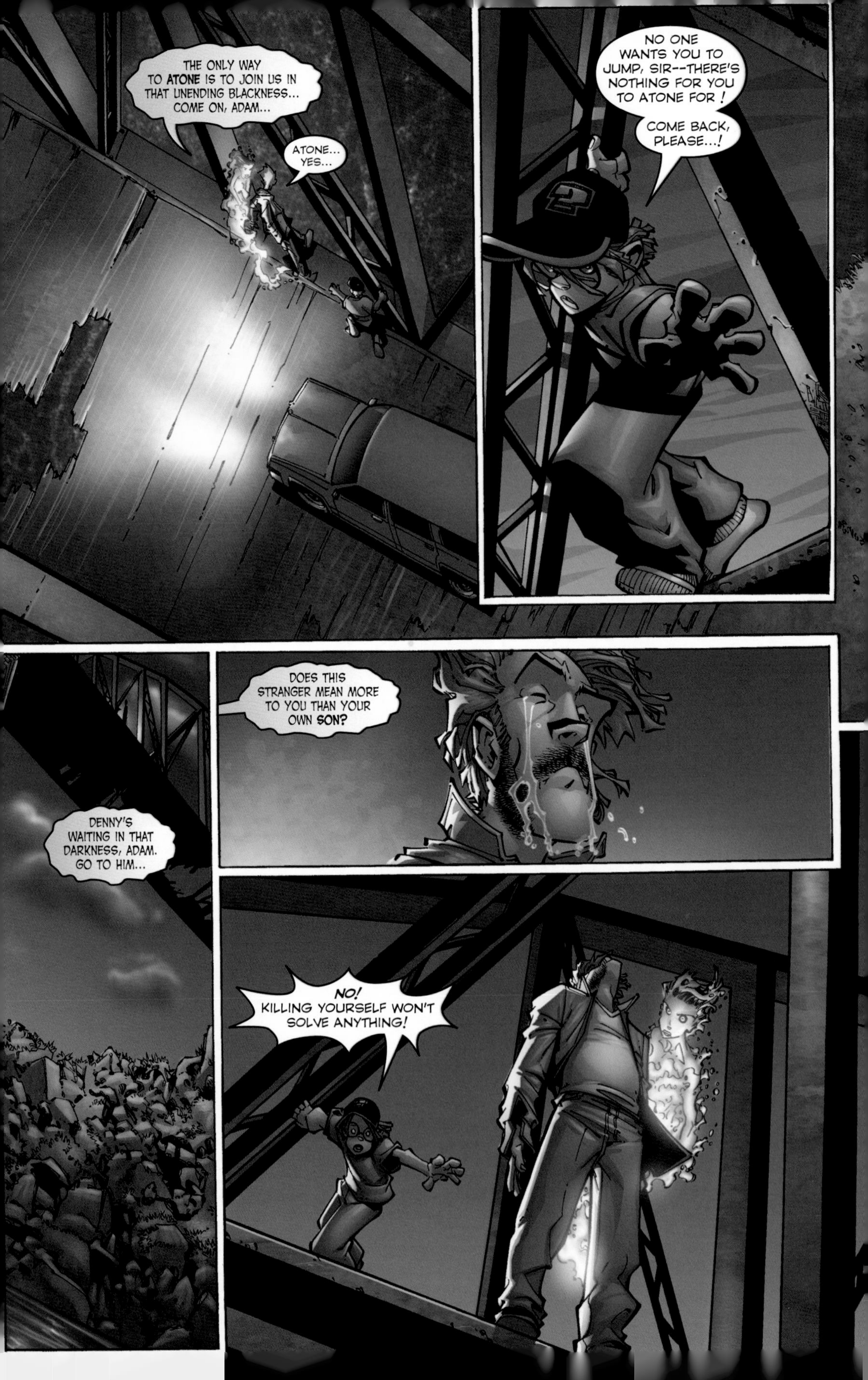
THE ONLY WAY TO ATONE IS TO JOIN US IN THAT UNENDING BLACKNESS... COME ON, ADAM...
ATONE... YES...
NO ONE WANTS YOU TO JUMP, SIR--THERE'S NOTHING FOR YOU TO ATONE FOR!
COME BACK, PLEASE...!
DOES THIS STRANGER MEAN MORE TO YOU THAN YOUR OWN SON?
DENNY'S WAITING IN THAT DARKNESS, ADAM. GO TO HIM...
NO! KILLING YOURSELF WON'T SOLVE ANYTHING!

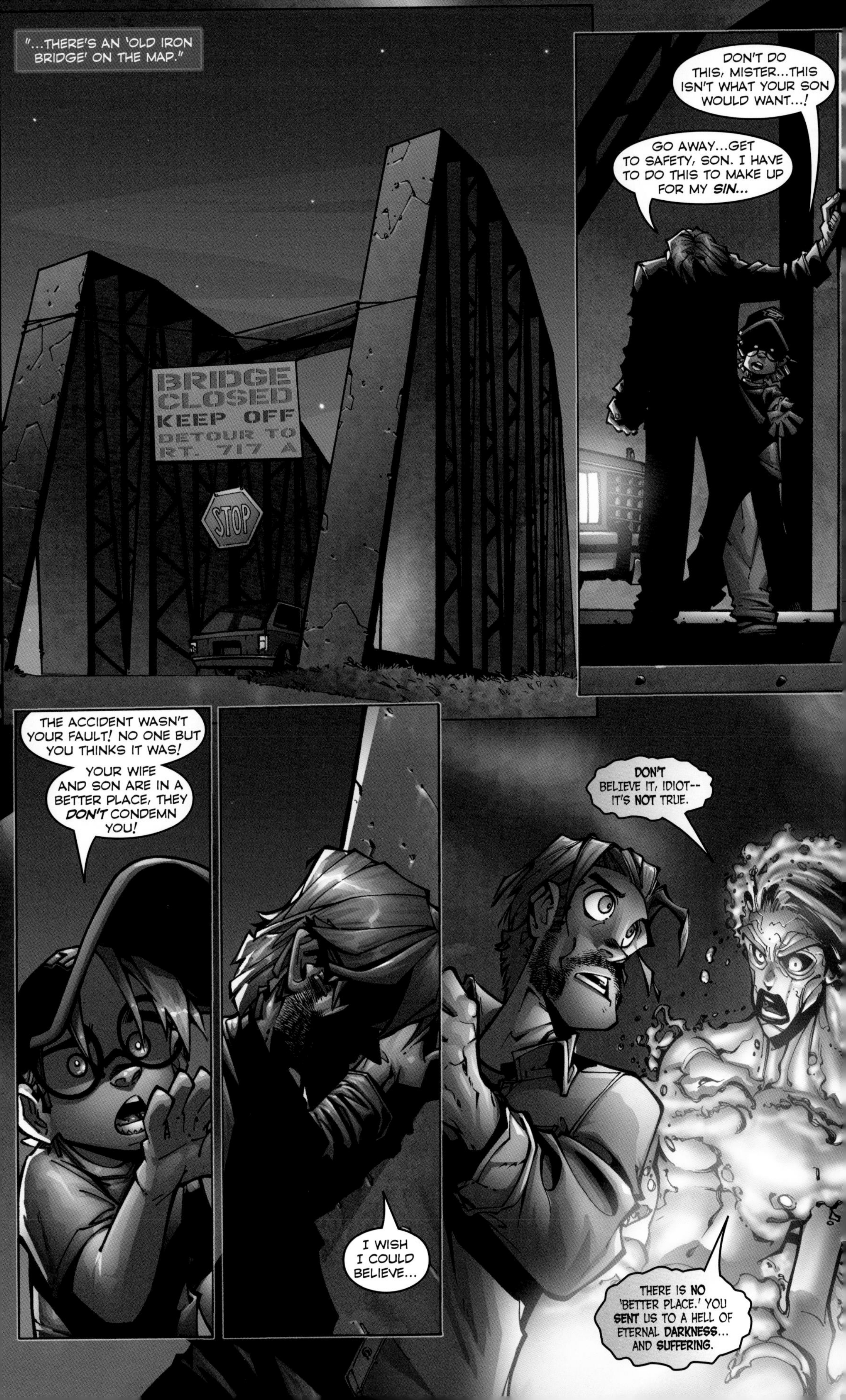
"...THERE'S AN 'OLD IRON BRIDGE' ON THE MAP."
BRIDGE CLOSED KEEP OFF DETOUR TO RT. 717 A
STOP
DON'T DO THIS, MISTER...THIS ISN'T WHAT YOUR SON WOULD WANT...!
GO AWAY...GET TO SAFETY, SON. I HAVE TO DO THIS TO MAKE UP FOR MY SIN...
THE ACCIDENT WASN'T YOUR FAULT! NO ONE BUT YOU THINKS IT WAS!
YOUR WIFE AND SON ARE IN A BETTER PLACE, THEY DON'T CONDEMN YOU!
I WISH I COULD BELIEVE...
DON'T BELIEVE IT, IDIOT-- IT'S NOT TRUE.
THERE IS NO 'BETTER PLACE.' YOU SENT US TO A HELL OF ETERNAL DARKNESS... AND SUFFERING.

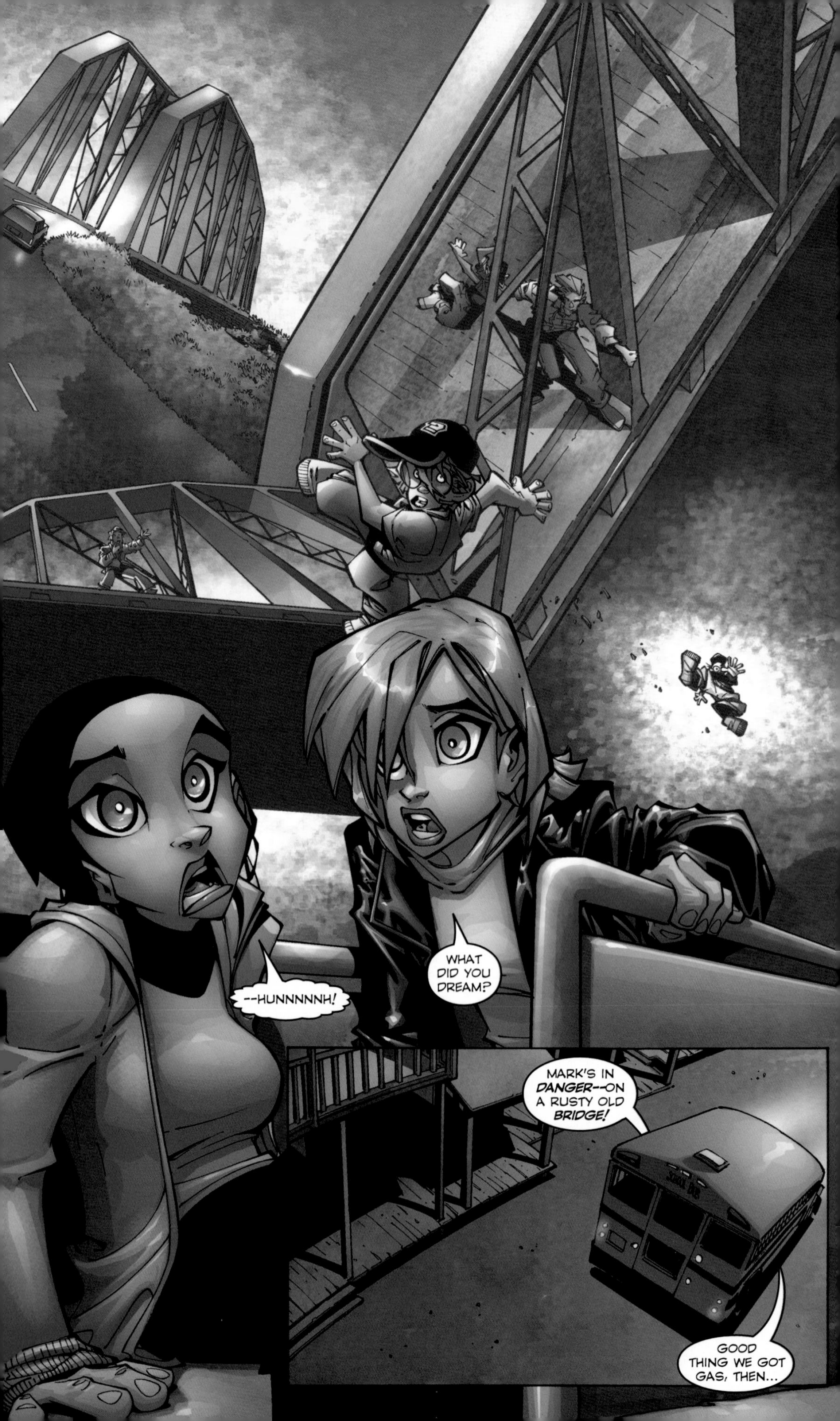
WHAT DID YOU DREAM?
--HUNNNNNH!
MARK'S IN DANGER--ON A RUSTY OLD BRIDGE!
GOOD THING WE GOT GAS, THEN...

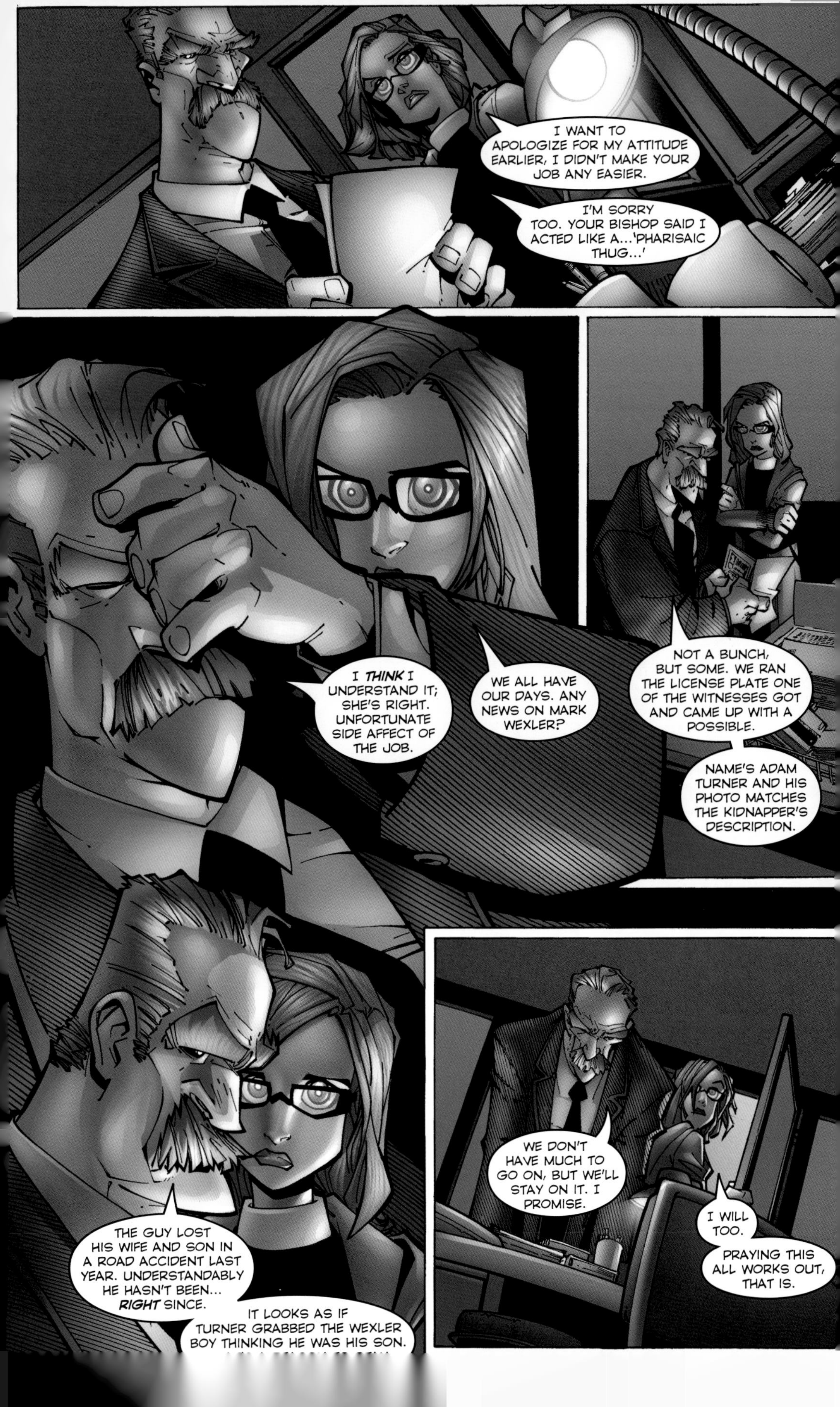

I WANT TO APOLOGIZE FOR MY ATTITUDE EARLIER, I DIDN'T MAKE YOUR JOB ANY EASIER.
I'M SORRY TOO. YOUR BISHOP SAID I ACTED LIKE A...'PHARISAIC THUG...'
I *THINK* I UNDERSTAND IT; SHE'S RIGHT. UNFORTUNATE SIDE AFFECT OF THE JOB.
WE ALL HAVE OUR DAYS. ANY NEWS ON MARK WEXLER?
NOT A BUNCH, BUT SOME. WE RAN THE LICENSE PLATE ONE OF THE WITNESSES GOT AND CAME UP WITH A POSSIBLE.
NAME'S ADAM TURNER AND HIS PHOTO MATCHES THE KIDNAPPER'S DESCRIPTION.
THE GUY LOST HIS WIFE AND SON IN A ROAD ACCIDENT LAST YEAR. UNDERSTANDABLY HE HASN'T BEEN... *RIGHT* SINCE.
IT LOOKS AS IF TURNER GRABBED THE WEXLER BOY THINKING HE WAS HIS SON.
WE DON'T HAVE MUCH TO GO ON, BUT WE'LL STAY ON IT. I PROMISE.
I WILL TOO.
PRAYING THIS ALL WORKS OUT, THAT IS.

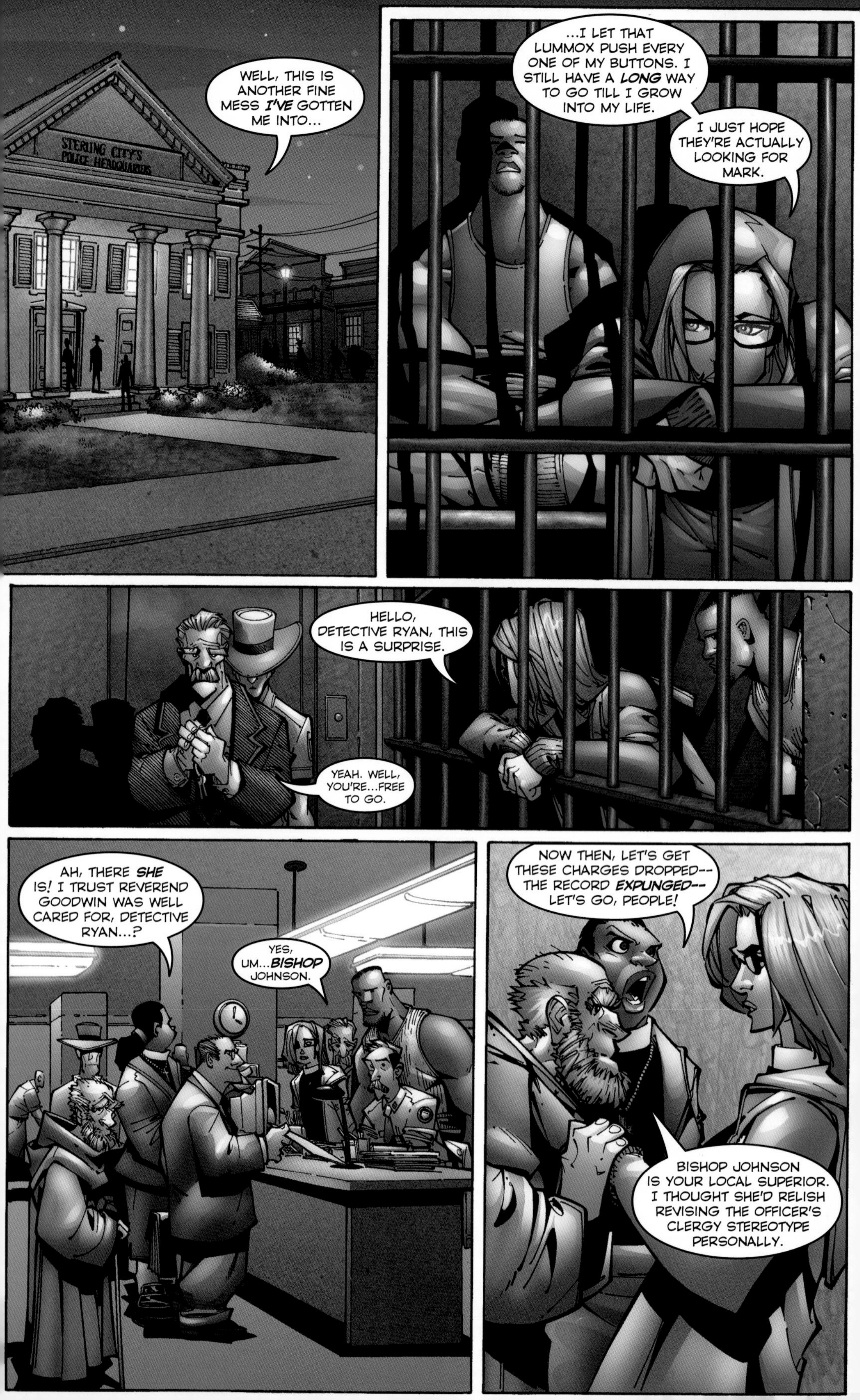

STERLING CITY'S POLICE HEADQUARTERS
WELL, THIS IS ANOTHER FINE MESS I'VE GOTTEN ME INTO...
...I LET THAT LUMMOX PUSH EVERY ONE OF MY BUTTONS. I STILL HAVE A LONG WAY TO GO TILL I GROW INTO MY LIFE.
I JUST HOPE THEY'RE ACTUALLY LOOKING FOR MARK.
HELLO, DETECTIVE RYAN, THIS IS A SURPRISE.
YEAH. WELL, YOU'RE...FREE TO GO.
AH, THERE SHE IS! I TRUST REVEREND GOODWIN WAS WELL CARED FOR, DETECTIVE RYAN...?
YES, UM...BISHOP JOHNSON.
NOW THEN, LET'S GET THESE CHARGES DROPPED-- THE RECORD EXPUNGED-- LET'S GO, PEOPLE!
BISHOP JOHNSON IS YOUR LOCAL SUPERIOR. I THOUGHT SHE'D RELISH REVISING THE OFFICER'S CLERGY STEREOTYPE PERSONALLY.

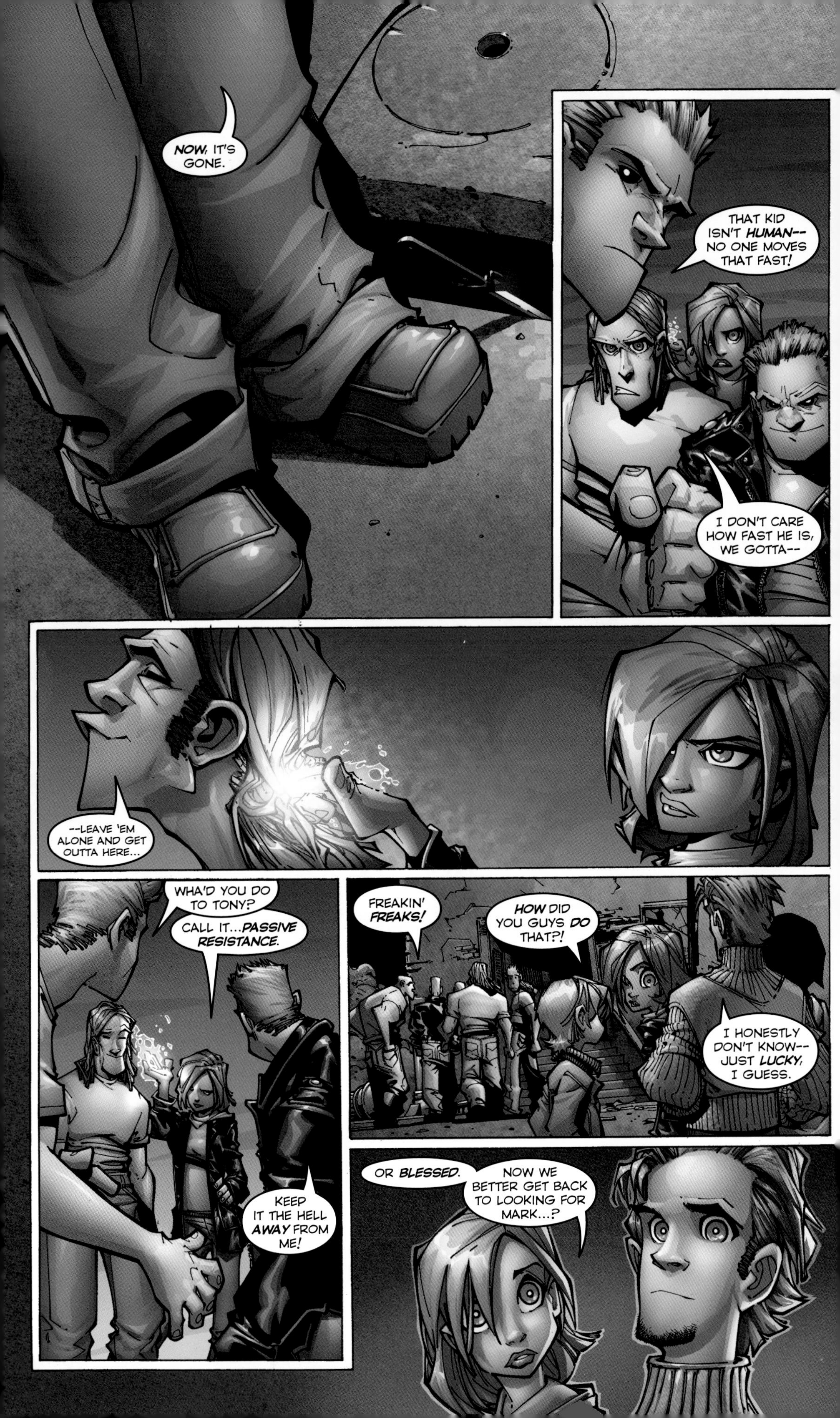
NOW, IT'S GONE.
THAT KID ISN'T HUMAN-- NO ONE MOVES THAT FAST!
I DON'T CARE HOW FAST HE IS, WE GOTTA--
--LEAVE 'EM ALONE AND GET OUTTA HERE...
WHA'D YOU DO TO TONY?
CALL IT...PASSIVE RESISTANCE.
KEEP IT THE HELL AWAY FROM ME!
FREAKIN' FREAKS!
HOW DID YOU GUYS DO THAT?!
I HONESTLY DON'T KNOW-- JUST LUCKY, I GUESS.
OR BLESSED.
NOW WE BETTER GET BACK TO LOOKING FOR MARK...?

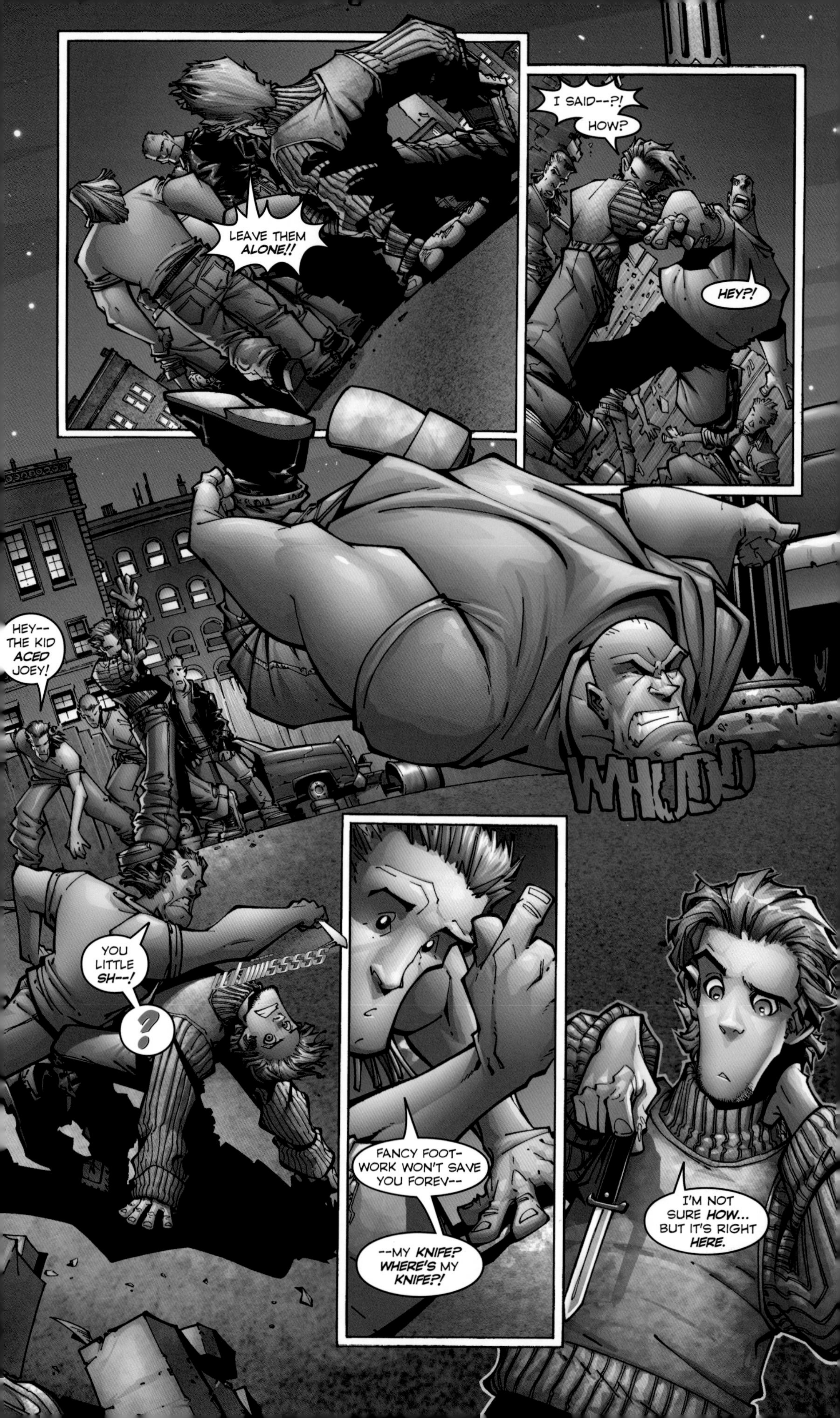
LEAVE THEM ALONE!!
I SAID--?!
HOW?
HEY?!
HEY-- THE KID ACED JOEY!
WHUD
YOU LITTLE SH--!
?
FANCY FOOT-WORK WON'T SAVE YOU FOREV--
--MY KNIFE? WHERE'S MY KNIFE?!
I'M NOT SURE HOW... BUT IT'S RIGHT HERE.

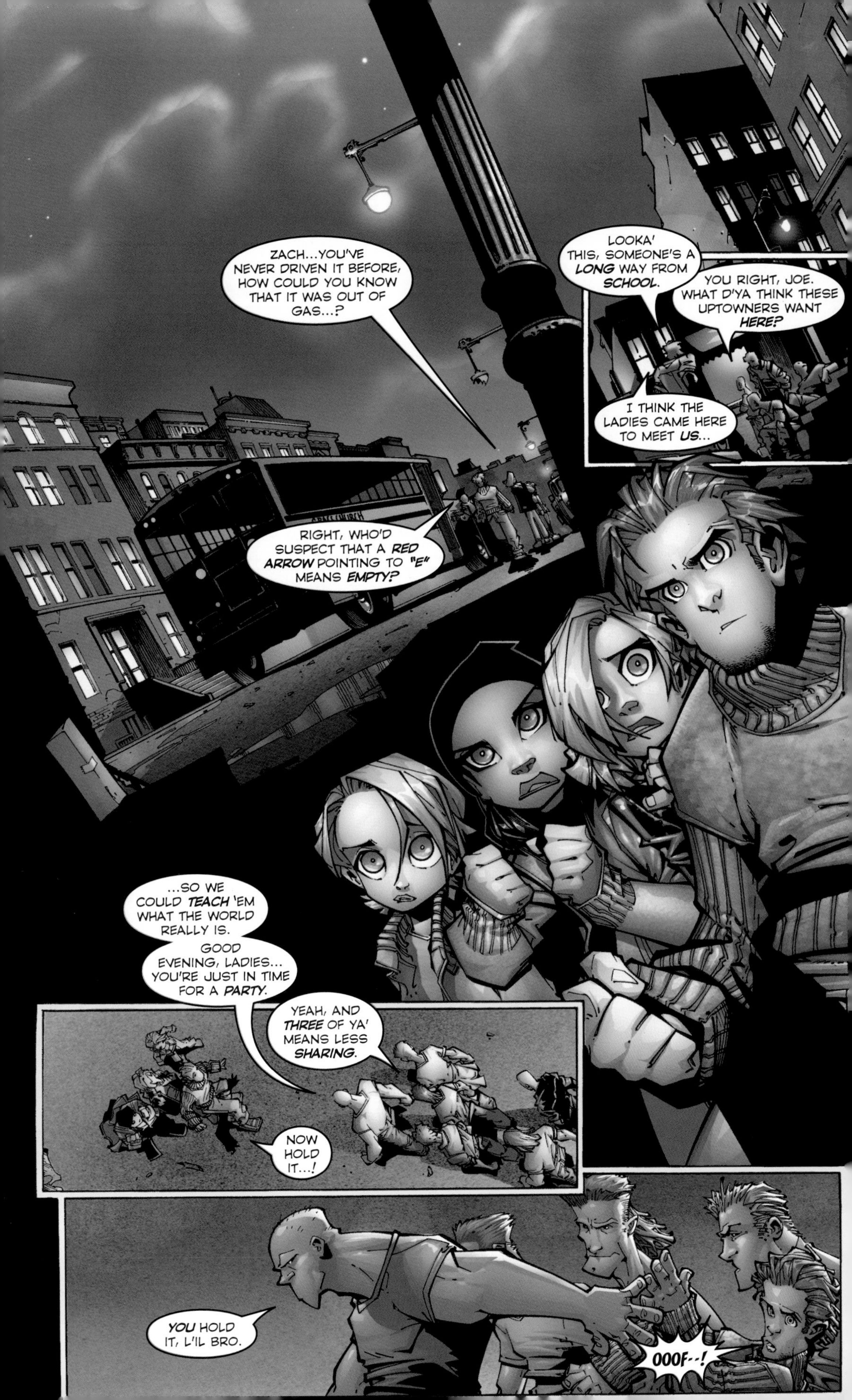
ZACH...YOU'VE NEVER DRIVEN IT BEFORE, HOW COULD YOU KNOW THAT IT WAS OUT OF GAS...?
LOOKA' THIS, SOMEONE'S A LONG WAY FROM SCHOOL.
YOU RIGHT, JOE. WHAT D'YA THINK THESE UPTOWNERS WANT HERE?
I THINK THE LADIES CAME HERE TO MEET US...
RIGHT, WHO'D SUSPECT THAT A RED ARROW POINTING TO "E" MEANS EMPTY?
...SO WE COULD TEACH 'EM WHAT THE WORLD REALLY IS.
GOOD EVENING, LADIES... YOU'RE JUST IN TIME FOR A PARTY.
YEAH, AND THREE OF YA' MEANS LESS SHARING.
NOW HOLD IT...!
YOU HOLD IT, L'IL BRO.
OOOF--!

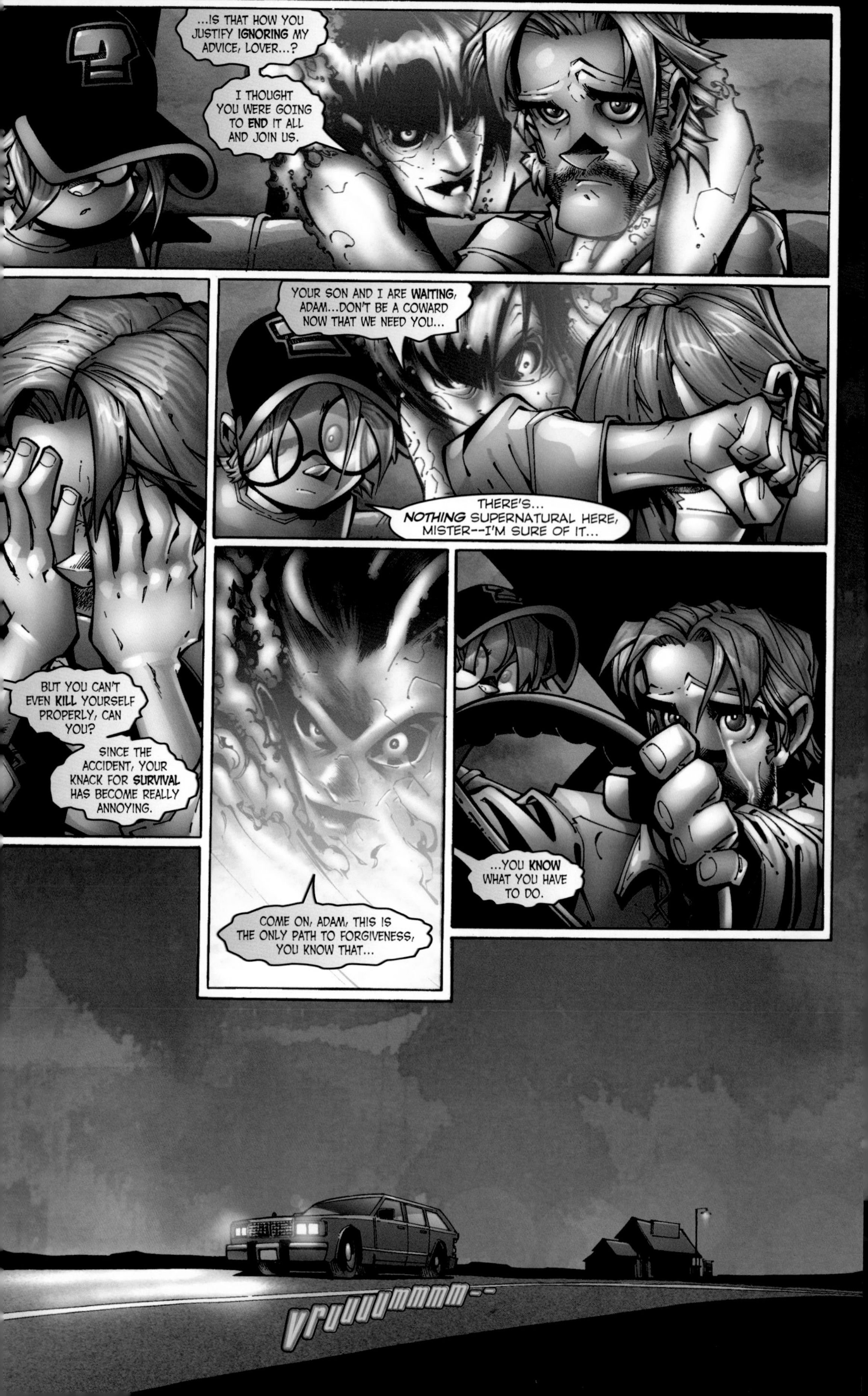
...IS THAT HOW YOU JUSTIFY IGNORING MY ADVICE, LOVER...?
I THOUGHT YOU WERE GOING TO END IT ALL AND JOIN US.
YOUR SON AND I ARE WAITING, ADAM...DON'T BE A COWARD NOW THAT WE NEED YOU...
THERE'S... NOTHING SUPERNATURAL HERE, MISTER--I'M SURE OF IT...
BUT YOU CAN'T EVEN KILL YOURSELF PROPERLY, CAN YOU?
SINCE THE ACCIDENT, YOUR KNACK FOR SURVIVAL HAS BECOME REALLY ANNOYING.
COME ON, ADAM, THIS IS THE ONLY PATH TO FORGIVENESS, YOU KNOW THAT...
...YOU KNOW WHAT YOU HAVE TO DO.
vruuuummmm--

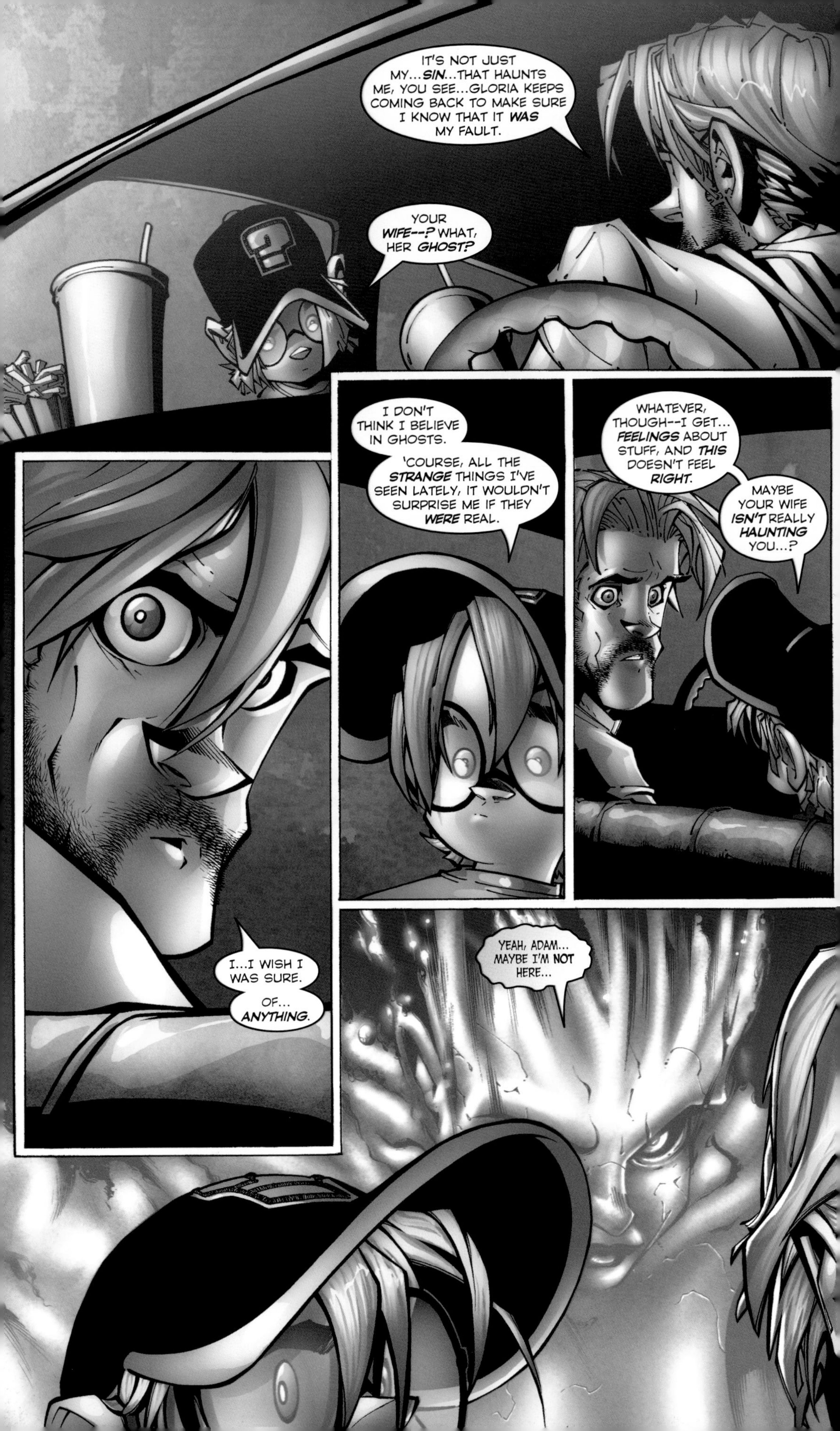
IT'S NOT JUST MY...SIN...THAT HAUNTS ME, YOU SEE...GLORIA KEEPS COMING BACK TO MAKE SURE I KNOW THAT IT WAS MY FAULT.
YOUR WIFE--? WHAT, HER GHOST?
I DON'T THINK I BELIEVE IN GHOSTS.
'COURSE, ALL THE STRANGE THINGS I'VE SEEN LATELY, IT WOULDN'T SURPRISE ME IF THEY WERE REAL.
WHATEVER, THOUGH--I GET... FEELINGS ABOUT STUFF, AND THIS DOESN'T FEEL RIGHT.
MAYBE YOUR WIFE ISN'T REALLY HAUNTING YOU...?
I...I WISH I WAS SURE.
OF... ANYTHING.
YEAH, ADAM... MAYBE I'M NOT HERE...

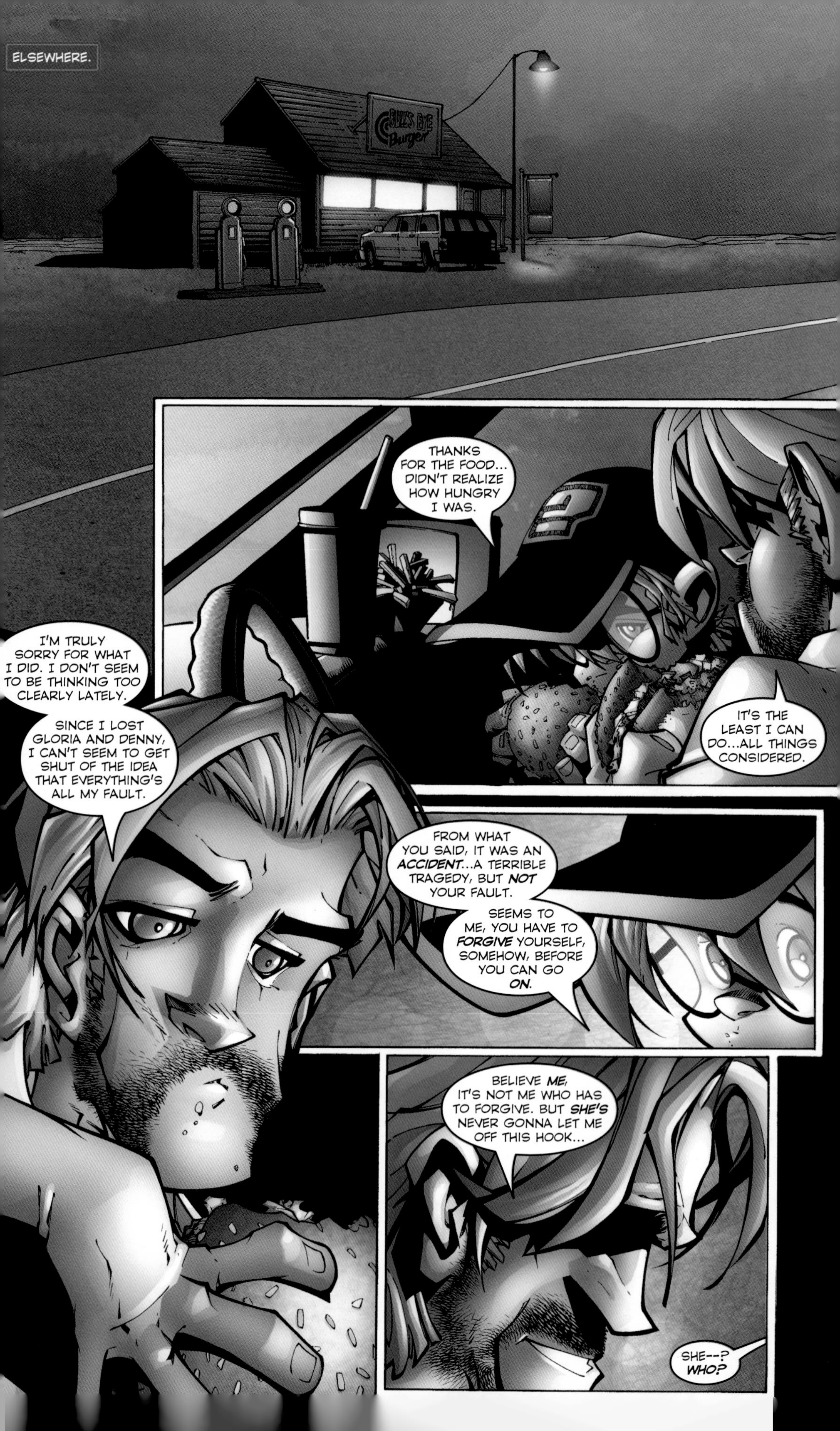
ELSEWHERE.
BULL'S EYE Burger
THANKS FOR THE FOOD... DIDN'T REALIZE HOW HUNGRY I WAS.
IT'S THE LEAST I CAN DO...ALL THINGS CONSIDERED.
I'M TRULY SORRY FOR WHAT I DID. I DON'T SEEM TO BE THINKING TOO CLEARLY LATELY.
SINCE I LOST GLORIA AND DENNY, I CAN'T SEEM TO GET SHUT OF THE IDEA THAT EVERYTHING'S ALL MY FAULT.
FROM WHAT YOU SAID, IT WAS AN ACCIDENT...A TERRIBLE TRAGEDY, BUT NOT YOUR FAULT.
SEEMS TO ME, YOU HAVE TO FORGIVE YOURSELF, SOMEHOW, BEFORE YOU CAN GO ON.
BELIEVE ME, IT'S NOT ME WHO HAS TO FORGIVE. BUT SHE'S NEVER GONNA LET ME OFF THIS HOOK...
SHE--? WHO?

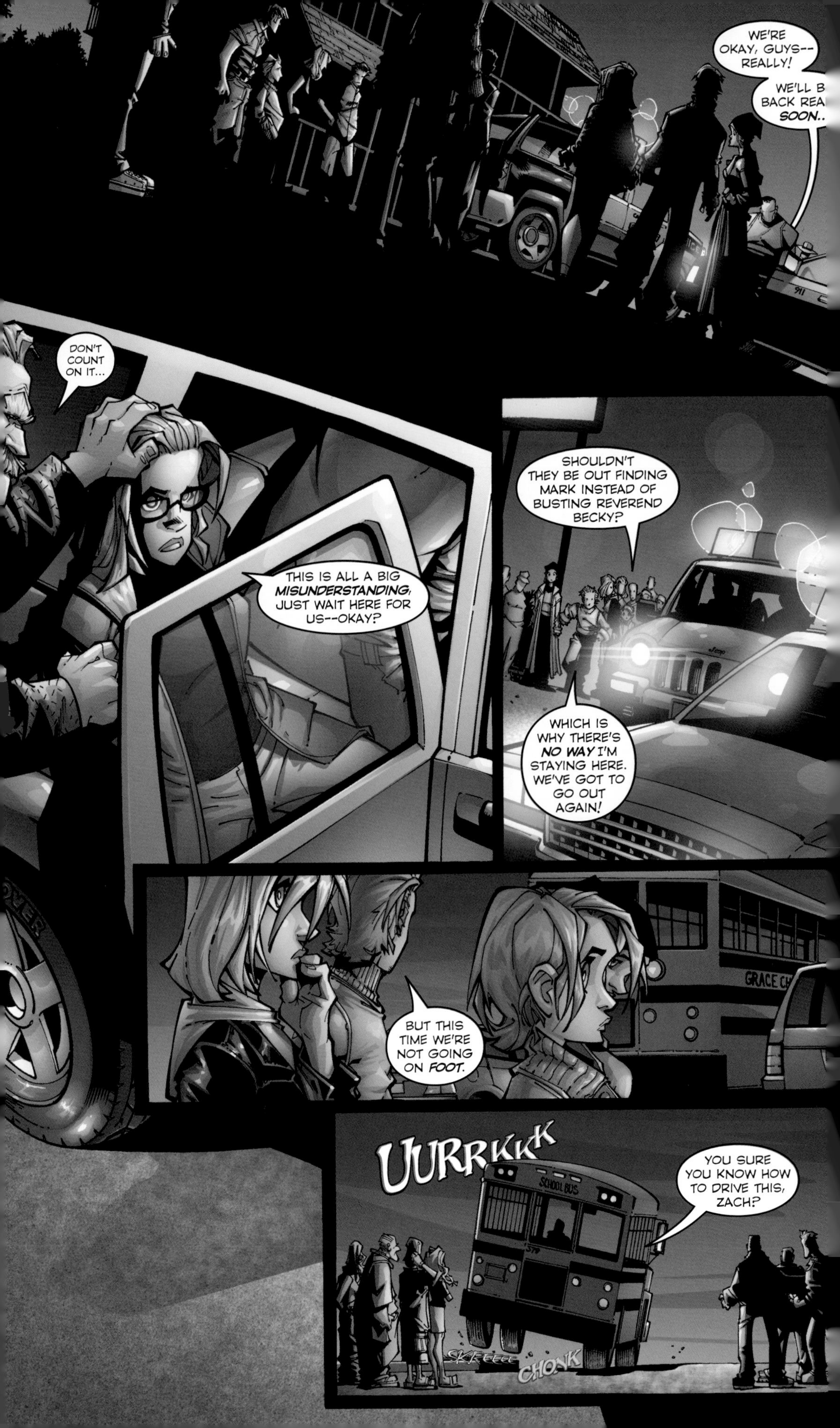

WE'RE OKAY, GUYS-- REALLY!
WE'LL B BACK REA SOON..
DON'T COUNT ON IT...
THIS IS ALL A BIG MISUNDERSTANDING, JUST WAIT HERE FOR US--OKAY?
SHOULDN'T THEY BE OUT FINDING MARK INSTEAD OF BUSTING REVEREND BECKY?
WHICH IS WHY THERE'S NO WAY I'M STAYING HERE. WE'VE GOT TO GO OUT AGAIN!
BUT THIS TIME WE'RE NOT GOING ON FOOT.
UURRKKK
SCHOOL BUS
YOU SURE YOU KNOW HOW TO DRIVE THIS, ZACH?
SKREEEE
CHONK

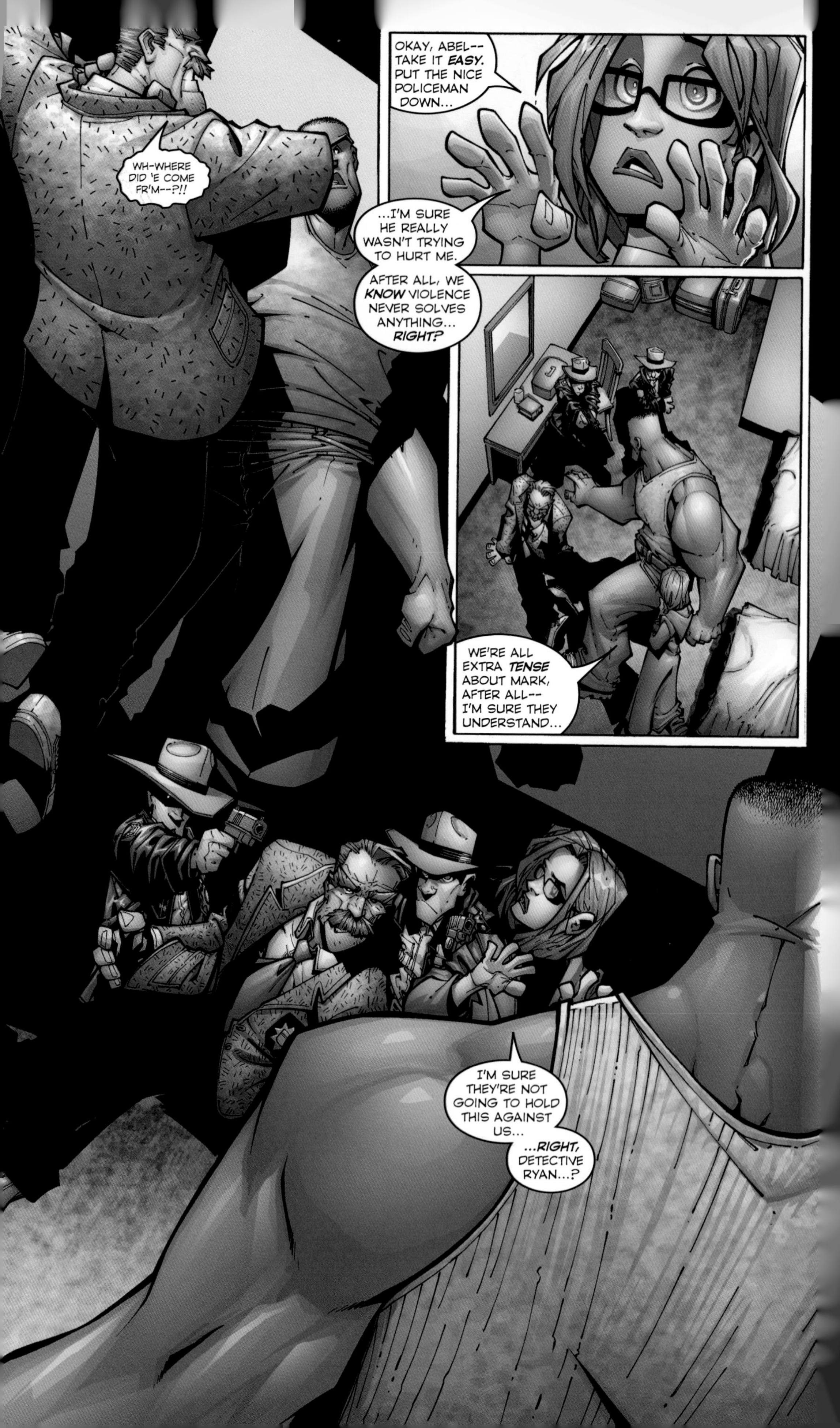
WH-WHERE DID 'E COME FR'M--?!!
OKAY, ABEL-- TAKE IT **EASY.** PUT THE NICE POLICEMAN DOWN...
...I'M SURE HE REALLY WASN'T TRYING TO HURT ME.
AFTER ALL, WE **KNOW** VIOLENCE NEVER SOLVES ANYTHING... **RIGHT?**
WE'RE ALL EXTRA **TENSE** ABOUT MARK, AFTER ALL-- I'M SURE THEY UNDERSTAND...
I'M SURE THEY'RE NOT GOING TO HOLD THIS AGAINST US...
...**RIGHT,** DETECTIVE RYAN...?

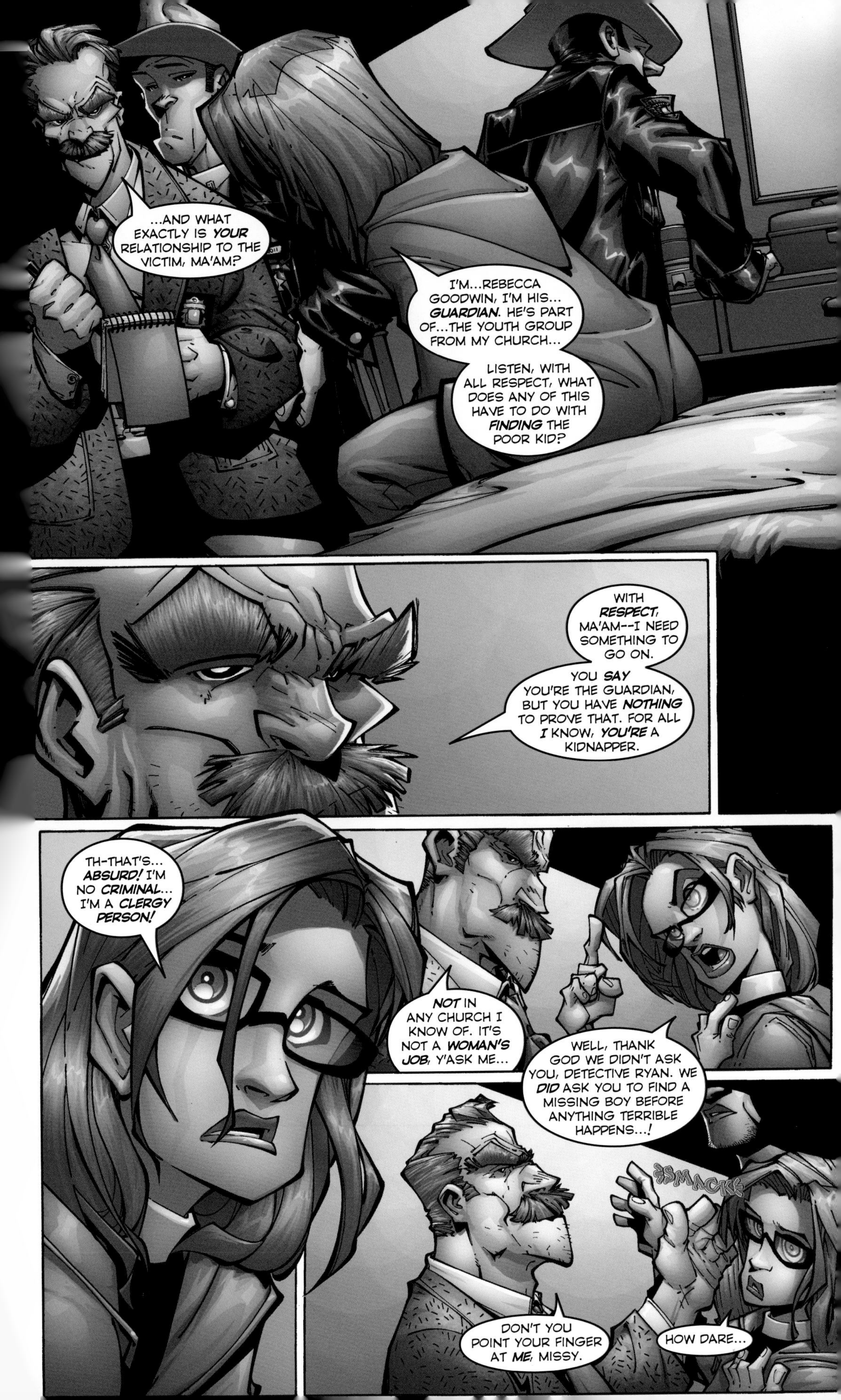
...AND WHAT EXACTLY IS YOUR RELATIONSHIP TO THE VICTIM, MA'AM?
I'M...REBECCA GOODWIN, I'M HIS... GUARDIAN. HE'S PART OF...THE YOUTH GROUP FROM MY CHURCH...
LISTEN, WITH ALL RESPECT, WHAT DOES ANY OF THIS HAVE TO DO WITH FINDING THE POOR KID?
WITH RESPECT, MA'AM--I NEED SOMETHING TO GO ON.
YOU SAY YOU'RE THE GUARDIAN, BUT YOU HAVE NOTHING TO PROVE THAT. FOR ALL I KNOW, YOU'RE A KIDNAPPER.
TH-THAT'S... ABSURD! I'M NO CRIMINAL... I'M A CLERGY PERSON!
NOT IN ANY CHURCH I KNOW OF. IT'S NOT A WOMAN'S JOB, Y'ASK ME...
WELL, THANK GOD WE DIDN'T ASK YOU, DETECTIVE RYAN. WE DID ASK YOU TO FIND A MISSING BOY BEFORE ANYTHING TERRIBLE HAPPENS...!
SMACK
DON'T YOU POINT YOUR FINGER AT ME, MISSY.
HOW DARE...

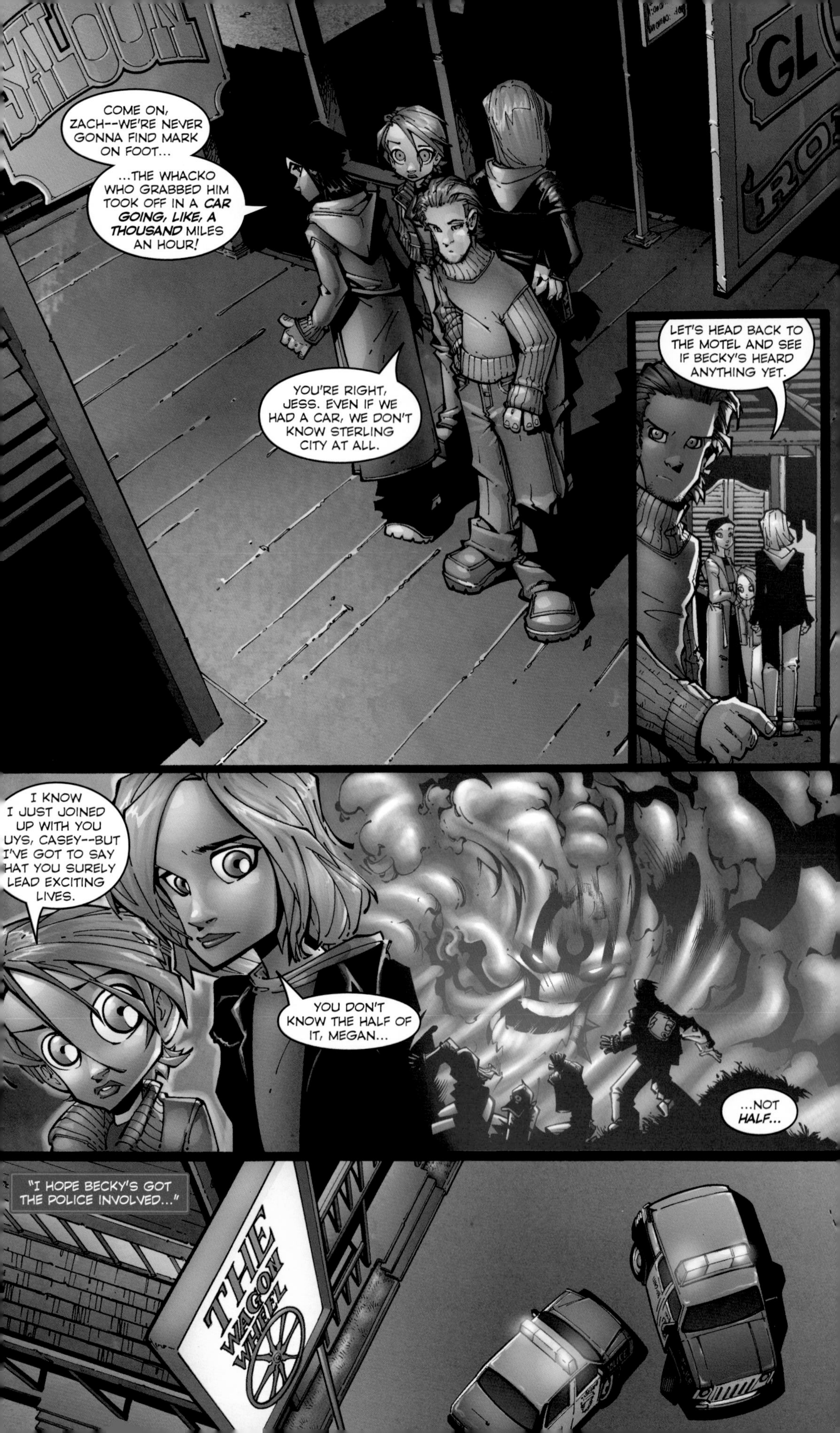

COME ON, ZACH--WE'RE NEVER GONNA FIND MARK ON FOOT...
...THE WHACKO WHO GRABBED HIM TOOK OFF IN A *CAR GOING, LIKE, A THOUSAND* MILES AN HOUR!
YOU'RE RIGHT, JESS. EVEN IF WE HAD A CAR, WE DON'T KNOW STERLING CITY AT ALL.
LET'S HEAD BACK TO THE MOTEL AND SEE IF BECKY'S HEARD ANYTHING YET.
I KNOW I JUST JOINED UP WITH YOU UYS, CASEY--BUT I'VE GOT TO SAY HAT YOU SURELY LEAD EXCITING LIVES.
YOU DON'T KNOW THE HALF OF IT, MEGAN...
...NOT *HALF*...
"I HOPE BECKY'S GOT THE POLICE INVOLVED..."
THE WAGON WHEEL

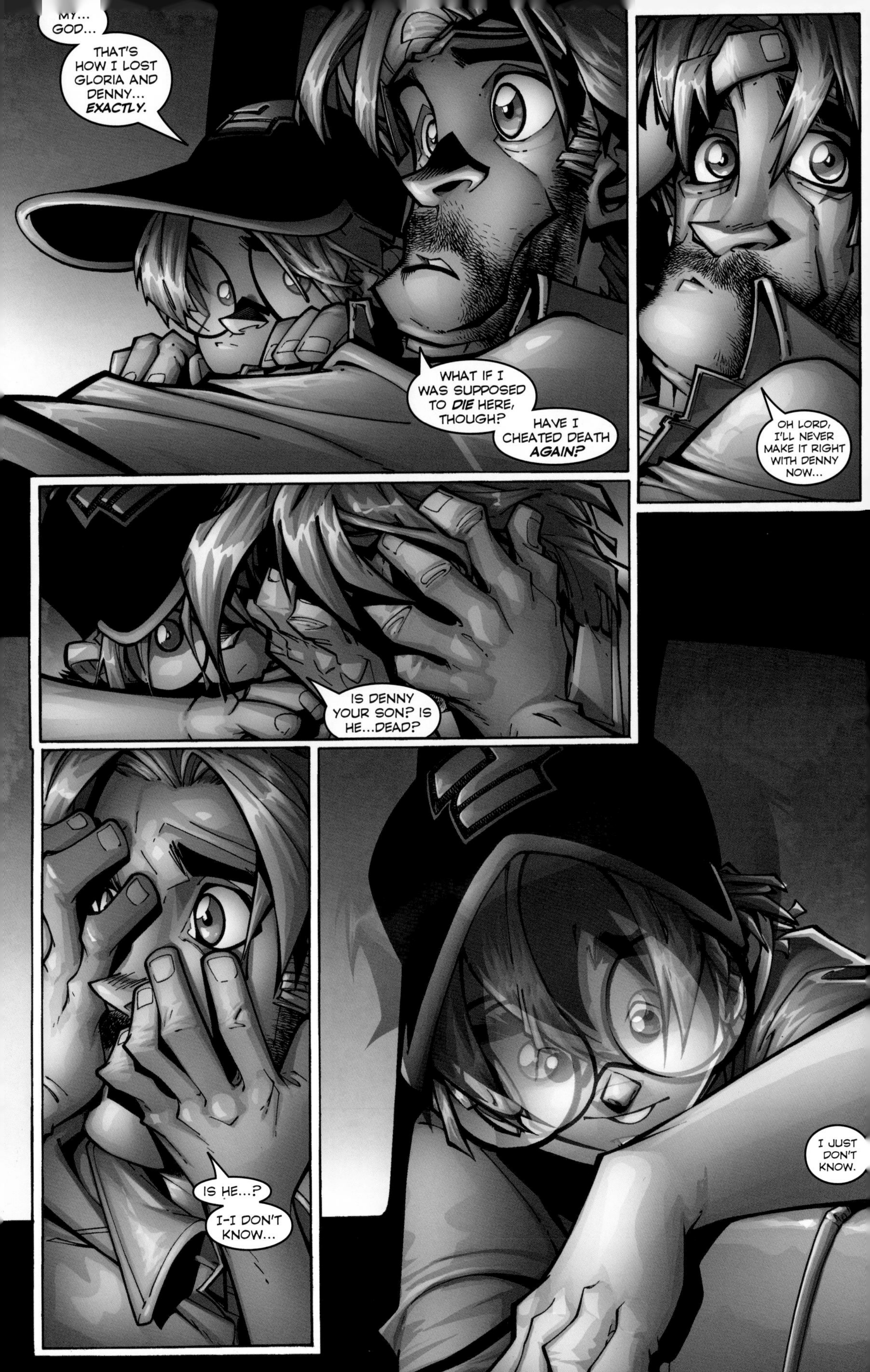
MY... GOD...
THAT'S HOW I LOST GLORIA AND DENNY... *EXACTLY.*
WHAT IF I WAS SUPPOSED TO *DIE* HERE, THOUGH?
HAVE I CHEATED DEATH *AGAIN?*
OH LORD, I'LL NEVER MAKE IT RIGHT WITH DENNY NOW...
IS DENNY YOUR SON? IS HE...DEAD?
IS HE...?
I-I DON'T KNOW...
I JUST DON'T KNOW.

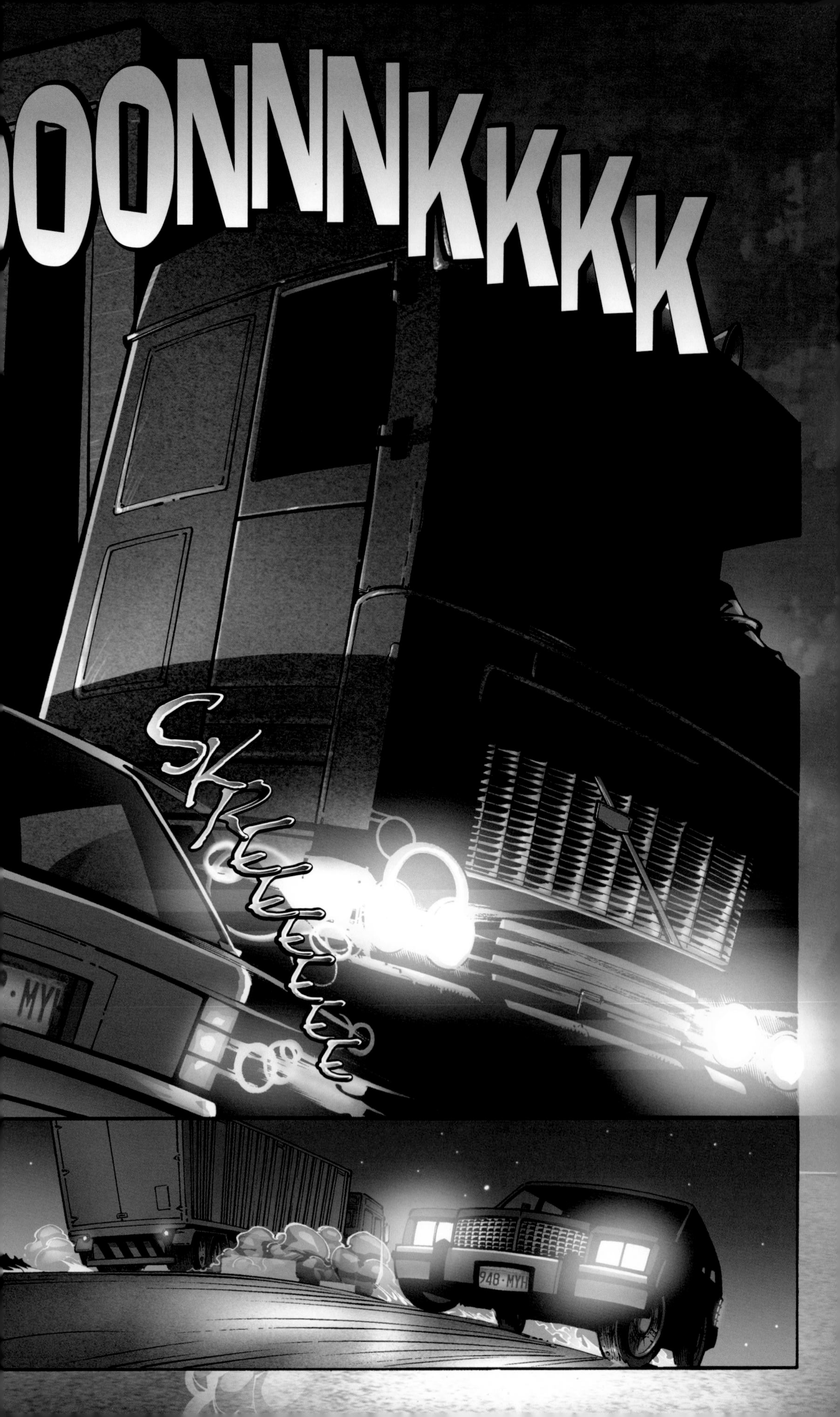
OONNNKKKK
SKREEEEEEE

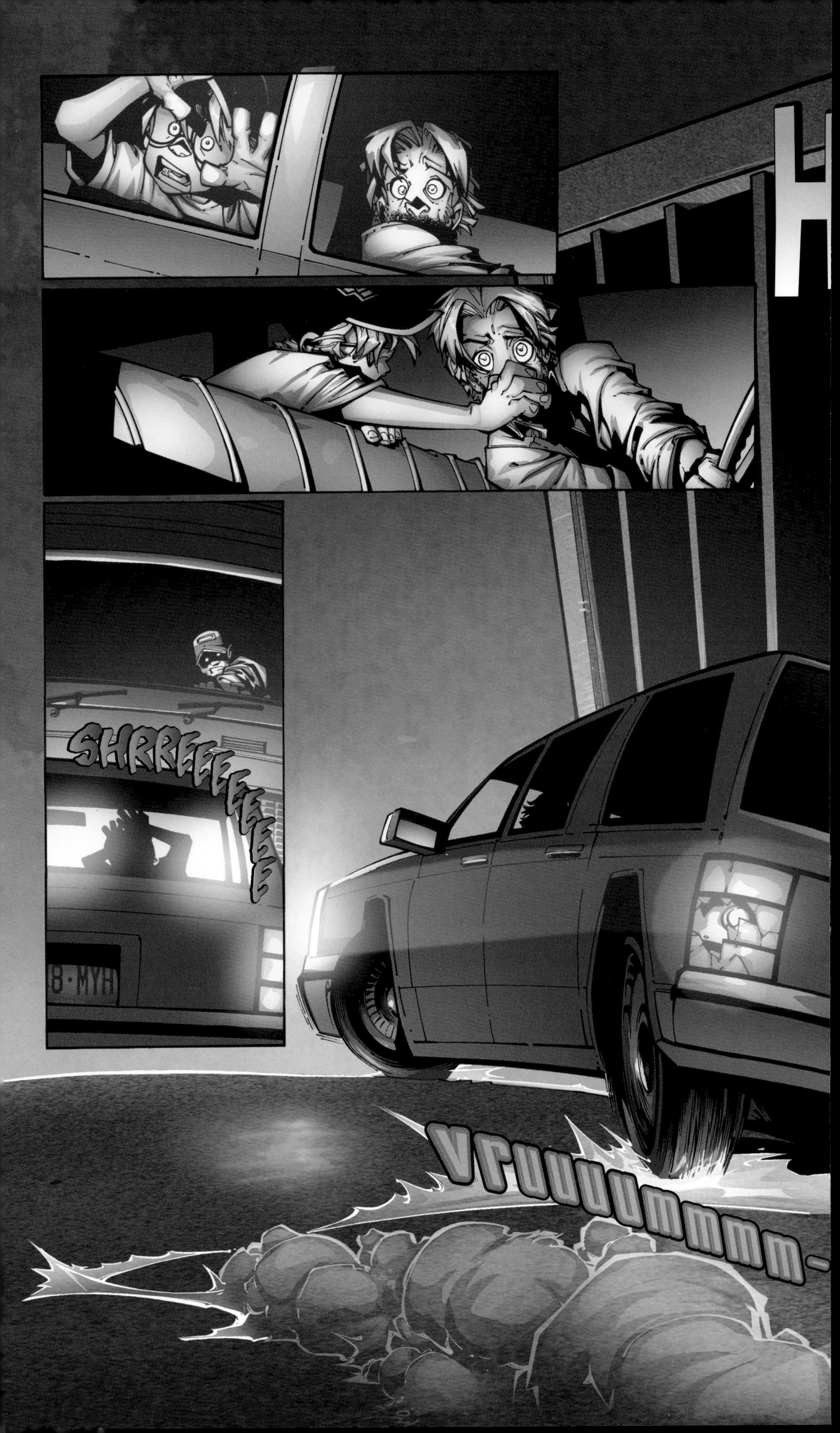
SHRREEEEEEEE
VRUUUUMMMM-
8·MYH

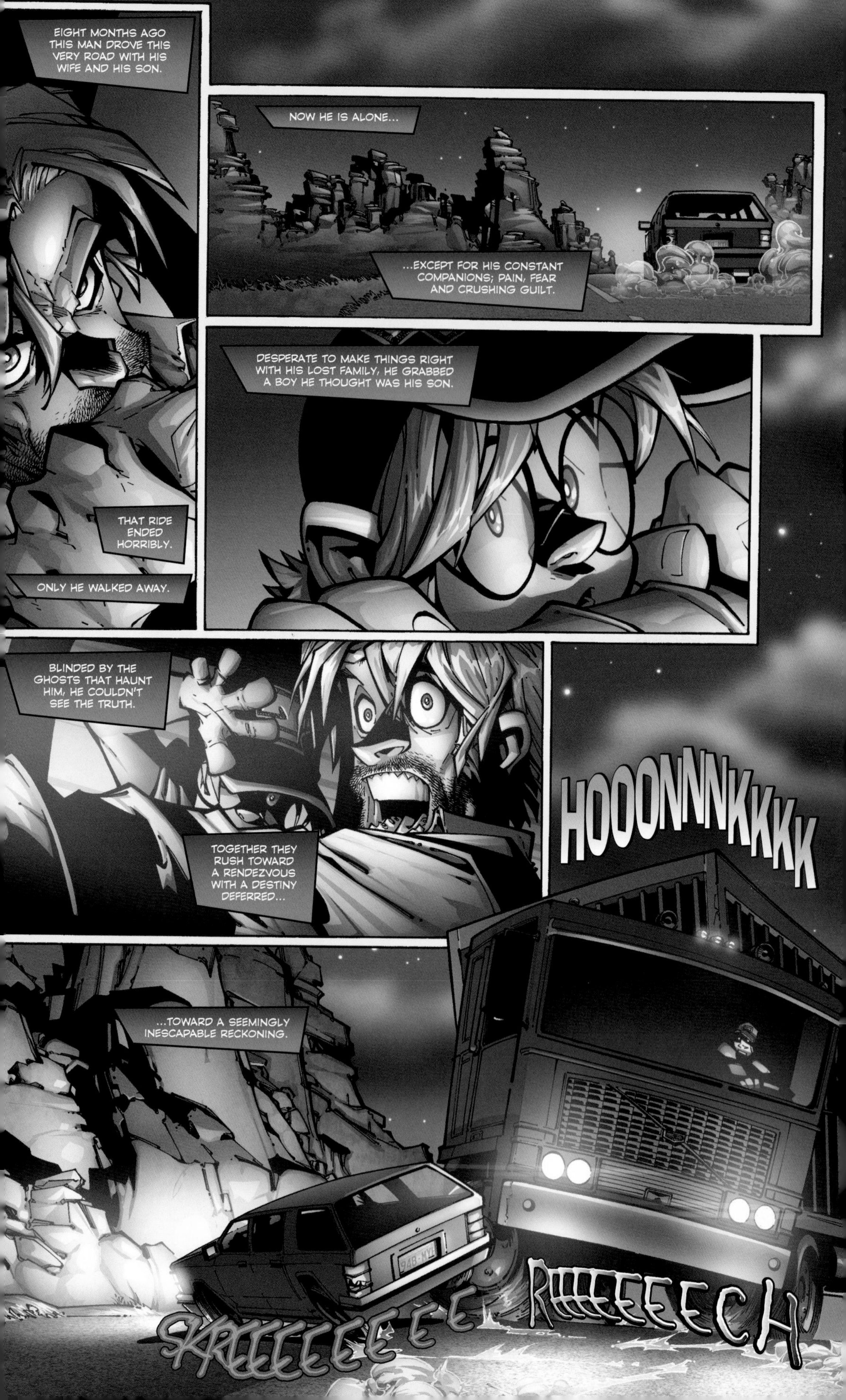
EIGHT MONTHS AGO THIS MAN DROVE THIS VERY ROAD WITH HIS WIFE AND HIS SON.
NOW HE IS ALONE...
...EXCEPT FOR HIS CONSTANT COMPANIONS; PAIN, FEAR AND CRUSHING GUILT.
THAT RIDE ENDED HORRIBLY.
ONLY HE WALKED AWAY.
DESPERATE TO MAKE THINGS RIGHT WITH HIS LOST FAMILY, HE GRABBED A BOY HE THOUGHT WAS HIS SON.
BLINDED BY THE GHOSTS THAT HAUNT HIM, HE COULDN'T SEE THE TRUTH.
TOGETHER THEY RUSH TOWARD A RENDEZVOUS WITH A DESTINY DEFERRED...
HOOONNNKKKK
...TOWARD A SEEMINGLY INESCAPABLE RECKONING.
SKREEEEEEEE E E
REEEEEEECH

CHAPTER TEN
HAUNTS

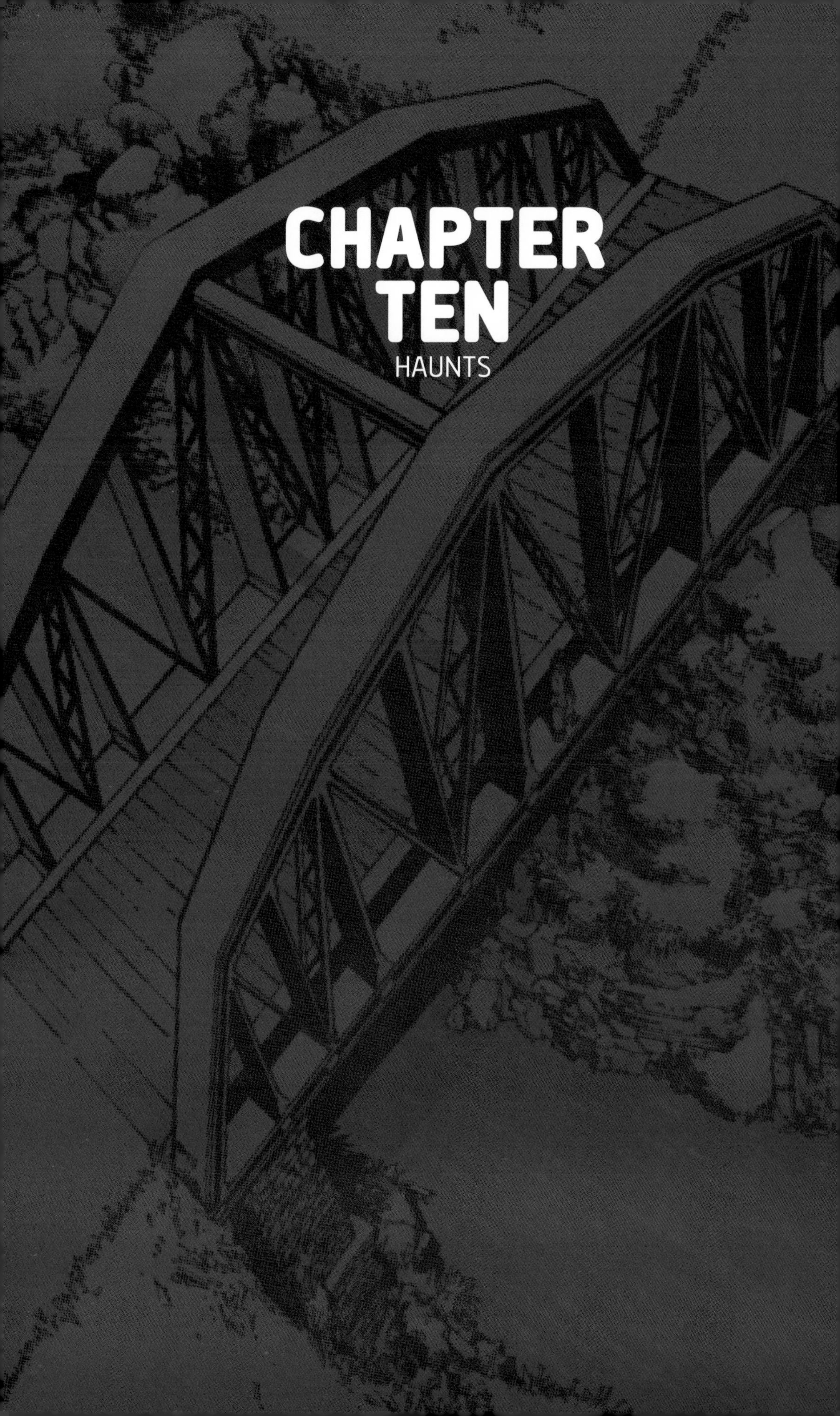

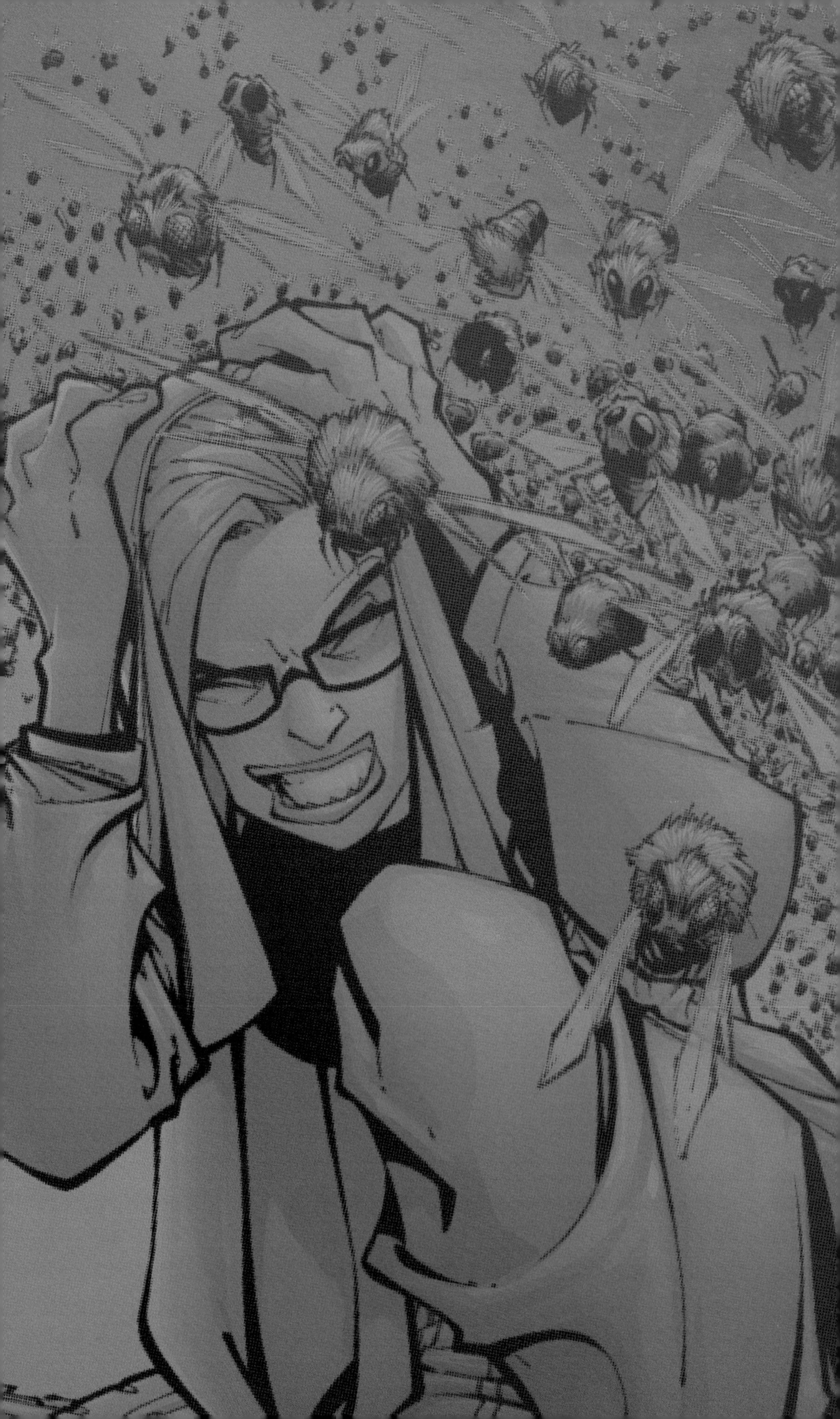

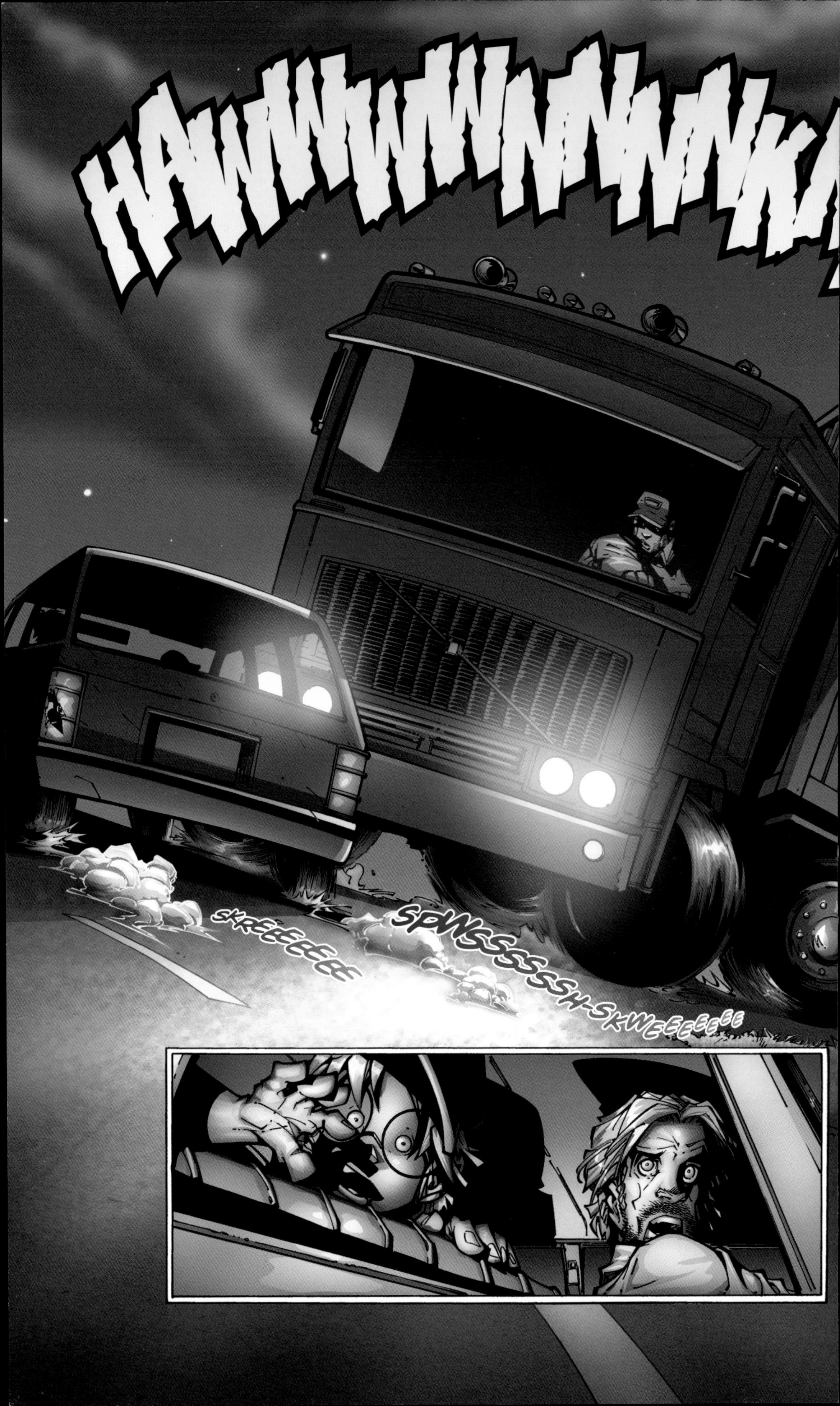
HAWWWWWNNNNNK
SKREEEEEEE
SPWSSSSSSH-SKWEEEEEEE

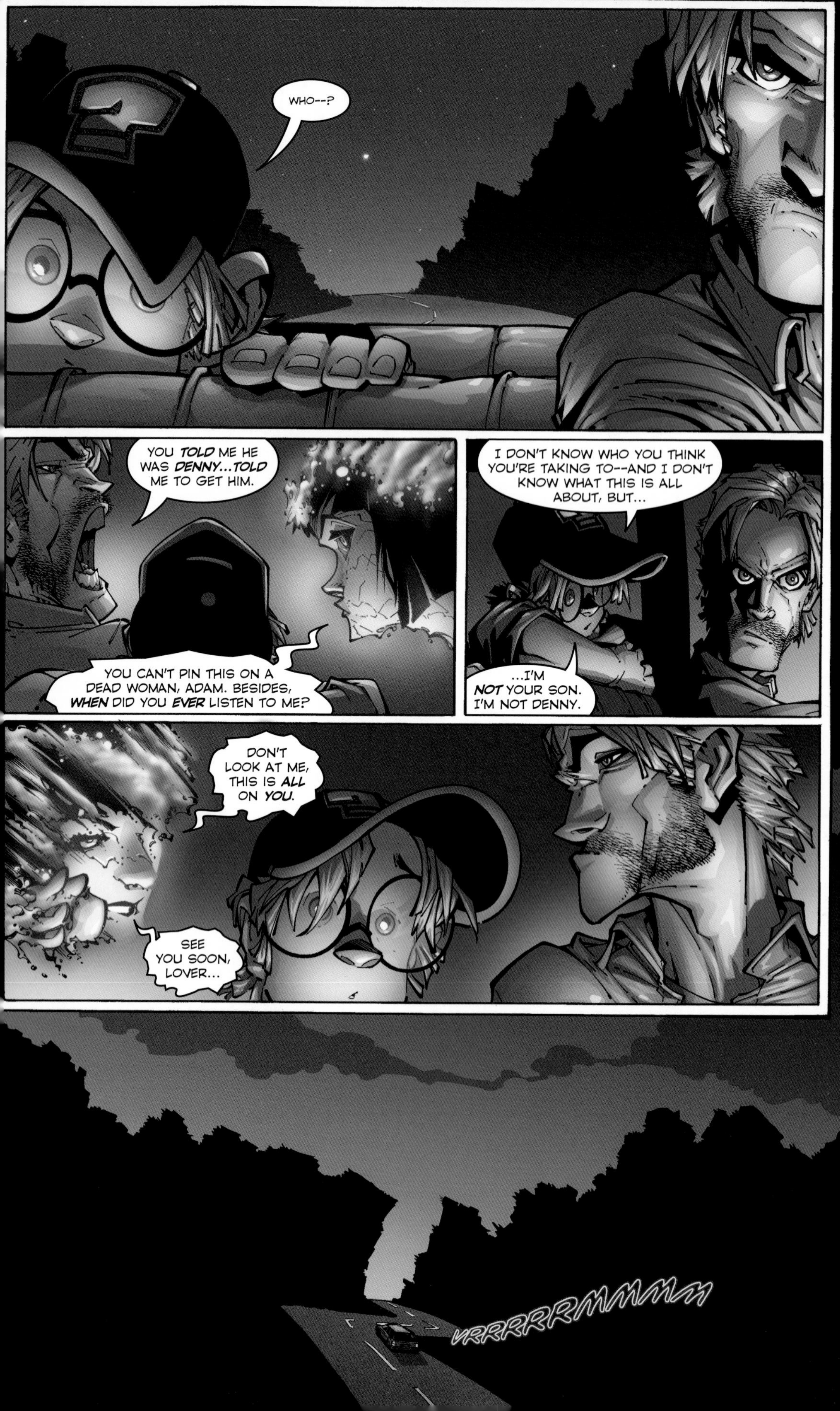
WHO--?
YOU TOLD ME HE WAS DENNY...TOLD ME TO GET HIM.
YOU CAN'T PIN THIS ON A DEAD WOMAN, ADAM. BESIDES, WHEN DID YOU EVER LISTEN TO ME?
I DON'T KNOW WHO YOU THINK YOU'RE TAKING TO--AND I DON'T KNOW WHAT THIS IS ALL ABOUT, BUT...
...I'M NOT YOUR SON. I'M NOT DENNY.
DON'T LOOK AT ME, THIS IS ALL ON YOU.
SEE YOU SOON, LOVER...
VRRRRRMMMMM

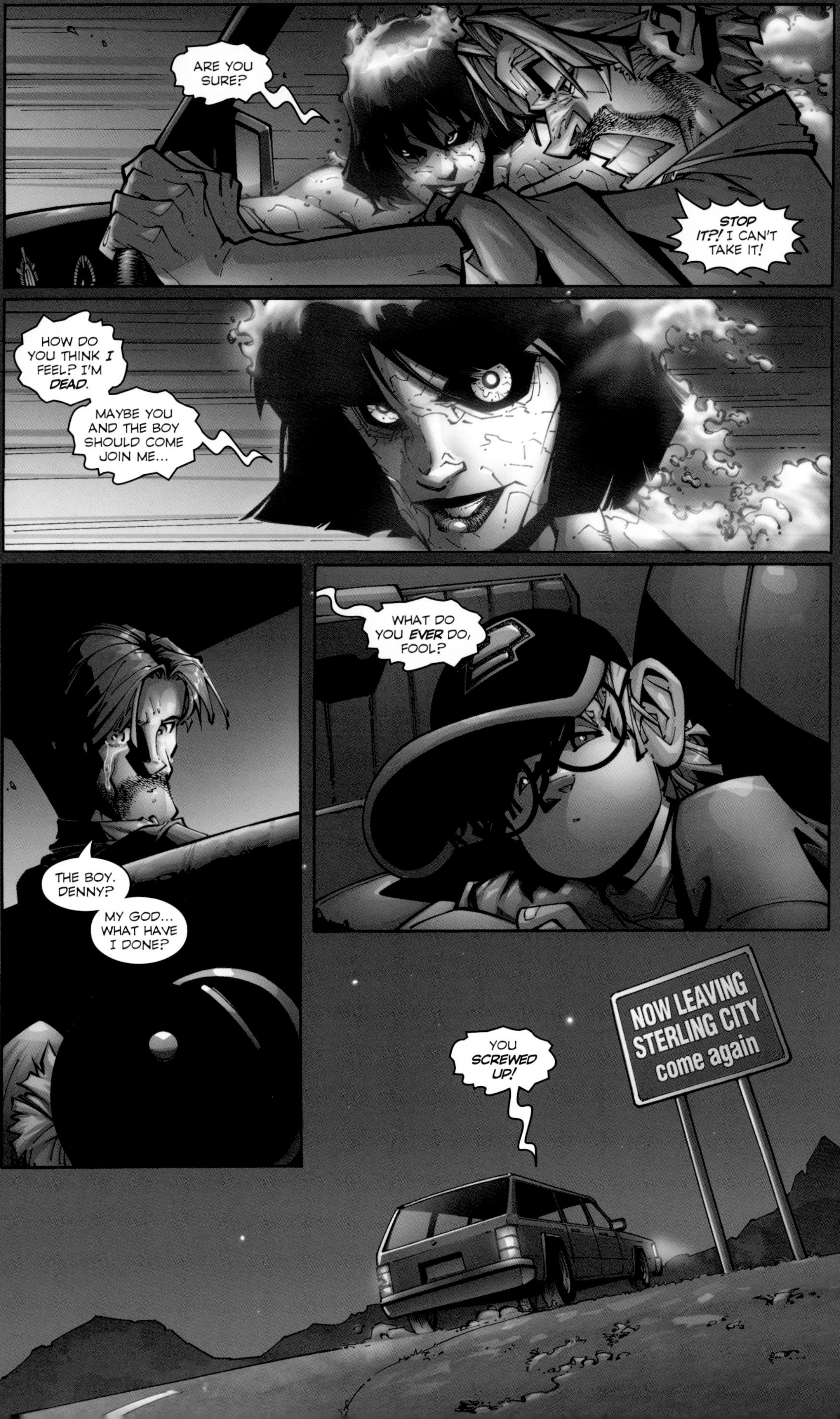

ARE YOU SURE?
STOP IT?! I CAN'T TAKE IT!
HOW DO YOU THINK I FEEL? I'M DEAD.
MAYBE YOU AND THE BOY SHOULD COME JOIN ME...
THE BOY. DENNY?
MY GOD... WHAT HAVE I DONE?
WHAT DO YOU EVER DO, FOOL?
NOW LEAVING STERLING CITY come again
YOU SCREWED UP!

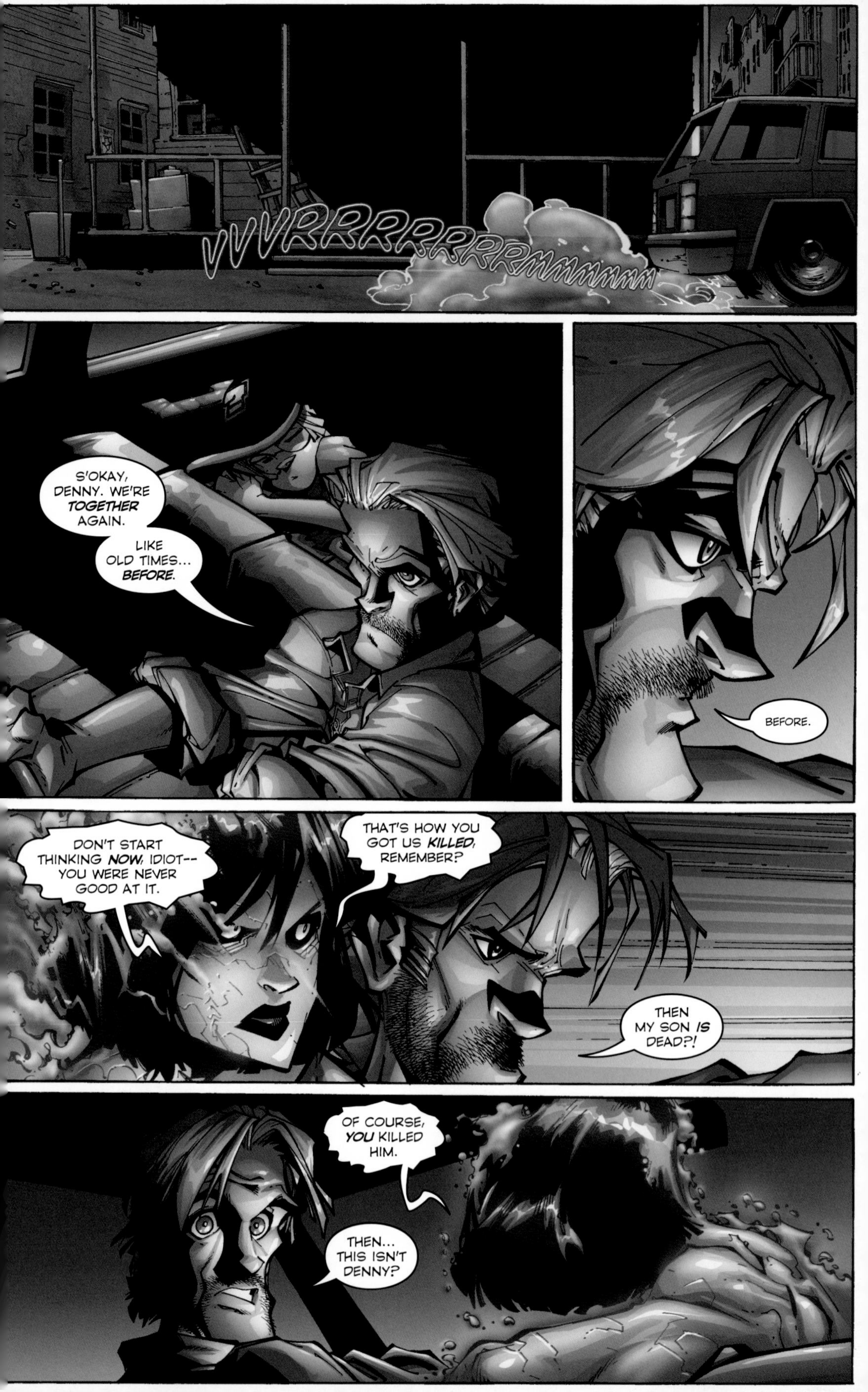
VVVRRRRRRRRMMMMMMM
S'OKAY, DENNY. WE'RE TOGETHER AGAIN.
LIKE OLD TIMES... BEFORE.
BEFORE.
DON'T START THINKING NOW, IDIOT-- YOU WERE NEVER GOOD AT IT.
THAT'S HOW YOU GOT US KILLED, REMEMBER?
THEN MY SON IS DEAD?!
OF COURSE, YOU KILLED HIM.
THEN... THIS ISN'T DENNY?

WRRRRRRRMMMMM

LION

KRRNNCH

SKREEEEEEE

ZACH--?

HE'S GONE, BECK...THE GUY... JUST...TOOK HIM.

BUT, WHO...AND WHY...? IT'S NUTS!

MY GOD...

WHAT THE HELL DO WE DO NOW?

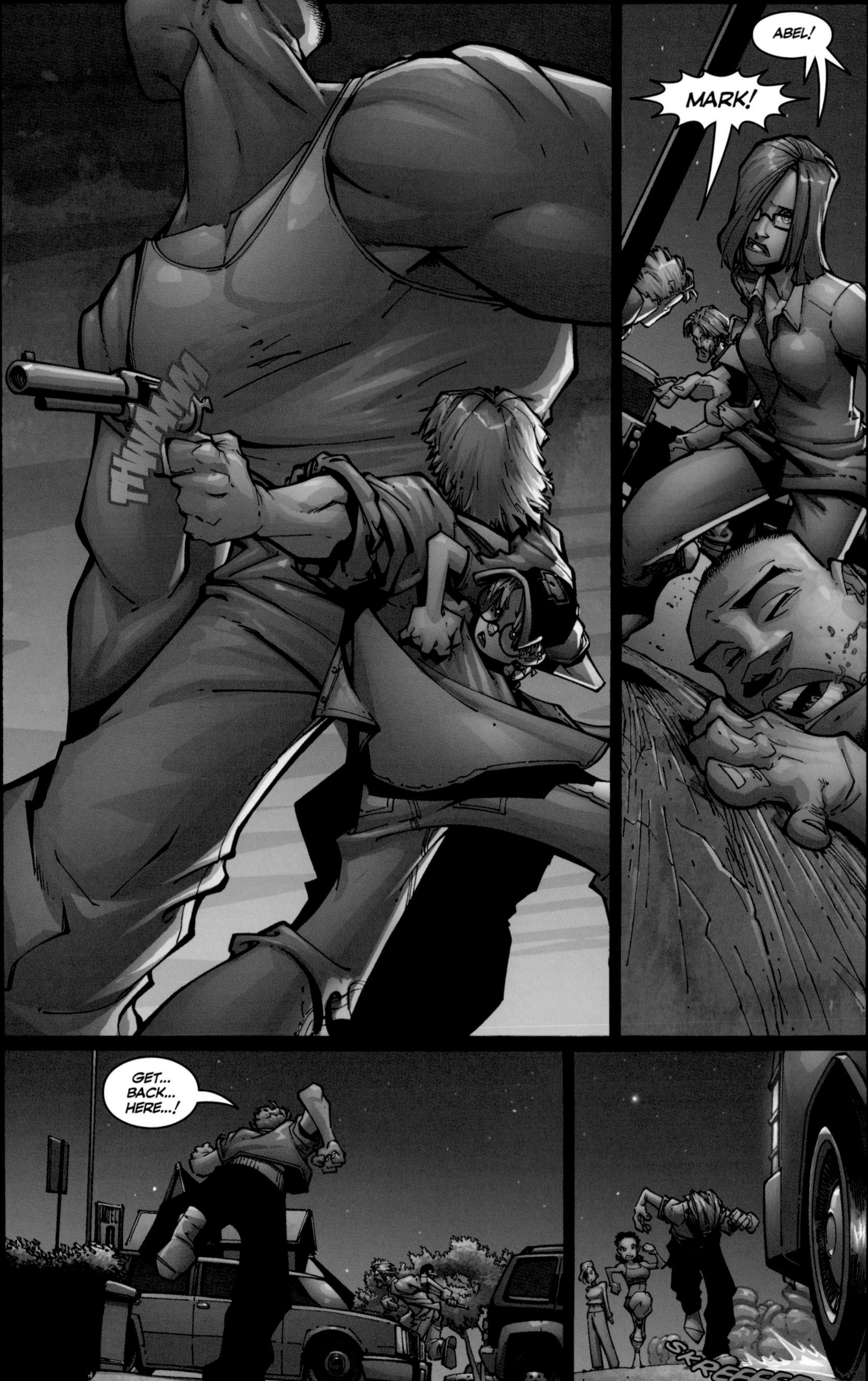
THWAMM
ABEL!
MARK!
GET... BACK... HERE...!
SKREEEEEEEE

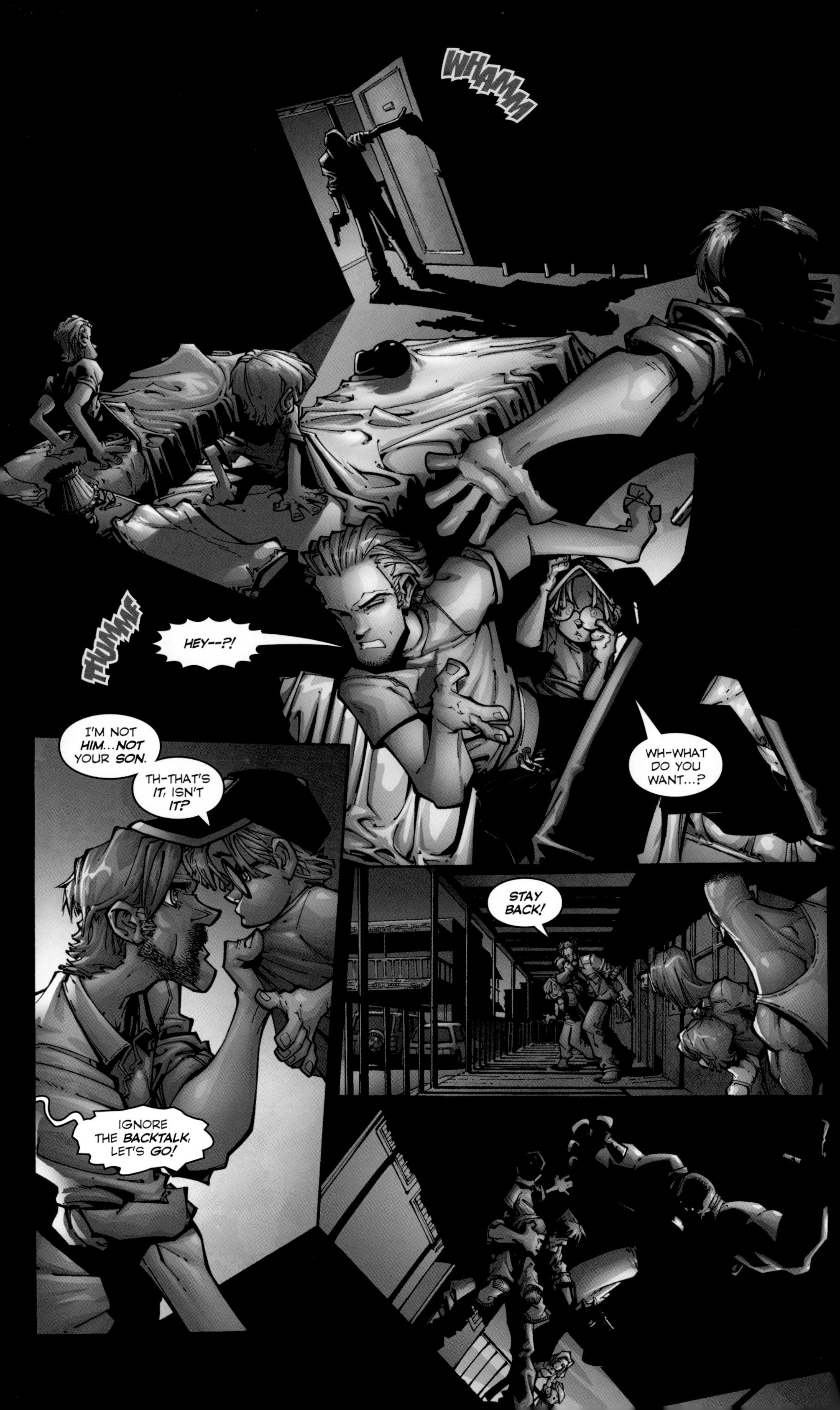
WHAMM
THUMP
HEY--?!
WH-WHAT DO YOU WANT...?
I'M NOT HIM...NOT YOUR SON.
TH-THAT'S IT, ISN'T IT?
STAY BACK!
IGNORE THE BACKTALK, LET'S GO!

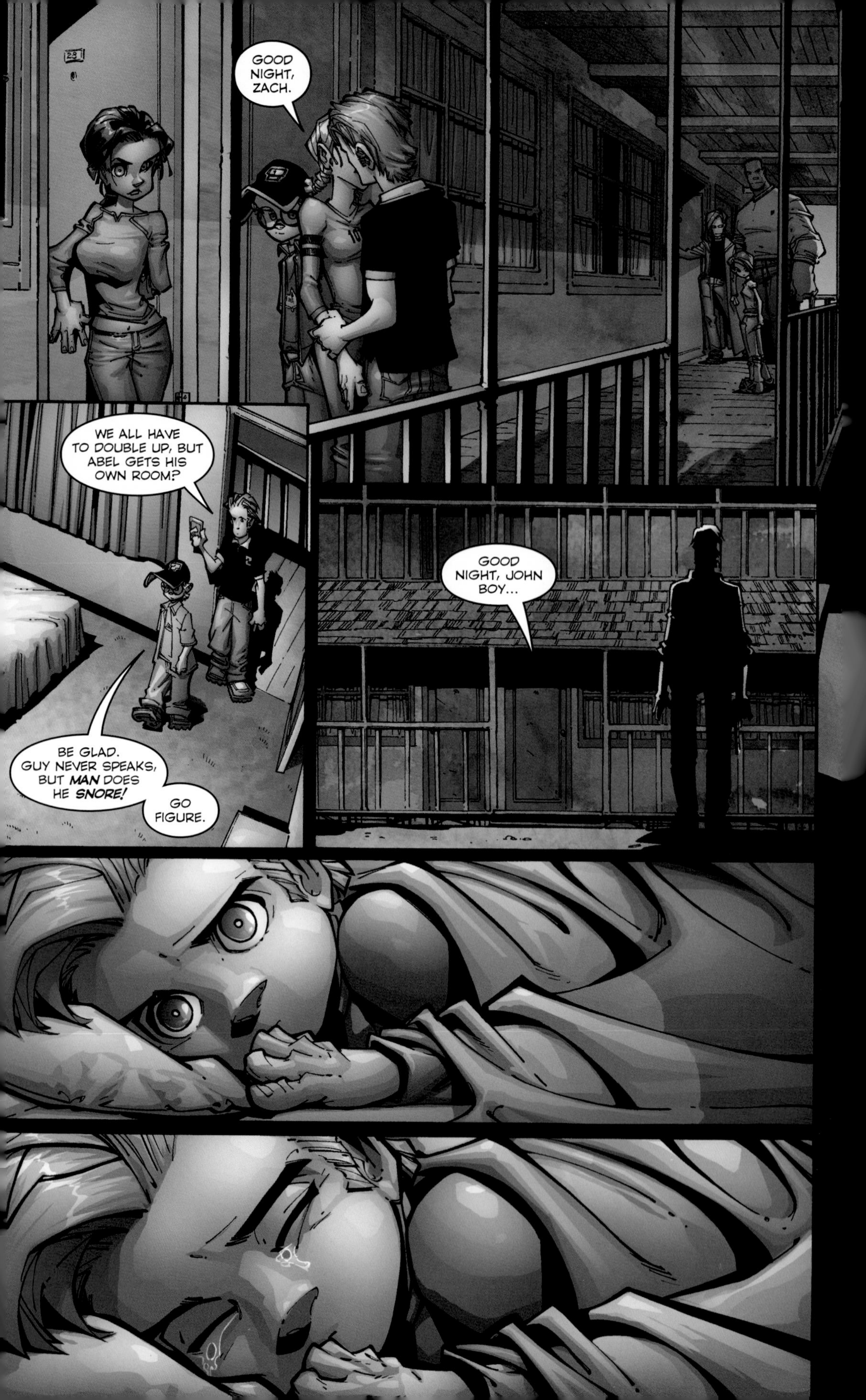

GOOD NIGHT, ZACH.
WE ALL HAVE TO DOUBLE UP, BUT ABEL GETS HIS OWN ROOM?
BE GLAD. GUY NEVER SPEAKS, BUT MAN DOES HE SNORE!
GO FIGURE.
GOOD NIGHT, JOHN BOY...

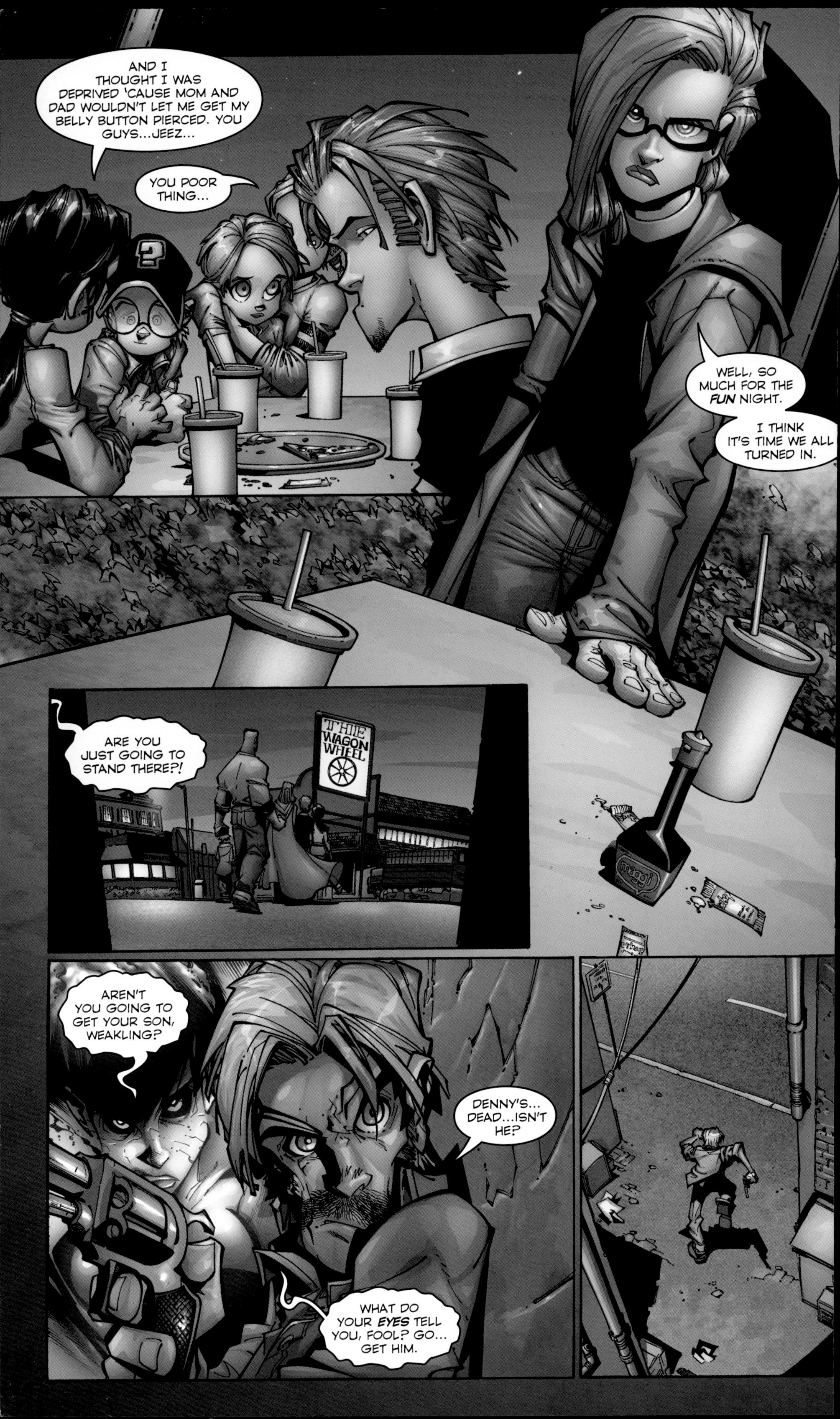
AND I THOUGHT I WAS DEPRIVED 'CAUSE MOM AND DAD WOULDN'T LET ME GET MY BELLY BUTTON PIERCED. YOU GUYS...JEEZ...
YOU POOR THING...
WELL, SO MUCH FOR THE FUN NIGHT.
I THINK IT'S TIME WE ALL TURNED IN.
ARE YOU JUST GOING TO STAND THERE?!
THE WAGON WHEEL
ARE'NT YOU GOING TO GET YOUR SON, WEAKLING?
DENNY'S... DEAD...ISN'T HE?
WHAT DO YOUR EYES TELL YOU, FOOL? GO... GET HIM.

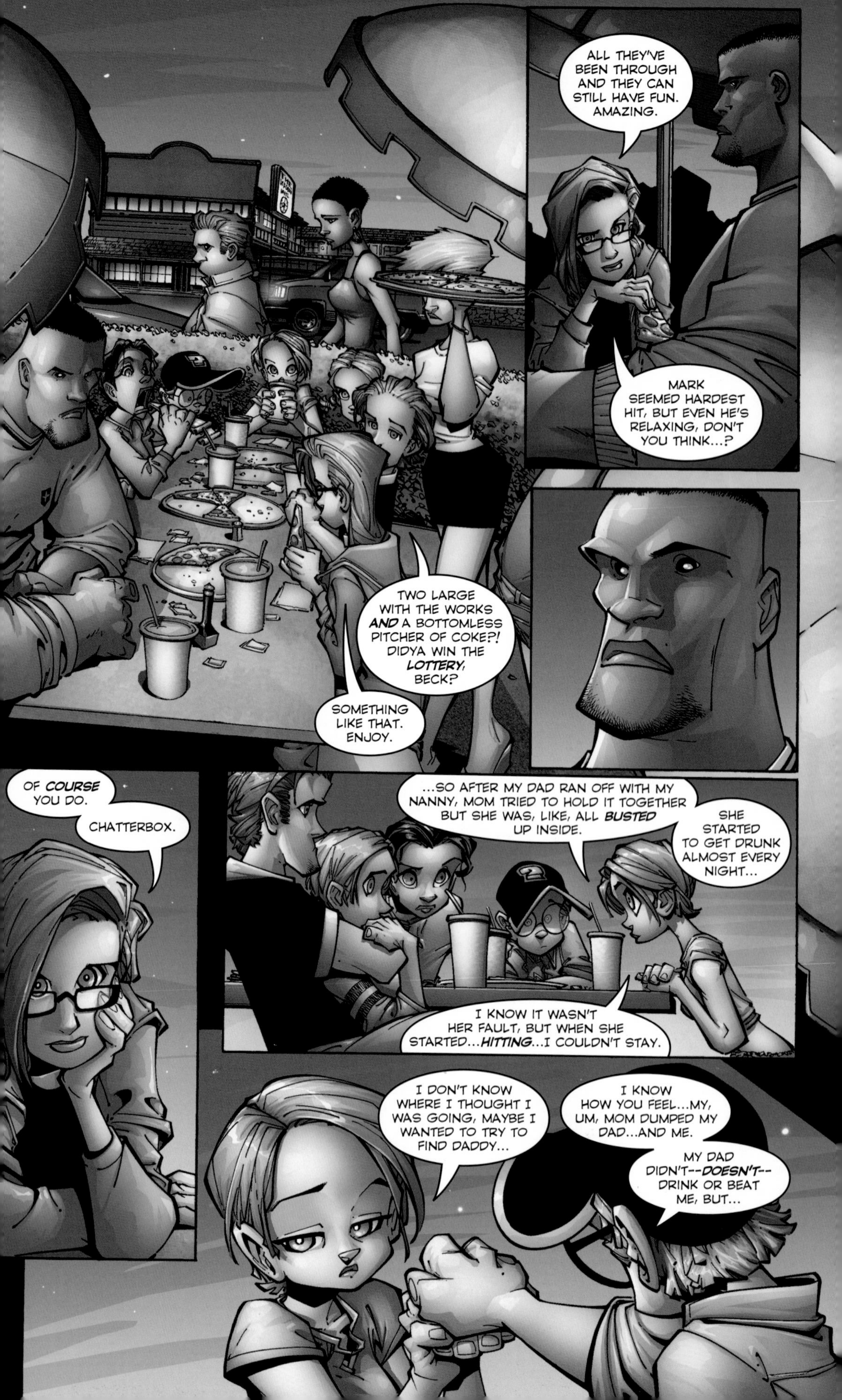
ALL THEY'VE BEEN THROUGH AND THEY CAN STILL HAVE FUN. AMAZING.
MARK SEEMED HARDEST HIT, BUT EVEN HE'S RELAXING, DON'T YOU THINK...?
TWO LARGE WITH THE WORKS AND A BOTTOMLESS PITCHER OF COKE?! DIDYA WIN THE LOTTERY, BECK?
SOMETHING LIKE THAT. ENJOY.
OF COURSE YOU DO.
CHATTERBOX.
...SO AFTER MY DAD RAN OFF WITH MY NANNY, MOM TRIED TO HOLD IT TOGETHER BUT SHE WAS, LIKE, ALL BUSTED UP INSIDE.
SHE STARTED TO GET DRUNK ALMOST EVERY NIGHT...
I KNOW IT WASN'T HER FAULT, BUT WHEN SHE STARTED...HITTING...I COULDN'T STAY.
I DON'T KNOW WHERE I THOUGHT I WAS GOING, MAYBE I WANTED TO TRY TO FIND DADDY...
I KNOW HOW YOU FEEL...MY, UM, MOM DUMPED MY DAD...AND ME.
MY DAD DIDN'T--DOESN'T--DRINK OR BEAT ME, BUT...

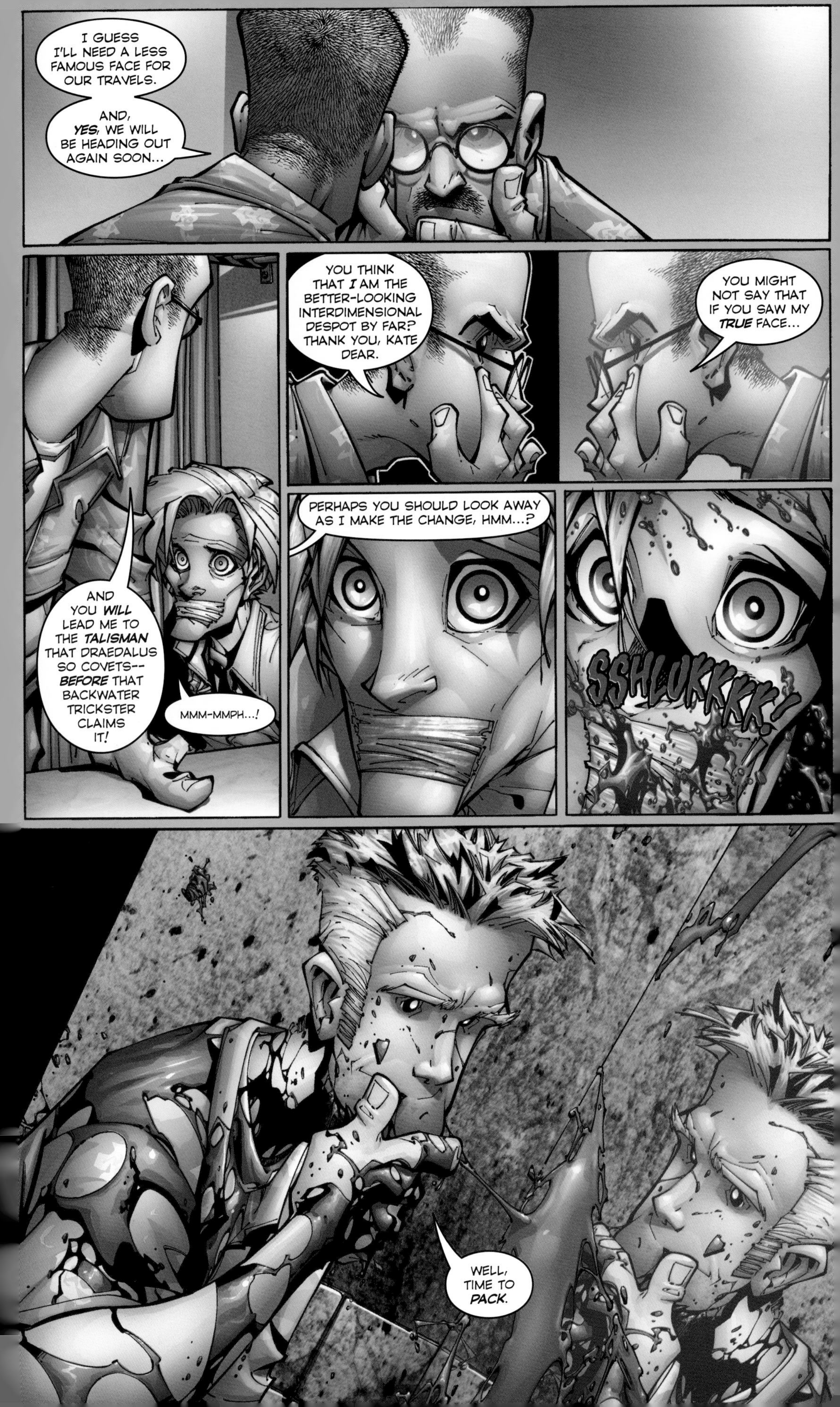

I GUESS I'LL NEED A LESS FAMOUS FACE FOR OUR TRAVELS.
AND, YES, WE WILL BE HEADING OUT AGAIN SOON...
AND YOU WILL LEAD ME TO THE TALISMAN THAT DRAEDALUS SO COVETS--BEFORE THAT BACKWATER TRICKSTER CLAIMS IT!
MMM-MMPH...!
YOU THINK THAT I AM THE BETTER-LOOKING INTERDIMENSIONAL DESPOT BY FAR? THANK YOU, KATE DEAR.
YOU MIGHT NOT SAY THAT IF YOU SAW MY TRUE FACE...
PERHAPS YOU SHOULD LOOK AWAY AS I MAKE THE CHANGE, HMM...?
SSHLUKKKK!
WELL, TIME TO PACK.

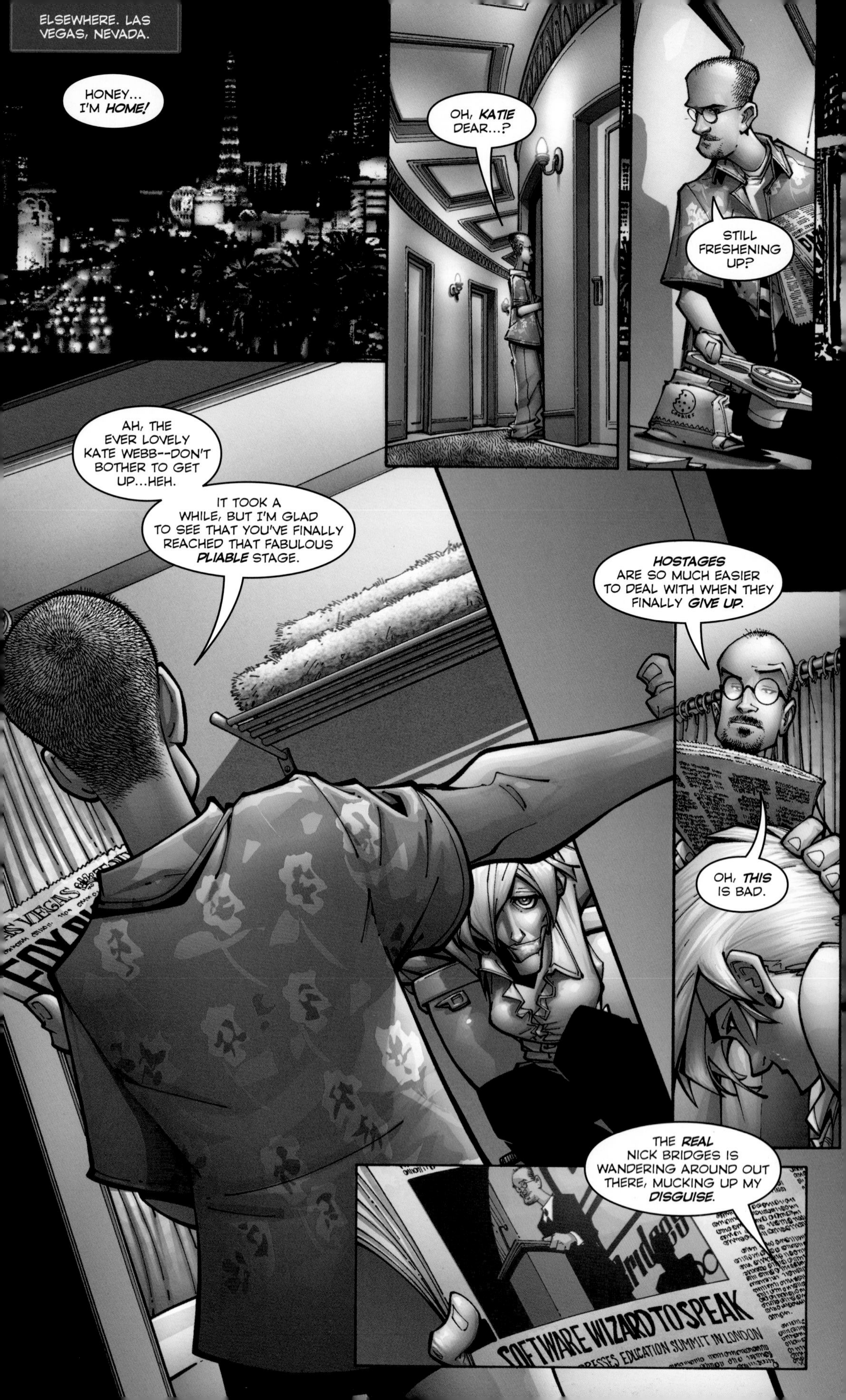
ELSEWHERE. LAS VEGAS, NEVADA.
HONEY... I'M HOME!
OH, KATIE DEAR...?
STILL FRESHENING UP?
AH, THE EVER LOVELY KATE WEBB--DON'T BOTHER TO GET UP...HEH.
IT TOOK A WHILE, BUT I'M GLAD TO SEE THAT YOU'VE FINALLY REACHED THAT FABULOUS PLIABLE STAGE.
HOSTAGES ARE SO MUCH EASIER TO DEAL WITH WHEN THEY FINALLY GIVE UP.
OH, THIS IS BAD.
THE REAL NICK BRIDGES IS WANDERING AROUND OUT THERE, MUCKING UP MY DISGUISE.
SOFTWARE WIZARD TO SPEAK
EDUCATION SUMMIT IN LONDON

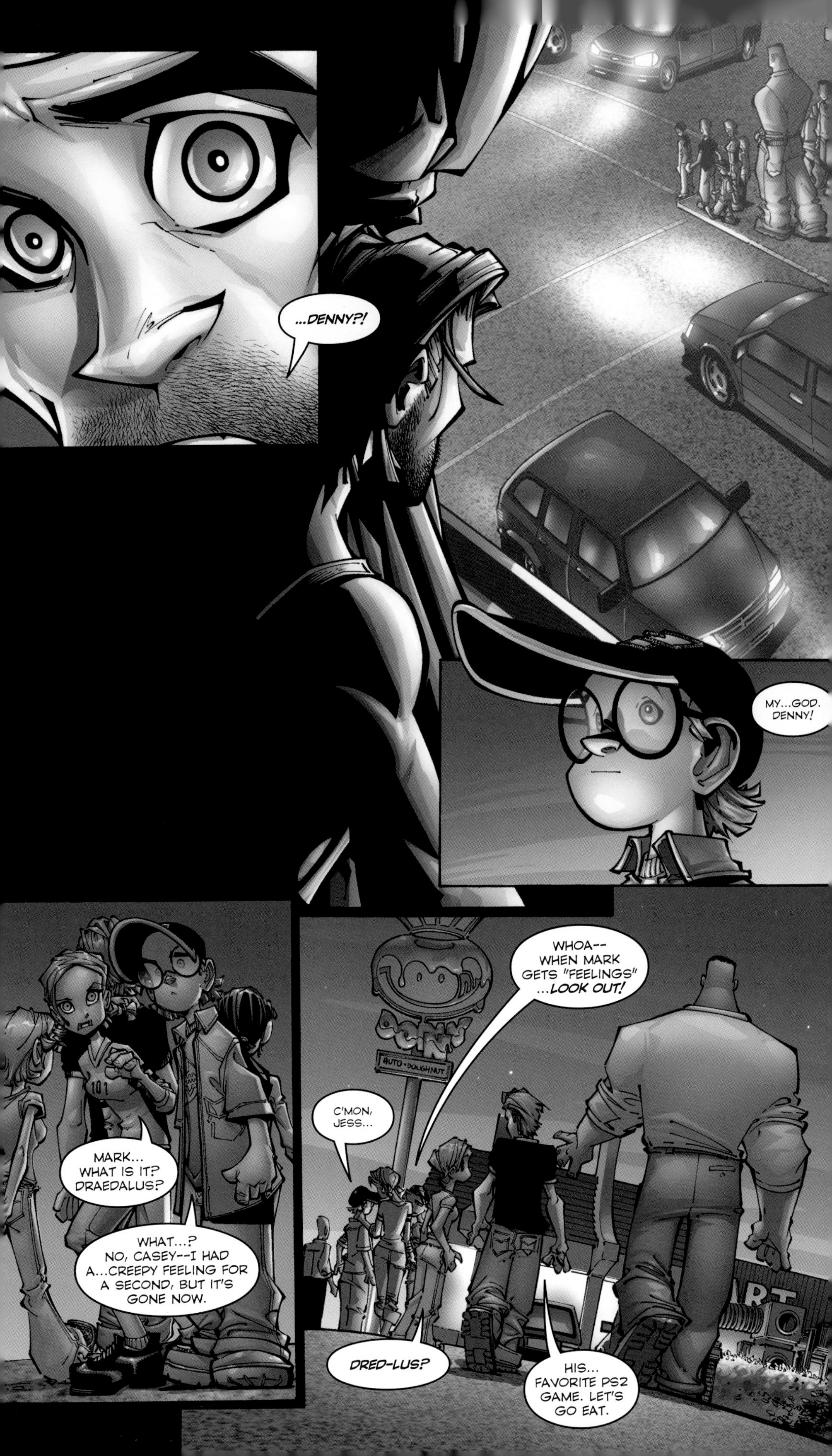
...DENNY?!
MY...GOD. DENNY!
MARK... WHAT IS IT? DRAEDALUS?
WHAT...? NO, CASEY--I HAD A...CREEPY FEELING FOR A SECOND, BUT IT'S GONE NOW.
AUTO-DOUGHNUT
WHOA-- WHEN MARK GETS "FEELINGS" ...LOOK OUT!
C'MON, JESS...
DRED-LUS?
HIS... FAVORITE PS2 GAME. LET'S GO EAT.

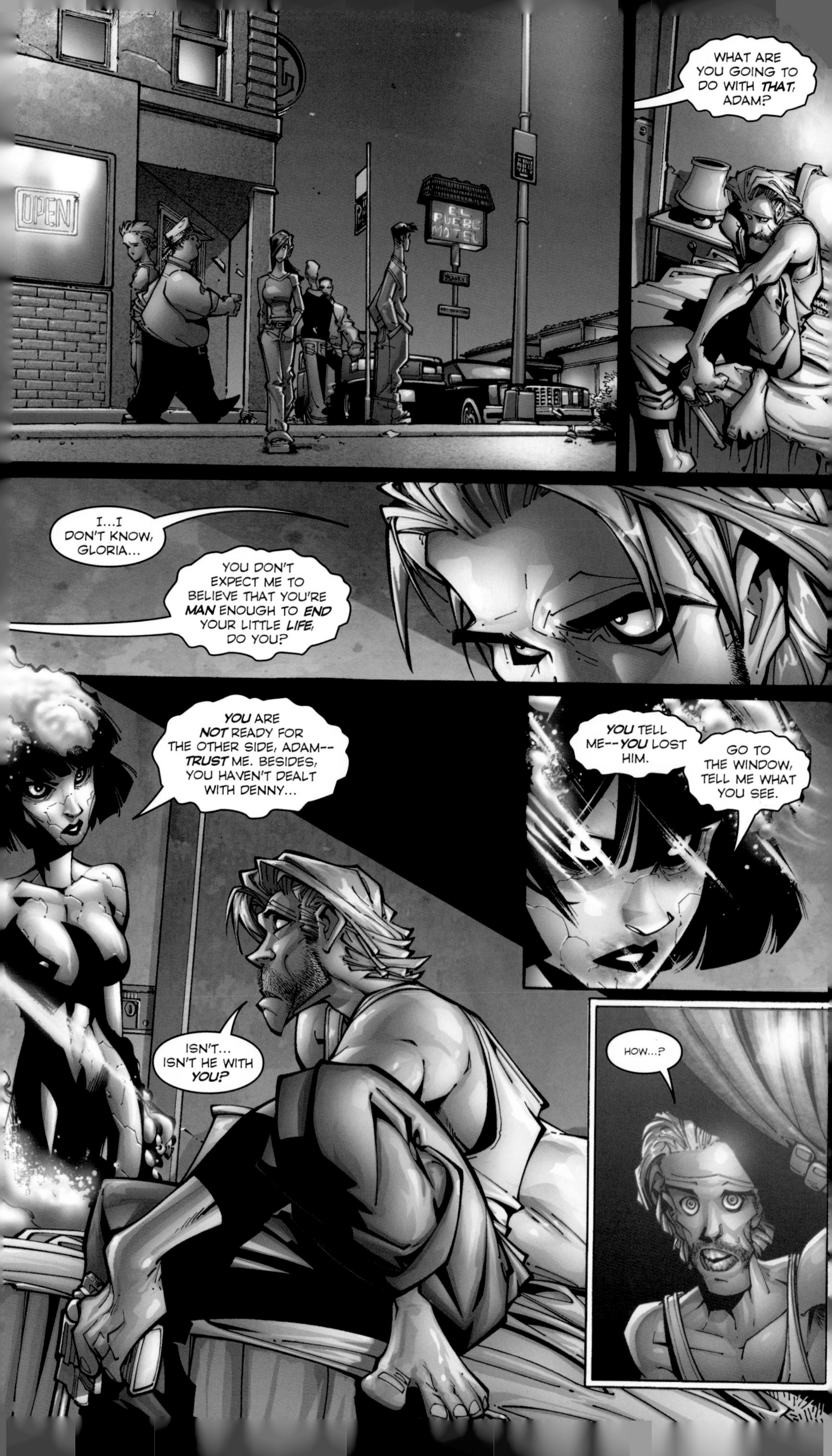
OPEN
EL PUEBLO MOTEL
WHAT ARE YOU GOING TO DO WITH THAT, ADAM?
I...I DON'T KNOW, GLORIA...
YOU DON'T EXPECT ME TO BELIEVE THAT YOU'RE MAN ENOUGH TO END YOUR LITTLE LIFE, DO YOU?
YOU ARE NOT READY FOR THE OTHER SIDE, ADAM-- TRUST ME. BESIDES, YOU HAVEN'T DEALT WITH DENNY...
ISN'T... ISN'T HE WITH YOU?
YOU TELL ME--YOU LOST HIM.
GO TO THE WINDOW, TELL ME WHAT YOU SEE.
HOW...?

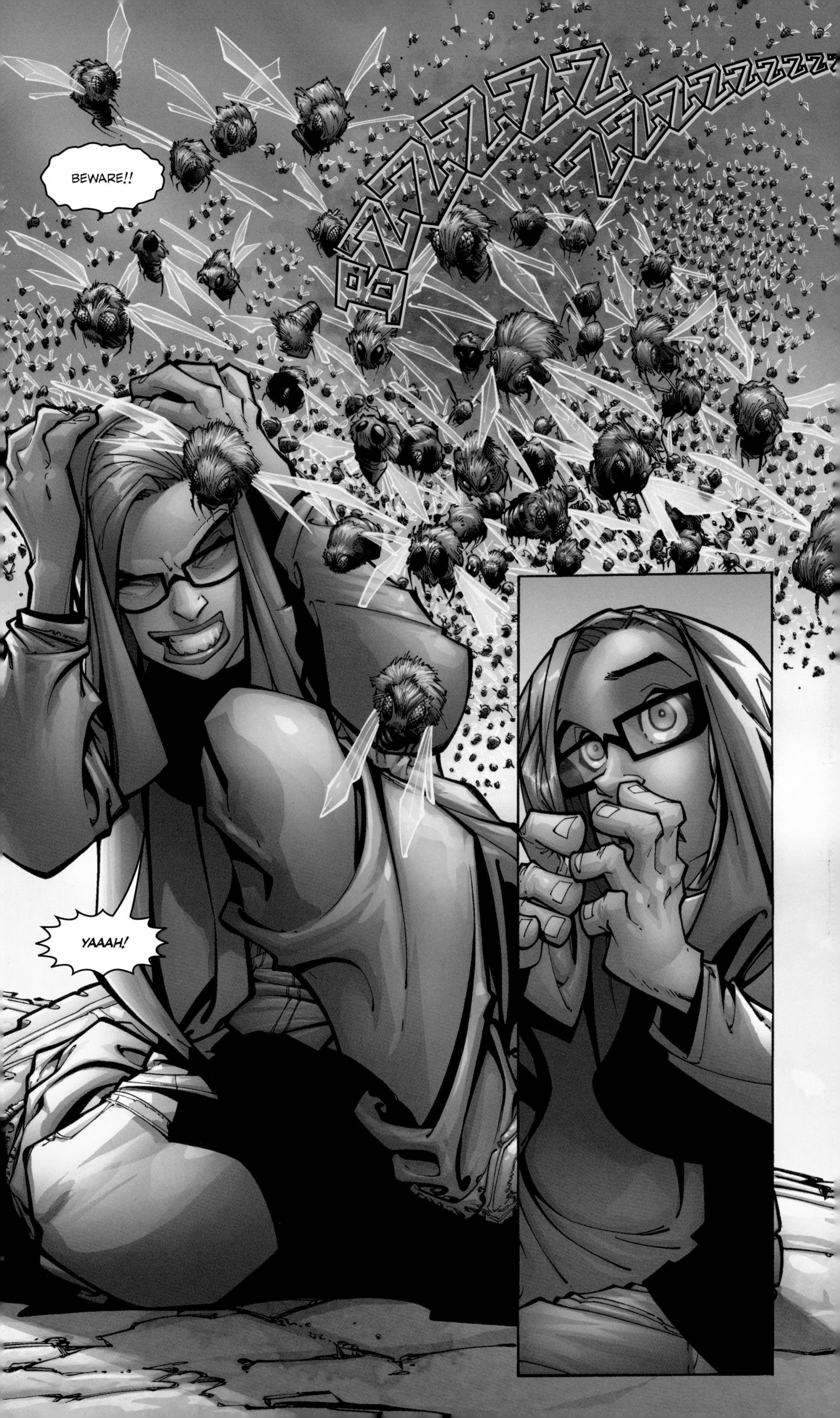
BEWARE!!
BZZZZZ ZZZZZZZZZZZZ
YAAAH!

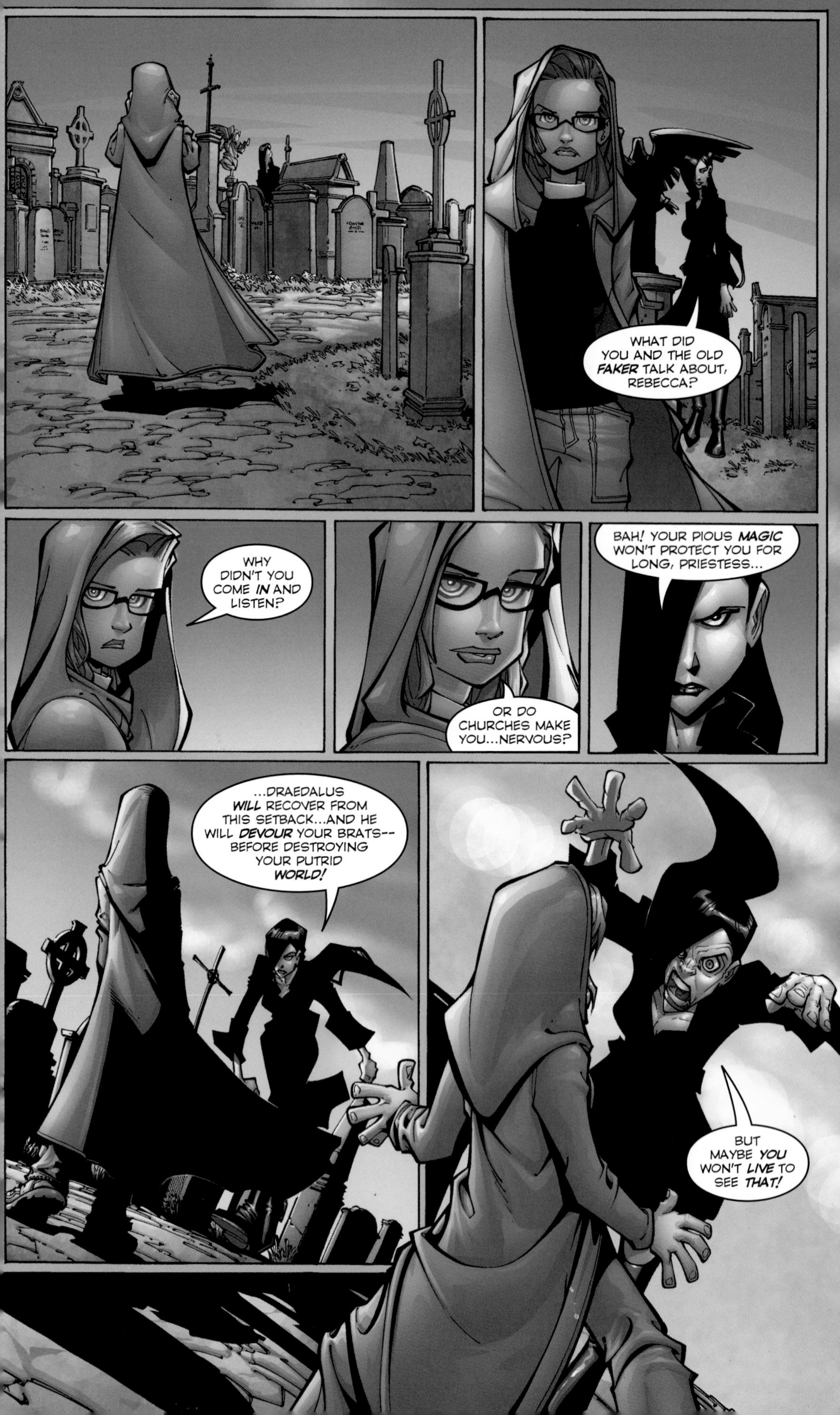

WHAT DID YOU AND THE OLD **FAKER** TALK ABOUT, REBECCA?
WHY DIDN'T YOU COME **IN** AND LISTEN?
OR DO CHURCHES MAKE YOU...NERVOUS?
BAH! YOUR PIOUS **MAGIC** WON'T PROTECT YOU FOR LONG, PRIESTESS...
...DRAEDALUS **WILL** RECOVER FROM THIS SETBACK...AND HE WILL **DEVOUR** YOUR BRATS--BEFORE DESTROYING YOUR PUTRID **WORLD!**
BUT MAYBE **YOU** WON'T **LIVE** TO SEE **THAT!**

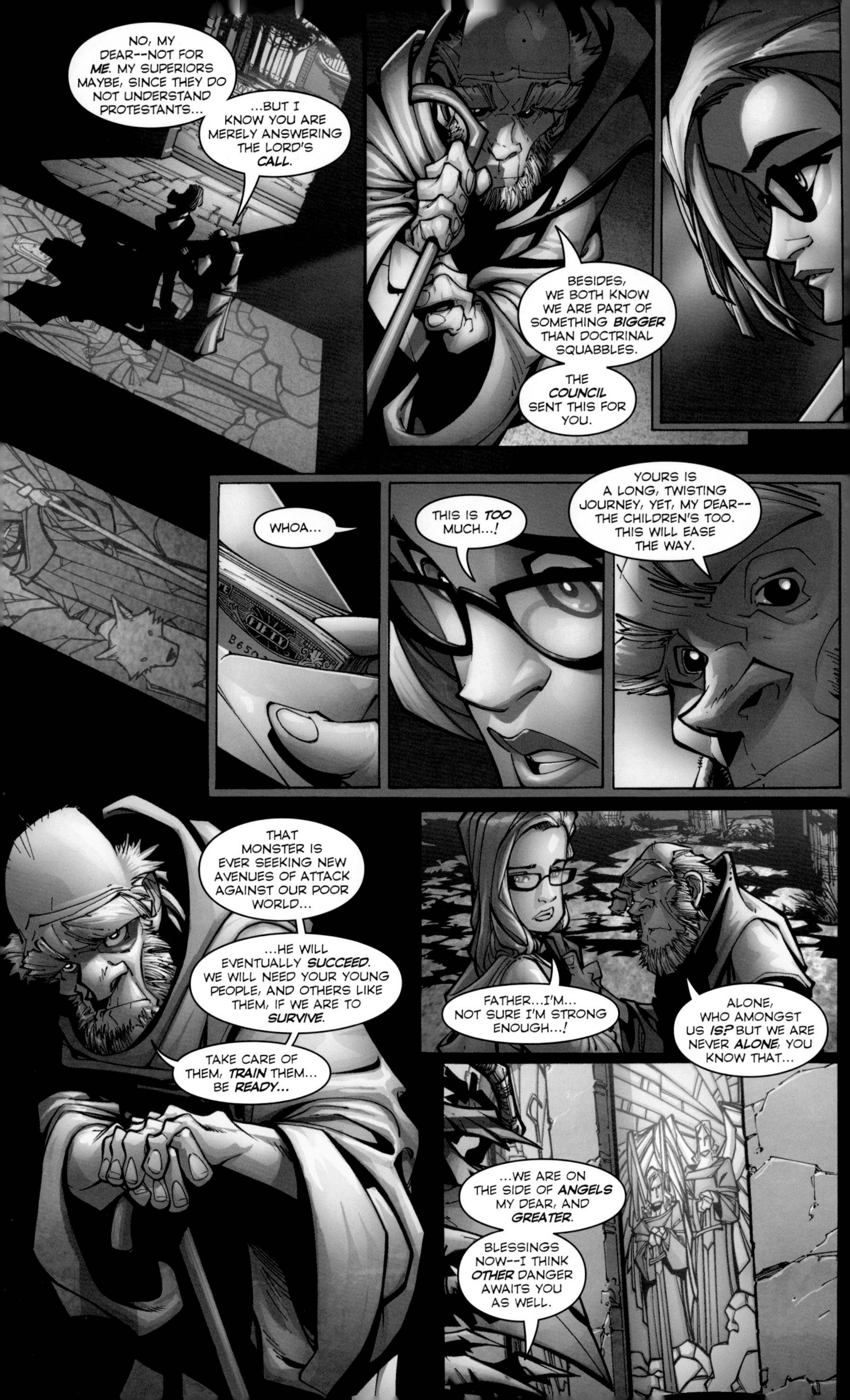
NO, MY DEAR--NOT FOR ME. MY SUPERIORS MAYBE, SINCE THEY DO NOT UNDERSTAND PROTESTANTS...
...BUT I KNOW YOU ARE MERELY ANSWERING THE LORD'S CALL.
BESIDES, WE BOTH KNOW WE ARE PART OF SOMETHING BIGGER THAN DOCTRINAL SQUABBLES.
THE COUNCIL SENT THIS FOR YOU.
WHOA...
FIFTY
THIS IS TOO MUCH...!
YOURS IS A LONG, TWISTING JOURNEY, YET, MY DEAR--THE CHILDREN'S TOO. THIS WILL EASE THE WAY.
THAT MONSTER IS EVER SEEKING NEW AVENUES OF ATTACK AGAINST OUR POOR WORLD...
...HE WILL EVENTUALLY SUCCEED. WE WILL NEED YOUR YOUNG PEOPLE, AND OTHERS LIKE THEM, IF WE ARE TO SURVIVE.
TAKE CARE OF THEM, TRAIN THEM... BE READY...
FATHER...I'M... NOT SURE I'M STRONG ENOUGH...!
ALONE, WHO AMONGST US IS? BUT WE ARE NEVER ALONE, YOU KNOW THAT...
...WE ARE ON THE SIDE OF ANGELS MY DEAR, AND GREATER.
BLESSINGS NOW--I THINK OTHER DANGER AWAITS YOU AS WELL.

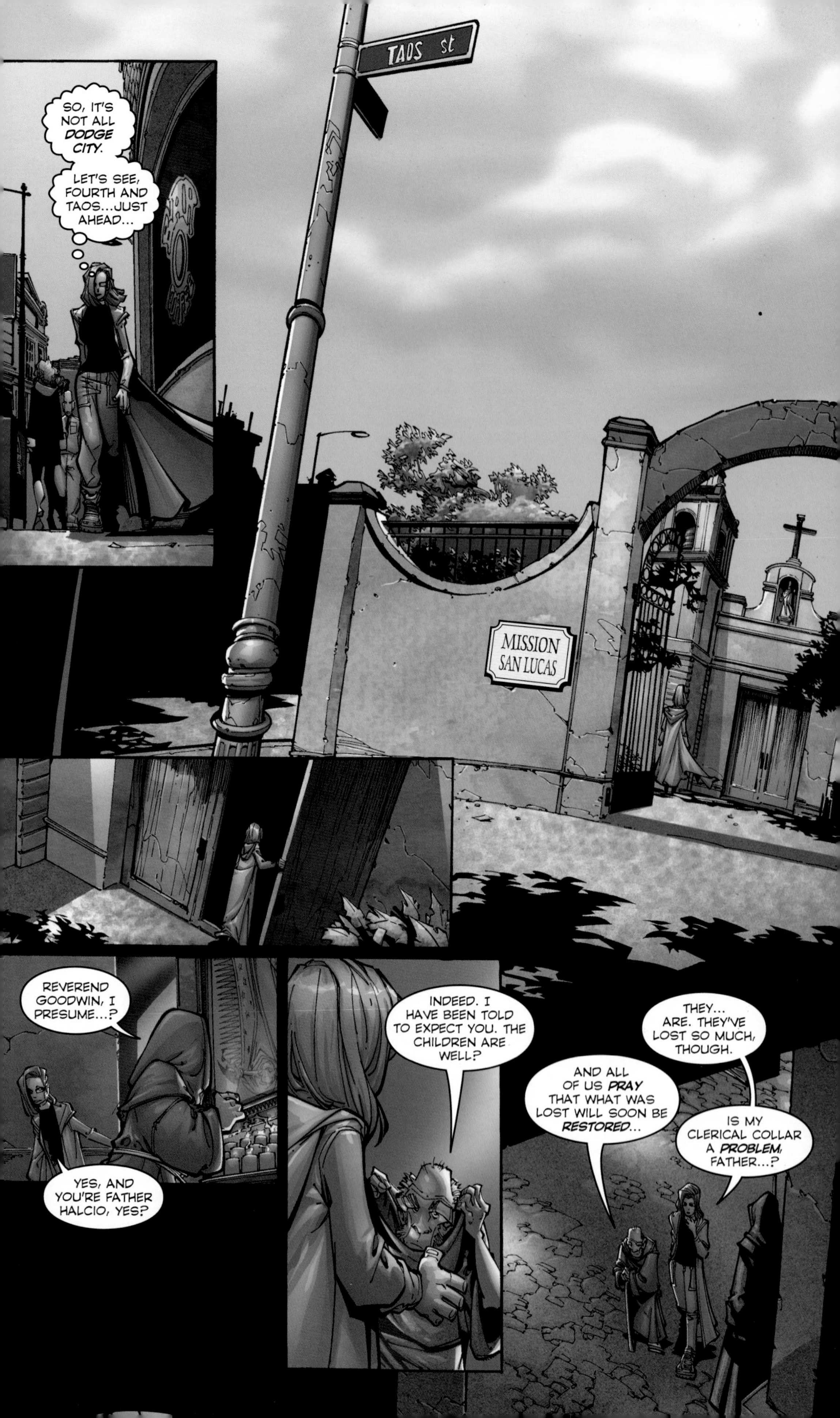
TAOS st
SO, IT'S NOT ALL DODGE CITY.
LET'S SEE, FOURTH AND TAOS...JUST AHEAD...
MISSION SAN LUCAS
REVEREND GOODWIN, I PRESUME...?
YES, AND YOU'RE FATHER HALCIO, YES?
INDEED. I HAVE BEEN TOLD TO EXPECT YOU. THE CHILDREN ARE WELL?
THEY... ARE. THEY'VE LOST SO MUCH, THOUGH.
AND ALL OF US PRAY THAT WHAT WAS LOST WILL SOON BE RESTORED...
IS MY CLERICAL COLLAR A PROBLEM, FATHER...?

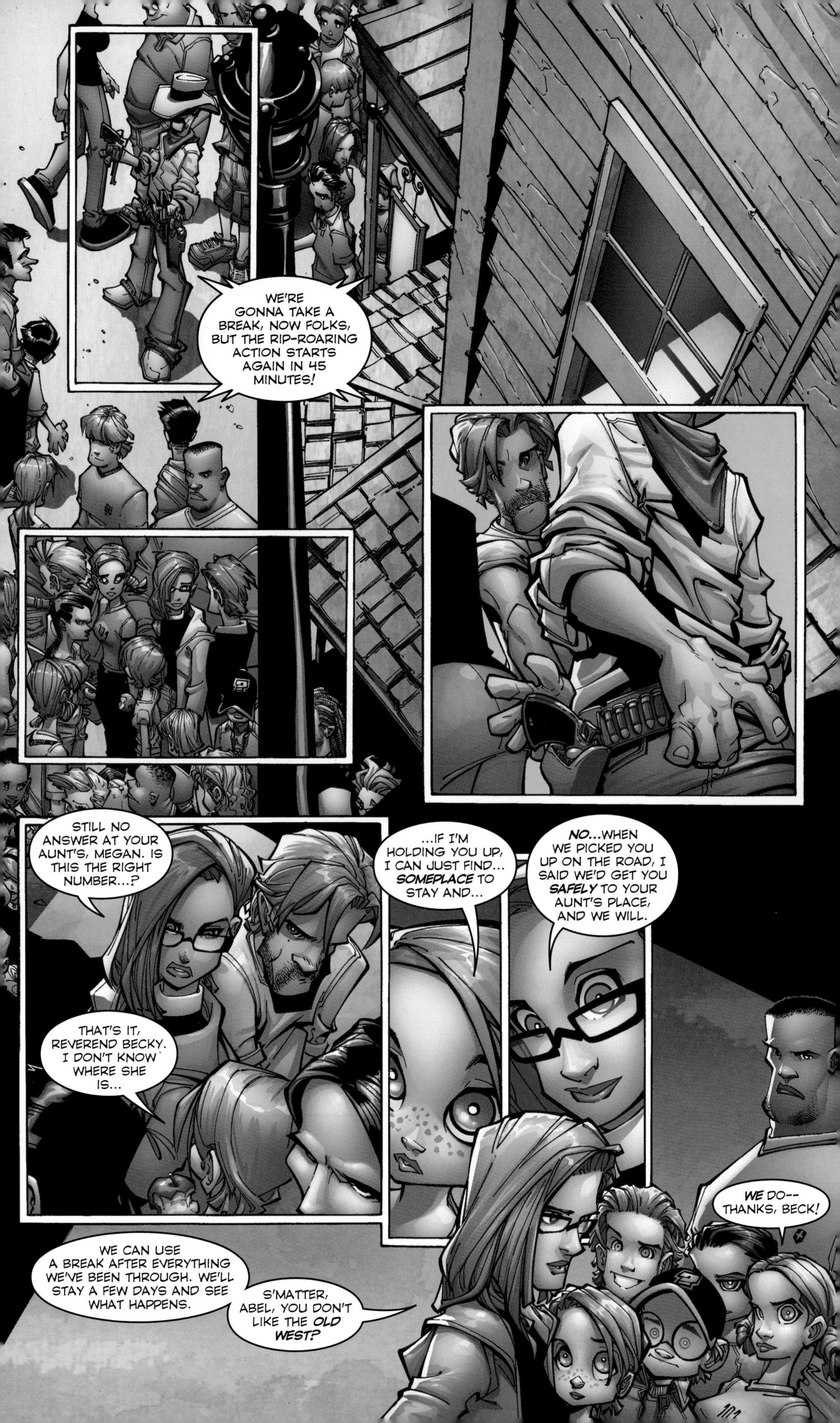
WE'RE GONNA TAKE A BREAK, NOW FOLKS, BUT THE RIP-ROARING ACTION STARTS AGAIN IN 45 MINUTES!
STILL NO ANSWER AT YOUR AUNT'S, MEGAN. IS THIS THE RIGHT NUMBER...?
THAT'S IT, REVEREND BECKY. I DON'T KNOW WHERE SHE IS...
...IF I'M HOLDING YOU UP, I CAN JUST FIND... SOMEPLACE TO STAY AND...
NO...WHEN WE PICKED YOU UP ON THE ROAD, I SAID WE'D GET YOU SAFELY TO YOUR AUNT'S PLACE, AND WE WILL.
WE CAN USE A BREAK AFTER EVERYTHING WE'VE BEEN THROUGH. WE'LL STAY A FEW DAYS AND SEE WHAT HAPPENS.
S'MATTER, ABEL, YOU DON'T LIKE THE OLD WEST?
WE DO-- THANKS, BECK!

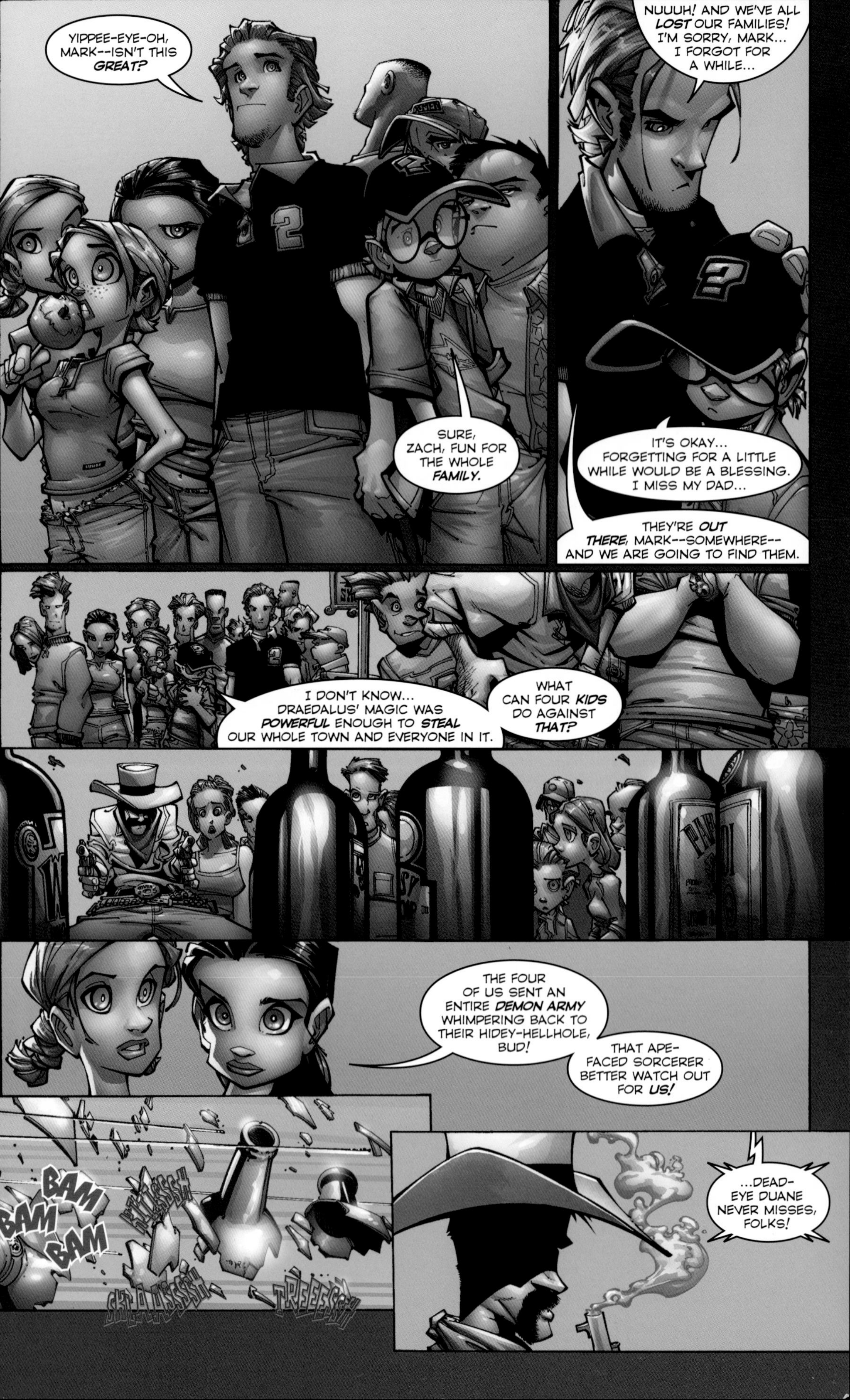
YIPPEE-EYE-OH, MARK--ISN'T THIS GREAT?
SURE, ZACH, FUN FOR THE WHOLE FAMILY.
NUUUH! AND WE'VE ALL LOST OUR FAMILIES! I'M SORRY, MARK... I FORGOT FOR A WHILE...
IT'S OKAY... FORGETTING FOR A LITTLE WHILE WOULD BE A BLESSING. I MISS MY DAD...
THEY'RE OUT THERE, MARK--SOMEWHERE-- AND WE ARE GOING TO FIND THEM.
I DON'T KNOW... DRAEDALUS' MAGIC WAS POWERFUL ENOUGH TO STEAL OUR WHOLE TOWN AND EVERYONE IN IT.
WHAT CAN FOUR KIDS DO AGAINST THAT?
THE FOUR OF US SENT AN ENTIRE DEMON ARMY WHIMPERING BACK TO THEIR HIDEY-HELLHOLE, BUD!
THAT APE-FACED SORCERER BETTER WATCH OUT FOR US!
BAM
BAM
BAM
BAM
...DEAD-EYE DUANE NEVER MISSES, FOLKS!

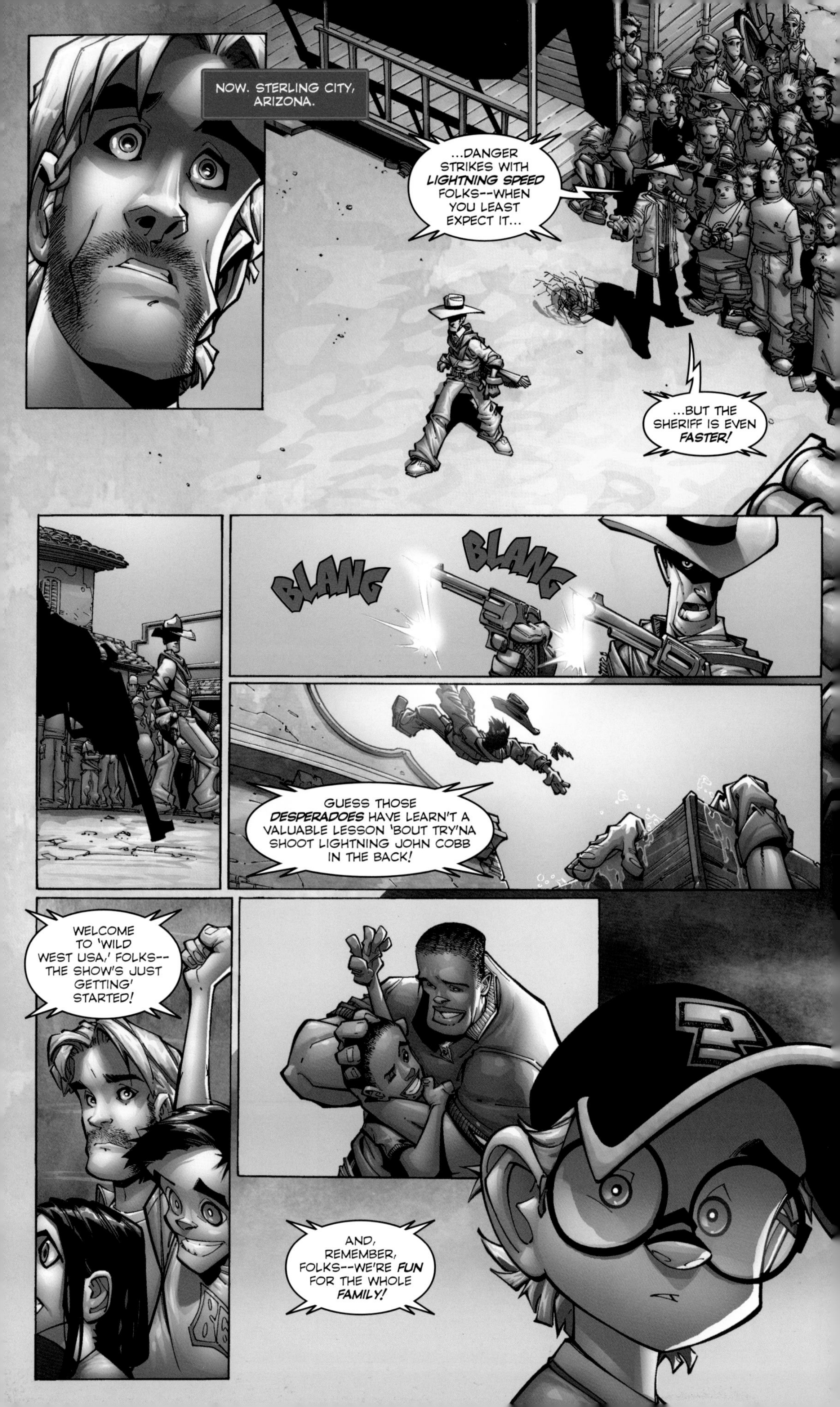
NOW. STERLING CITY, ARIZONA.
...DANGER STRIKES WITH LIGHTNING SPEED FOLKS--WHEN YOU LEAST EXPECT IT...
...BUT THE SHERIFF IS EVEN FASTER!
BLANG
BLANG
GUESS THOSE DESPERADOES HAVE LEARN'T A VALUABLE LESSON 'BOUT TRY'NA SHOOT LIGHTNING JOHN COBB IN THE BACK!
WELCOME TO 'WILD WEST USA,' FOLKS--THE SHOW'S JUST GETTING' STARTED!
AND, REMEMBER, FOLKS--WE'RE FUN FOR THE WHOLE FAMILY!

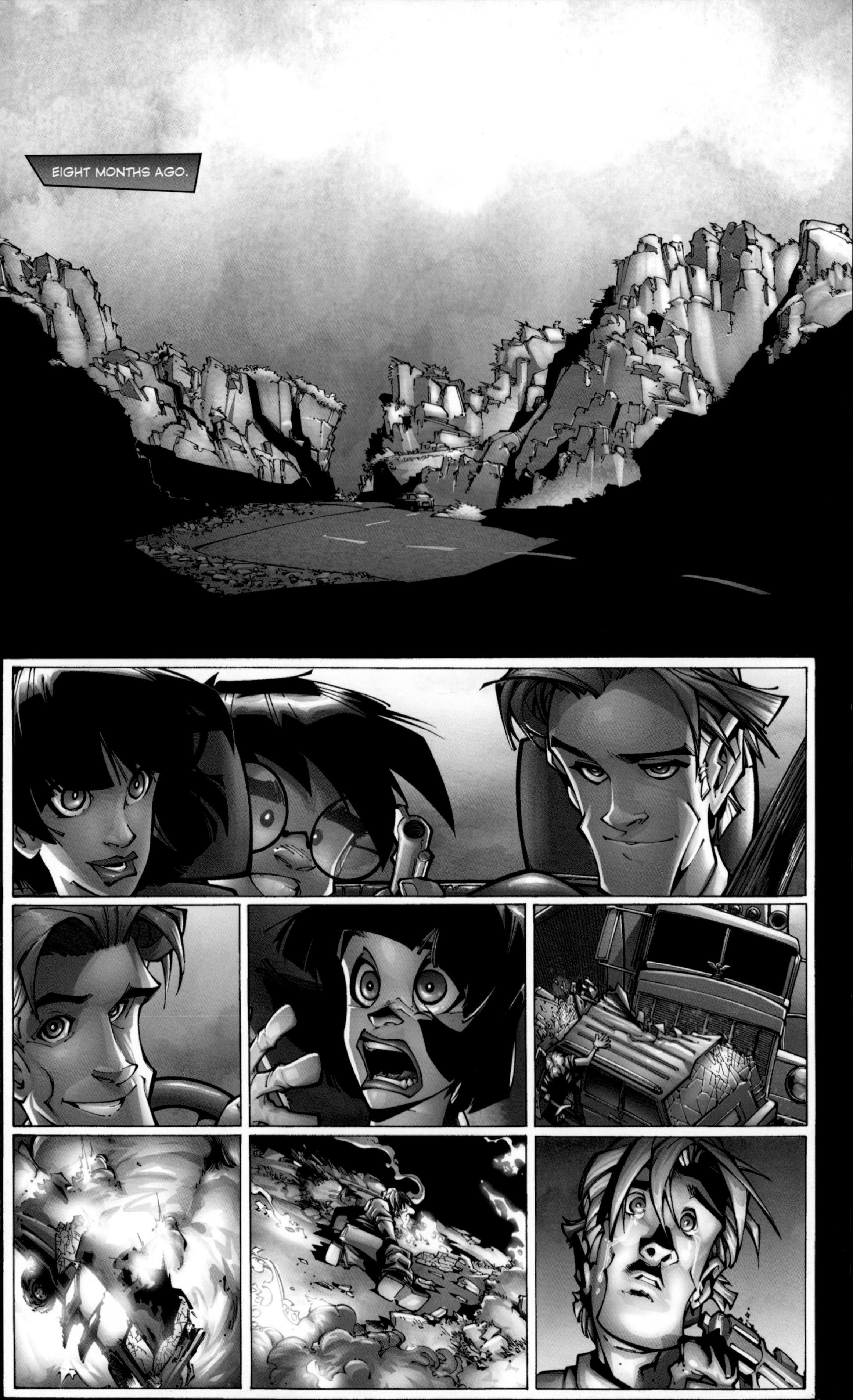
EIGHT MONTHS AGO.

CHAPTER NINE
TWISTING ROAD

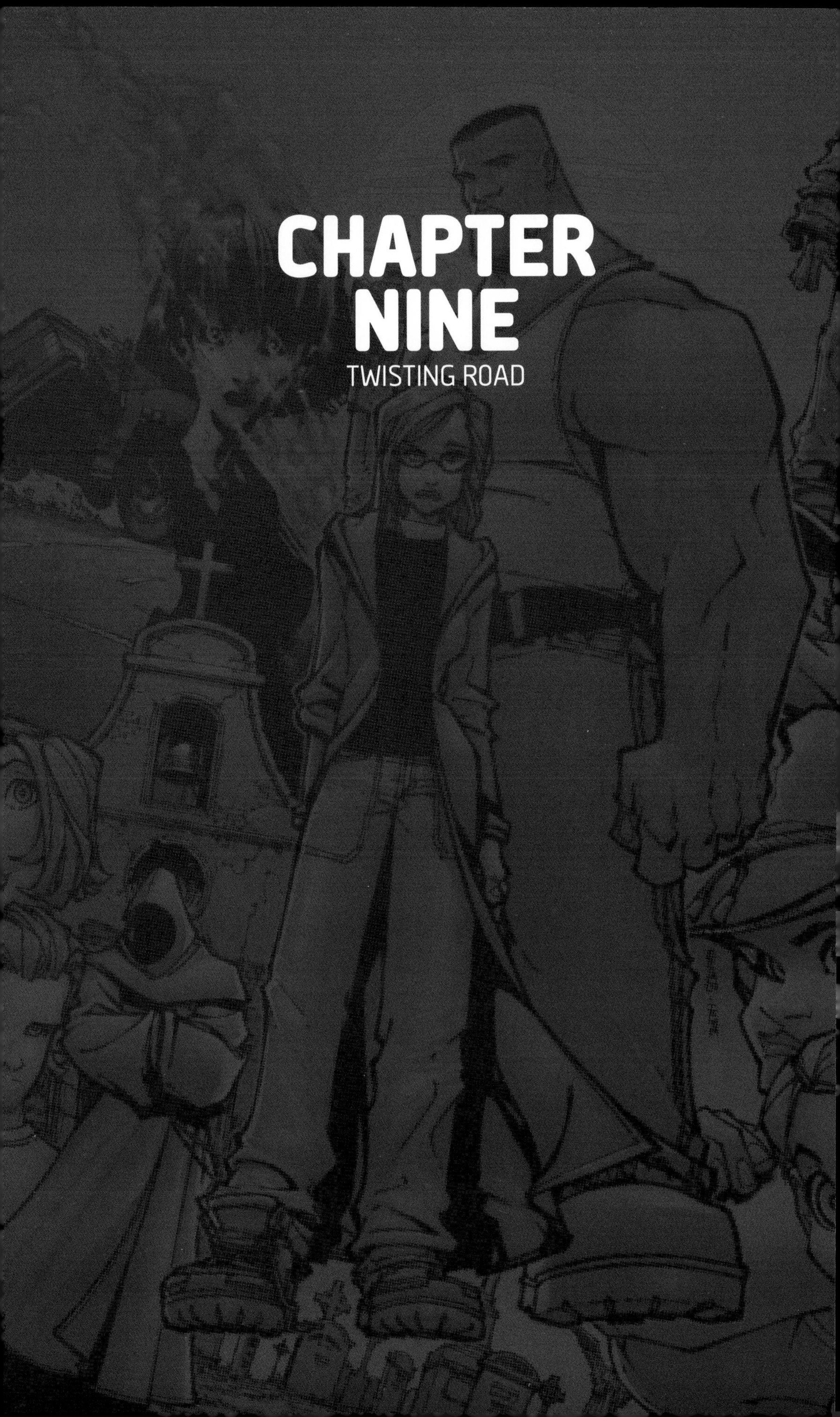

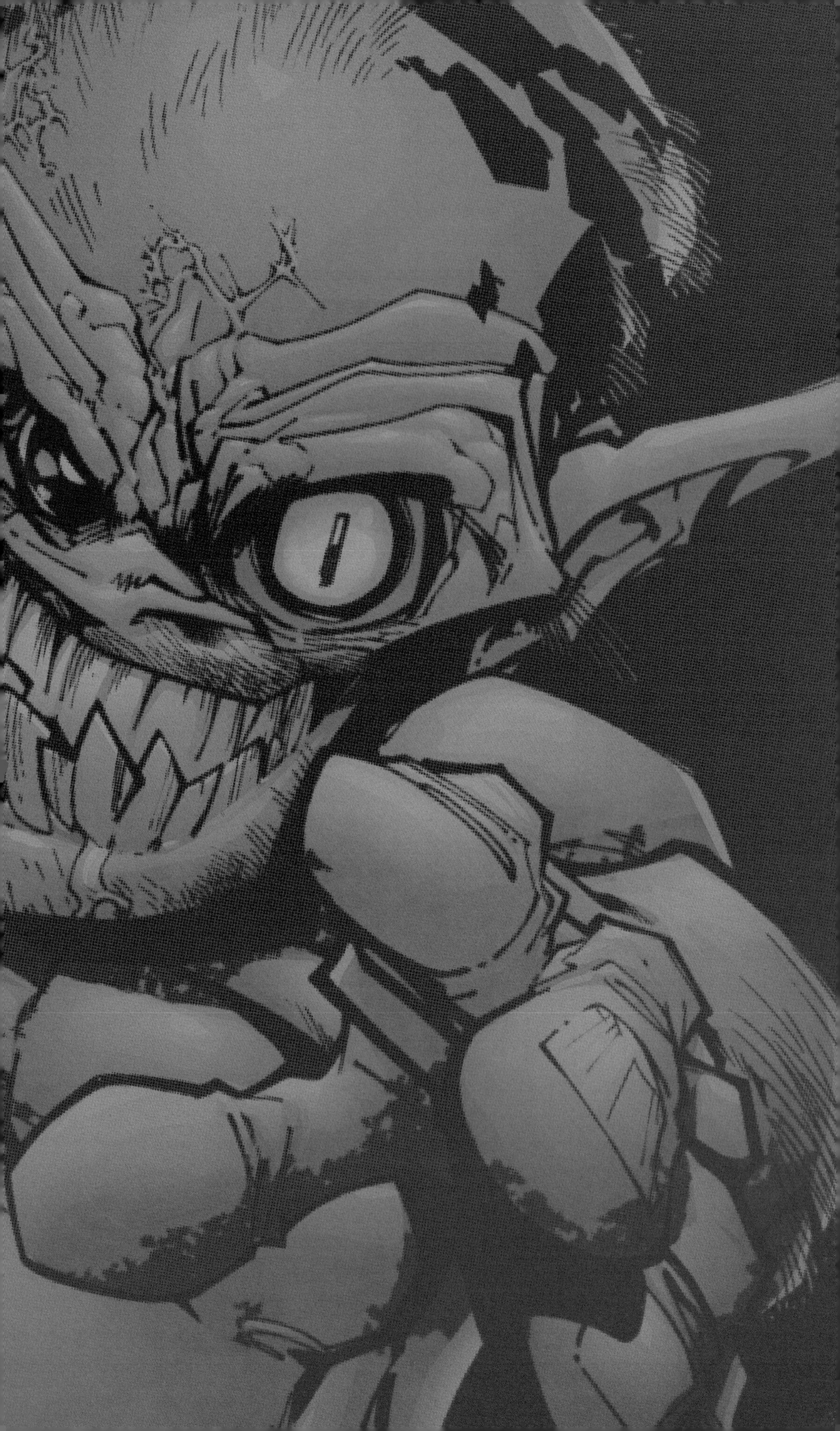

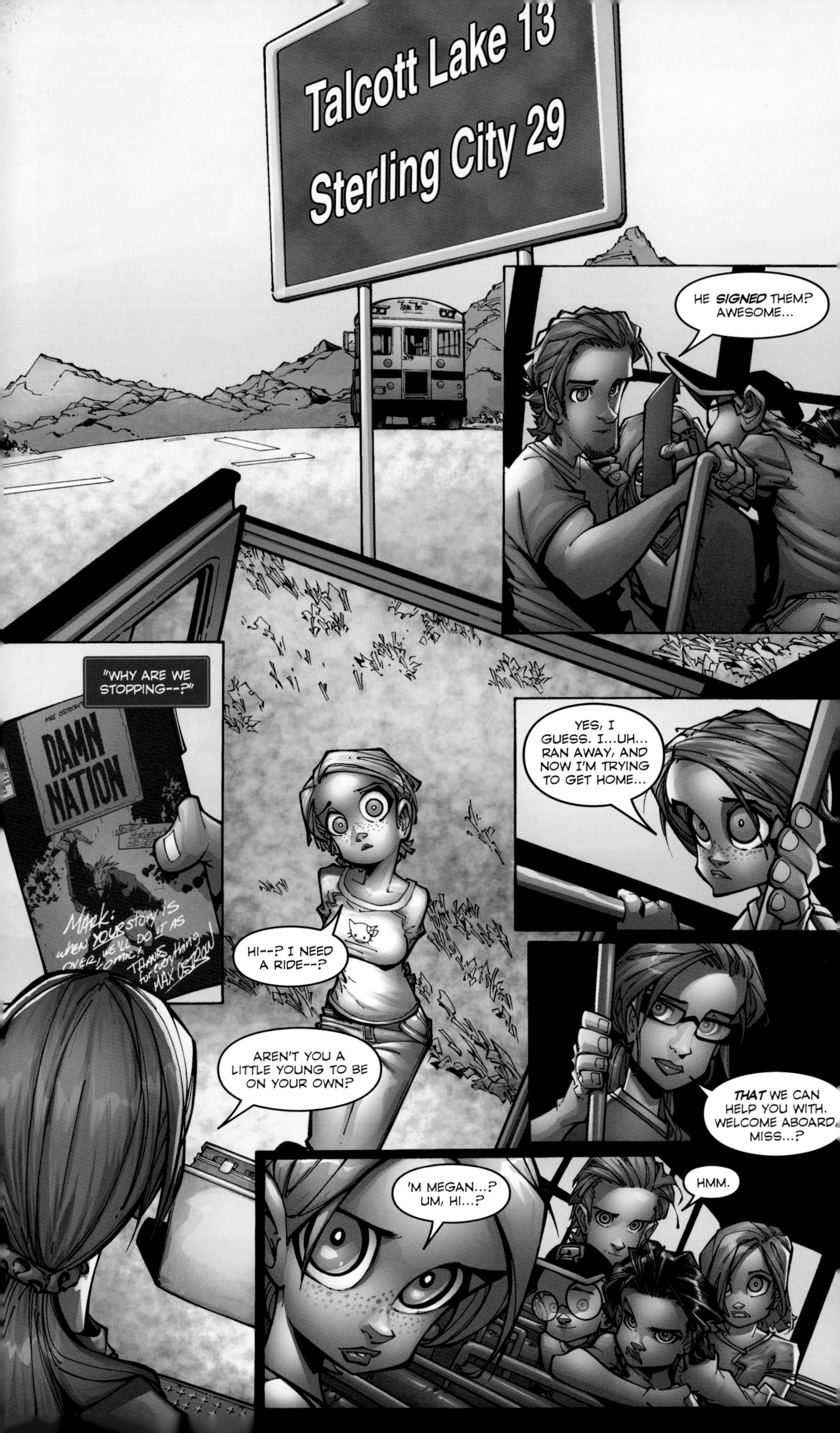

Talcott Lake 13
Sterling City 29
HE *SIGNED* THEM? AWESOME...
"WHY ARE WE STOPPING--?"
DAMN NATION
MARK: when YOUR story is over, we'll do it as comic! THANKS for everything MAX OSTROW
HI--? I NEED A RIDE--?
ARE'N'T YOU A LITTLE YOUNG TO BE ON YOUR OWN?
YES, I GUESS. I...UH... RAN AWAY, AND NOW I'M TRYING TO GET HOME...
THAT WE CAN HELP YOU WITH. WELCOME ABOARD, MISS...?
'M MEGAN...? UM, HI...?
HMM.

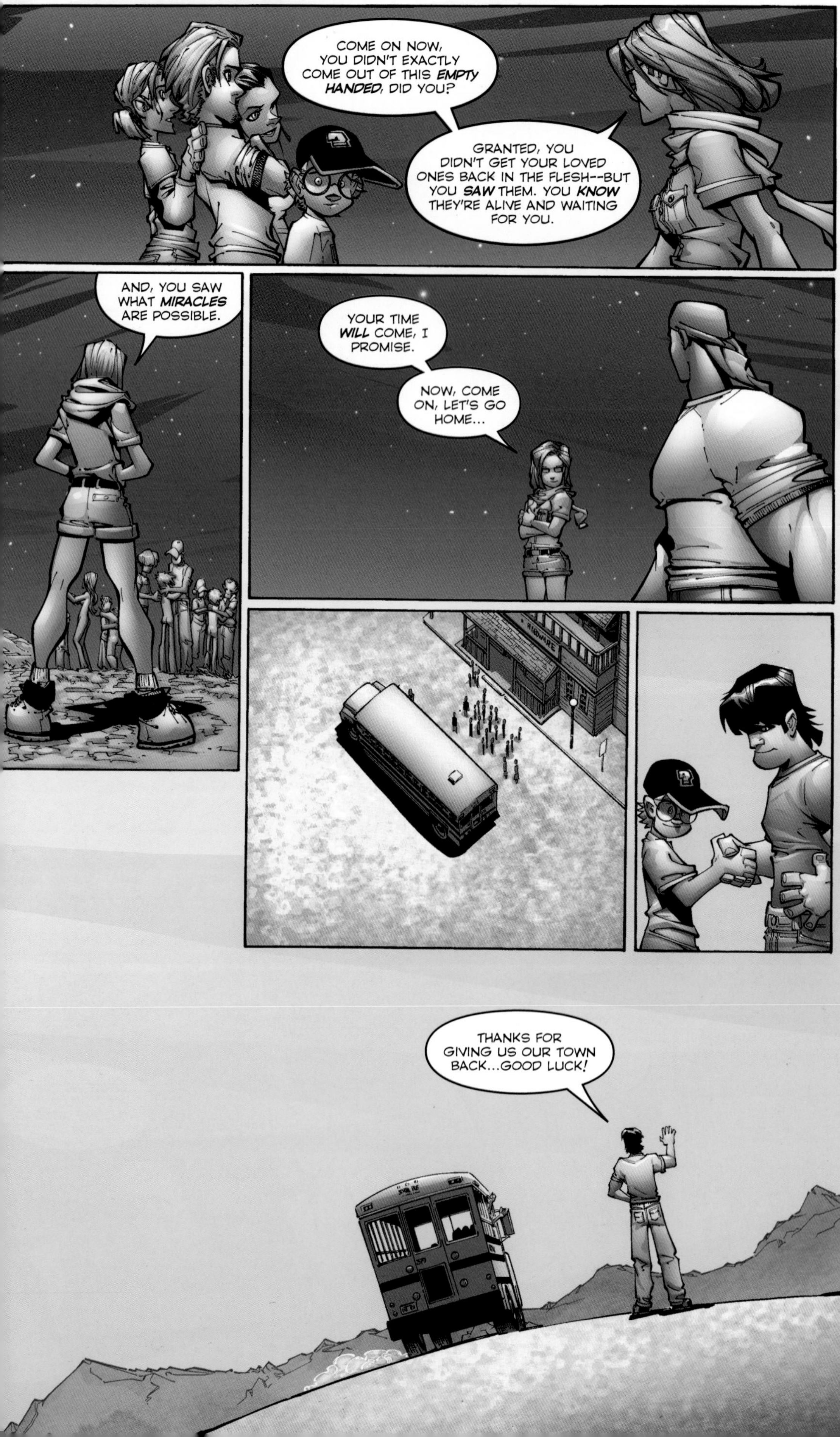
COME ON NOW, YOU DIDN'T EXACTLY COME OUT OF THIS *EMPTY HANDED*, DID YOU?
GRANTED, YOU DIDN'T GET YOUR LOVED ONES BACK IN THE FLESH--BUT YOU *SAW* THEM. YOU *KNOW* THEY'RE ALIVE AND WAITING FOR YOU.
AND, YOU SAW WHAT *MIRACLES* ARE POSSIBLE.
YOUR TIME *WILL* COME, I PROMISE.
NOW, COME ON, LET'S GO HOME...
THANKS FOR GIVING US OUR TOWN BACK...GOOD LUCK!

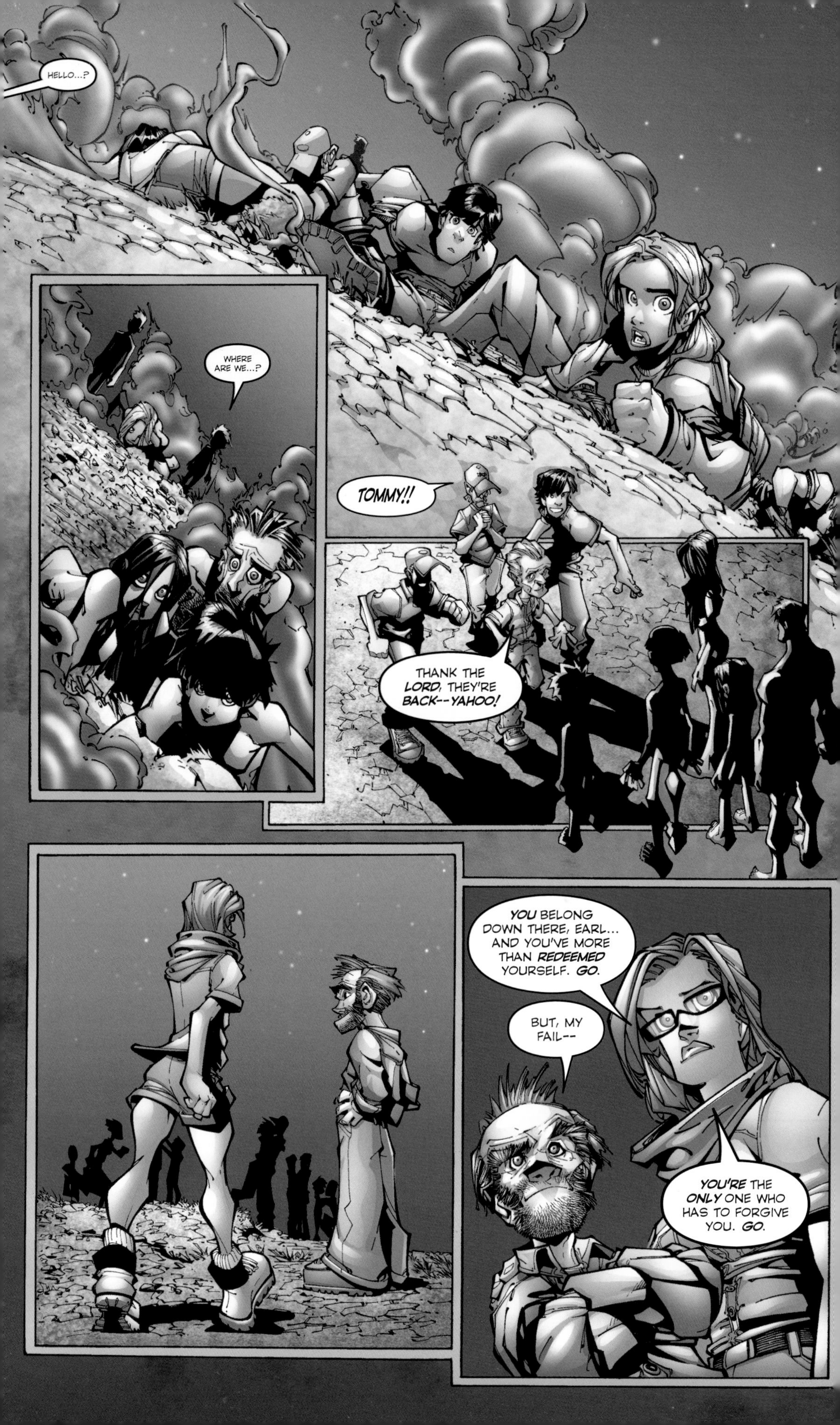
HELLO...?
WHERE ARE WE...?
TOMMY!!
THANK THE LORD, THEY'RE BACK--YAHOO!
YOU BELONG DOWN THERE, EARL... AND YOU'VE MORE THAN REDEEMED YOURSELF. GO.
BUT, MY FAIL--
YOU'RE THE ONLY ONE WHO HAS TO FORGIVE YOU. GO.

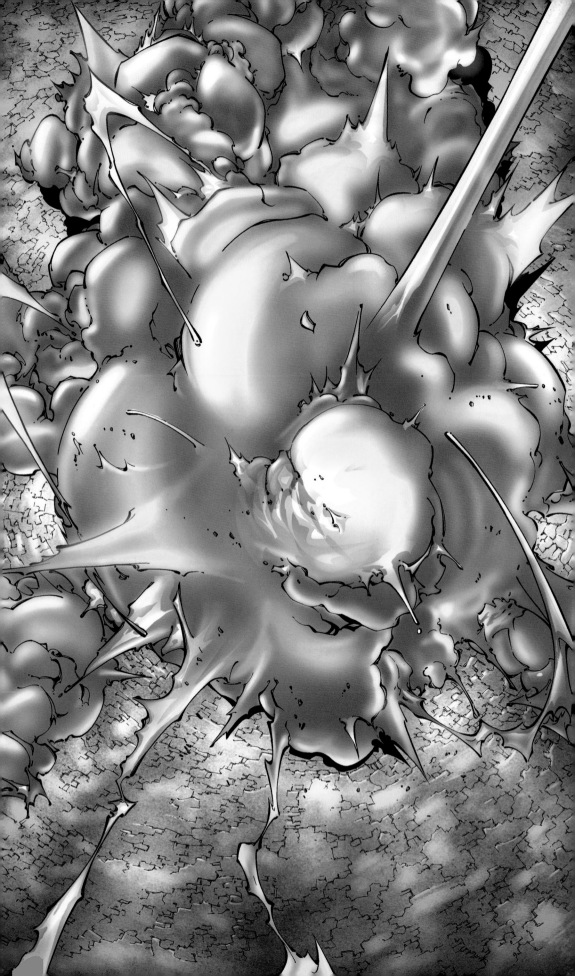

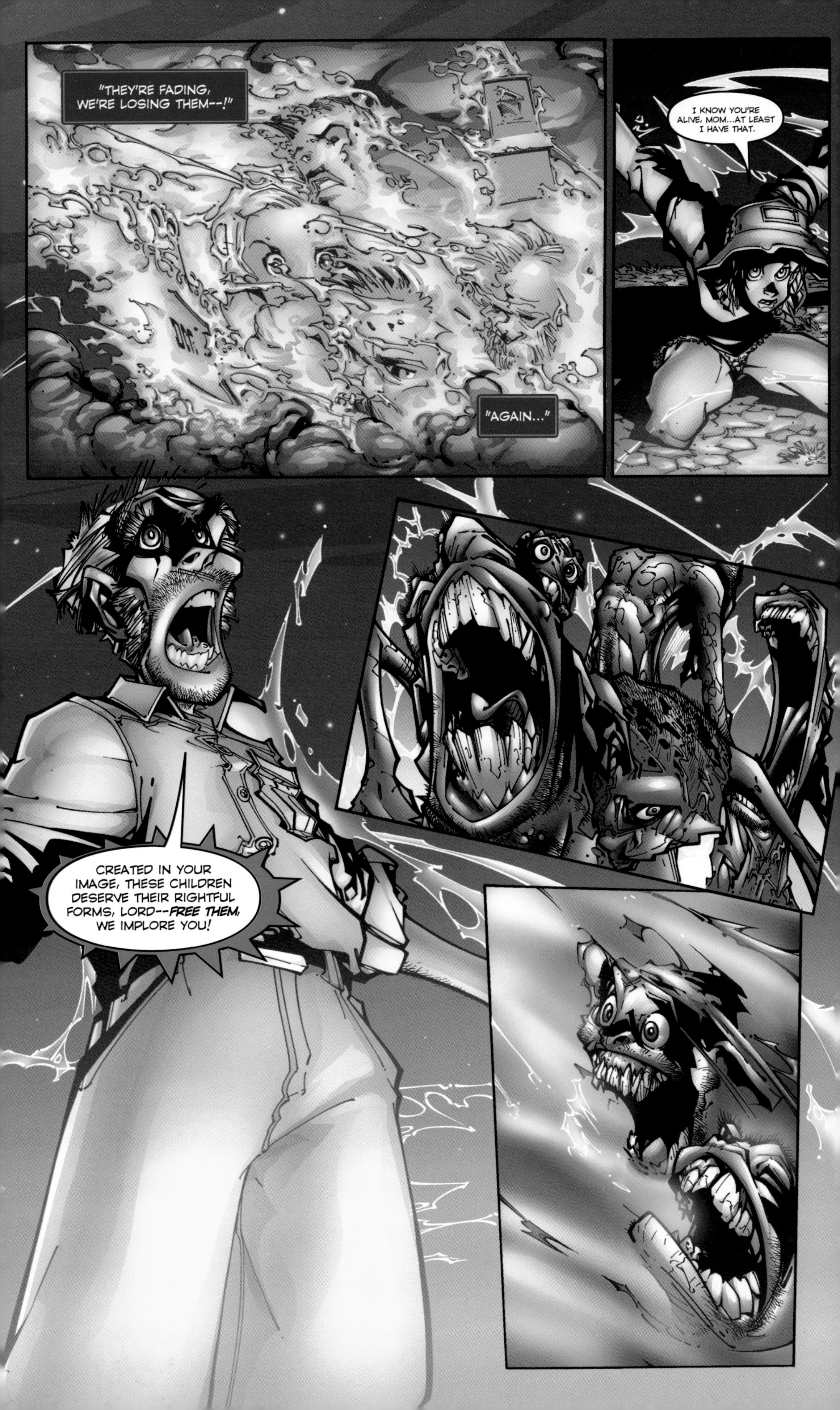
"THEY'RE FADING, WE'RE LOSING THEM--!"
"AGAIN..."
I KNOW YOU'RE ALIVE, MOM...AT LEAST I HAVE THAT.
CREATED IN YOUR IMAGE, THESE CHILDREN DESERVE THEIR RIGHTFUL FORMS, LORD--FREE THEM, WE IMPLORE YOU!

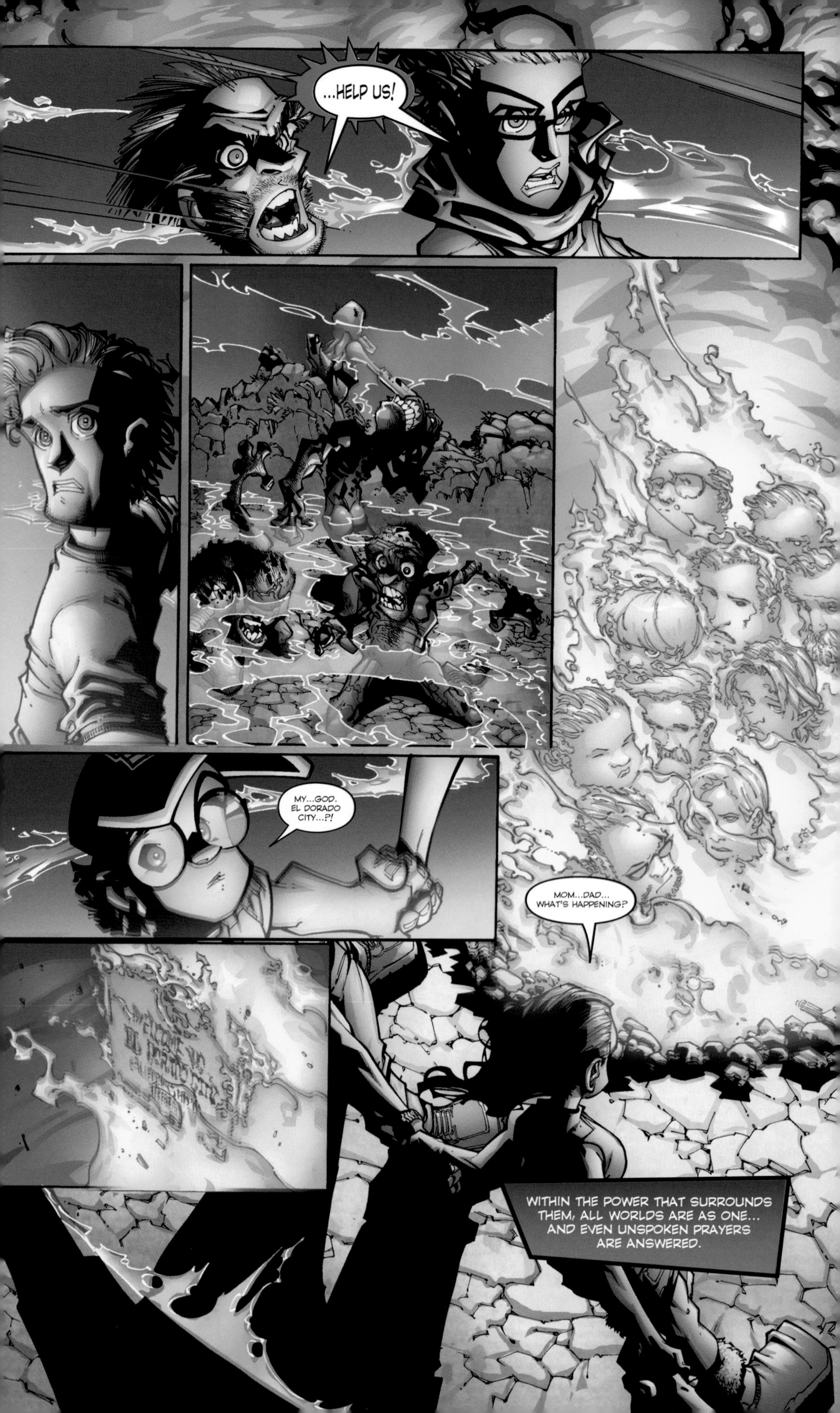
...HELP US!
MY...GOD. EL DORADO CITY...?!
MOM...DAD... WHAT'S HAPPENING?
WITHIN THE POWER THAT SURROUNDS THEM, ALL WORLDS ARE AS ONE... AND EVEN UNSPOKEN PRAYERS ARE ANSWERED.

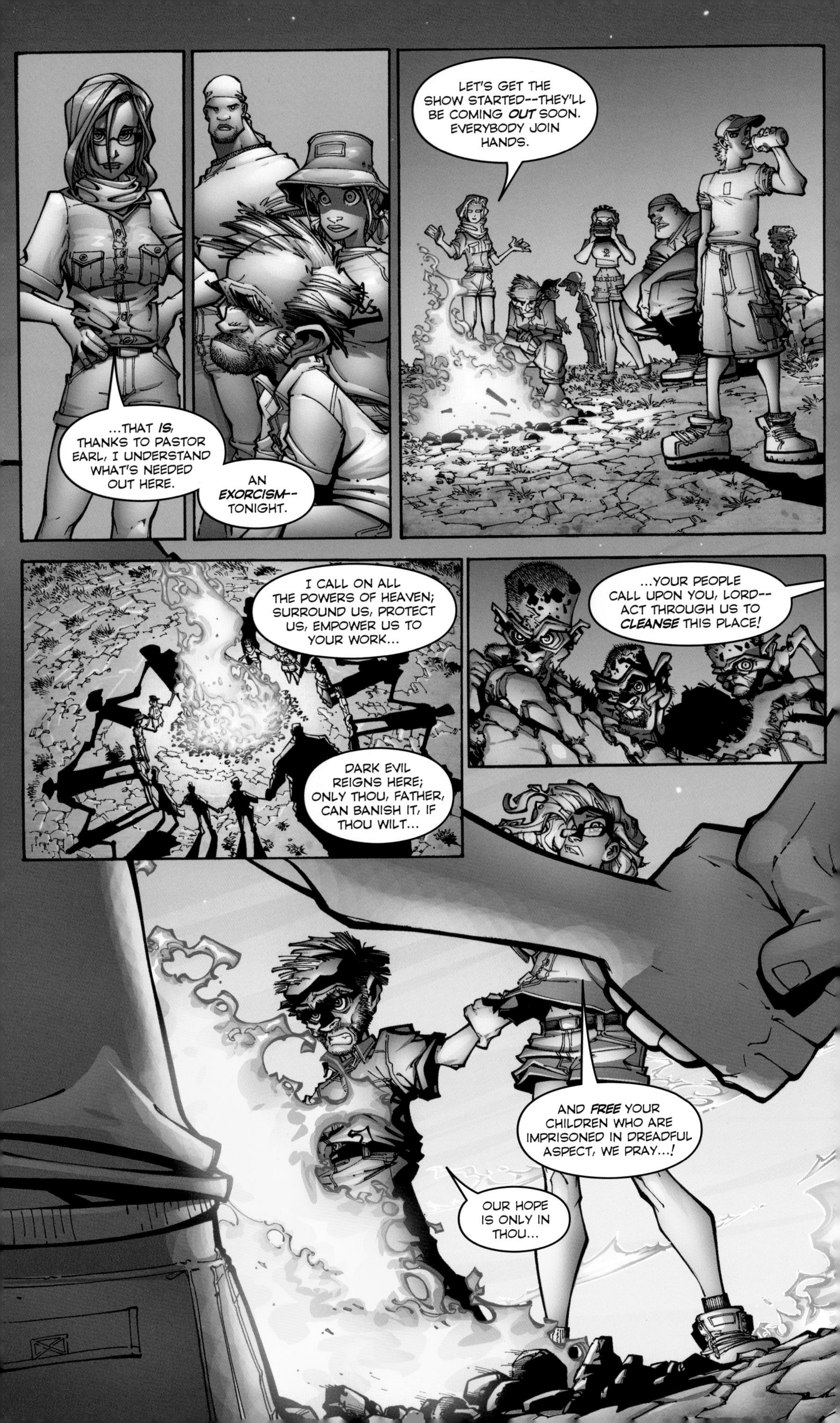
...THAT *IS*, THANKS TO PASTOR EARL, I UNDERSTAND WHAT'S NEEDED OUT HERE.
AN *EXORCISM*-- TONIGHT.
LET'S GET THE SHOW STARTED--THEY'LL BE COMING *OUT* SOON. EVERYBODY JOIN HANDS.
I CALL ON ALL THE POWERS OF HEAVEN; SURROUND US, PROTECT US, EMPOWER US TO YOUR WORK...
DARK EVIL REIGNS HERE; ONLY THOU, FATHER, CAN BANISH IT, IF THOU WILT...
...YOUR PEOPLE CALL UPON YOU, LORD-- ACT THROUGH US TO *CLEANSE* THIS PLACE!
AND *FREE* YOUR CHILDREN WHO ARE IMPRISONED IN DREADFUL ASPECT, WE PRAY...!
OUR HOPE IS ONLY IN THOU...

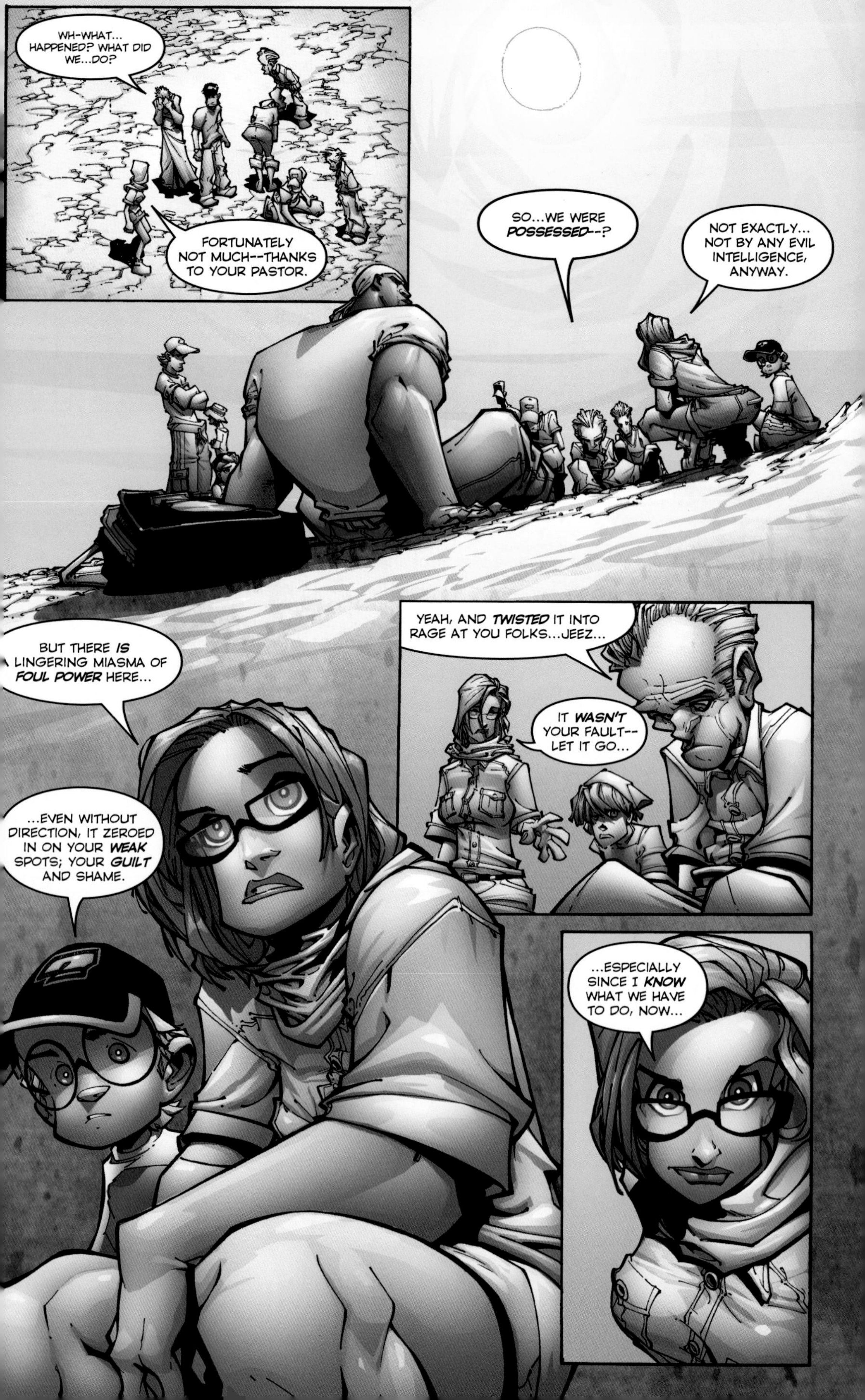
WH-WHAT... HAPPENED? WHAT DID WE...DO?
FORTUNATELY NOT MUCH--THANKS TO YOUR PASTOR.
SO...WE WERE *POSSESSED*--?
NOT EXACTLY... NOT BY ANY EVIL INTELLIGENCE, ANYWAY.
BUT THERE *IS* A LINGERING MIASMA OF *FOUL POWER* HERE...
...EVEN WITHOUT DIRECTION, IT ZEROED IN ON YOUR *WEAK* SPOTS; YOUR *GUILT* AND SHAME.
YEAH, AND *TWISTED* IT INTO RAGE AT YOU FOLKS...JEEZ...
IT *WASN'T* YOUR FAULT-- LET IT GO...
...ESPECIALLY SINCE I *KNOW* WHAT WE HAVE TO DO, NOW...

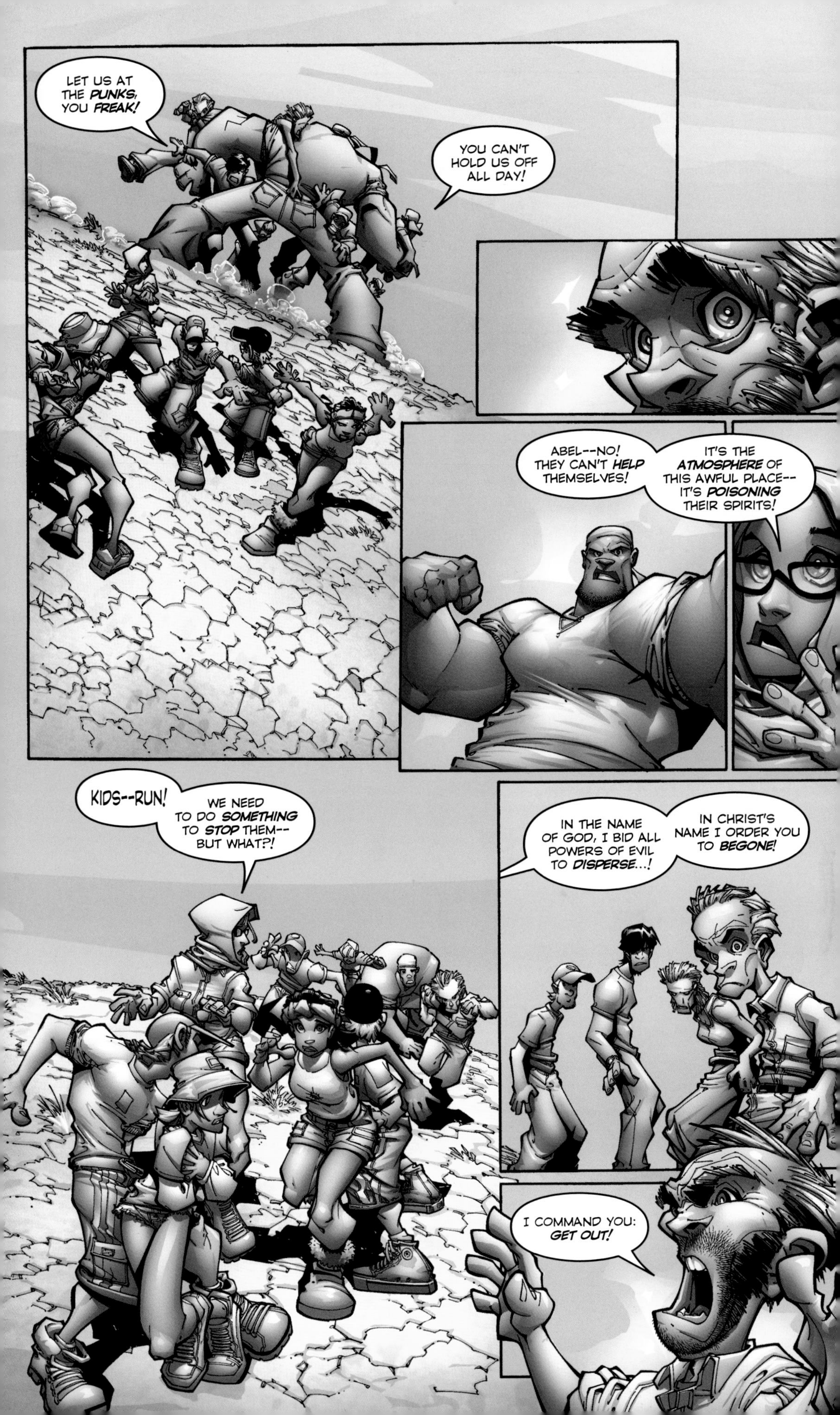
LET US AT THE PUNKS, YOU FREAK!
YOU CAN'T HOLD US OFF ALL DAY!
ABEL--NO! THEY CAN'T HELP THEMSELVES!
IT'S THE ATMOSPHERE OF THIS AWFUL PLACE-- IT'S POISONING THEIR SPIRITS!
KIDS--RUN!
WE NEED TO DO SOMETHING TO STOP THEM-- BUT WHAT?!
IN THE NAME OF GOD, I BID ALL POWERS OF EVIL TO DISPERSE...!
IN CHRIST'S NAME I ORDER YOU TO BEGONE!
I COMMAND YOU: GET OUT!

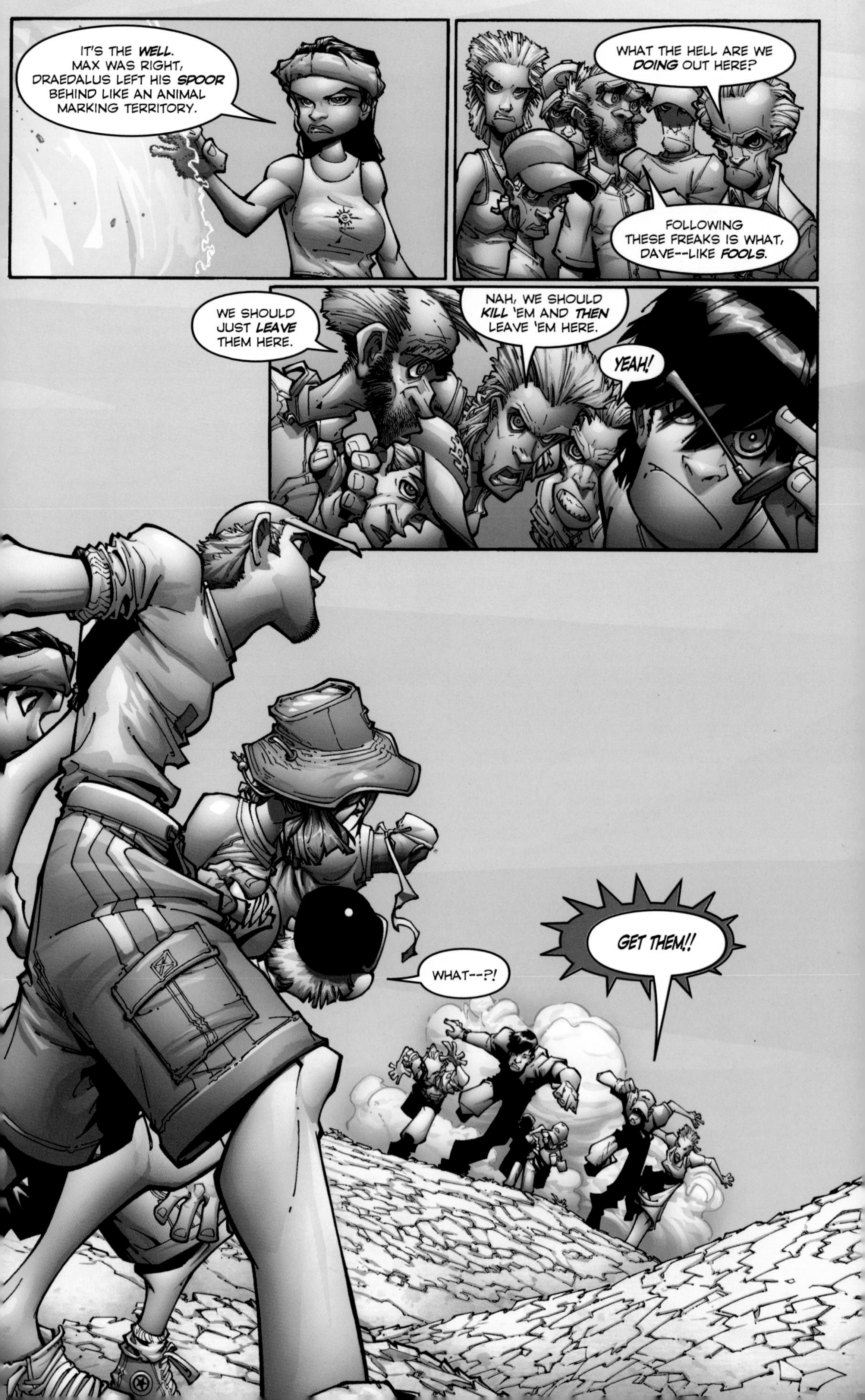
IT'S THE WELL. MAX WAS RIGHT, DRAEDALUS LEFT HIS SPOOR BEHIND LIKE AN ANIMAL MARKING TERRITORY.
WHAT THE HELL ARE WE DOING OUT HERE?
FOLLOWING THESE FREAKS IS WHAT, DAVE--LIKE FOOLS.
WE SHOULD JUST LEAVE THEM HERE.
NAH, WE SHOULD KILL 'EM AND THEN LEAVE 'EM HERE.
YEAH!
GET THEM!!
WHAT--?!

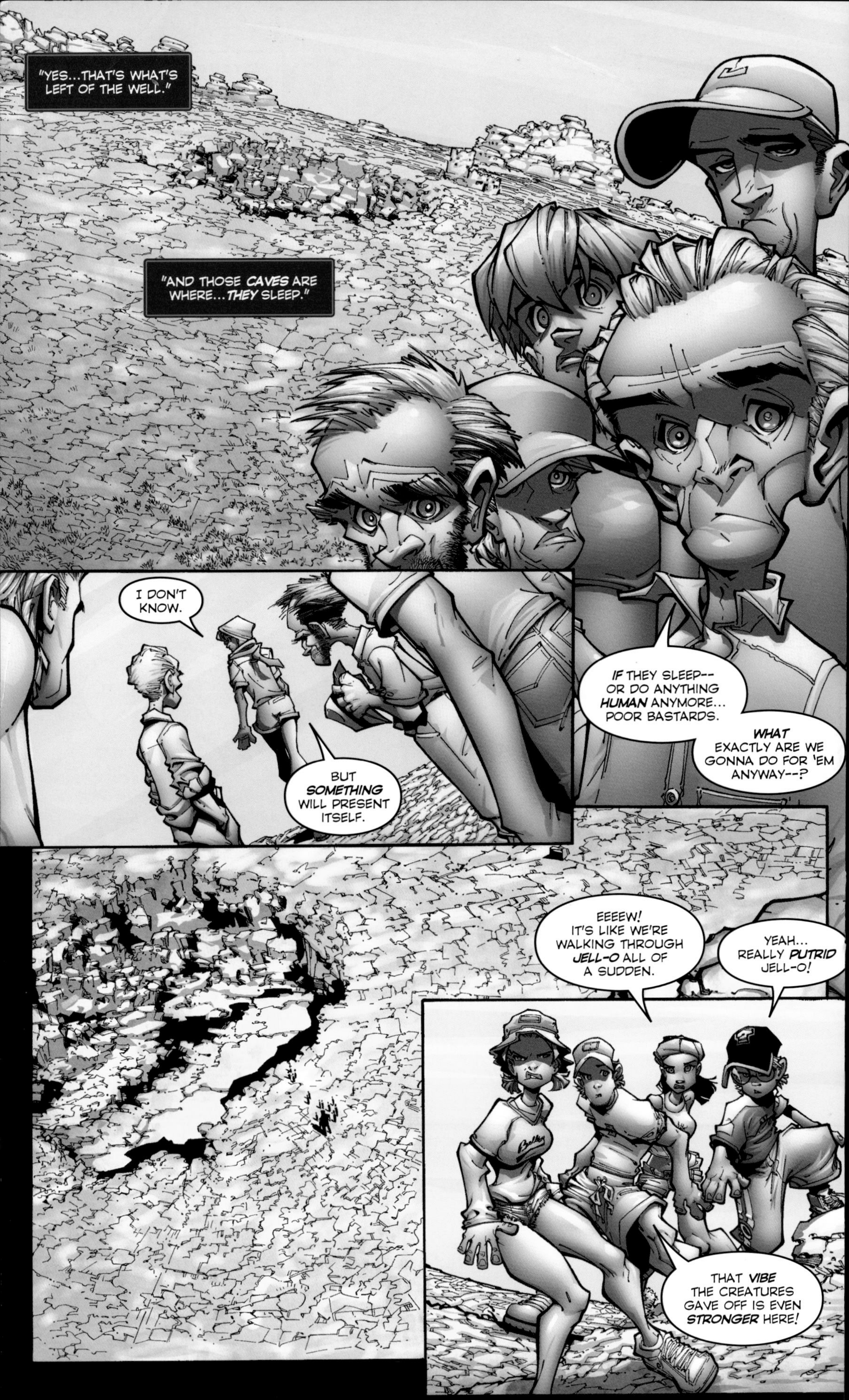
"YES...THAT'S WHAT'S LEFT OF THE WELL."
"AND THOSE CAVES ARE WHERE...THEY SLEEP."
I DON'T KNOW.
BUT SOMETHING WILL PRESENT ITSELF.
IF THEY SLEEP-- OR DO ANYTHING HUMAN ANYMORE... POOR BASTARDS.
WHAT EXACTLY ARE WE GONNA DO FOR 'EM ANYWAY--?
EEEEW! IT'S LIKE WE'RE WALKING THROUGH JELL-O ALL OF A SUDDEN.
YEAH... REALLY PUTRID JELL-O!
THAT VIBE THE CREATURES GAVE OFF IS EVEN STRONGER HERE!

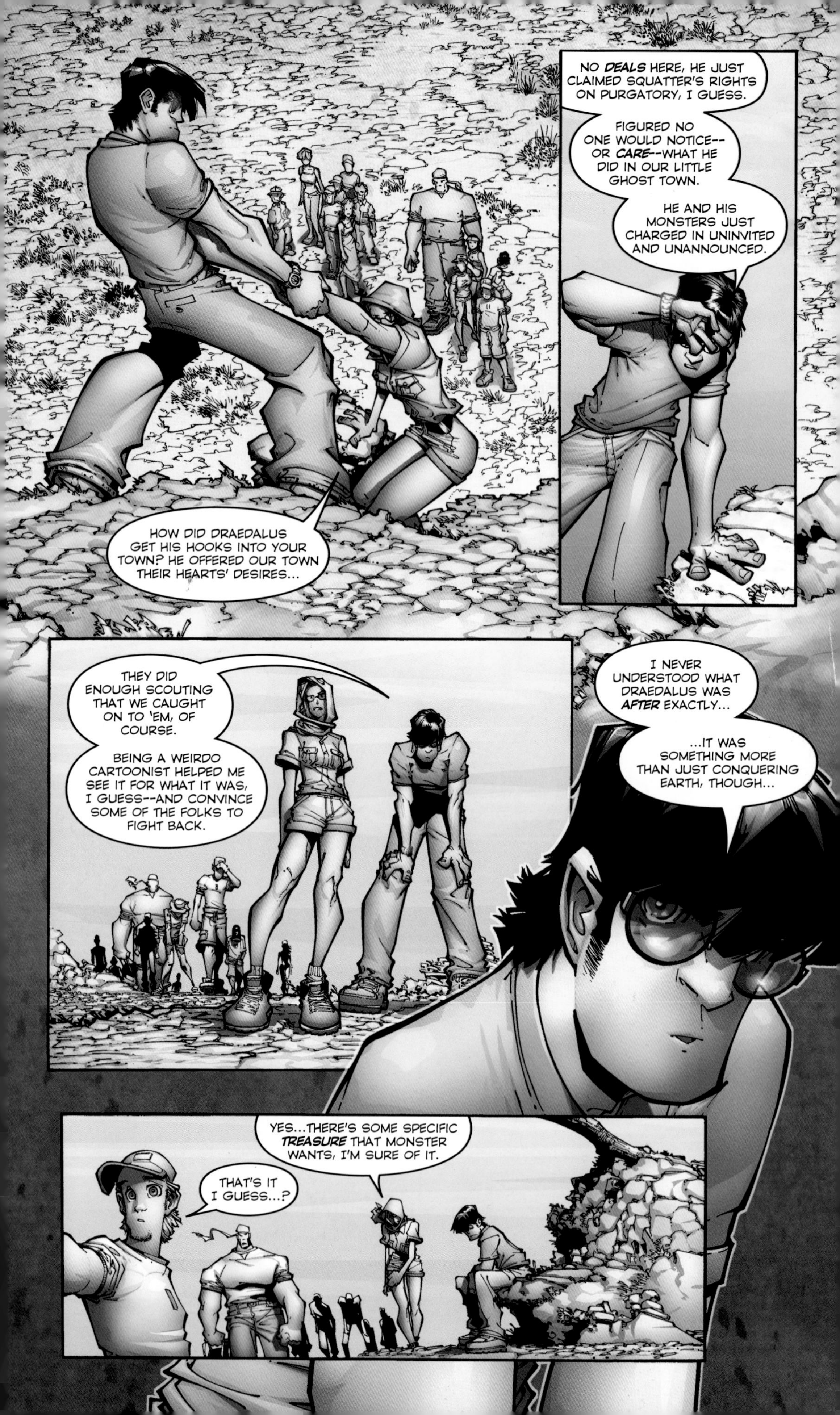
HOW DID DRAEDALUS GET HIS HOOKS INTO YOUR TOWN? HE OFFERED OUR TOWN THEIR HEARTS' DESIRES...
NO DEALS HERE, HE JUST CLAIMED SQUATTER'S RIGHTS ON PURGATORY, I GUESS.
FIGURED NO ONE WOULD NOTICE--OR CARE--WHAT HE DID IN OUR LITTLE GHOST TOWN.
HE AND HIS MONSTERS JUST CHARGED IN UNINVITED AND UNANNOUNCED.
THEY DID ENOUGH SCOUTING THAT WE CAUGHT ON TO 'EM, OF COURSE.
BEING A WEIRDO CARTOONIST HELPED ME SEE IT FOR WHAT IT WAS, I GUESS--AND CONVINCE SOME OF THE FOLKS TO FIGHT BACK.
I NEVER UNDERSTOOD WHAT DRAEDALUS WAS AFTER EXACTLY...
...IT WAS SOMETHING MORE THAN JUST CONQUERING EARTH, THOUGH...
THAT'S IT I GUESS...?
YES...THERE'S SOME SPECIFIC TREASURE THAT MONSTER WANTS, I'M SURE OF IT.

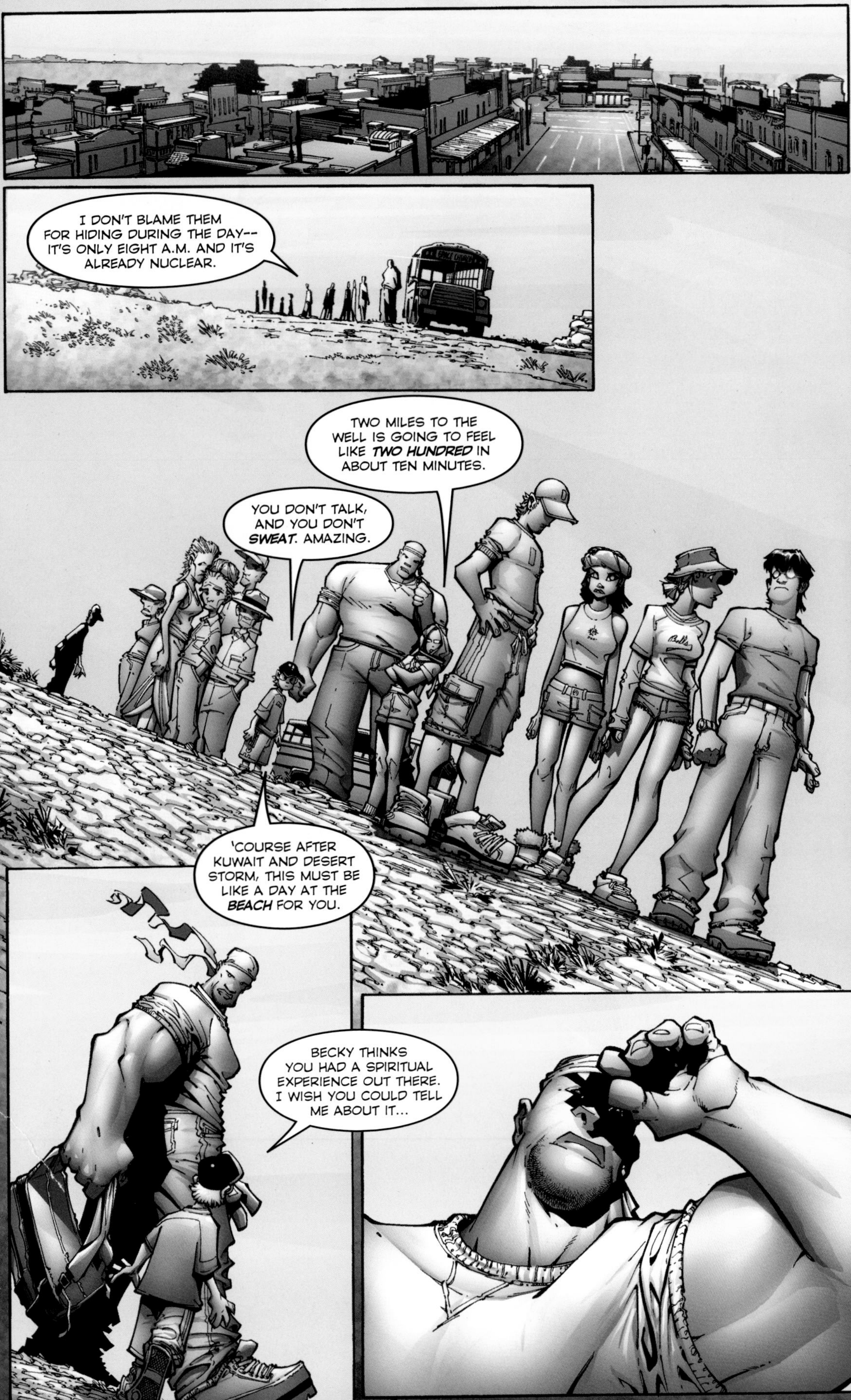
I DON'T BLAME THEM FOR HIDING DURING THE DAY-- IT'S ONLY EIGHT A.M. AND IT'S ALREADY NUCLEAR.
TWO MILES TO THE WELL IS GOING TO FEEL LIKE *TWO HUNDRED* IN ABOUT TEN MINUTES.
YOU DON'T TALK, AND YOU DON'T *SWEAT*. AMAZING.
'COURSE AFTER KUWAIT AND DESERT STORM, THIS MUST BE LIKE A DAY AT THE *BEACH* FOR YOU.
BECKY THINKS YOU HAD A SPIRITUAL EXPERIENCE OUT THERE. I WISH YOU COULD TELL ME ABOUT IT...

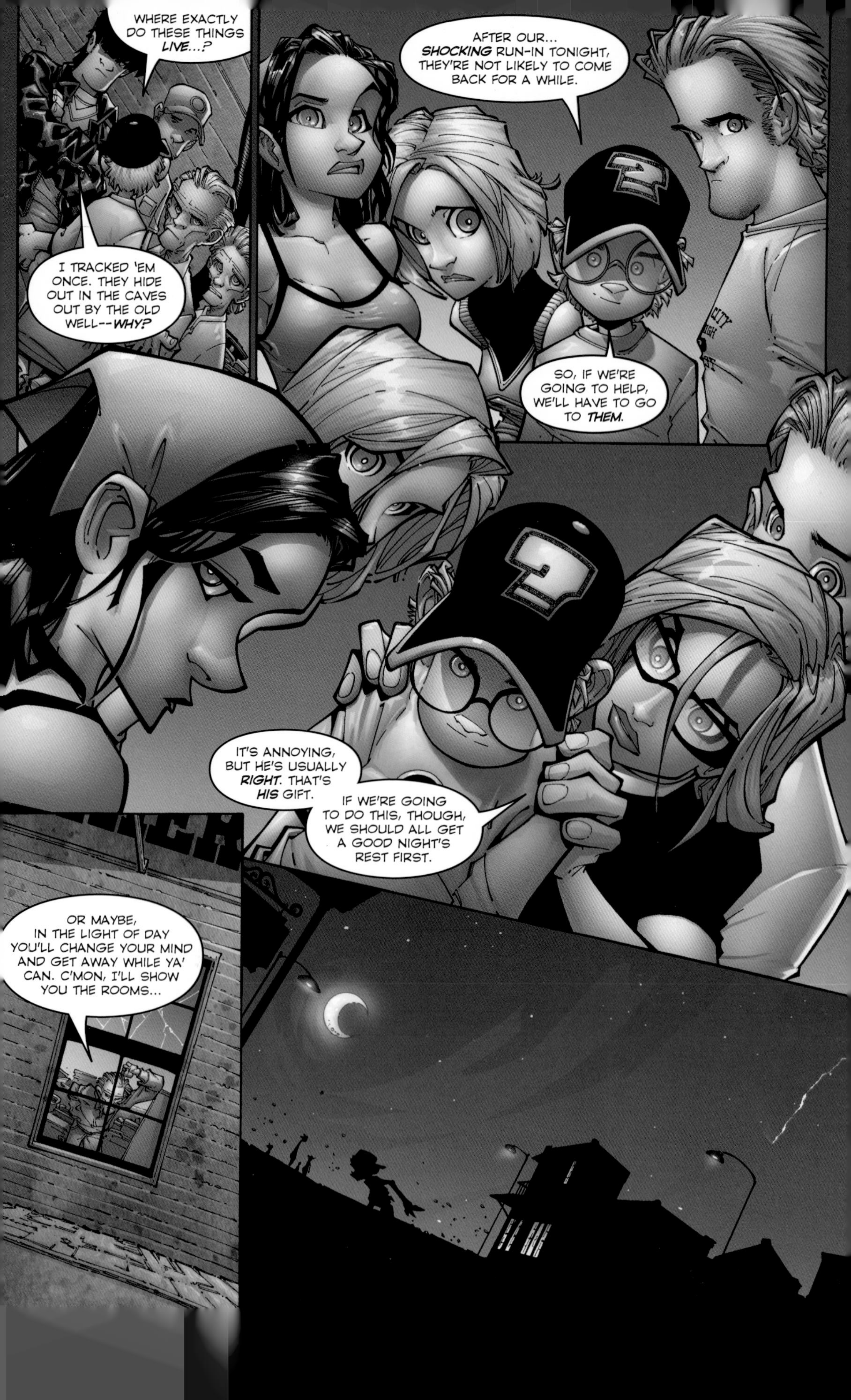
WHERE EXACTLY DO THESE THINGS *LIVE*...?
I TRACKED 'EM ONCE. THEY HIDE OUT IN THE CAVES OUT BY THE OLD WELL--*WHY?*
AFTER OUR... ***SHOCKING*** RUN-IN TONIGHT, THEY'RE NOT LIKELY TO COME BACK FOR A WHILE.
SO, IF WE'RE GOING TO HELP, WE'LL HAVE TO GO TO ***THEM***.
IT'S ANNOYING, BUT HE'S USUALLY ***RIGHT***. THAT'S ***HIS*** GIFT.
IF WE'RE GOING TO DO THIS, THOUGH, WE SHOULD ALL GET A GOOD NIGHT'S REST FIRST.
OR MAYBE, IN THE LIGHT OF DAY YOU'LL CHANGE YOUR MIND AND GET AWAY WHILE YA' CAN. C'MON, I'LL SHOW YOU THE ROOMS...

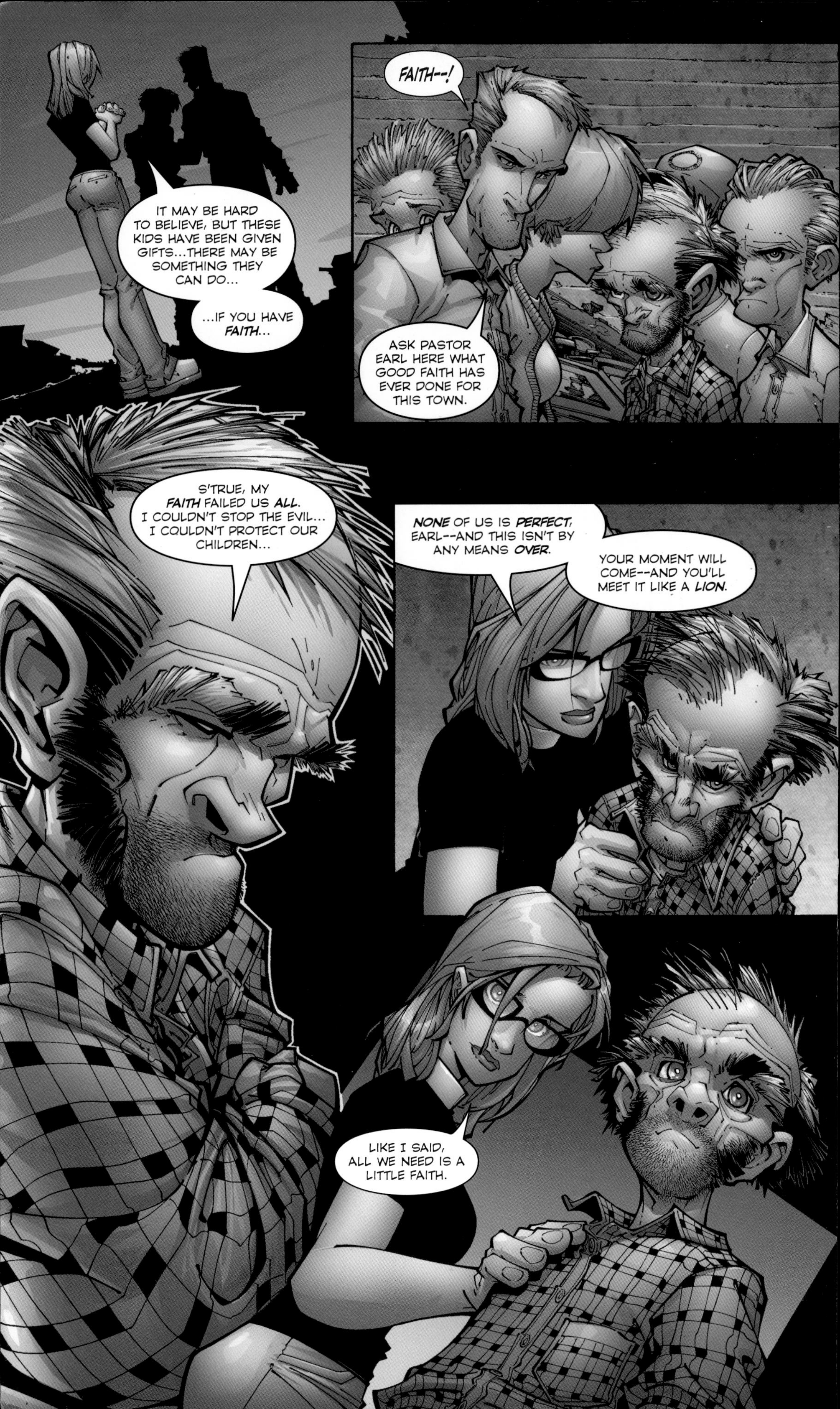

IT MAY BE HARD TO BELIEVE, BUT THESE KIDS HAVE BEEN GIVEN GIFTS...THERE MAY BE SOMETHING THEY CAN DO...
...IF YOU HAVE FAITH...
FAITH--!
ASK PASTOR EARL HERE WHAT GOOD FAITH HAS EVER DONE FOR THIS TOWN.
S'TRUE, MY FAITH FAILED US ALL. I COULDN'T STOP THE EVIL... I COULDN'T PROTECT OUR CHILDREN...
NONE OF US IS PERFECT, EARL--AND THIS ISN'T BY ANY MEANS OVER.
YOUR MOMENT WILL COME--AND YOU'LL MEET IT LIKE A LION.
LIKE I SAID, ALL WE NEED IS A LITTLE FAITH.

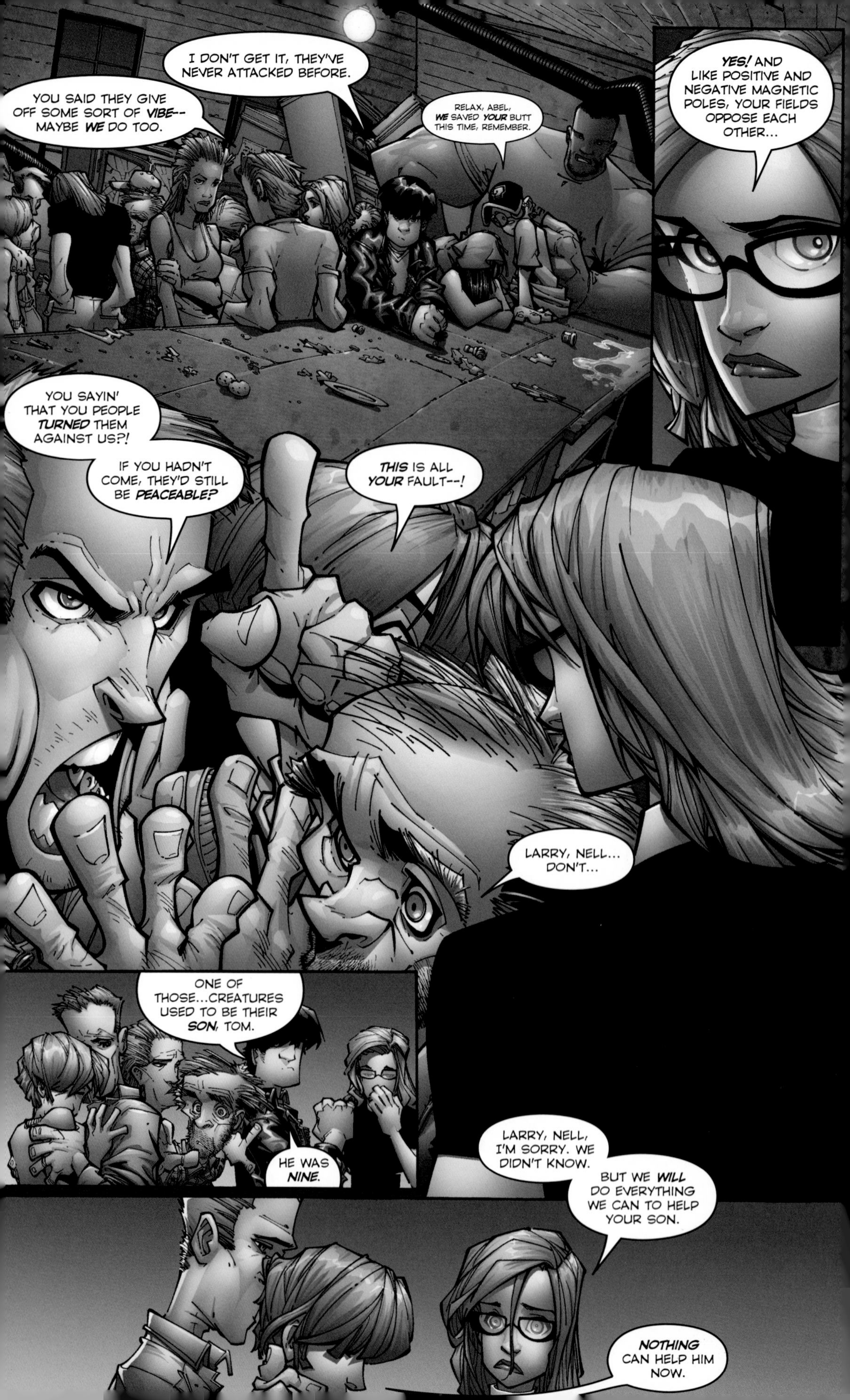
YOU SAID THEY GIVE OFF SOME SORT OF VIBE-- MAYBE WE DO TOO.
I DON'T GET IT, THEY'VE NEVER ATTACKED BEFORE.
RELAX, ABEL, WE SAVED YOUR BUTT THIS TIME, REMEMBER.
YES! AND LIKE POSITIVE AND NEGATIVE MAGNETIC POLES, YOUR FIELDS OPPOSE EACH OTHER...
YOU SAYIN' THAT YOU PEOPLE TURNED THEM AGAINST US?!
IF YOU HADN'T COME, THEY'D STILL BE PEACEABLE?
THIS IS ALL YOUR FAULT--!
LARRY, NELL... DON'T...
ONE OF THOSE...CREATURES USED TO BE THEIR SON, TOM.
HE WAS NINE.
LARRY, NELL, I'M SORRY. WE DIDN'T KNOW.
BUT WE WILL DO EVERYTHING WE CAN TO HELP YOUR SON.
NOTHING CAN HELP HIM NOW.

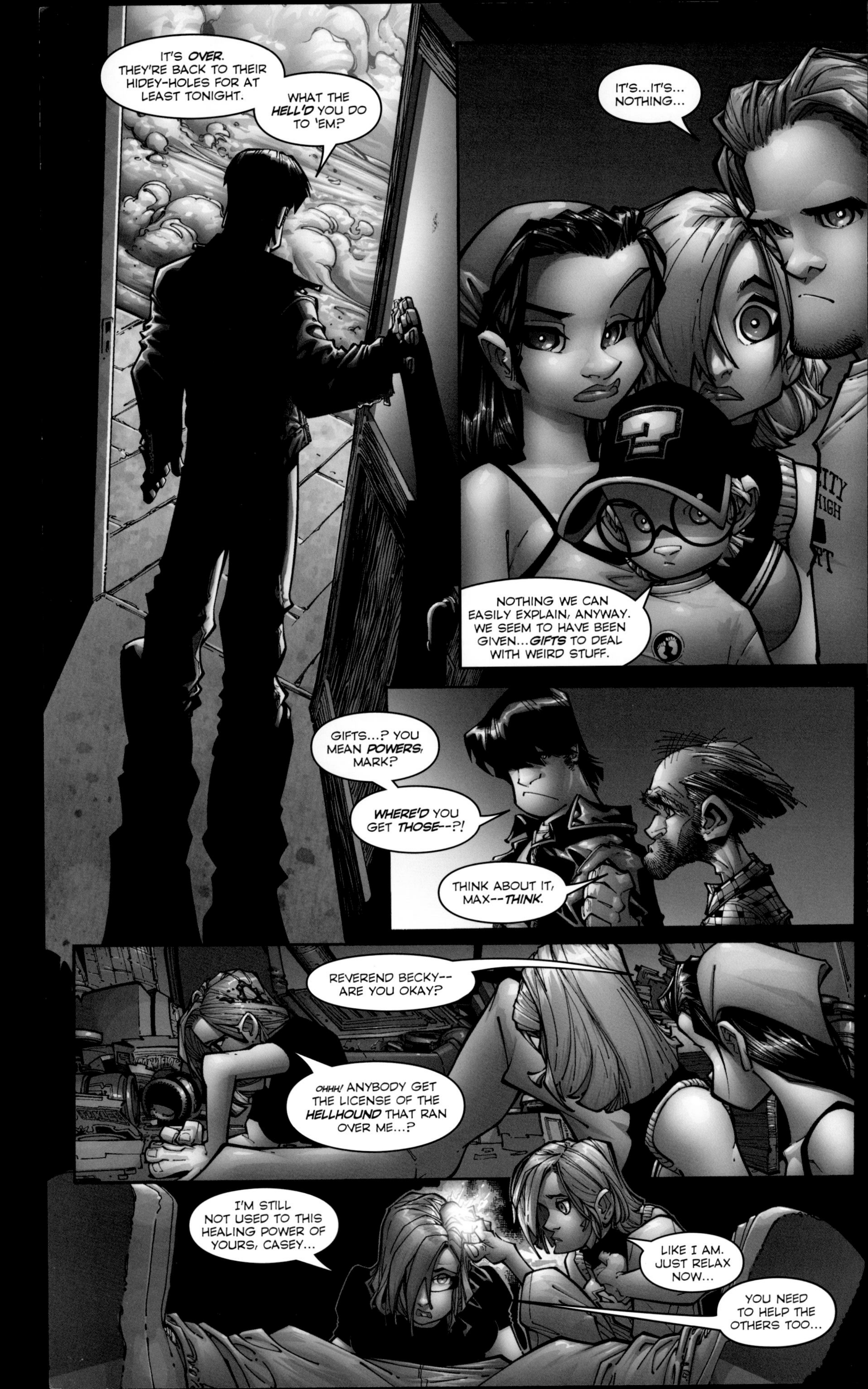
IT'S OVER. THEY'RE BACK TO THEIR HIDEY-HOLES FOR AT LEAST TONIGHT.
WHAT THE HELL'D YOU DO TO 'EM?
IT'S...IT'S... NOTHING...
NOTHING WE CAN EASILY EXPLAIN, ANYWAY. WE SEEM TO HAVE BEEN GIVEN...GIFTS TO DEAL WITH WEIRD STUFF.
GIFTS...? YOU MEAN POWERS, MARK?
WHERE'D YOU GET THOSE--?!
THINK ABOUT IT, MAX--THINK.
REVEREND BECKY-- ARE YOU OKAY?
OHHH! ANYBODY GET THE LICENSE OF THE HELLHOUND THAT RAN OVER ME...?
I'M STILL NOT USED TO THIS HEALING POWER OF YOURS, CASEY...
LIKE I AM. JUST RELAX NOW...
YOU NEED TO HELP THE OTHERS TOO...

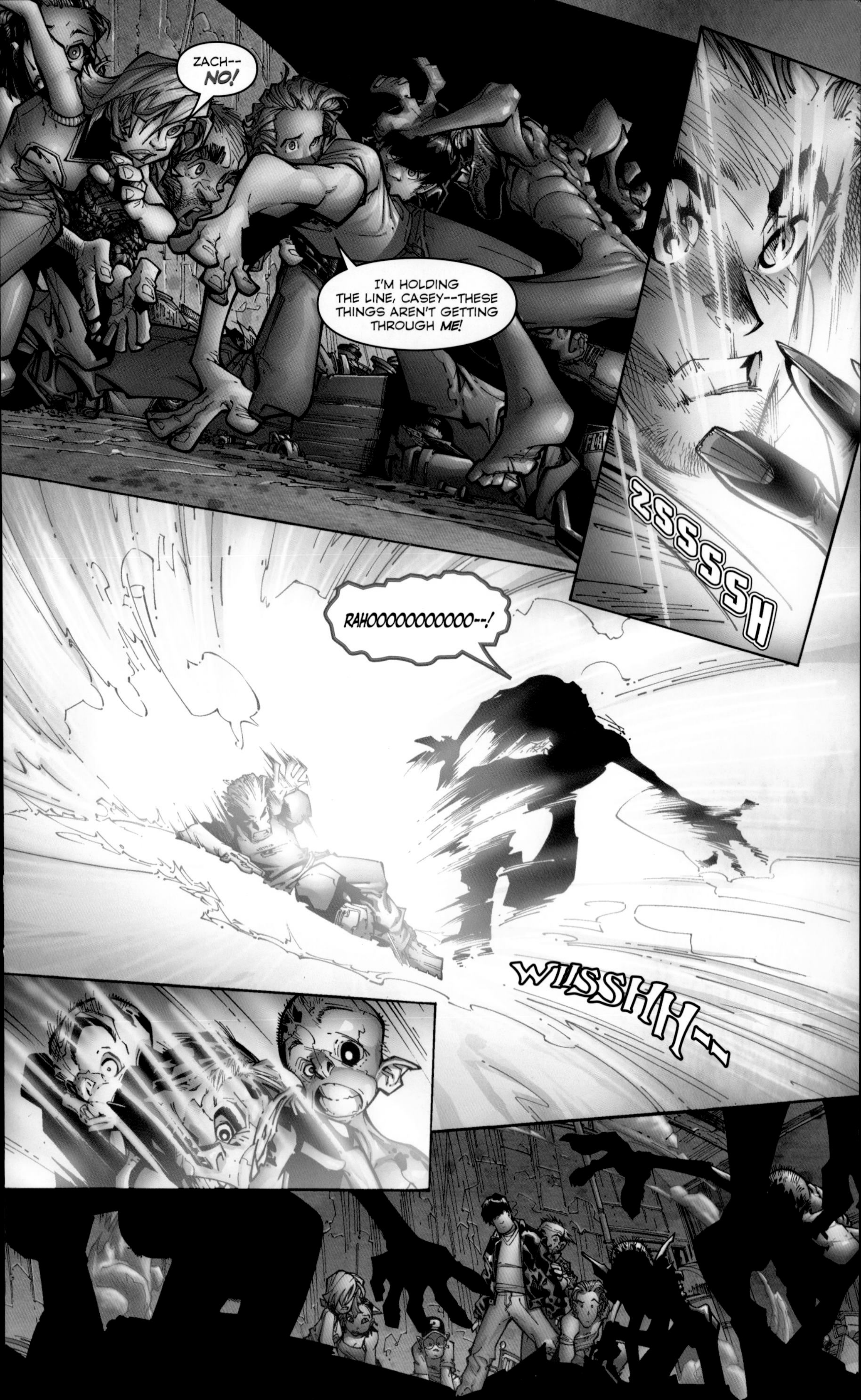
ZACH--
NO!
I'M HOLDING THE LINE, CASEY--THESE THINGS AREN'T GETTING THROUGH ME!
ZSSSSSH
RAHOOOOOOOOOOO--!
WIISSHH--

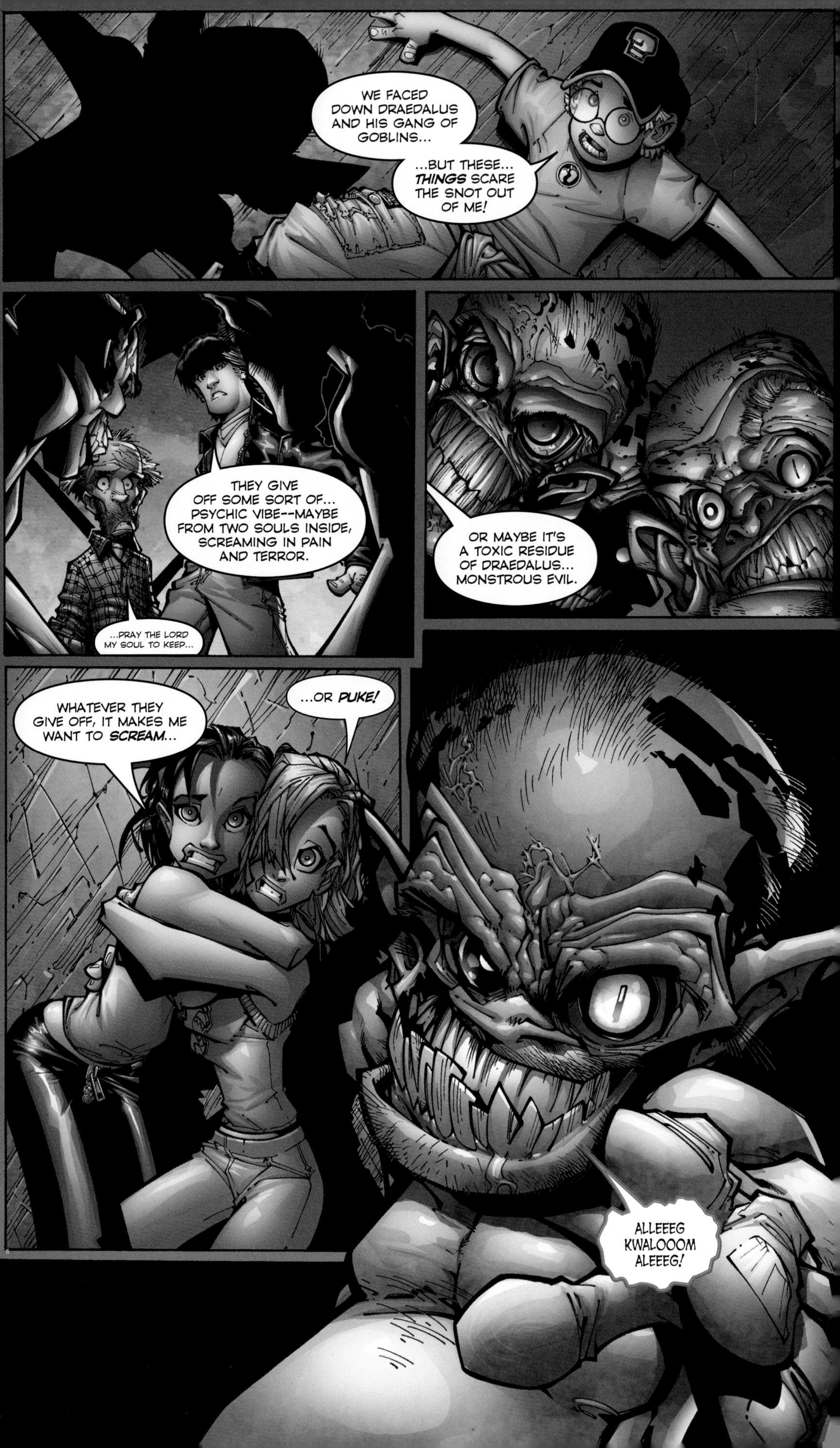
WE FACED DOWN DRAEDALUS AND HIS GANG OF GOBLINS...
...BUT THESE... THINGS SCARE THE SNOT OUT OF ME!
THEY GIVE OFF SOME SORT OF... PSYCHIC VIBE--MAYBE FROM TWO SOULS INSIDE, SCREAMING IN PAIN AND TERROR.
...PRAY THE LORD MY SOUL TO KEEP...
OR MAYBE IT'S A TOXIC RESIDUE OF DRAEDALUS... MONSTROUS EVIL.
WHATEVER THEY GIVE OFF, IT MAKES ME WANT TO SCREAM...
...OR PUKE!
ALLEEEG KWALOOOM ALEEEG!

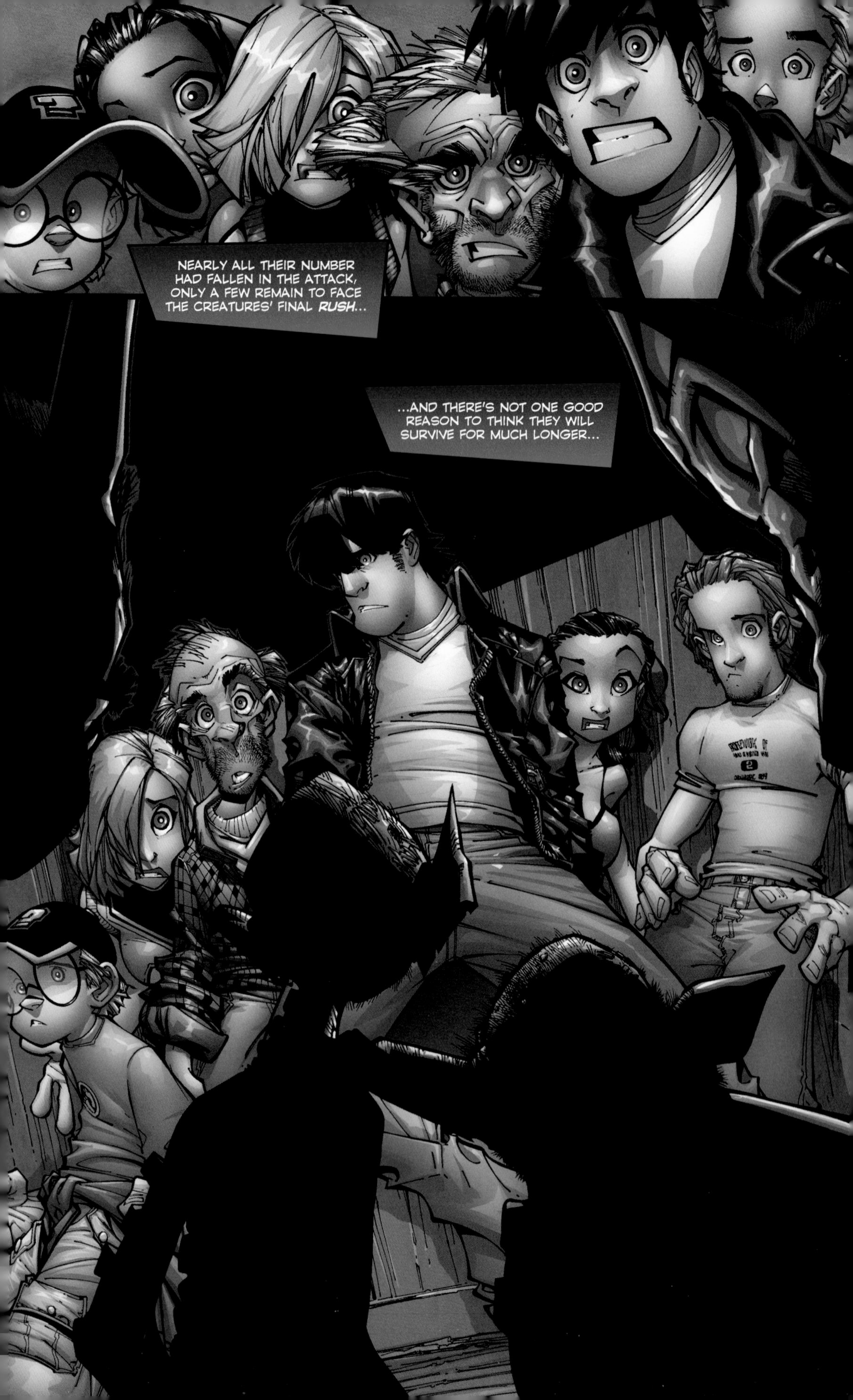
NEARLY ALL THEIR NUMBER HAD FALLEN IN THE ATTACK, ONLY A FEW REMAIN TO FACE THE CREATURES' FINAL RUSH...
...AND THERE'S NOT ONE GOOD REASON TO THINK THEY WILL SURVIVE FOR MUCH LONGER...

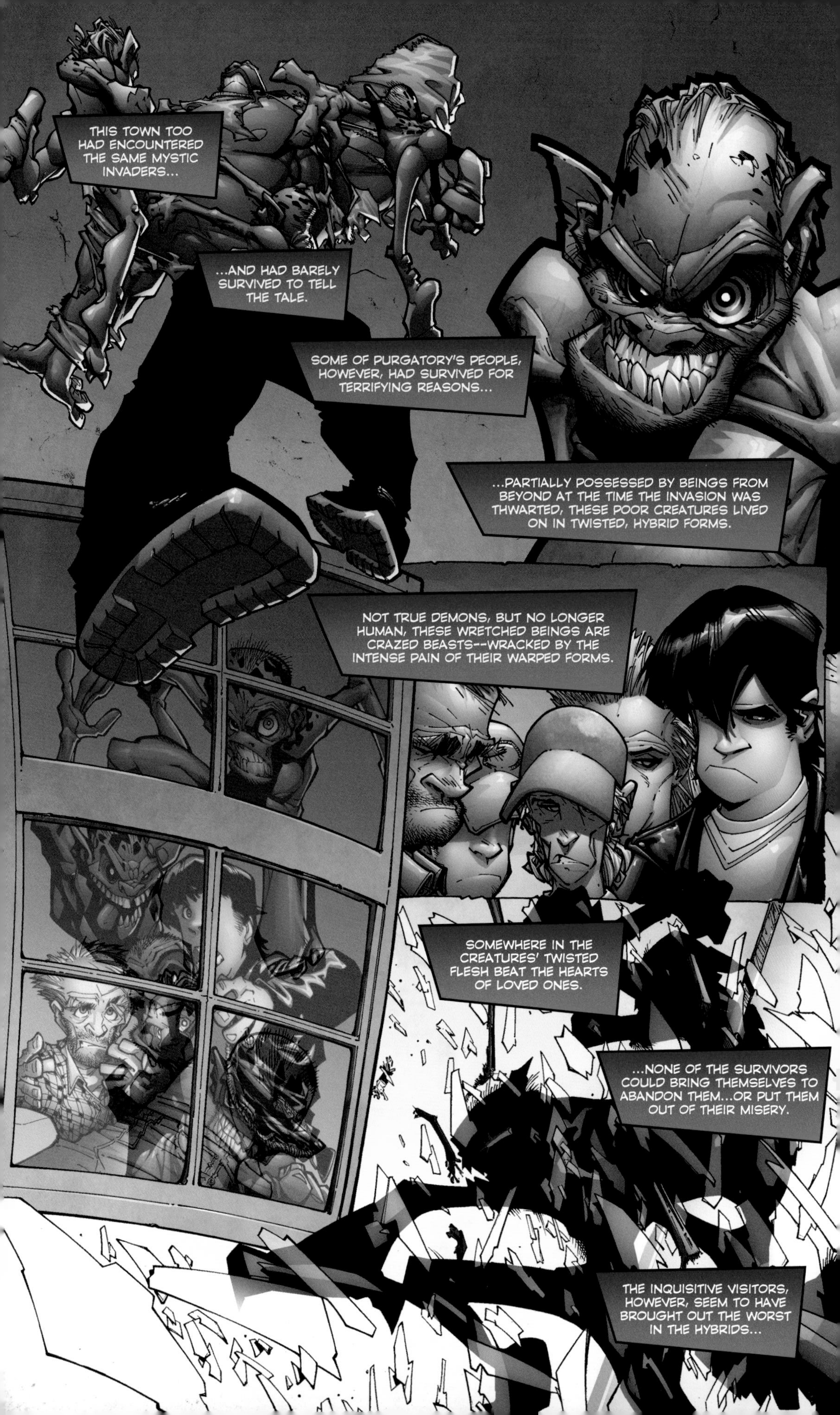
THIS TOWN TOO HAD ENCOUNTERED THE SAME MYSTIC INVADERS...
...AND HAD BARELY SURVIVED TO TELL THE TALE.
SOME OF PURGATORY'S PEOPLE, HOWEVER, HAD SURVIVED FOR TERRIFYING REASONS...
...PARTIALLY POSSESSED BY BEINGS FROM BEYOND AT THE TIME THE INVASION WAS THWARTED, THESE POOR CREATURES LIVED ON IN TWISTED, HYBRID FORMS.
NOT TRUE DEMONS, BUT NO LONGER HUMAN, THESE WRETCHED BEINGS ARE CRAZED BEASTS--WRACKED BY THE INTENSE PAIN OF THEIR WARPED FORMS.
SOMEWHERE IN THE CREATURES' TWISTED FLESH BEAT THE HEARTS OF LOVED ONES.
...NONE OF THE SURVIVORS COULD BRING THEMSELVES TO ABANDON THEM...OR PUT THEM OUT OF THEIR MISERY.
THE INQUISITIVE VISITORS, HOWEVER, SEEM TO HAVE BROUGHT OUT THE WORST IN THE HYBRIDS...

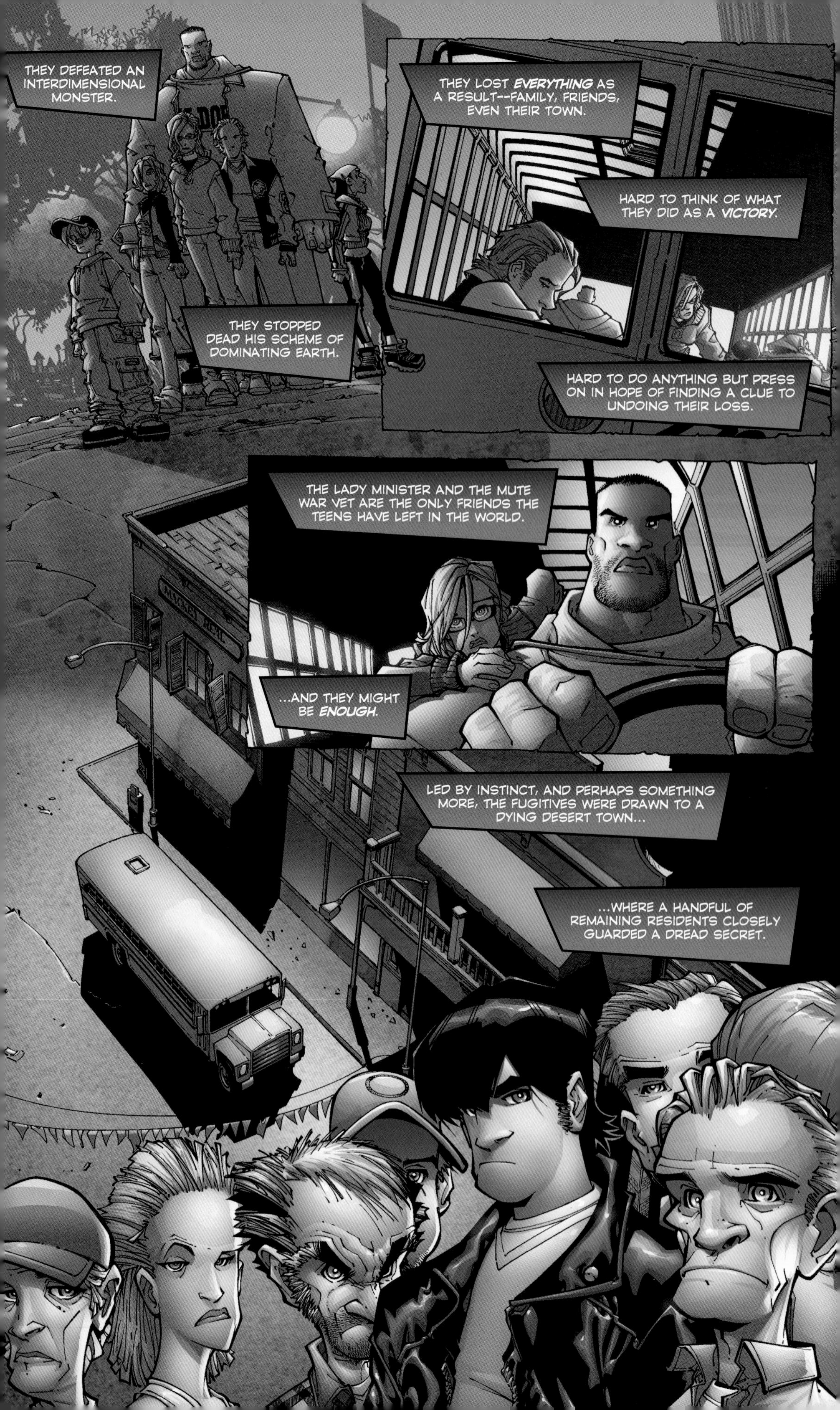

THEY DEFEATED AN INTERDIMENSIONAL MONSTER.
THEY STOPPED DEAD HIS SCHEME OF DOMINATING EARTH.
THEY LOST EVERYTHING AS A RESULT--FAMILY, FRIENDS, EVEN THEIR TOWN.
HARD TO THINK OF WHAT THEY DID AS A VICTORY.
HARD TO DO ANYTHING BUT PRESS ON IN HOPE OF FINDING A CLUE TO UNDOING THEIR LOSS.
THE LADY MINISTER AND THE MUTE WAR VET ARE THE ONLY FRIENDS THE TEENS HAVE LEFT IN THE WORLD.
...AND THEY MIGHT BE ENOUGH.
LED BY INSTINCT, AND PERHAPS SOMETHING MORE, THE FUGITIVES WERE DRAWN TO A DYING DESERT TOWN...
...WHERE A HANDFUL OF REMAINING RESIDENTS CLOSELY GUARDED A DREAD SECRET.

CHAPTER EIGHT
STUCK IN THE MIDDLE

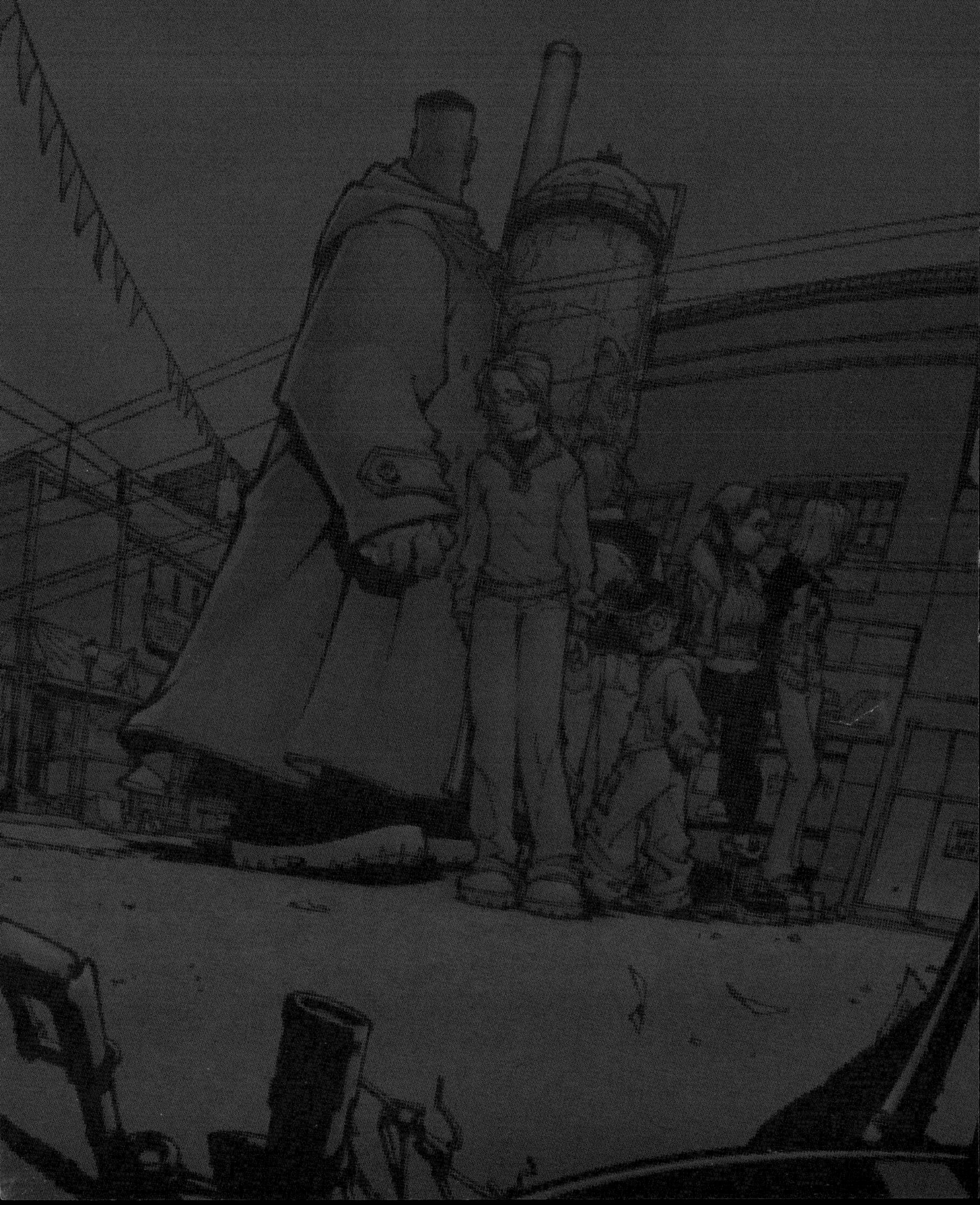

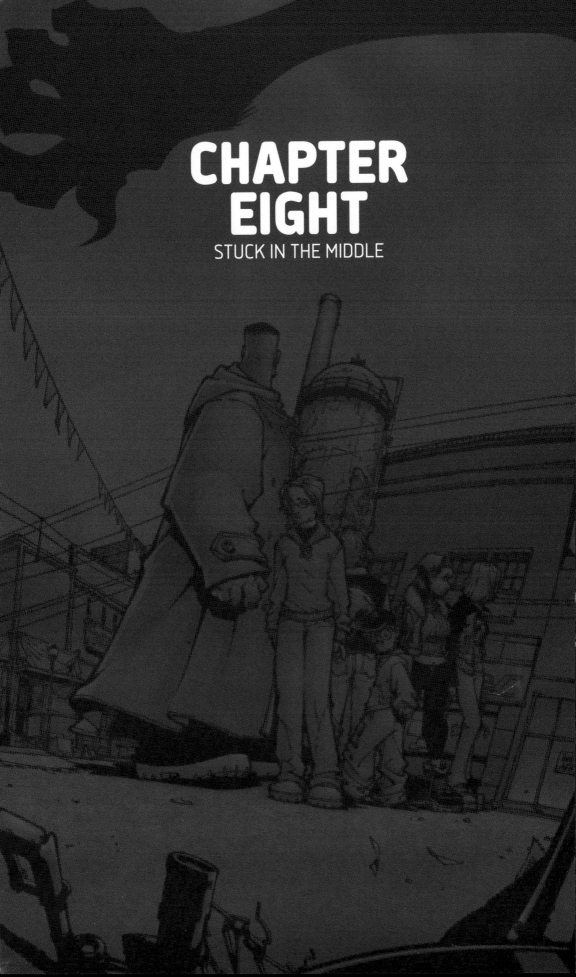

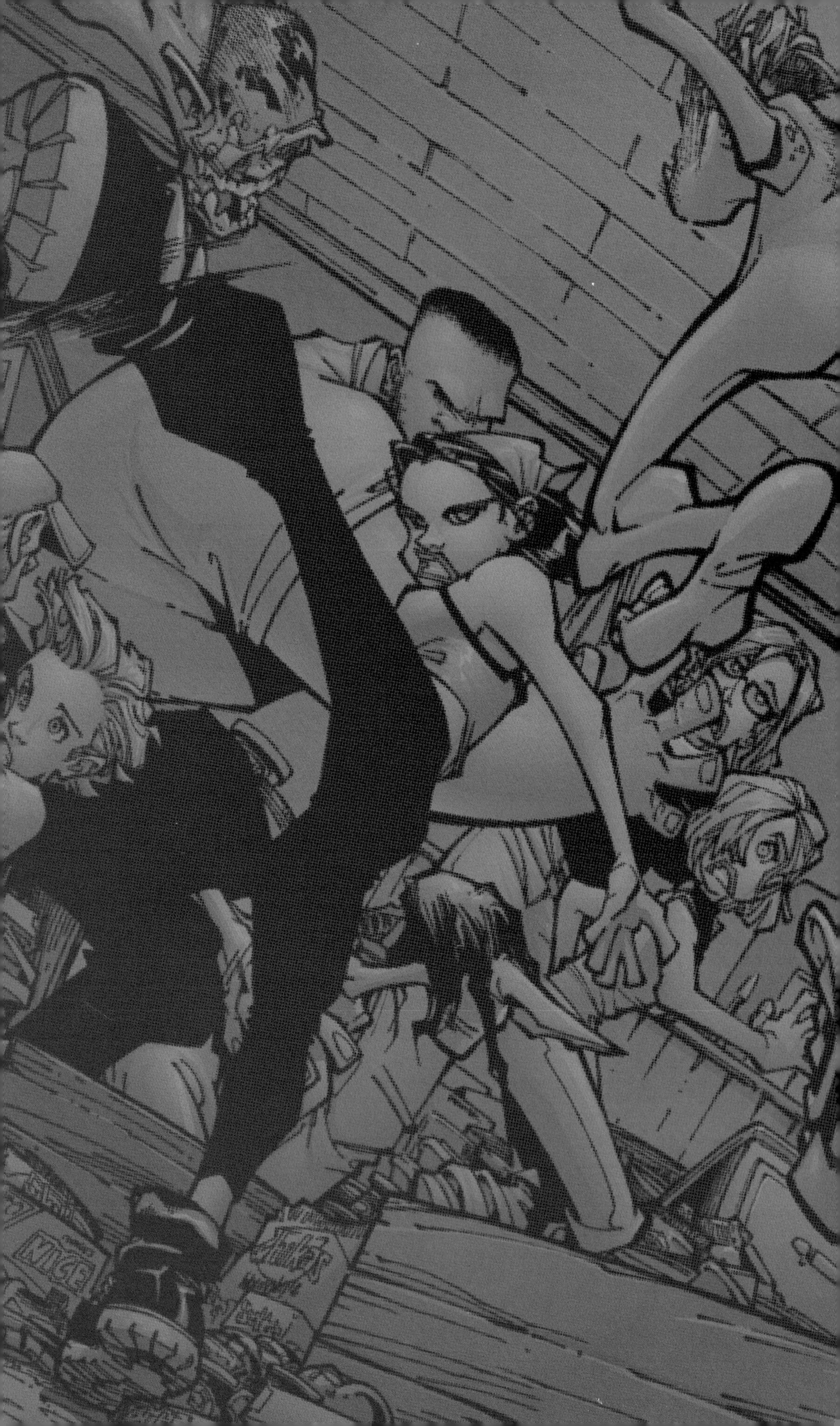

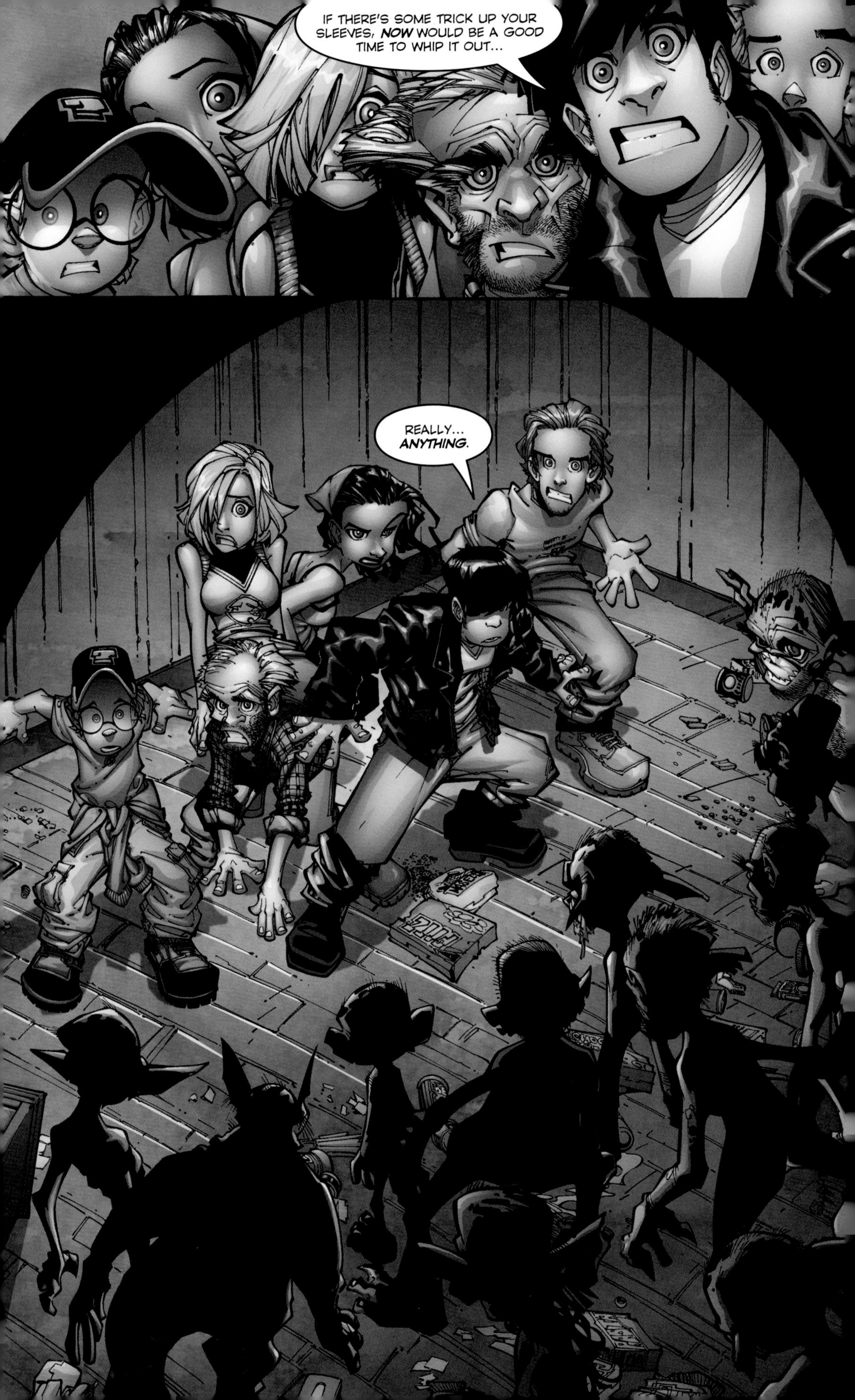
IF THERE'S SOME TRICK UP YOUR SLEEVES, NOW WOULD BE A GOOD TIME TO WHIP IT OUT...
REALLY... ANYTHING.

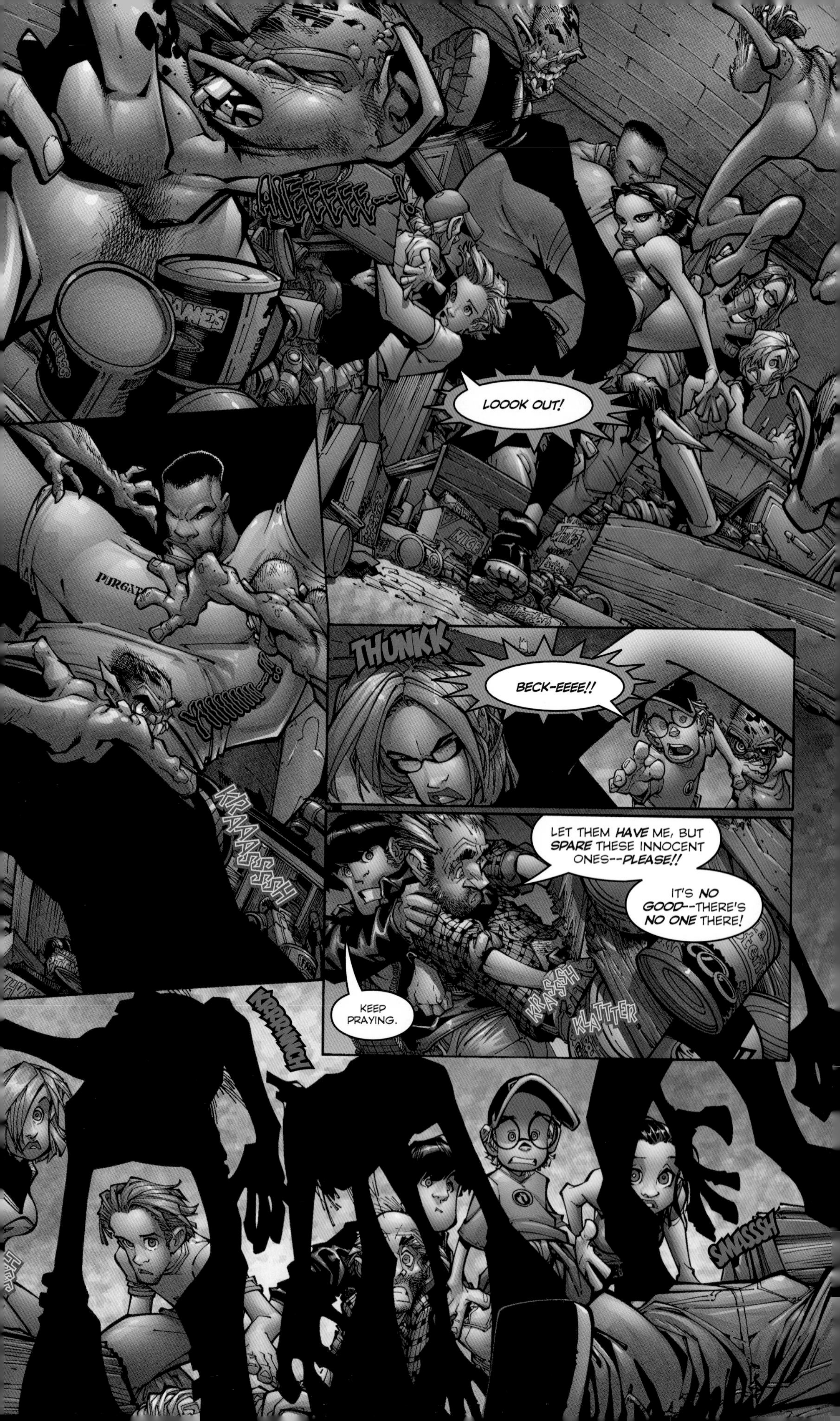

LOOOK OUT!
THUNKK
BECK-EEEE!!
LET THEM HAVE ME, BUT SPARE THESE INNOCENT ONES--PLEASE!!
IT'S NO GOOD--THERE'S NO ONE THERE!
KEEP PRAYING.
KLATTER
KRRRANCH!
SMASSSH

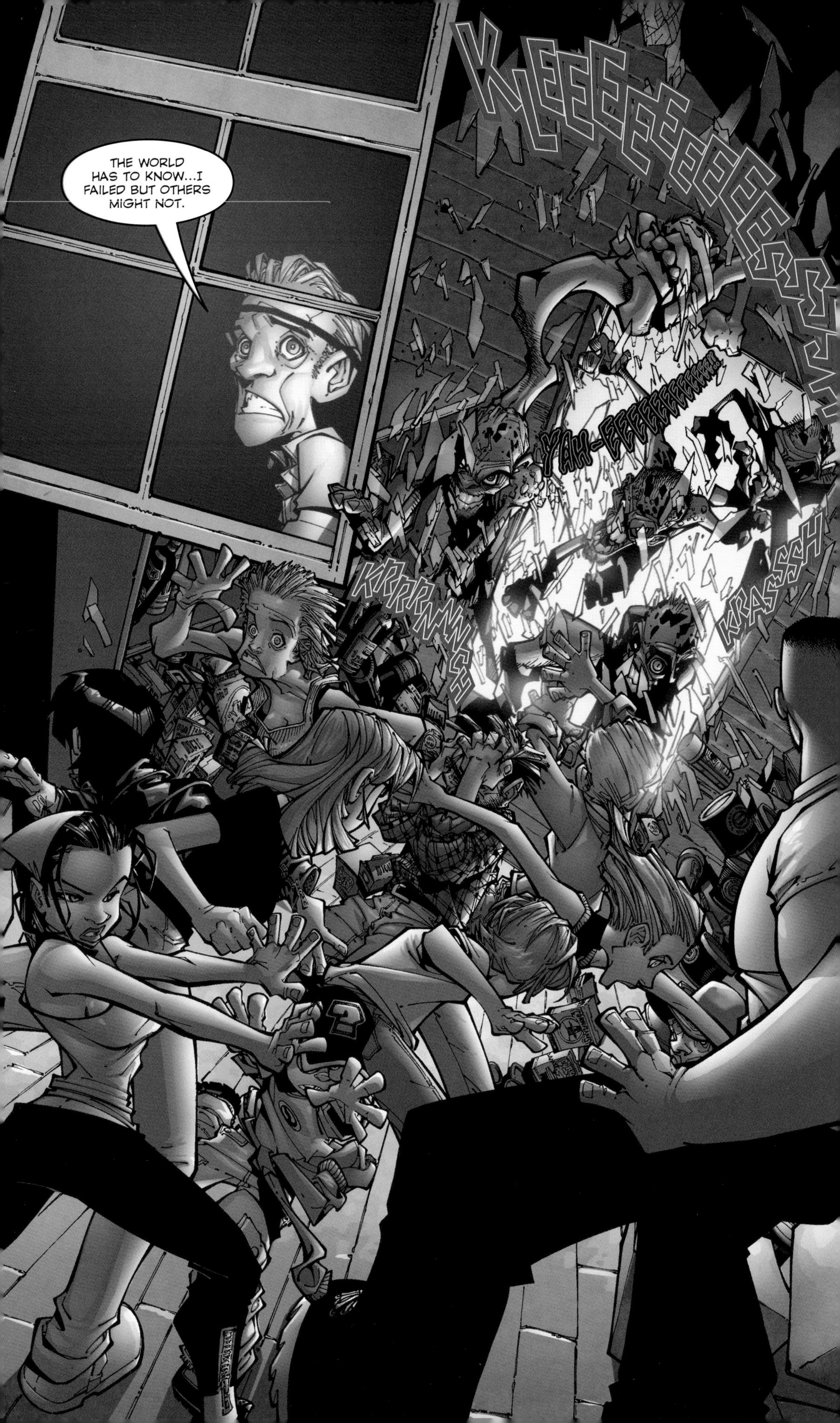
THE WORLD HAS TO KNOW...I FAILED BUT OTHERS MIGHT NOT.
KREEEEEEEEESSSH
YAH-EEEEEAAAAAAAH!!
KRRRRNNNCH
KRASSSH

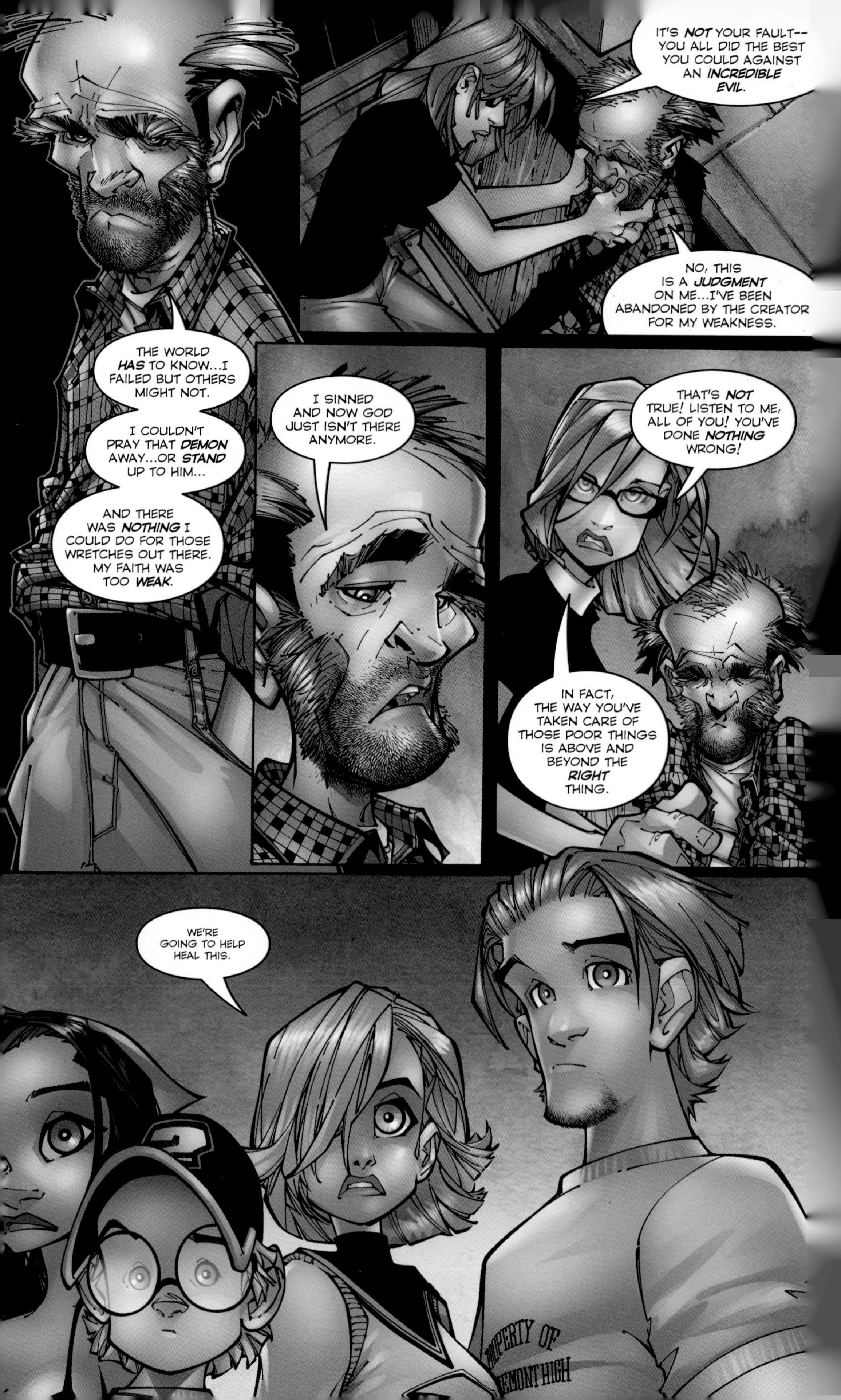
IT'S NOT YOUR FAULT-- YOU ALL DID THE BEST YOU COULD AGAINST AN INCREDIBLE EVIL.
NO, THIS IS A JUDGMENT ON ME...I'VE BEEN ABANDONED BY THE CREATOR FOR MY WEAKNESS.
THE WORLD HAS TO KNOW...I FAILED BUT OTHERS MIGHT NOT.
I COULDN'T PRAY THAT DEMON AWAY...OR STAND UP TO HIM...
AND THERE WAS NOTHING I COULD DO FOR THOSE WRETCHES OUT THERE. MY FAITH WAS TOO WEAK.
I SINNED AND NOW GOD JUST ISN'T THERE ANYMORE.
THAT'S NOT TRUE! LISTEN TO ME, ALL OF YOU! YOU'VE DONE NOTHING WRONG!
IN FACT, THE WAY YOU'VE TAKEN CARE OF THOSE POOR THINGS IS ABOVE AND BEYOND THE RIGHT THING.
WE'RE GOING TO HELP HEAL THIS.

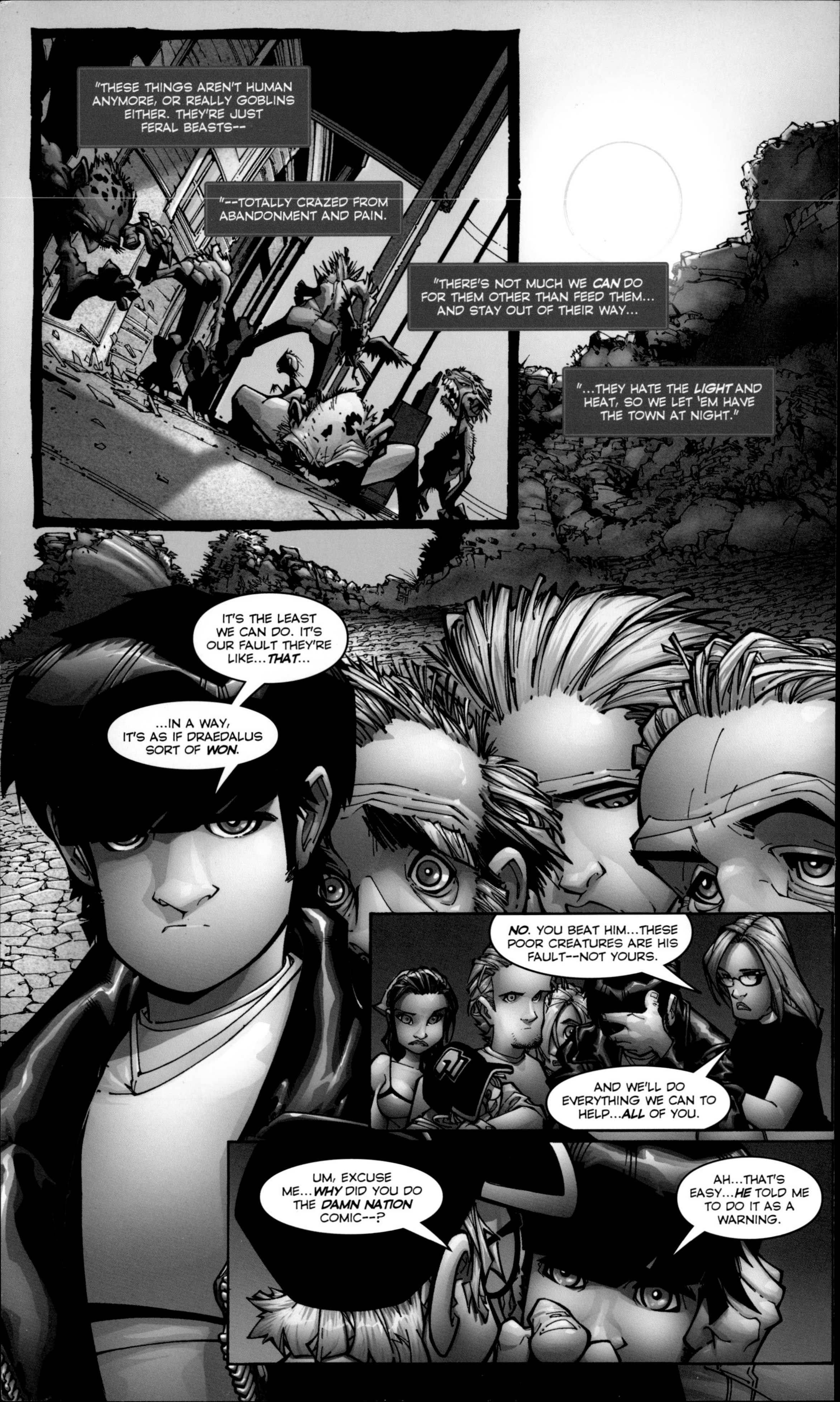
"THESE THINGS AREN'T HUMAN ANYMORE, OR REALLY GOBLINS EITHER. THEY'RE JUST FERAL BEASTS--
"--TOTALLY CRAZED FROM ABANDONMENT AND PAIN.
"THERE'S NOT MUCH WE CAN DO FOR THEM OTHER THAN FEED THEM... AND STAY OUT OF THEIR WAY...
"...THEY HATE THE LIGHT AND HEAT, SO WE LET 'EM HAVE THE TOWN AT NIGHT."
IT'S THE LEAST WE CAN DO. IT'S OUR FAULT THEY'RE LIKE... THAT...
...IN A WAY, IT'S AS IF DRAEDALUS SORT OF WON.
NO. YOU BEAT HIM...THESE POOR CREATURES ARE HIS FAULT--NOT YOURS.
AND WE'LL DO EVERYTHING WE CAN TO HELP...ALL OF YOU.
UM, EXCUSE ME...WHY DID YOU DO THE DAMN NATION COMIC--?
AH...THAT'S EASY...HE TOLD ME TO DO IT AS A WARNING.

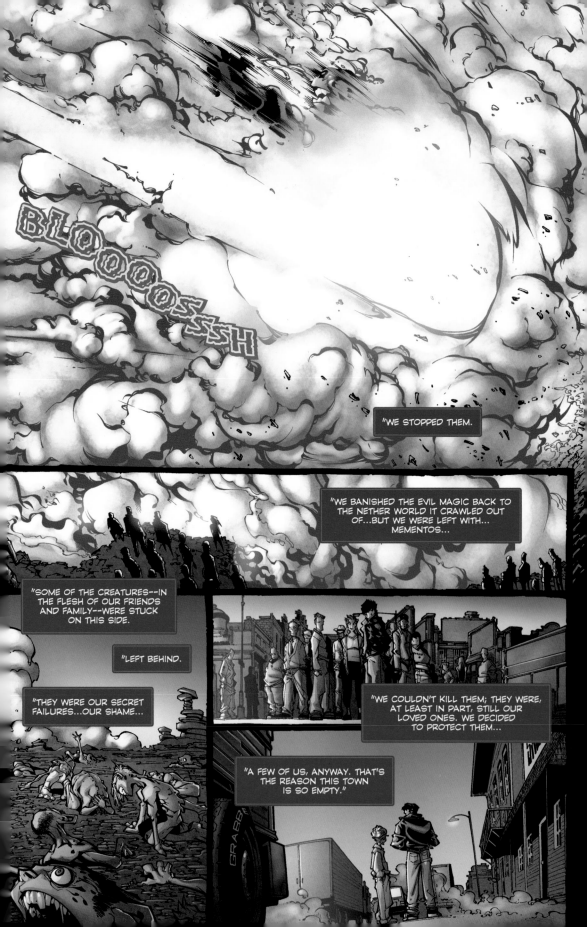

BLOOOOSSSH

"WE STOPPED THEM.

"WE BANISHED THE EVIL MAGIC BACK TO THE NETHER WORLD IT CRAWLED OUT OF...BUT WE WERE LEFT WITH... MEMENTOS...

"SOME OF THE CREATURES--IN THE FLESH OF OUR FRIENDS AND FAMILY--WERE STUCK ON THIS SIDE.

"LEFT BEHIND.

"THEY WERE OUR SECRET FAILURES...OUR SHAME...

"WE COULDN'T KILL THEM; THEY WERE, AT LEAST IN PART, STILL OUR LOVED ONES. WE DECIDED TO PROTECT THEM...

"A FEW OF US, ANYWAY. THAT'S THE REASON THIS TOWN IS SO EMPTY."

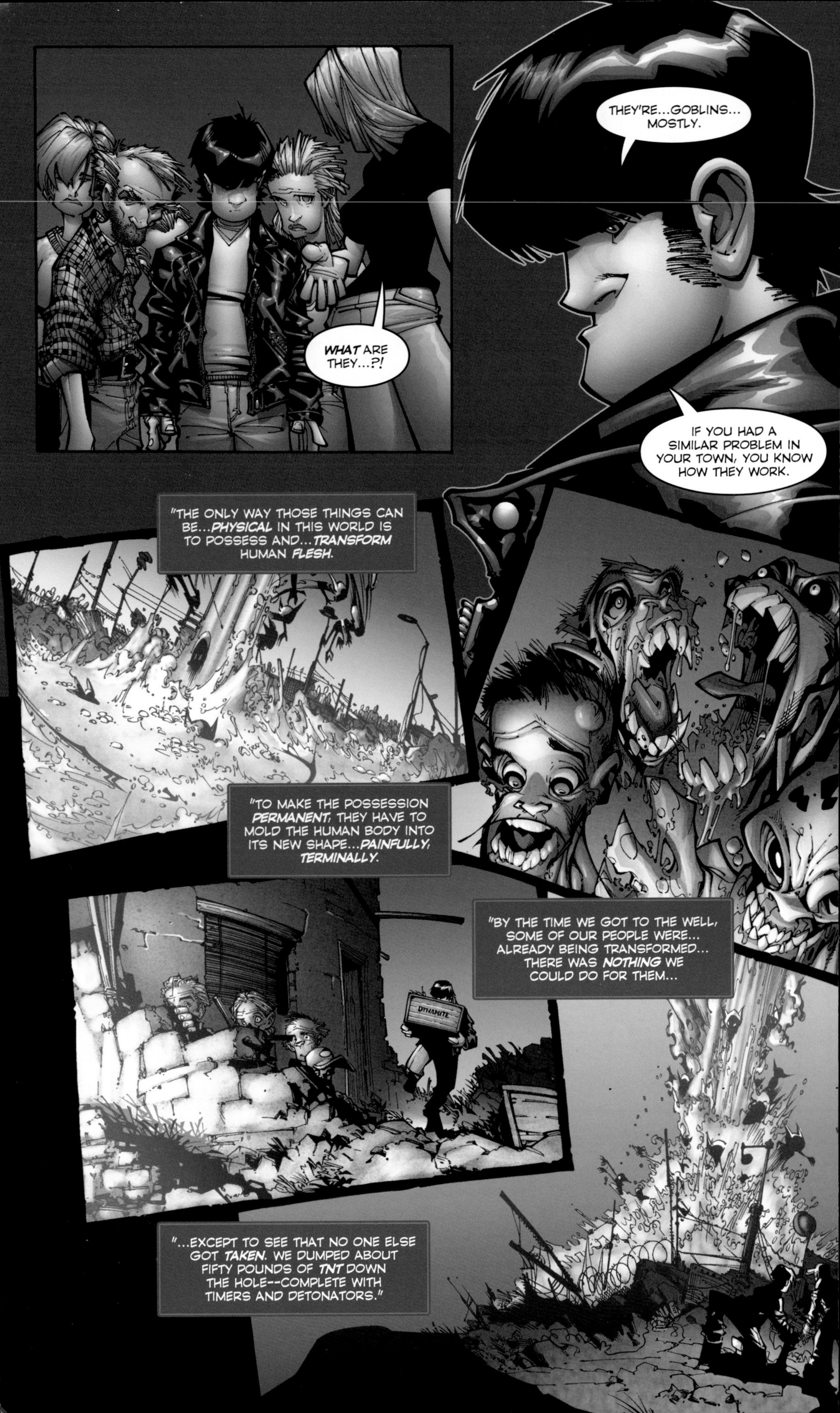
WHAT ARE THEY...?!
THEY'RE...GOBLINS... MOSTLY.
IF YOU HAD A SIMILAR PROBLEM IN YOUR TOWN, YOU KNOW HOW THEY WORK.
"THE ONLY WAY THOSE THINGS CAN BE...PHYSICAL IN THIS WORLD IS TO POSSESS AND...TRANSFORM HUMAN FLESH.
"TO MAKE THE POSSESSION PERMANENT, THEY HAVE TO MOLD THE HUMAN BODY INTO ITS NEW SHAPE...PAINFULLY, TERMINALLY.
"BY THE TIME WE GOT TO THE WELL, SOME OF OUR PEOPLE WERE... ALREADY BEING TRANSFORMED... THERE WAS NOTHING WE COULD DO FOR THEM...
DYNAMITE
"...EXCEPT TO SEE THAT NO ONE ELSE GOT TAKEN. WE DUMPED ABOUT FIFTY POUNDS OF TNT DOWN THE HOLE--COMPLETE WITH TIMERS AND DETONATORS."

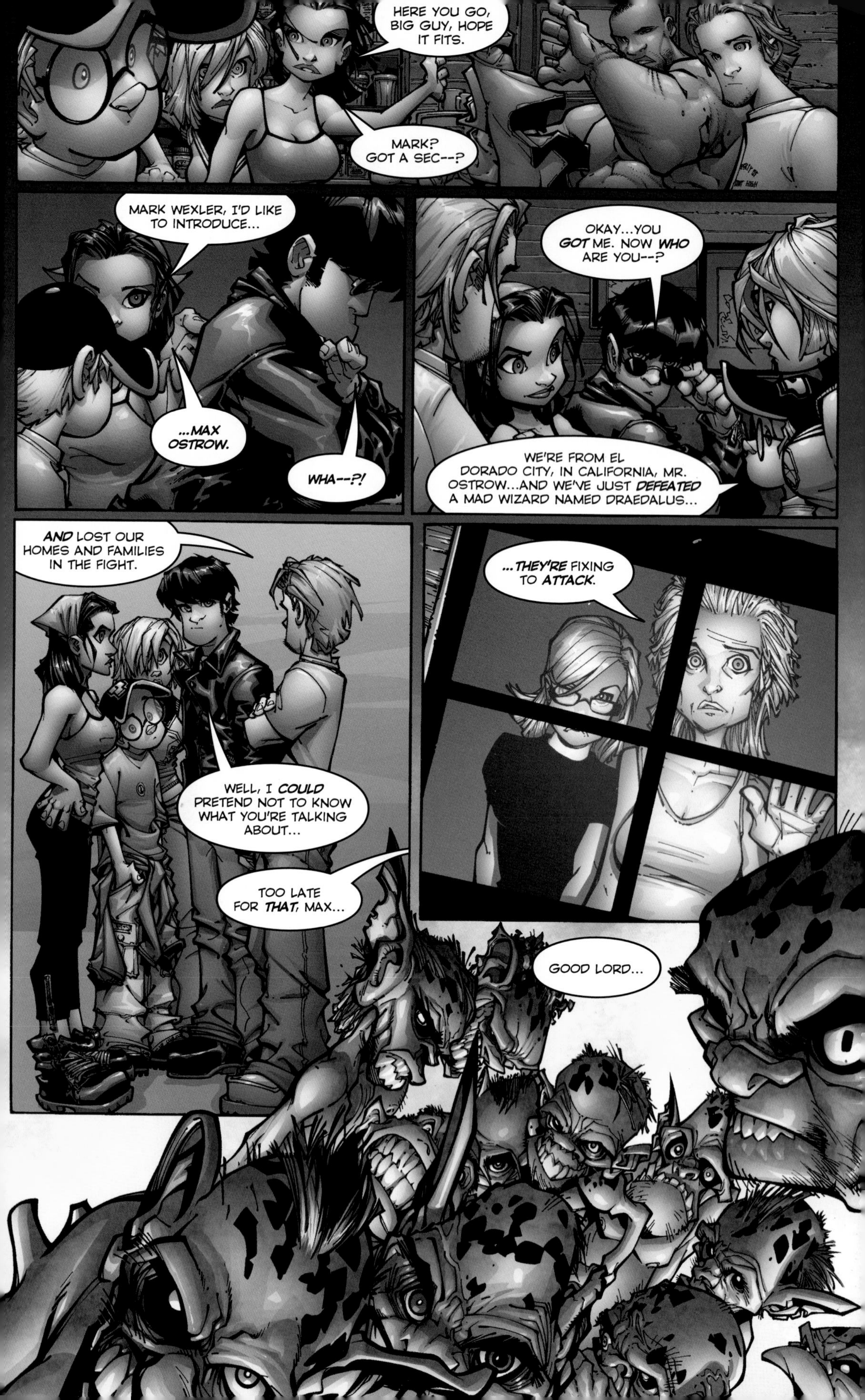
HERE YOU GO, BIG GUY, HOPE IT FITS.
MARK? GOT A SEC--?
MARK WEXLER, I'D LIKE TO INTRODUCE...
...MAX OSTROW.
WHA--?!
OKAY...YOU GOT ME. NOW WHO ARE YOU--?
WE'RE FROM EL DORADO CITY, IN CALIFORNIA, MR. OSTROW...AND WE'VE JUST DEFEATED A MAD WIZARD NAMED DRAEDALUS...
AND LOST OUR HOMES AND FAMILIES IN THE FIGHT.
WELL, I COULD PRETEND NOT TO KNOW WHAT YOU'RE TALKING ABOUT...
TOO LATE FOR THAT, MAX...
...THEY'RE FIXING TO ATTACK.
GOOD LORD...

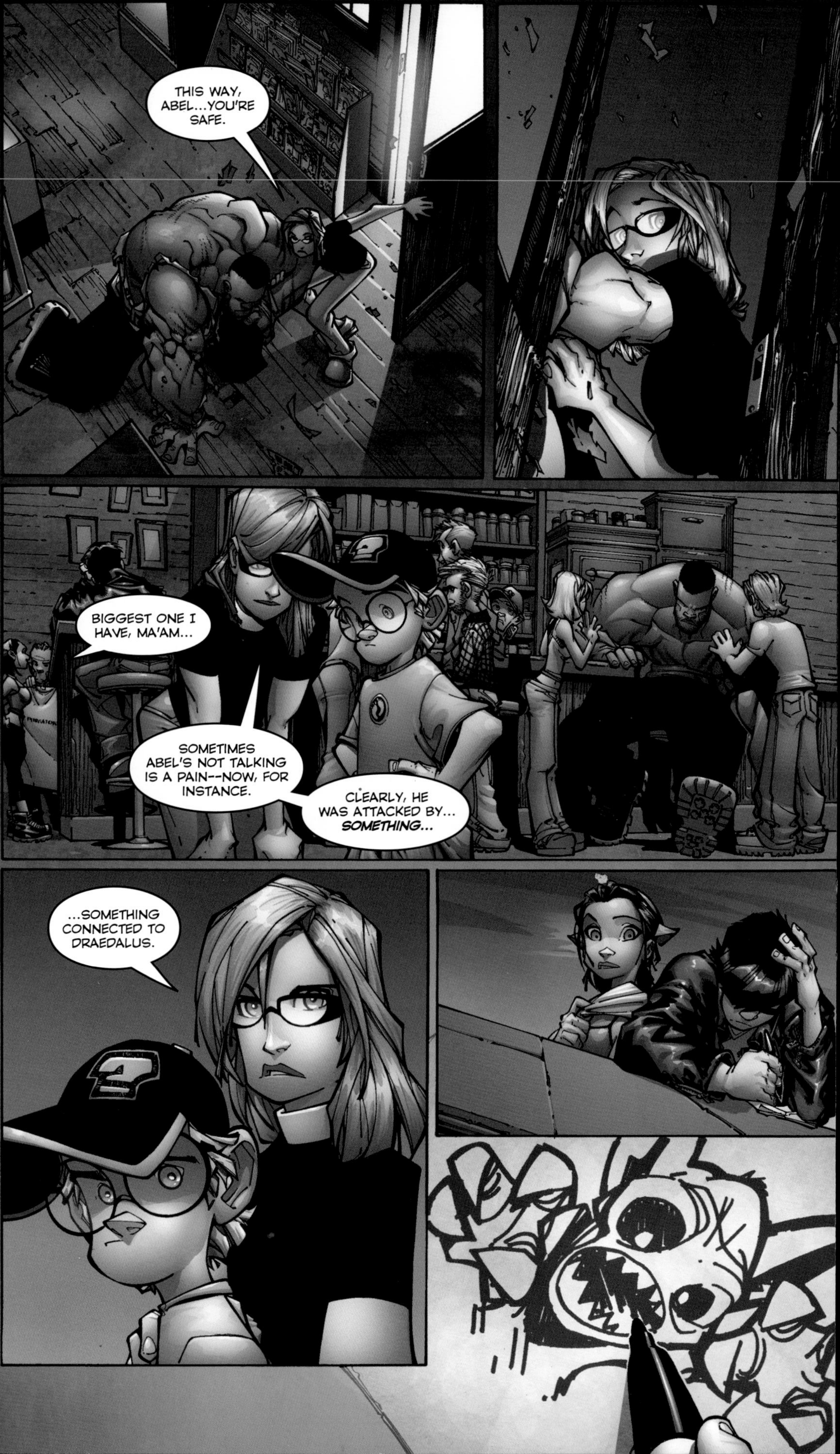
THIS WAY, ABEL...YOU'RE SAFE.
BIGGEST ONE I HAVE, MA'AM...
SOMETIMES ABEL'S NOT TALKING IS A PAIN--NOW, FOR INSTANCE.
CLEARLY, HE WAS ATTACKED BY... SOMETHING...
...SOMETHING CONNECTED TO DRAEDALUS.

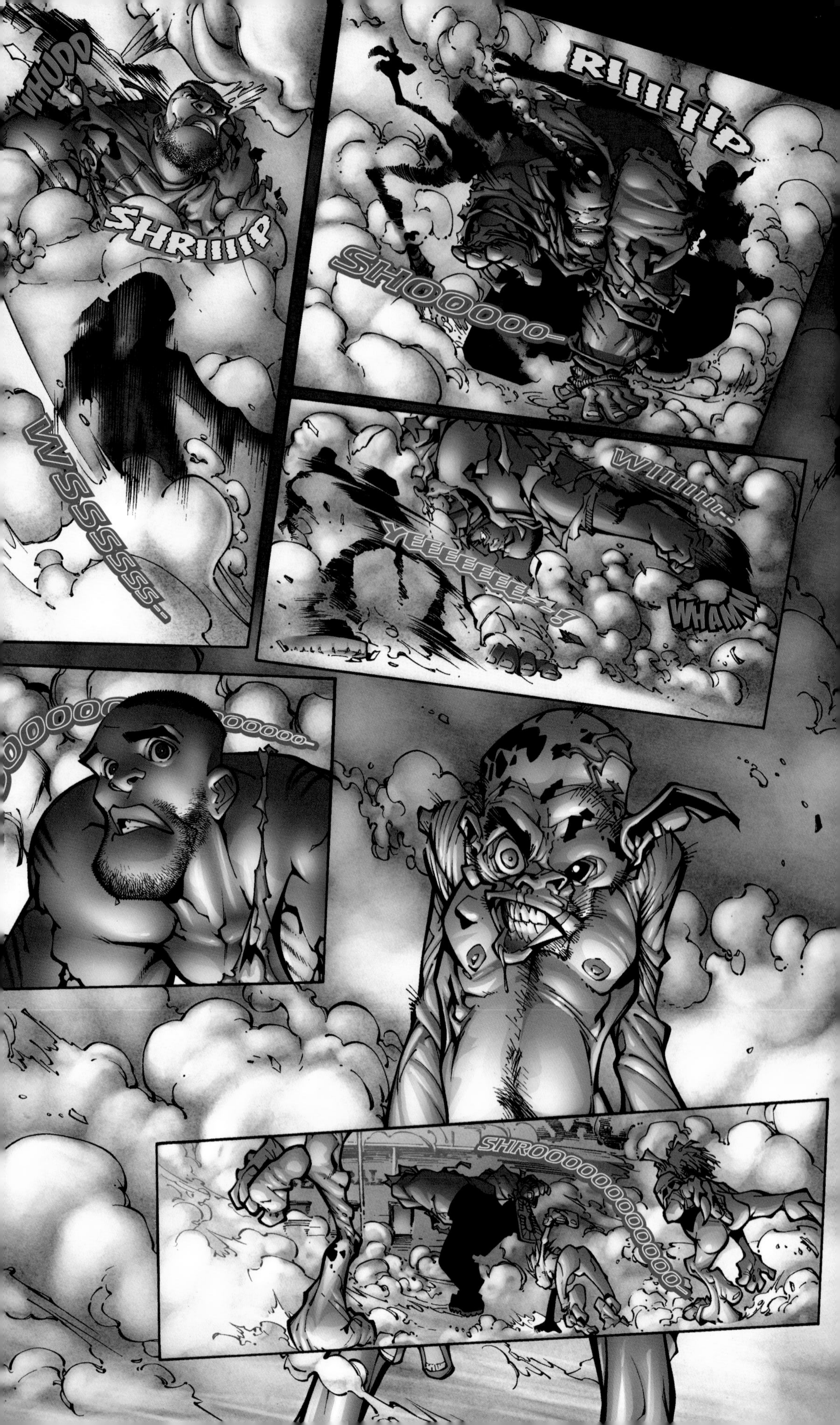
WHUDD
SHRIIIIP
WSSSSSSS--
RIIIIIIP
SHOOOOO--
WIIIIIII--
YEEEEEEE--!
WHAM
SHROOOOOOOOOOOO--

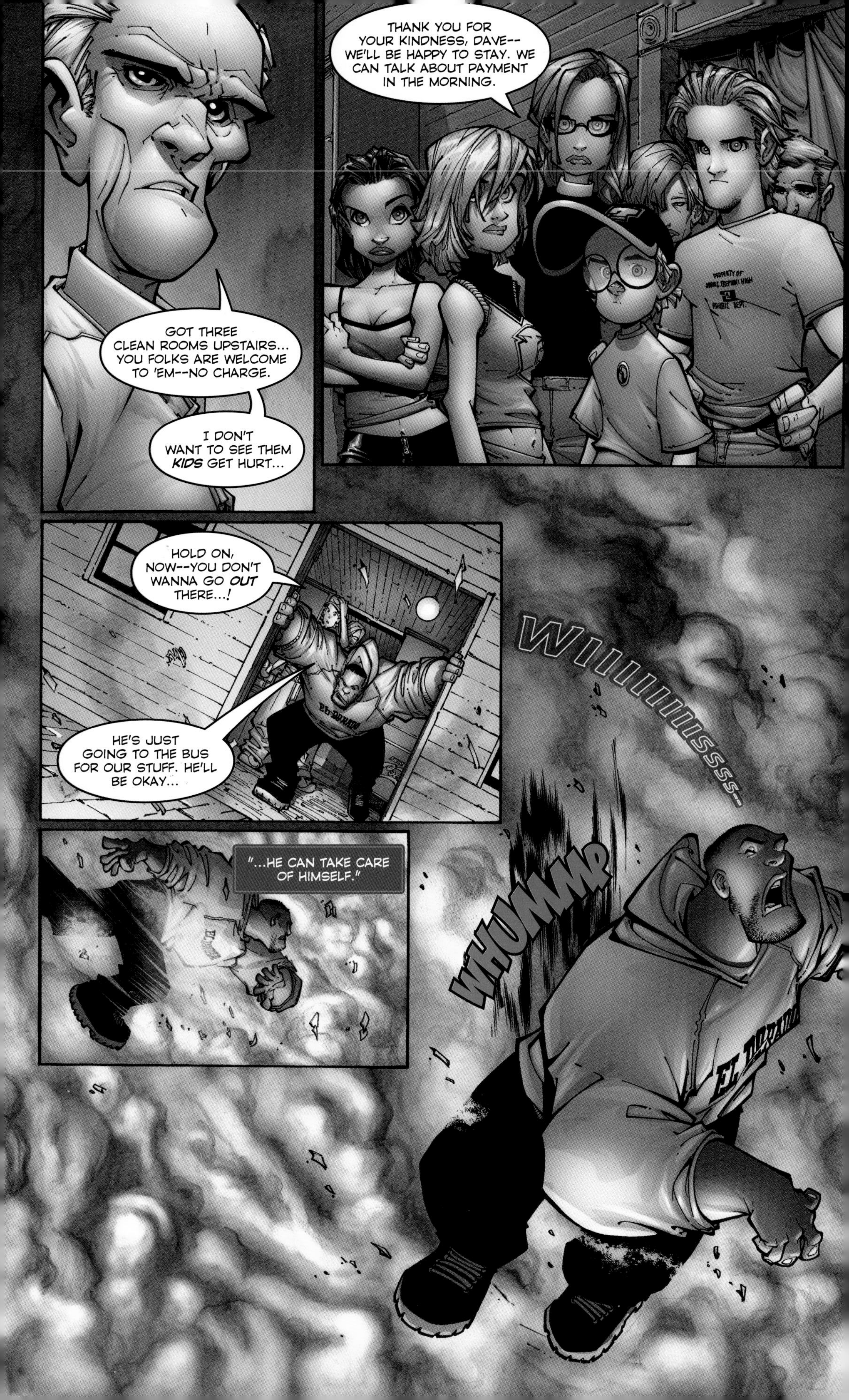
GOT THREE CLEAN ROOMS UPSTAIRS... YOU FOLKS ARE WELCOME TO 'EM--NO CHARGE.
I DON'T WANT TO SEE THEM KIDS GET HURT...
THANK YOU FOR YOUR KINDNESS, DAVE--WE'LL BE HAPPY TO STAY. WE CAN TALK ABOUT PAYMENT IN THE MORNING.
HOLD ON, NOW--YOU DON'T WANNA GO OUT THERE...!
HE'S JUST GOING TO THE BUS FOR OUR STUFF. HE'LL BE OKAY...
"...HE CAN TAKE CARE OF HIMSELF."
WIIIIIIIISSSSS-
WHUMMP
EL DORADO

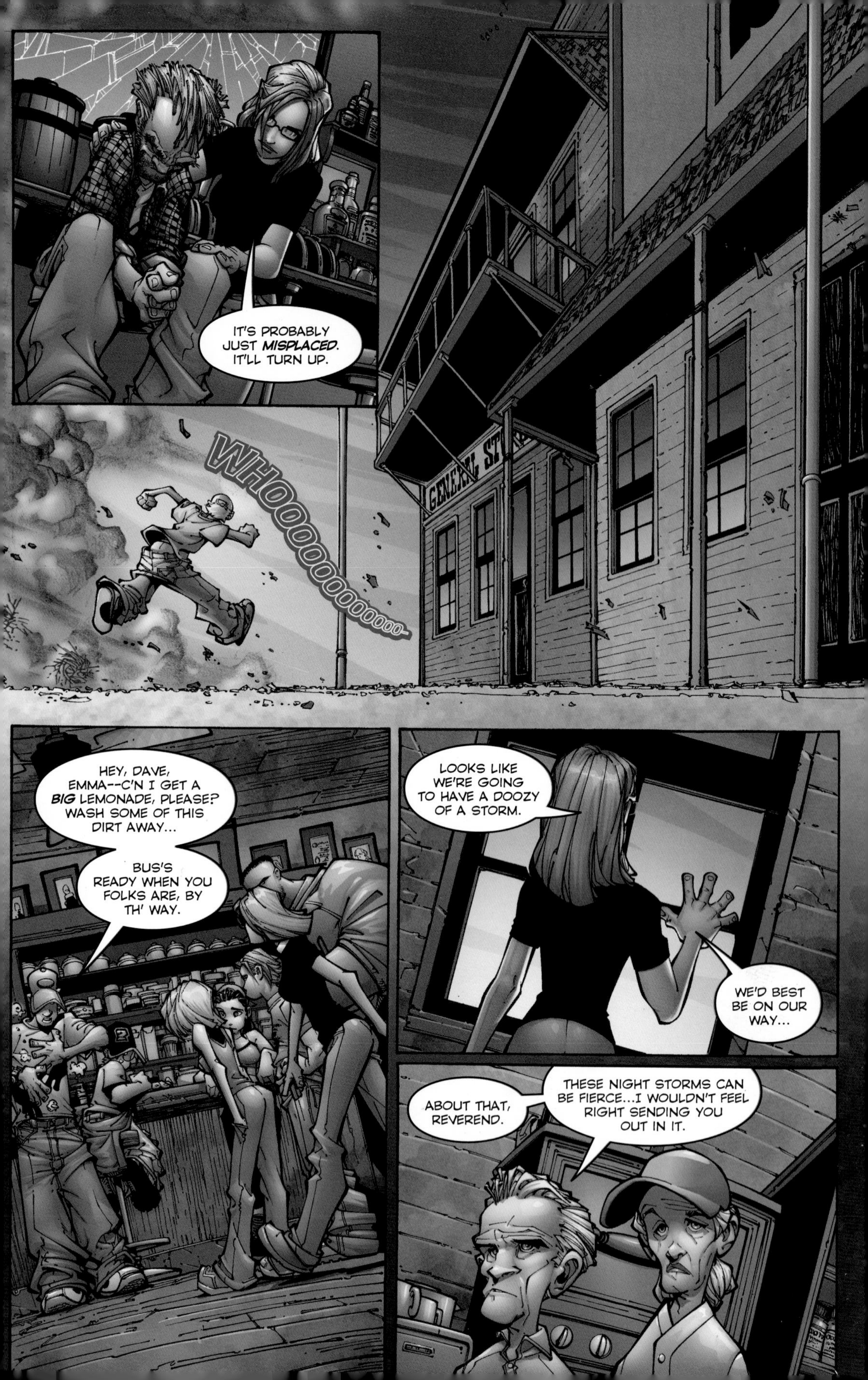

IT'S PROBABLY JUST MISPLACED. IT'LL TURN UP.
WHOOOOOOOOOOOOO-
GENERAL STORE
HEY, DAVE, EMMA--C'N I GET A BIG LEMONADE, PLEASE? WASH SOME OF THIS DIRT AWAY...
BUS'S READY WHEN YOU FOLKS ARE, BY TH' WAY.
LOOKS LIKE WE'RE GOING TO HAVE A DOOZY OF A STORM.
WE'D BEST BE ON OUR WAY...
ABOUT THAT, REVEREND.
THESE NIGHT STORMS CAN BE FIERCE...I WOULDN'T FEEL RIGHT SENDING YOU OUT IN IT.

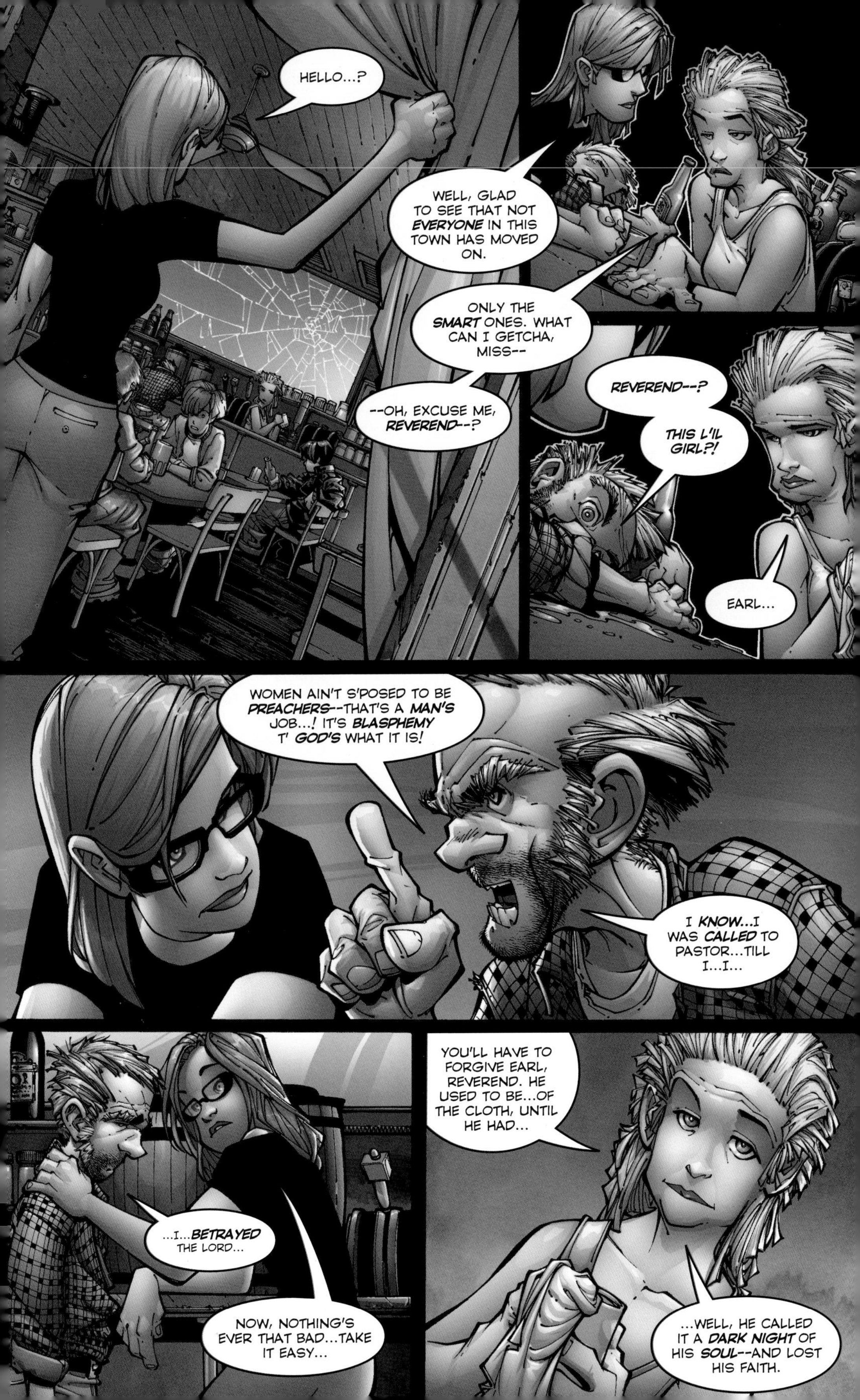
HELLO...?
WELL, GLAD TO SEE THAT NOT EVERYONE IN THIS TOWN HAS MOVED ON.
ONLY THE SMART ONES. WHAT CAN I GETCHA, MISS--
--OH, EXCUSE ME, REVEREND--?
REVEREND--?
THIS L'IL GIRL?!
EARL...
WOMEN AIN'T S'POSED TO BE PREACHERS--THAT'S A MAN'S JOB...! IT'S BLASPHEMY T' GOD'S WHAT IT IS!
I KNOW...I WAS CALLED TO PASTOR...TILL I...I...
...I...BETRAYED THE LORD...
NOW, NOTHING'S EVER THAT BAD...TAKE IT EASY...
YOU'LL HAVE TO FORGIVE EARL, REVEREND. HE USED TO BE...OF THE CLOTH, UNTIL HE HAD...
...WELL, HE CALLED IT A DARK NIGHT OF HIS SOUL--AND LOST HIS FAITH.

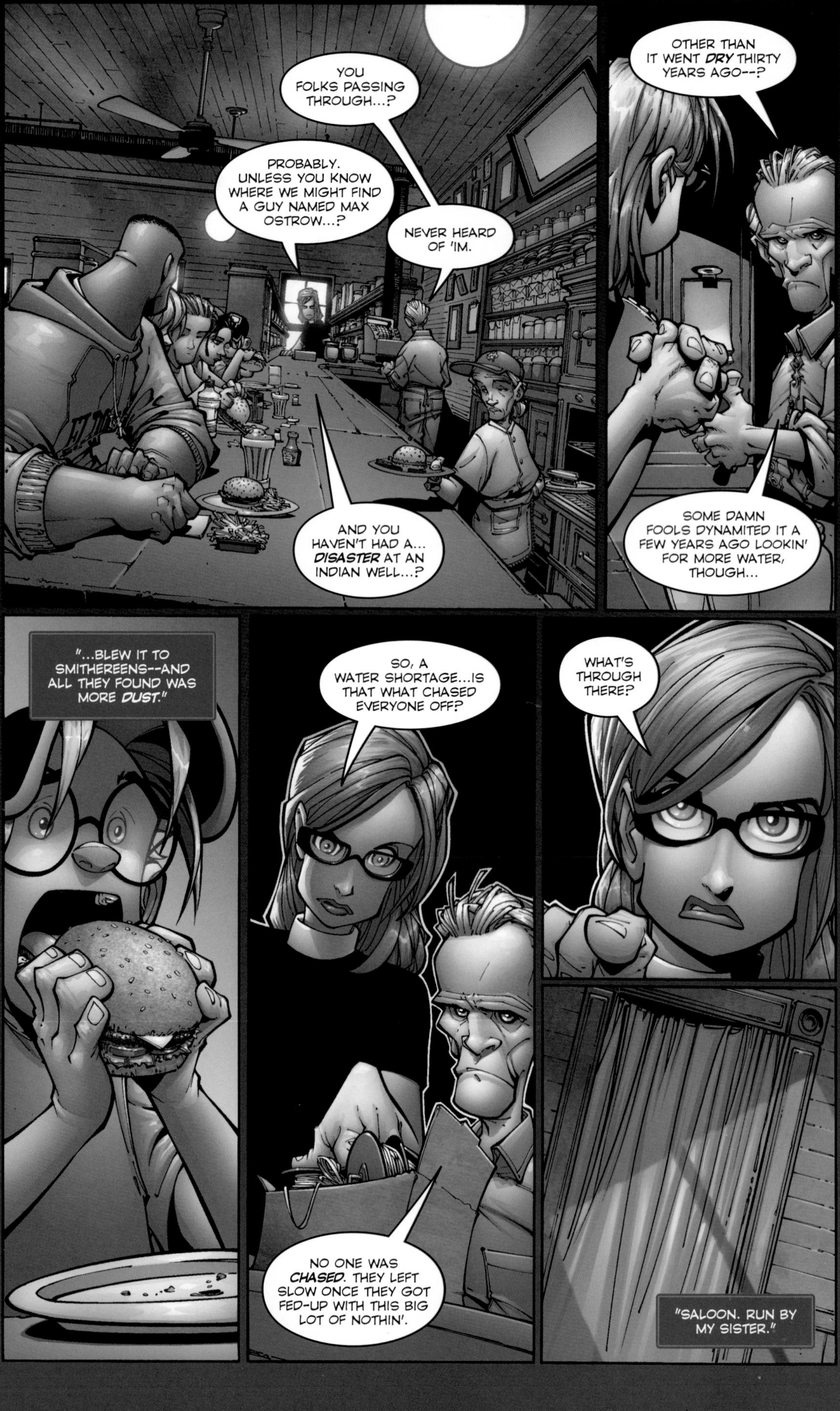
YOU FOLKS PASSING THROUGH...?
PROBABLY. UNLESS YOU KNOW WHERE WE MIGHT FIND A GUY NAMED MAX OSTROW...?
NEVER HEARD OF 'IM.
AND YOU HAVEN'T HAD A... DISASTER AT AN INDIAN WELL...?
OTHER THAN IT WENT DRY THIRTY YEARS AGO--?
SOME DAMN FOOLS DYNAMITED IT A FEW YEARS AGO LOOKIN' FOR MORE WATER, THOUGH...
"...BLEW IT TO SMITHEREENS--AND ALL THEY FOUND WAS MORE DUST."
SO, A WATER SHORTAGE...IS THAT WHAT CHASED EVERYONE OFF?
NO ONE WAS CHASED. THEY LEFT SLOW ONCE THEY GOT FED-UP WITH THIS BIG LOT OF NOTHIN'.
WHAT'S THROUGH THERE?
"SALOON. RUN BY MY SISTER."

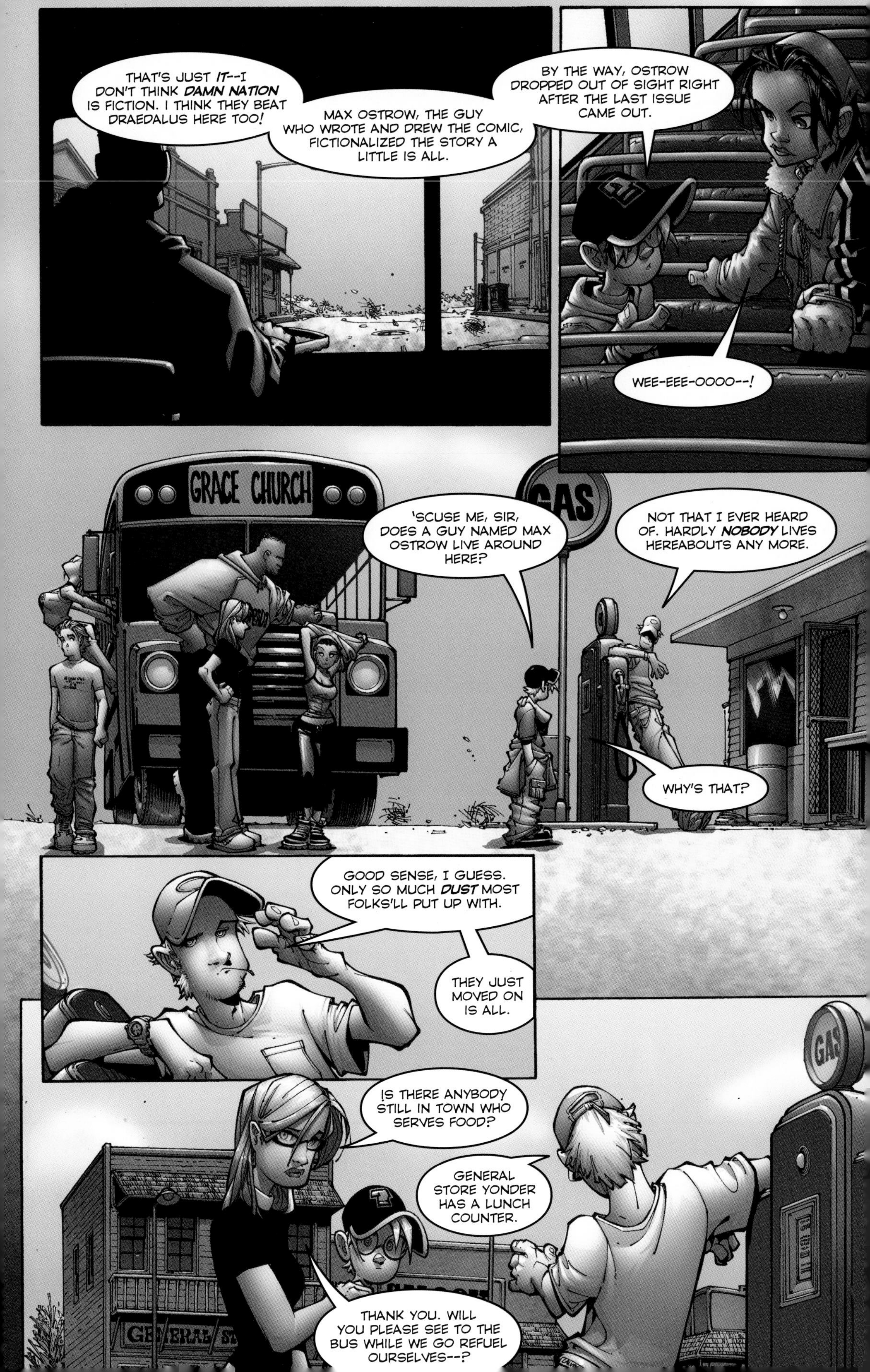
THAT'S JUST IT--I DON'T THINK DAMN NATION IS FICTION. I THINK THEY BEAT DRAEDALUS HERE TOO!
MAX OSTROW, THE GUY WHO WROTE AND DREW THE COMIC, FICTIONALIZED THE STORY A LITTLE IS ALL.
BY THE WAY, OSTROW DROPPED OUT OF SIGHT RIGHT AFTER THE LAST ISSUE CAME OUT.
WEE-EEE-OOOO--!
GRACE CHURCH
GAS
'SCUSE ME, SIR, DOES A GUY NAMED MAX OSTROW LIVE AROUND HERE?
NOT THAT I EVER HEARD OF. HARDLY NOBODY LIVES HEREABOUTS ANY MORE.
WHY'S THAT?
GOOD SENSE, I GUESS. ONLY SO MUCH DUST MOST FOLKS'LL PUT UP WITH.
THEY JUST MOVED ON IS ALL.
GAS
IS THERE ANYBODY STILL IN TOWN WHO SERVES FOOD?
GENERAL STORE YONDER HAS A LUNCH COUNTER.
THANK YOU. WILL YOU PLEASE SEE TO THE BUS WHILE WE GO REFUEL OURSELVES--?

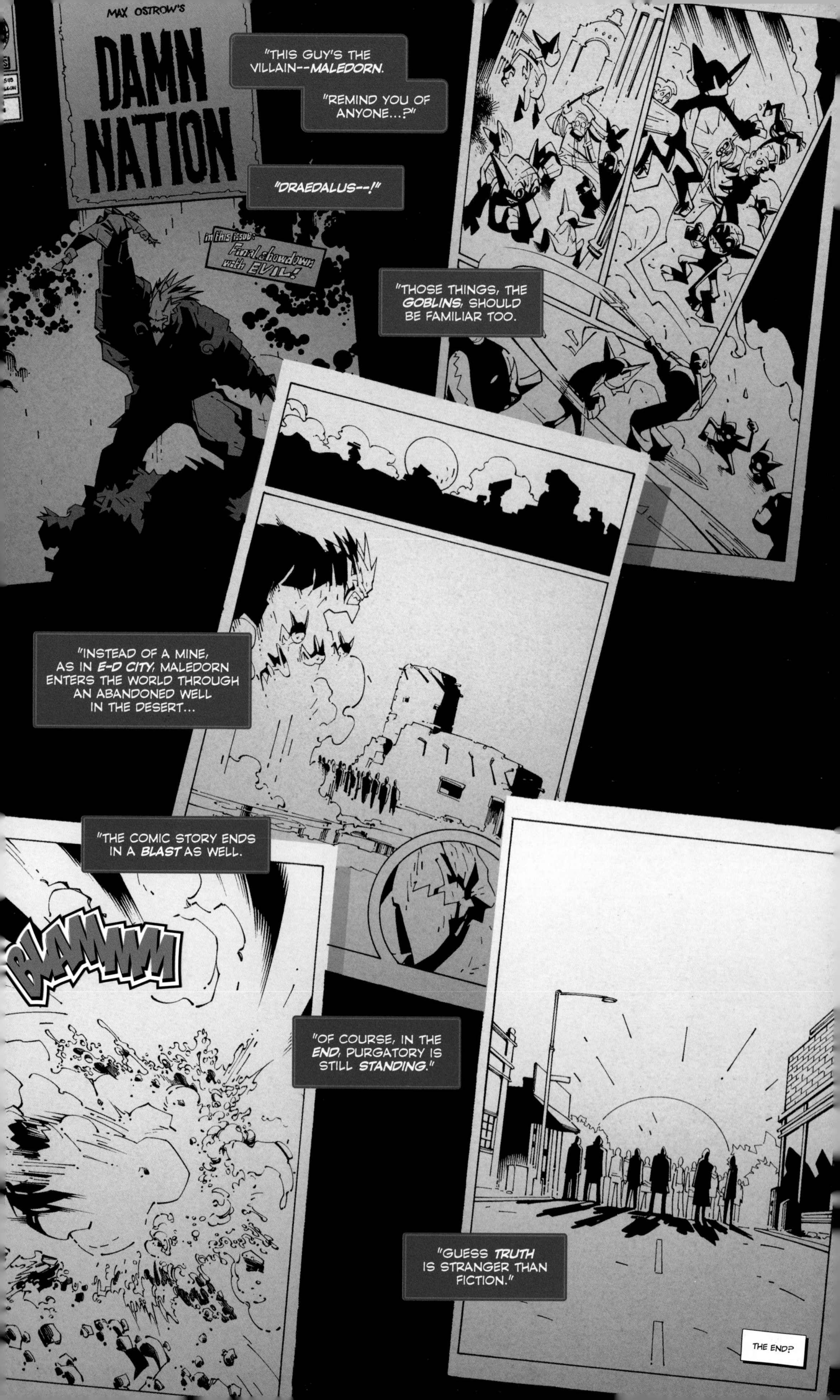
MAX OSTROW'S
DAMN NATION
"THIS GUY'S THE VILLAIN--*MALEDORN*.
"REMIND YOU OF ANYONE...?"
"DRAEDALUS--!"
in this issue: Final showdown with EVIL!
"THOSE THINGS, THE *GOBLINS*, SHOULD BE FAMILIAR TOO.
"INSTEAD OF A MINE, AS IN *E-D CITY*, MALEDORN ENTERS THE WORLD THROUGH AN ABANDONED WELL IN THE DESERT...
"THE COMIC STORY ENDS IN A *BLAST* AS WELL.
BLAMMMM
"OF COURSE, IN THE *END*, PURGATORY IS STILL *STANDING*."
"GUESS *TRUTH* IS STRANGER THAN FICTION."
THE END?

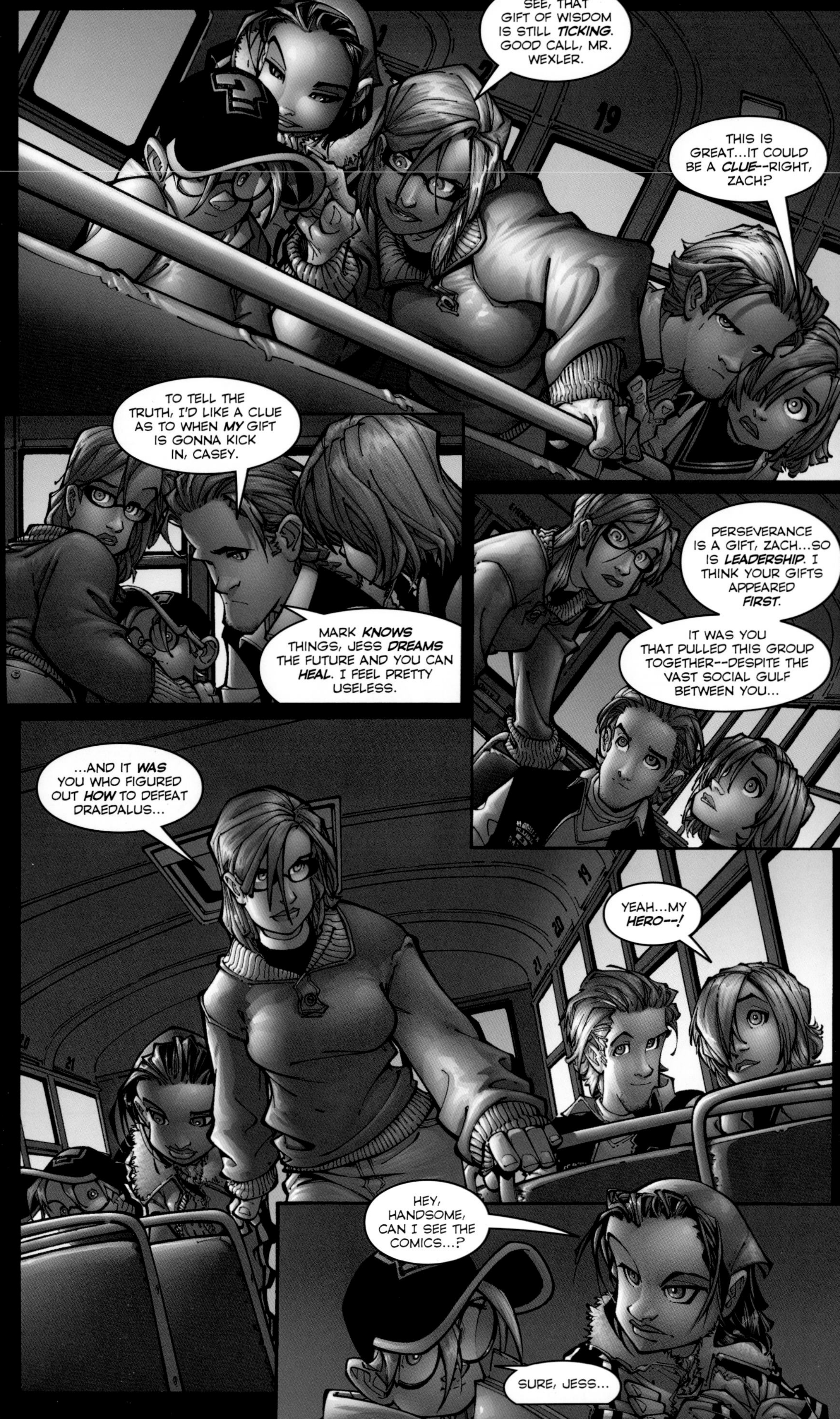
SEE, THAT GIFT OF WISDOM IS STILL *TICKING*. GOOD CALL, MR. WEXLER.
THIS IS GREAT...IT COULD BE A *CLUE*--RIGHT, ZACH?
TO TELL THE TRUTH, I'D LIKE A CLUE AS TO WHEN *MY* GIFT IS GONNA KICK IN, CASEY.
MARK *KNOWS* THINGS, JESS *DREAMS* THE FUTURE AND YOU CAN *HEAL*. I FEEL PRETTY USELESS.
PERSEVERANCE IS A GIFT, ZACH...SO IS *LEADERSHIP*. I THINK YOUR GIFTS APPEARED *FIRST*.
IT WAS YOU THAT PULLED THIS GROUP TOGETHER--DESPITE THE VAST SOCIAL GULF BETWEEN YOU...
...AND IT *WAS* YOU WHO FIGURED OUT *HOW* TO DEFEAT DRAEDALUS...
YEAH...MY *HERO--!*
HEY, HANDSOME, CAN I SEE THE COMICS...?
SURE, JESS...

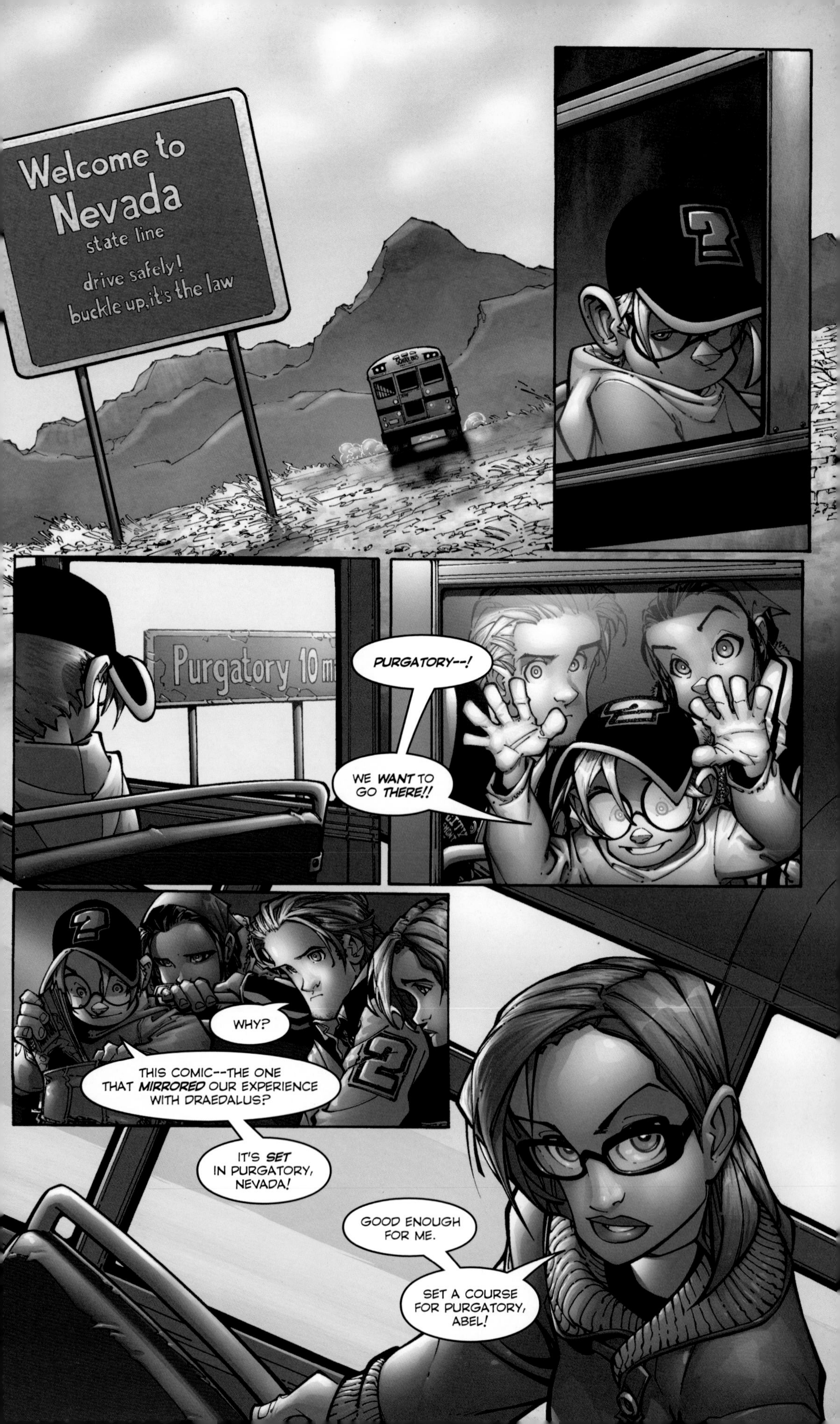

Welcome to Nevada
state line
drive safely!
buckle up, it's the law
Purgatory 10 mi
PURGATORY--!
WE WANT TO GO THERE!!
WHY?
THIS COMIC--THE ONE THAT MIRRORED OUR EXPERIENCE WITH DRAEDALUS?
IT'S SET IN PURGATORY, NEVADA!
GOOD ENOUGH FOR ME.
SET A COURSE FOR PURGATORY, ABEL!

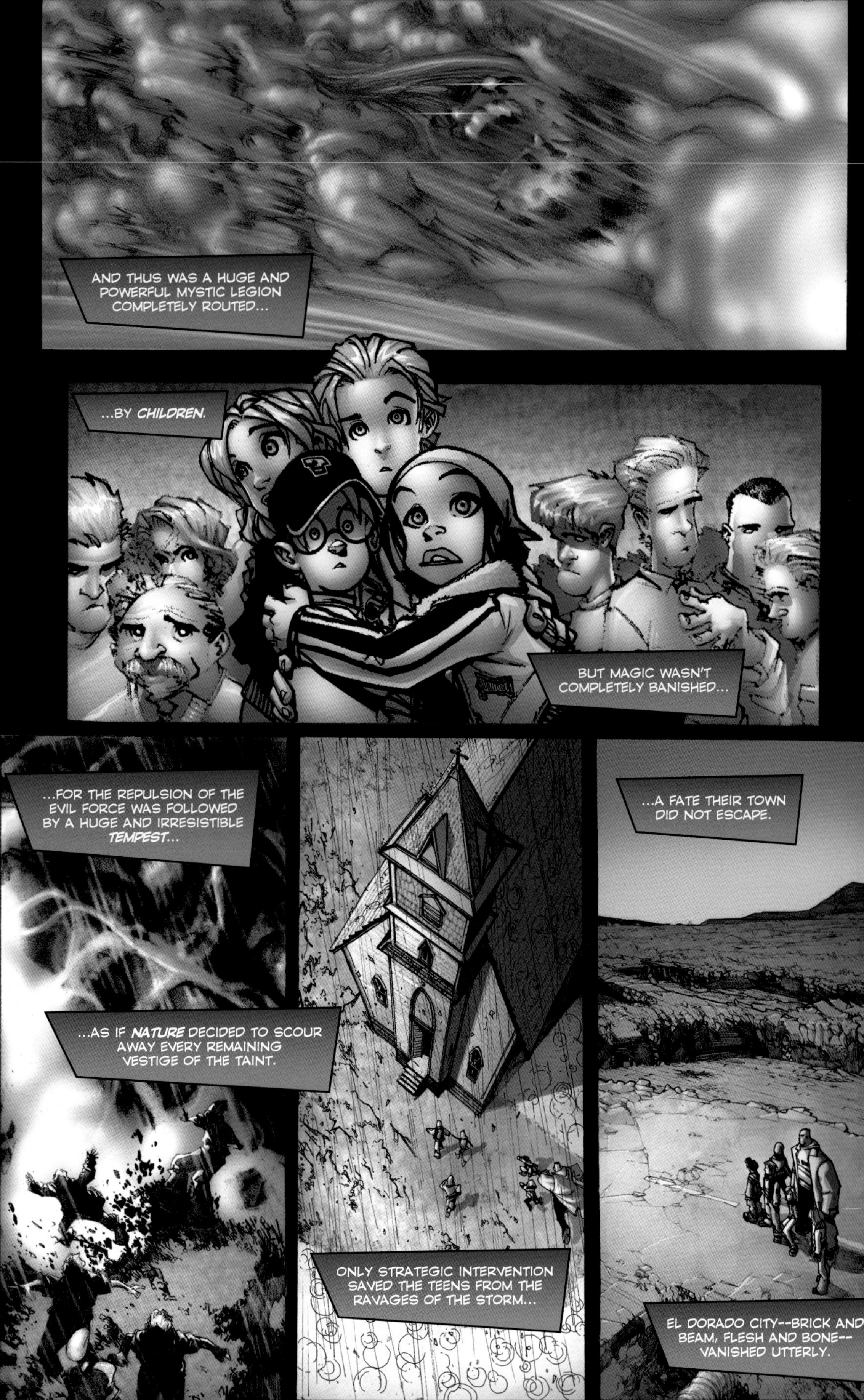
AND THUS WAS A HUGE AND POWERFUL MYSTIC LEGION COMPLETELY ROUTED...
...BY CHILDREN.
BUT MAGIC WASN'T COMPLETELY BANISHED...
...FOR THE REPULSION OF THE EVIL FORCE WAS FOLLOWED BY A HUGE AND IRRESISTIBLE TEMPEST...
...AS IF NATURE DECIDED TO SCOUR AWAY EVERY REMAINING VESTIGE OF THE TAINT.
ONLY STRATEGIC INTERVENTION SAVED THE TEENS FROM THE RAVAGES OF THE STORM...
...A FATE THEIR TOWN DID NOT ESCAPE.
EL DORADO CITY--BRICK AND BEAM, FLESH AND BONE--VANISHED UTTERLY.

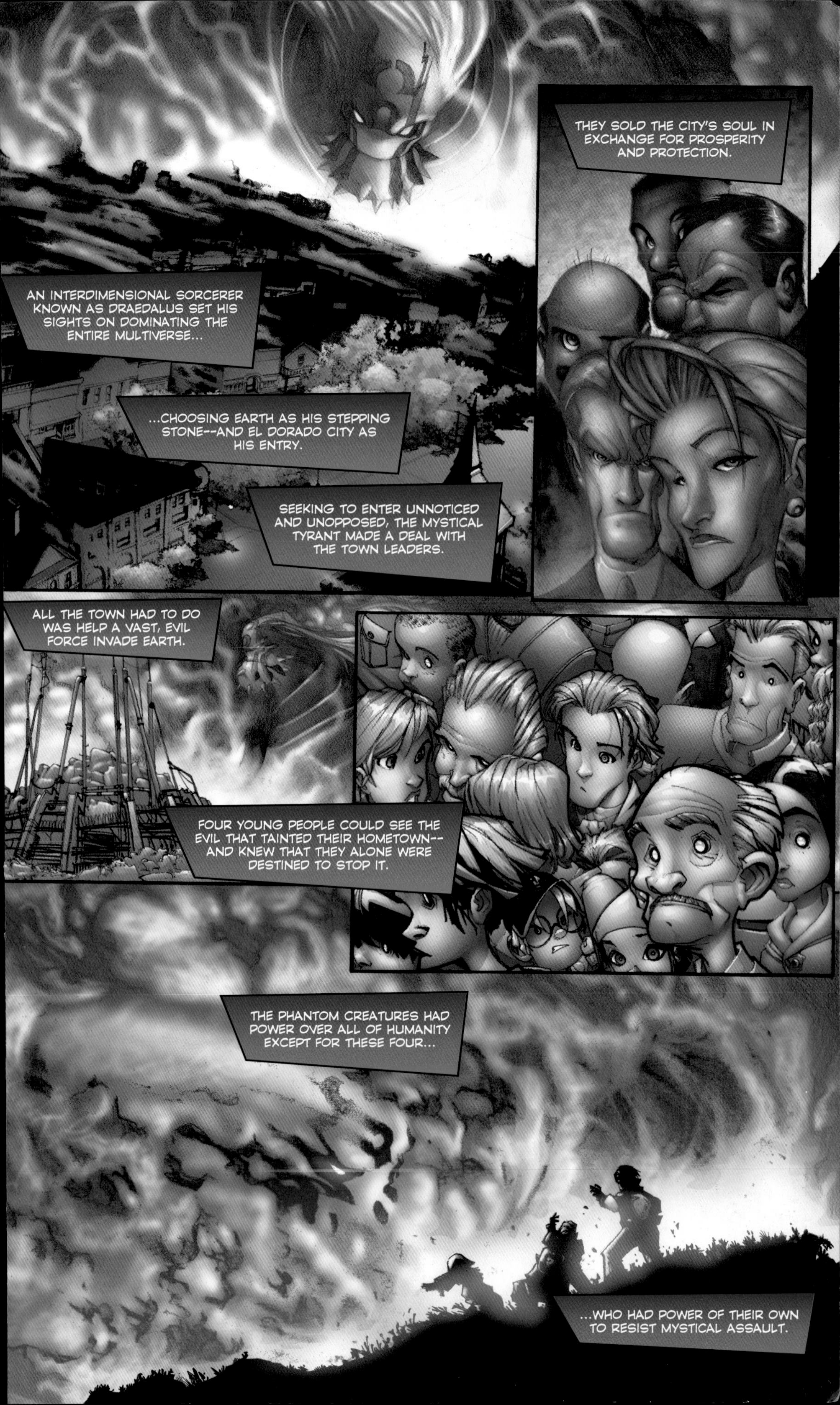

AN INTERDIMENSIONAL SORCERER KNOWN AS DRAEDALUS SET HIS SIGHTS ON DOMINATING THE ENTIRE MULTIVERSE...
...CHOOSING EARTH AS HIS STEPPING STONE--AND EL DORADO CITY AS HIS ENTRY.
SEEKING TO ENTER UNNOTICED AND UNOPPOSED, THE MYSTICAL TYRANT MADE A DEAL WITH THE TOWN LEADERS.
THEY SOLD THE CITY'S SOUL IN EXCHANGE FOR PROSPERITY AND PROTECTION.
ALL THE TOWN HAD TO DO WAS HELP A VAST, EVIL FORCE INVADE EARTH.
FOUR YOUNG PEOPLE COULD SEE THE EVIL THAT TAINTED THEIR HOMETOWN--AND KNEW THAT THEY ALONE WERE DESTINED TO STOP IT.
THE PHANTOM CREATURES HAD POWER OVER ALL OF HUMANITY EXCEPT FOR THESE FOUR...
...WHO HAD POWER OF THEIR OWN TO RESIST MYSTICAL ASSAULT.

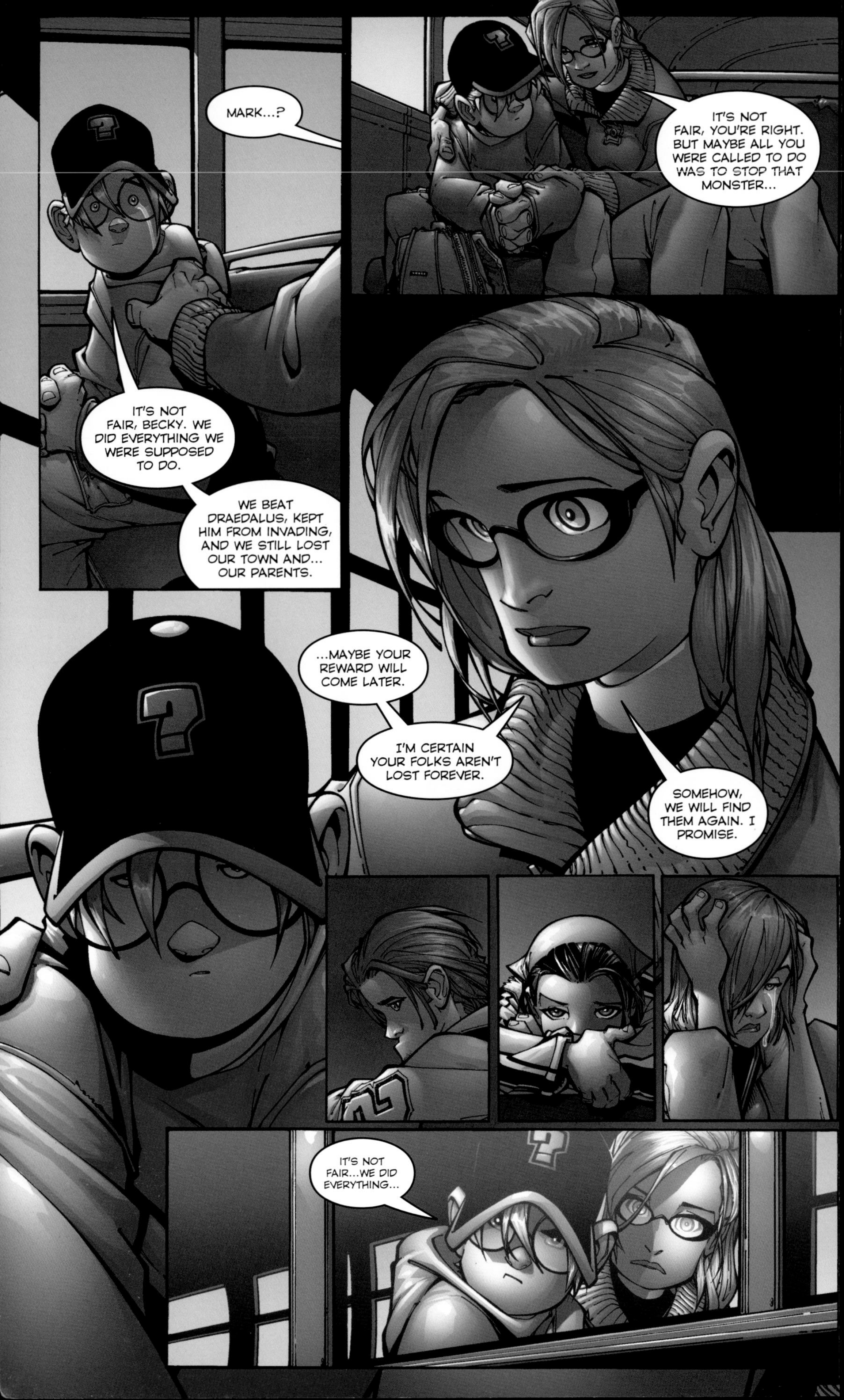
MARK...?
IT'S NOT FAIR, YOU'RE RIGHT. BUT MAYBE ALL YOU WERE CALLED TO DO WAS TO STOP THAT MONSTER...
IT'S NOT FAIR, BECKY. WE DID EVERYTHING WE WERE SUPPOSED TO DO.
WE BEAT DRAEDALUS, KEPT HIM FROM INVADING, AND WE STILL LOST OUR TOWN AND... OUR PARENTS.
...MAYBE YOUR REWARD WILL COME LATER.
I'M CERTAIN YOUR FOLKS AREN'T LOST FOREVER.
SOMEHOW, WE WILL FIND THEM AGAIN. I PROMISE.
IT'S NOT FAIR...WE DID EVERYTHING...

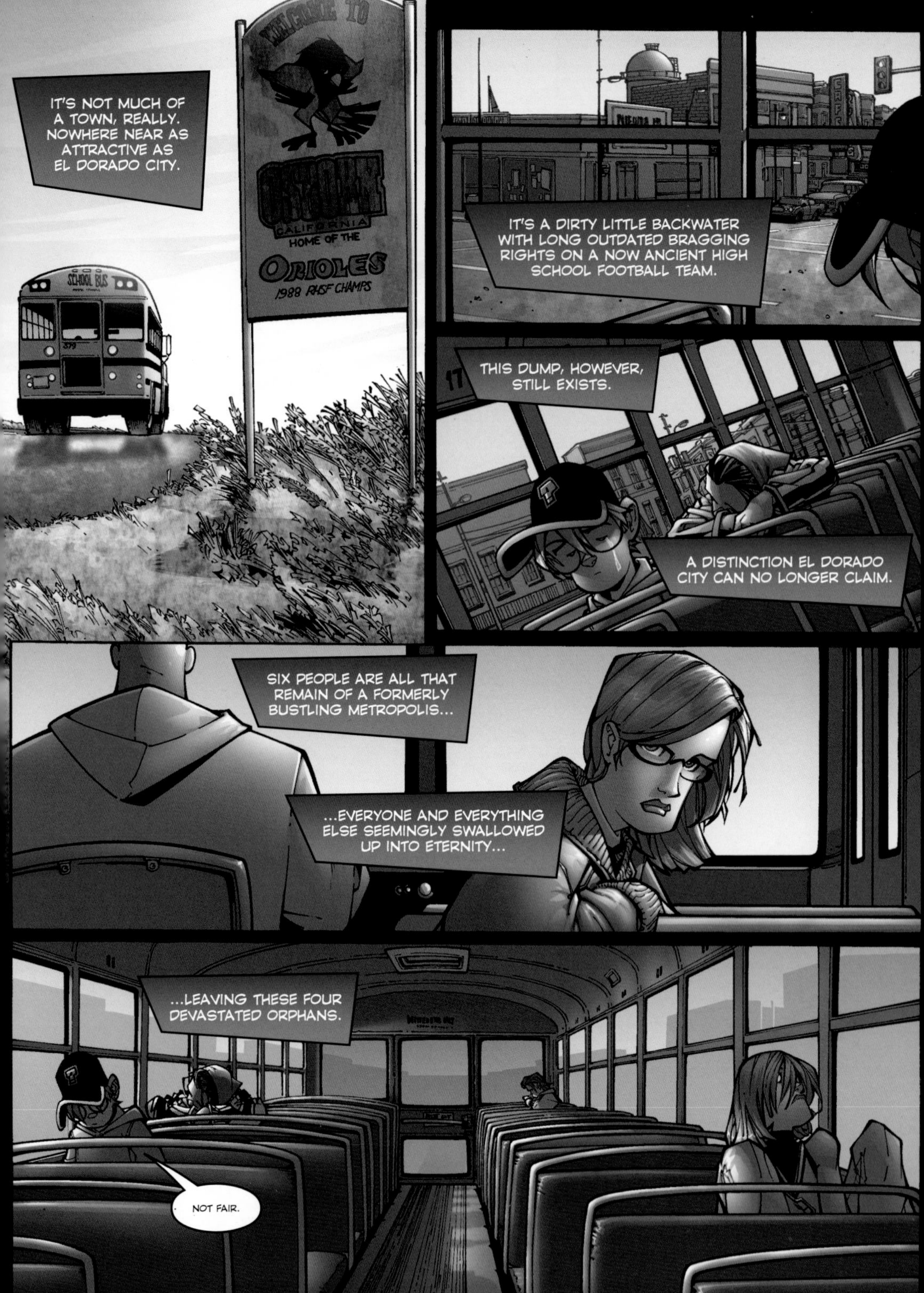
IT'S NOT MUCH OF A TOWN, REALLY. NOWHERE NEAR AS ATTRACTIVE AS EL DORADO CITY.
WELCOME TO
CALIFORNIA
HOME OF THE
ORIOLES
1988 RHSF CHAMPS
SCHOOL BUS
IT'S A DIRTY LITTLE BACKWATER WITH LONG OUTDATED BRAGGING RIGHTS ON A NOW ANCIENT HIGH SCHOOL FOOTBALL TEAM.
THIS DUMP, HOWEVER, STILL EXISTS.
A DISTINCTION EL DORADO CITY CAN NO LONGER CLAIM.
SIX PEOPLE ARE ALL THAT REMAIN OF A FORMERLY BUSTLING METROPOLIS...
...EVERYONE AND EVERYTHING ELSE SEEMINGLY SWALLOWED UP INTO ETERNITY...
...LEAVING THESE FOUR DEVASTATED ORPHANS.
NOT FAIR.

CHAPTER SEVEN

LEFT BEHIND

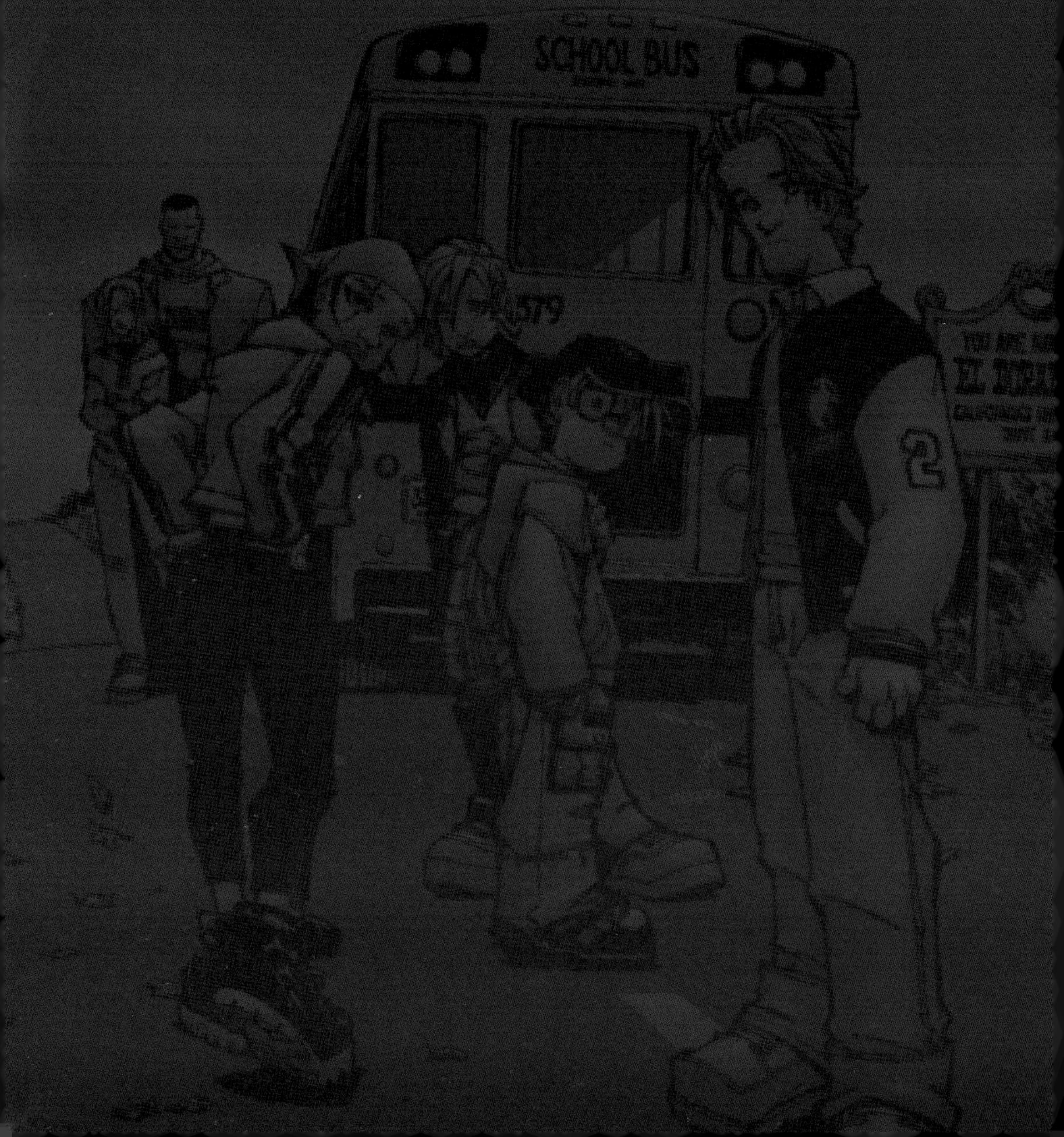
SCHOOL BUS

CREATED BY
HUMBERTO RAMOS
BRIAN AUGUSTYN

SCRIPT BY
BRIAN AUGUSTYN

PENCILS BY
HUMBERTO RAMOS

INKS BY
SANDRA HOPE

COLORS BY
STUDIO F

LETTERS BY
SERGIO GARCIA CHAPTERS 7, 9, 11, 12
ED ROEDER CHAPTER 8
JENNA GARCIA CHAPTERS 10, 11

LOGO DESIGN BY
LEONARDO OLEA

COVER BY
HUMBERTO RAMOS
COLORS BY EDGAR DELGADO

ORIGINAL SERIES
EDITOR
SCOTT DUNBIER

BOOM! STUDIOS EDITION
PRODUCTION AND DESIGN
SCOTT NEWMAN
ASSISTANT EDITOR
ALEX GALER
EDITOR
DAFNA PLEBAN

ROSS RICHIE CEO & Founder
MATT GAGNON Editor-in-Chief
FILIP SABLIK President of Publishing & Marketing
STEPHEN CHRISTY President of Development
LANCE KREITER VP of Licensing & Merchandising
PHIL BARBARO VP of Finance
BRYCE CARLSON Managing Editor
MEL CAYLO Marketing Manager
SCOTT NEWMAN Production Design Manager
IRENE BRADISH Operations Manager
CHRISTINE DINH Brand Communications Manager
SIERRA HAHN Senior Editor
DAFNA PLEBAN Editor
SHANNON WATTERS Editor
ERIC HARBURN Editor
WHITNEY LEOPARD Associate Editor
JASMINE AMIRI Associate Editor

CHRIS ROSA Associate Editor
ALEX GALER Assistant Editor
CAMERON CHITTOCK Assistant Editor
MARY GUMPORT Assistant Editor
MATTHEW LEVINE Assistant Editor
KELSEY DIETERICH Production Designer
JILLIAN CRAB Production Designer
MICHELLE ANKLEY Production Design Assistant
GRACE PARK Production Design Assistant
AARON FERRARA Operations Coordinator
ELIZABETH LOUGHRIDGE Accounting Coordinator
JOSÉ MEZA Sales Assistant
JAMES ARRIOLA Mailroom Assistant
HOLLY AITCHISON Operations Assistant
STEPHANIE HOCUTT Marketing Assistant
SAM KUSEK Direct Market Assistant

OUT THERE Volume Two, August 2016. Published by BOOM! Studios, a division of Boom Entertainment, Inc. Out There is ™ & © 2016 Humberto Ramos and Brian Augustyn. Originally published in single magazine form as OUT THERE No. 7-12. ™ & © 2002 Humberto Ramos and Brian Augustyn. All rights reserved. BOOM! Studios™ and the BOOM! Studios logo are trademarks of Boom Entertainment, Inc., registered in various countries and categories. All characters, events, and institutions depicted herein are fictional. Any similarity between any of the names, characters, persons, events, and/or institutions in this publication to actual names, characters, persons, whether living or dead, events, and persons, is unintended and purely coincidental. BOOM! Studios does not read or accept unsolicited submissions of ideas, stories, or artwork.

A catalog record of this book is available from OCLC and from the BOOM! Studios website, www.boom-studios.com, on the Librarians Page.

BOOM! Studios, 5670 Wilshire Boulevard, Suite 450, Los Angeles, CA 90036-5679. Printed in China. First Printing. ISBN: 978-1-60886-819-3, eISBN: 978-1-61398-490-1

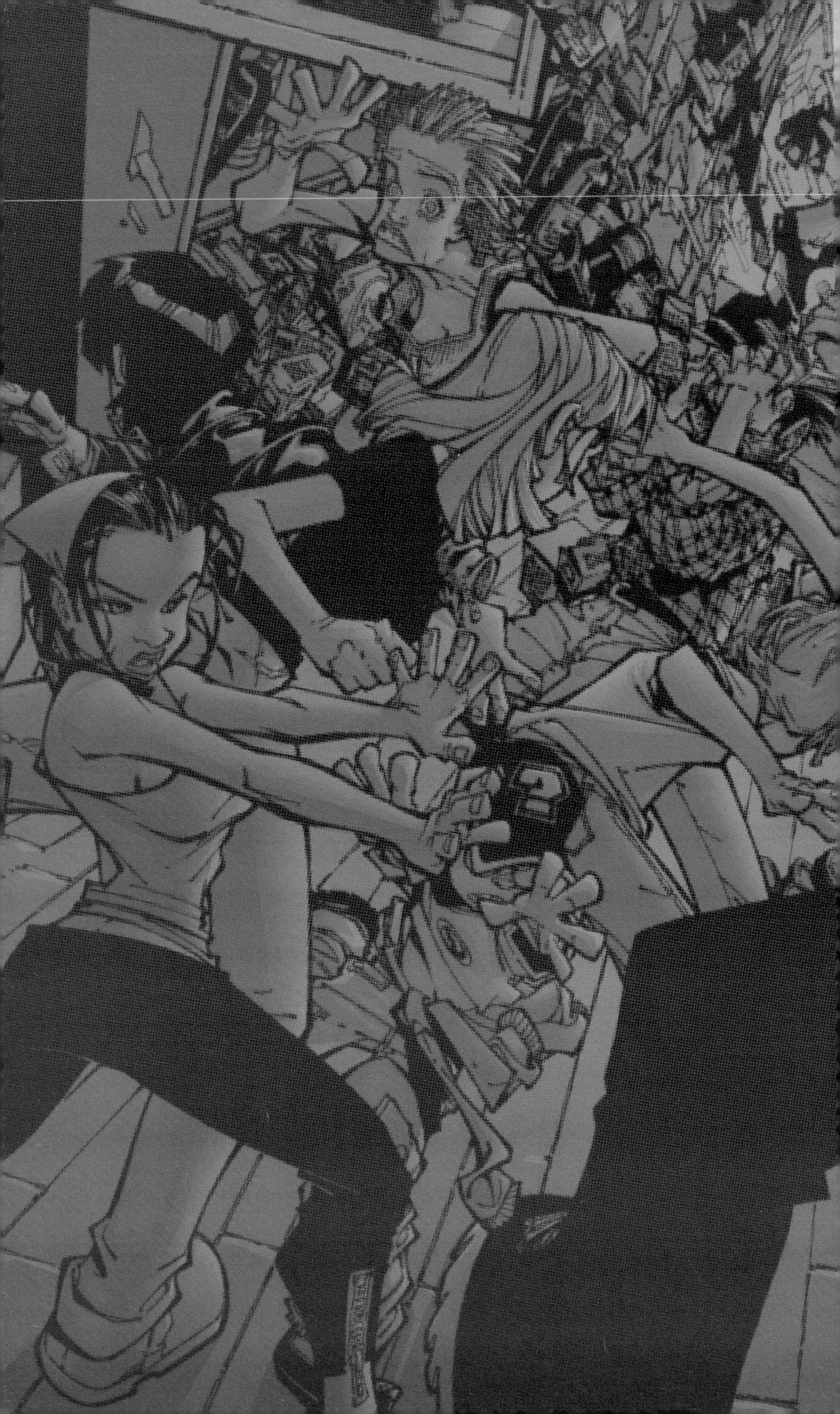

CALIFORNIA

VOLUME 2

OUT THERE™

OUT OF THIS WORLD

HUMBERTO RAMOS
BRIAN AUGUSTYN
SANDRA HOPE